Surveying Victims

Surveying Victims

A study of the measurement of criminal victimization, perceptions of crime, and attitudes to criminal justice

Richard F. Sparks
Rutgers University

Hazel G. Genn
Wolfson College, Oxford

David J. Dodd
University of Guyana

JOHN WILEY & SONS
Chichester · New York · Brisbane · Toronto

2694959

Library of Congress Cataloging in Publication Data:

Sparks, Richard F.
  Surveying victims.

  Bibliography: p.
  Includes index.
  1. Victims of crimes—England—London.
2. Crime and criminals—England—London—Public
opinion.   3.   Criminal justice, Administration of—
England—London—Public opinion.   4.   Public opinion
—England—London.
I.   Genn, Hazel G., joint author. II.   Dodd,
David J., joint author. III.   Title.
HV6250.3.G7S68   364   76-52393

ISBN 0 471 99494 4

Photosetting by Thomson Press (India) Limited, New Delhi

Printed by The Pitman Press, Bath, Avon.

Preface

This is a book about a new method of criminological research. More strictly, it is about the recent application of a long-established social science research technique—the sample survey—to the measurement and explanation of crime. By using this technique to ask samples of the general public directly about their experiences as victims of crime, researchers in a number of countries are now obtaining a wealth of information about crime and society's reactions to crime, of a kind which could not be obtained in any other way. In particular, they are learning much, for the first time, about the so-called 'dark figure' of crime—those offences which are not reported to the police and not recorded in official criminal statistics.

Surveys of this kind—known as surveys of victimization, or 'victim surveys'—were first carried out only ten years ago. Within a mere decade, therefore, some of the oldest problems in criminology have come at last within reach of solution. Surveys like the one described in this book can also provide valuable information about the public's perceptions of crime and attitudes to the criminal justice system. Even more importantly, however, by giving a fuller picture of the incidence, nature, and distribution of crime, they can themselves help to transform those perceptions, and can thus radically alter what the public learns and thinks about 'the crime problem'. For this reason, it is obviously important that the picture of crime presented by victim surveys be as accurate as possible.

Unfortunately, social science research methods are notoriously imprecise; moreover, because of the complex nature of most social phenomena, the findings obtained by using those methods are often uncertain and open to differing interpretations. These problems are apt to be compounded when a new research strategy or technique is introduced (or when, as has happened with the victim survey, an established method is applied to new subject-matter). Even in the physical sciences, where the objects of study are generally quite tractable and theories about them comparatively well-developed, new methods of research must often undergo extensive testing before their results can be accepted with confidence: this is all the more necessary in the social sciences, where such extensive pre-testing is unfortunately less likely to take place.

Because of the relative novelty of the victim survey method, the aim of our research was primarily methodological: that is, we were—at least initially—

more interested in trying to discover how well social survey techniques worked in this field, than in the substantive findings of a victim survey of a particular English population. Will people who have been victims of crime really remember accurately what happened to them, and when it happened—and will they tell a survey interviewer about it? When our project was first conceived, we knew of no other large-scale studies which had seriously tried to answer these questions, and to discover how accurate the victim survey method was likely to be: that objective was, therefore, our first priority. At the same time, we were seeking to learn something—more than anyone knew at the time— about the magnitude and nature of criminal victimization in some part of the English population; and in taking at least the initial steps toward some kind of explanation as to why victims of crime (as identified by a victim survey) responded to their experiences as they did. This in turn required the development and testing of other survey techniques, aimed at measuring people's perceptions and attitudes relating to crime and the criminal justice system. The resulting project was thus both methodological and exploratory in its aims. In addition, we feel that we learned something about the extent to which our respondents—adults living in three inner London areas in 1973—were victims of crimes of different kinds; and about the ways in which these experiences affected their attitudes and their social lives. But our efforts here were only a first step at measuring criminal victimization in London: and our findings on this point should not be generalized beyond the limits indicated in the text.

Our research officially began early in 1972, at the Cambridge University Institute of Criminology. As with many university research projects, our time-table was a tight one; and as happens in most such projects, we did not succeed in meeting it. All three of us participated fully in the design of questionnaires, pilot studies, fieldwork and analyses of data, which occupied us until the end of 1973. At that time, however, Dr. Dodd had to leave Cambridge to take up a Lectureship in Criminology at the University of Guyana. It was thus impossible for him to participate fully in the drafting of the final report on the research, which was carried out by the other two authors. (By the time the manuscript was completed, one of those authors had moved from Cambridge to the United States, and the other had moved to Oxford; considerable centripetal force was thus needed in order to assemble the final version.) The ordering of the authors' names thus reflects, roughly, their respective shares in the writing of this book; it does *not* reflect their intellectual contributions to the research on which the book is based. That research was a joint venture, shared equally among the three of us.

As is usual with research projects undertaken at the Cambridge Institute, we had the benefit of a Consultative and Reviewing Committee, whose members gave generously of their time to read and comment upon early drafts of our report, and who helped us in many other ways during the life of the proejct. The Chairman of this Committee was Mr. I. J. Croft, Head of the Home Office Research Unit (which was responsible for funding the project). Its members included Dr. Mark Abrams, head of the Social Science Research Council's

Survey Unit; Dr. A. N. Oppenheim, Reader in Social Psychology at the London School of Economics and Political Science; Professor F. H. McClintock, now Professor of Criminology in the University of Edinburgh; Professor Nigel Walker, Director of the Cambridge Institute of Criminology; Miss Margaret Guy, also of the Cambridge Institute; Dr. R. V. G. Clarke of the Home Office Research Unit; (now) Deputy Assistant Commissioner H. D. Walton of the Metropolitan Police; Mrs. J. E. Reisz of the Home Office Police Department; and Mr. J. A. Chilcot, at that time of the Home Office Criminal Policy Department. We should like to record our gratitude to all of the members of this Committee for their support and assistance.

In addition, many academic colleagues commented on earlier drafts of this book, gave us valuable advice and criticism, and made available to us the results of their own research. We should especially like to thank Dr. Kauko Aromaa; Dr. Albert D. Biderman; Mr. A. E. Bottoms, Mr. Ron Mawby and Dr. Monica Walker; Dr. R. W. Burnham; Professor Marshall Clinard; Professor Desmond Ellis; Dr. J. P. Fiselier; Professor Michael Hindelang; Dr. Günther Kaiser and Dr. Egon Stephan; Professor J. P. Martin; Professor Albert J. Reiss, Jr.; Professor Paul Davidson Reynolds; Dr. Irvin Waller and Mr. Norm Okihiro; and Dr. Preben Wolf. Collectively, they provided us with much information, and saved us from many mistakes; such ignorance and error as may remain is, of course, entirely our responsibility.

Last but not least, our thanks must go to Mrs. Dorothy Feula, who typed the final version of the manuscript.

RICHARD F. SPARKS
HAZEL G. GENN
DAVID J. DODD

Contents

CHAPTER I

Counting Crimes and Counting Victims

1. The Measurement of Crime

The first motive for collecting and publishing official statistics of crime and criminals was a political one. Bentham,[1] among others, had argued vigorously that such a means of measuring the moral health of the nation was a necessary tool of the legislator; and the development of 'moral statistics' in France and other European countries during the nineteenth century was animated chiefly by a concern for tracing the effects of legislation and of other forms of social change.[2] This concern appears, in a slightly altered form, in the present-day use of criminal statistics as a kind of 'social indicator': a high crime rate, like high rates of unemployment or illiteracy, being widely interpreted by politicians and plain men alike as a sign of 'social pathology' or a decline in the quality of life.[3]

In addition, since social scientists first began to study crime, about 150 years ago, they have relied to a considerable extent on official statistics—kept by the police, courts, prisons or other government agencies—for their data on crimes and criminals. Such statistics (for example, those published annually in Britain by the Home Office, or the *Uniform Crime Reports* published by the Federal Bureau of Investigation in the United States) are not collected for research purposes. Yet beginning with the earliest studies of Guerry[4] and Quetelet,[5] the picture of law-breaking which such statistics provide—for example, of variations in crime rates over time, or in different areas—has been the *explanandum* of many different sociological and psychological theories, and the testing-ground for many more.

At the same time, however, most criminologists have argued that the official statistics are certainly incomplete and probably biased, in particular because many crimes are never reported to the police or recorded (in official statistics) by them. Moreover, it has long been recognized that this 'dark figure' of un-recorded crime is probably not constant, over time or in different areas, even for the same type of crime. Thus an increase in crime rates according to the statistics might well be due merely to an increase in the proportion of crime being reported to the police (or recorded in the official statistics by them), and not to a real change in the volume of criminal behaviour.

For most of the past century, the 'dark figure' of unrecorded crime has been rather like the weather: criminologists all talked about it, at least in the first chapters of their textbooks, but none of them did very much about it. In recent years, however, a number of researchers have tried to overcome the problem of the 'dark figure' by the technique of asking people directly about their experience of crime. The first studies of this kind were 'self-report' studies, in which samples of people (in most cases, school children or adolescents) were asked about crimes which they themselves might have committed. Among other things, these studies invariably revealed the existence of much greater amounts of crime than were disclosed by official statistics; more importantly, they showed that a large amount of crime is committed by persons—especially middle-class persons—who are never arrested or convicted.[6] They were thus of great value in correcting the picture of the typical delinquent which emerges from studies based on apprehended offenders. For a number of reasons, however, most self-report studies provide only limited information about the number of *offences* which may have been committed in a particular area and period of time. For this purpose, it is better to ask a representative sample of people in the area about crimes which may have been committed against them in (say) a one-year period. Estimates based on the numbers of crimes disclosed in this way can then be compared with the numbers recorded in police statistics for the same area and time period; and the difference between these two magnitudes represents, at least approximately, the 'dark figure' of unrecorded crime. Studies of this kind are called surveys of victimization, or 'victim surveys.' It is with research of this kind that this book is concerned.

The use of social survey or 'Gallup poll' methods in the measurement and study of crime is fairly recent.[7] The first major surveys of this kind were actually carried out in the United States, for the President's Commission on Law Enforcement and Administration of Justice, in 1966. One, conducted by the National Opinion Research Center, was based on a national sample of 10,000 households;[8] similar but smaller surveys were also carried out, for the same Commission, in Boston, Chicago and Washington, D.C.[9] These surveys produced evidence that the volume of serious crime in the areas surveyed was, at a minimum, between three and ten times as great as that shown by police statistics; they also threw light on a number of important related matters, in particular on the reasons why victims of crime did not report the matter to the police. For the first time, real progress had been made toward overcoming the problem of the 'dark figure' by empirical research.

In the ten years since the President's Commission surveys were published, the victim survey has become the basis of a growth industry of substantial proportions. In the United States, by far the most ambitious programme of victim survey research is the National Crime Panel study now being carried out by the U. S. Census Bureau on behalf of the Law Enforcement Assistance Administration (an agency of the U. S. Department of Justice). This project, which began in 1972, involves interviews with a national sample of about 60,000 households and 15,000 businesses; the panel design calls for each household and business to be reinterviewed every six months, on a continuing basis. Similar surveys have also been carried out by the Census Bureau in a number of selected American cities, and several other victim surveys have been done by academic researchers and commercial organizations. As a result, data on criminal victimization are now available for about 30 American cities;[10] in principle, these data could be compared with the *Uniform Crime Reports*, so as to provide both cross-sectional and over-time data on unrecorded crime and on variations in the 'dark figure.'

Similar research has been carried out or is in progress, in Canada, Australia, and a number of European countries. By the end of 1974, victim surveys had been conducted by academic researchers in Sweden, Norway, Denmark, Finland, Switzerland, Holland, West Germany and Belgium.[11] In England, the Government Social Survey (a division of the Office of Population Censuses and Surveys) carried out a large-sized survey of the adult population of England and Wales in 1966 which included a number of questions on the respondents' experiences of criminal victimization;[12] and in 1972 and 1973 the General Household Survey carried out by the same organization also included questions on criminal victimization of certain kinds.[13] All of these surveys relate to crimes committed against individuals or households; but the same techniques have also been used to study crimes against business and public organizations.[14] Within a very few years, therefore, there has been a substantial expenditure on victim survey research, and an abundance of data on victimization has been collected which may illuminate the 'dark figure' of crime. Seldom, in the history of social science research, can so much have been done about a single problem by so many in so short a time.

Plainly these surveys may make an important contribution to the understanding of crime and the development of criminological theories. But they also have political implications which may be of far greater importance. Victim surveys provide an alternative picture of the amount and nature of crime, to that which emerges from police and other official statistics. They can thus have a powerful impact on the general public's perception of 'the crime problem', and on public attitudes and beliefs concerning social order and the system of social control. To the extent that this new picture of crime is more accurate and complete than the old one, the change is of course a beneficial one. But as we shall see, the victim survey also has definite limitations as a method of measuring crime, so that the information which it can provide is still necessarily incomplete in certain crucial respects; and even for crimes which it can be used to find out about, its accuracy still remains to be finally established.

2. Methodological Questions

In view of the size of the investment to date in the victim survey technique, it is perhaps surprising that very little research had previously been done on a simple but crucial question, to wit: Does the technique actually work? More specifically, to what extent can survey respondents remember incidents—even fairly recent ones—in which crimes were committed against them? If they do remember such incidents, how accurately and precisely will they remember *when* the incidents took place? Will they tell a survey interviewer about them? Will they describe the incidents accurately—and will their descriptions generally be the same as (or at least be compatible or reconcilable with) those which would be given by the police or the courts? To what extent will respondents report spurious incidents of victimization—through fantasy, or through misinterpretation of the situation or misunderstanding of the criminal law?

When our research was first planned, early in 1971, we knew of only one small study[1] which had been done on the crucial question of respondents' recall of offences. While some other important methodological issues had received attention during the President's Commission studies,[2] others had not been investigated at all, at least in a criminological context. Admittedly many of the methodological problems of victim surveys are not peculiar to the study of crime, but are quite general problems of retrospective social surveys (i.e. surveys in which respondents are asked questions about events which may have happened to them at some time in the past). Questions of recall, and of the 'telescoping' of remembered incidents either forward or backward in time, have been investigated to some extent by sociologists, psychologists, economists and market researchers; other problems, such as those concerning response bias and the sampling of rare events, have been investigated by statisticians and students of survey methodology. But for several reasons it is doubtful how far the findings of these studies (which are not always clear in any case) can be applied to surveys about crime: and there are some problems—for example, concerning the possible repression and falsification of incidents by respondents, and the definition of situations as involving 'crimes' or 'offences'—in which studies of surveys on other subjects furnish no guidance at all.

In order to investigate these problems, we selected from police records a sample of persons in three inner London areas, who had reported to the police an incident involving an alleged offense occuring within the fifteen months preceding our survey. We then interviewed these persons, to see how many of them would mention the incidents in question to our interviewers and how accurately the incidents themselves would be described. This research strategy—sometimes known as a 'reverse record check'—can admittedly achieve only a partial validation of the victim survey method. It deals only with incidents which were reported to the police, which may well be more readily recalled (and disclosed to an interviewer) than incidents of which the police were not notified. But as a practical matter it would have been difficult, if not impossible, for us to select a sample of victims of unreported incidents; and in view of the limited information available even about reported ones, we felt that a study of them was worthwhile. It would enable us to clarify many methodological questions, and to help assess the usefulness and the limitations of this new (and relatively expensive) technique. If a substantial proportion of reported incidents were not mentioned to interviewers, the utility of the method would be seriously called into question; for in that case its results might well be no more accurate or precise than the official statistics it is meant to validate.[3]

After we began our research, results from pilot surveys (done as part of the U. S. Census Bureau project referred to earlier) became available to us. These pilot studies, which also involve reverse record checks, bear on some of the questions which we investigated; their results, which are discussed in detail in Chapter III, provide a valuable comparison with our own work. But it is unclear just how far the results of these American studies are valid in the rather different conditions applying to social surveys on crime in England; and in any case, as we shall see, their findings on certain crucial questions differ markedly from our own.

The first objective of our research, then, was purely methodological. We were concerned to investigate the feasibility of using the victim survey as a means of measuring crime, and to summarize what is known about this technique for the benefit of others who may wish to use it. But the victim survey need not be (and in our view should not be) thought of merely as a measuring instrument. In addition, such a survey can be used to obtain information relating to a wide range of criminological problems, and to develop and test explanatory theories. In addition to a sample of known victims, therefore, we interviewed random samples of adults (in a provincial city and three areas of London); and in addition to obtaining information about our respondents' experiences of victimization, we collected data on their perceptions and definitions of crime, and their attitudes to the criminal justice system. The problems which we explored fall into three broad groups: the reaction of victims (and of society generally) to crime; the attributes of the victims themselves; and the impact of crime on the community.

3. Theoretical Issues

(1) Societal Reaction to Crime

The recording of an event or state of affairs in the statistics of 'crime known to the police' is the outcome of a sequence of social and psychological processes. First, the act or state of affairs must be *perceived* by someone: property must be missed in suspicious circumstances, A's fist much be seen to collide with B's nose. Next, the person who perceives such a thing must *recognize* or *interpret* what he sees, or *classify* it as being a thing of a certain kind. In Wittgenstein's terminology,[1] he must not only *see* the event in the most literal sense of 'seeing,' but must also see it *as* something; in the jargon of social psychology, he must *define* the situation in some way. (For example, what he sees may be an act of physical violence; he may define this as an argument, a fight, a joke, a bit of childish misbehaviour, a justified response to provocation, an assault or an attempted murder.) Assuming that he defines it as an illegal act of some sort, he must decide whether or not to *report* it to the police. If the police do learn of

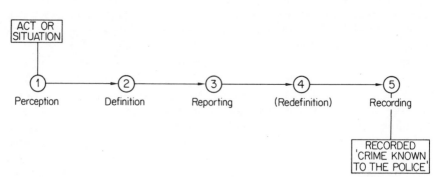

Figure I.1. The processes of societal reaction to crime and recording by police

the incident, a separate process of *redefinition* may take place, since the police may take a very different view of what happened from that taken by the person who called them. Finally, if the police do define the act as an illegal one, they must *record* it in the appropriate way in the official statistics. Diagrammatically, this process can be represented as in Figure I.1.

This diagram is deliberately oversimplified in a number of ways; and it is important to stress that it is *not* intended to reflect all of the possible actions and actors who may be involved in dealing with a situation involving a crime. In particular, it must not be assumed that the same person must perceive, define and report the crime, or that the person(s) doing any of those things must be the victim of that crime in a legal (or any other) sense. These may be reasonable hypotheses for some types of crime; but there are many ways in which the processes shown in the diagram may take place. For example, A may believe that some of his property is missing; he may tell this to B, who on learning of the circumstances classifies the situation as a theft; B may then mention the matter to C, who—acting independently—notifies the police. Or again, A may be found lying in the road, badly injured and unconscious; B, a hospital doctor, may conclude that the injuries resulted from a criminal assult; he may record this in hospital case papers which are later seen—quite fortuitously— by someone else who tells a police officer. A policeman may be the first to perceive and define a crime (which does not rule out the possibility of later redefinition of the situation by a superior officer). It must also be remembered that an event may be misperceived or wrongly defined as involving a crime, and that non-events may be reported to the police or recorded by them: it is not the case that a crime must in fact have occurred, for the processes of perception, definition and reporting to take place.

What is true is those processes must occur in the order shown in Figure I.1, if they occur at all; the diagram gives the sequence in which certain things must happen, if a crime which has in fact taken place is recorded in the statistics. At each of steps (1) to (5), some situations which do in fact involve crimes may, so to speak, fail to survive to the next step; the sum of such failures at all five steps is of course the 'dark figure' of unrecorded crime.[2]

It is important to note, however, that victim surveys only attempt to obtain directly information about those events which have successfully passed through step (2) of this process; they do not—indeed *ex hypothesi* they could not—attempt directly to measure the total volume of illegal acts which in fact take place.[3] Instead, survey respondents are asked whether or not certain events or types of event have been perceived and appropriately defined by them, usually within certain limits of time and place. But such surveys can also be used to study the working of the process itself—or at least its first three steps—since they can provide information on the ways in which respondents tend to perceive and define certain classes of events, and on the factors which lead such events to be reported (or not reported) to the police.[4] So far as step (3) is concerned, respondents can be asked directly about their reasons for reporting or not reporting, as the case may be; and those who do report offences to the police (or who claim to) can be compared with those who do not. But estimates can also be obtained from a victim survey of the 'reportability' of different sorts of offenses, *viz.* the conditional probability that an event—say, an apparent burglary—will be reported to the police, *if* it has been perceived and suitably defined. The sample estimate of this probability is of course just the proportion of burglaries mentioned by respondents which were reported by them to the police (or, more strictly, which the respondents *say* they reported). The probabilities associated with steps (1) and (2) of the process obviously cannot be obtained in the same way; but victim survey data on respondents' attitudes, evaluations and perceptions may make it possible to get at least a rough idea of the magnitude of those probabilities, which is more than criminologists have at present.

It should be obvious that understanding the process of societal reaction to crime is an important objective in its own right, and is not merely a matter of correcting some unfortunate deficiencies in the official criminal statistics. Essentially, the problem is this: why do different social groups react as they do, to violations of the criminal law or analogous social norms? Probably there is no single, straightforward answer to this question: much depends, no doubt, on the type of rule-violation involved. Where property crimes are concerned, for example, questions of ownership seem likely to be important: there is evidence that (at least in Western industrial societies) there are differences in attitudes to theft from persons and theft from impersonal agencies such as corporations.[5] In the case of traditional types of violent crime (such as assault or murder), the processes of perception and definition depend largely on such matters as intention and consent, and on patterns of norms concerning justification and excuse: for example, when does verbal or physical provocation make the use of physical force permissible, or even necessary, in retaliation? In theories of societal reaction, the dependent variable is neither the commission of crimes nor the experience of victimization; instead it is the victims' responses to such experiences, and the perceptions, definitions and attitudes of victims and non-victims in different social groups. Survey data on these are badly needed.

In the present research, in addition to asking about respondents' experiences of victimization, and about the respondents themselves, we collected information about a number of matters which seemed to us to be relevant to the explanation of societal reaction to crime. Several American studies have suggested that an important factor in determining whether or not a victim reports what he believes to be an offence is his attitude to the police. Relations between the police and the public are of course a matter of general importance, and (in this context) attitudes to the police have been the subject of a number of surveys in both Britain and the United States within the past ten years. It is clear that these attitudes are the product of many factors, of which actual contact with the police (e.g. in reporting a crime) is probably not the most important. But whatever their causes, victims' attitudes to the criminal law and its enforcement must plainly be a central element in the explanation of societal reaction to crime. We thus obtained data—discussed in Chapter V—on our respondents' knowledge of, attitudes to and contact with the police, both generally and in relation to the specific incidents in which they were victims of crime.

In addition, we included a number of questions aimed at measuring respondents' attitudes and beliefs relating to different sorts of crime and criminals, and to their immediate neighbourhood social environments. In one respect our survey had special reference to the violent behaviour. This was not primarily because of contemporary concern about 'the problem of violence' (whatever exactly that problem may be); rather it was because we believed that many of the theoretical problems of perception and definition of criminal behaviour are more acute with violent than with property crime.[6] Thus our questionnaire included a number of questions of a projective or quasi-projective type, aimed at discovering the extent to which our respondents believed that violence is permissible or legitimate, given certain sorts of provocation or justification. These data are discussed in Chapter VII.

Clearly it was not possible for us to investigate, in this study, all of the factors which may determine the process of societal reaction to crime; probably some of them are not capable of being studied effectively by survey methods. (For example, recent experimental research by Latané[7] and his colleagues has shown that there are important situational determinants—such as the number of persons present—of the processes of perception and reporting of crime and deviance.) Nonetheless, survey data may provide some evidence on both individual and ecological factors which may help to explain why the same type of act is treated as a crime in one part of town, while being ignored or tolerated in another. Thus, *a priori*, it seemed to us likely that the processes of definition and reporting are influenced by the perceived seriousness of different *types* of crime; to study this, we used a rating technique first suggested by Sellin and Wolfgang[8] to obtain rankings according to seriousness of a number of violent and property crimes. Again, this issue is of general theoretical interest in its own right, quite apart from its possible effect on the reporting of victimization. To what extent is there consensus, among different groups in the population, on the relative seriousness (in some sense) of different types of crime? And to what extent do the norms of the criminal law reflect generally held values? Several theorists in recent years have contended that there is conflict, rather than consensus, among different social classes on this point. It has been argued that 'for the most part, middle- and upper-class groups, who control the power of state legislatures, use the legal definitions of crimes in an attempt to control the kinds of things lower-class individuals commit against them, in particular property crimes and certain acts of violence.'[9] This, if true, would seem to imply that middle- and upper-class persons regard crimes like robbery, burglary and theft as more serious than do 'lower-class' persons (who presumably have less property). This is an empirical question, which can to some extent be studied by survey methods; we describe our findings on this point in Chapter VII.

Since a person's own criminality may well be an important factor in determining his response to crimes committed against him, we included some self-report questions in which respondents were asked about offences which they themselves might have committed. (The validity of these data, and their implications for the perception and reporting of crime, are discussed in Chapter IV.) Necessarily, our approach to this subject was a very crude one; but it seemed worthwhile, since until now there have been no self-report data of any kind relating to representative samples of the adult population. Finally, of course, there are many individual and attitudinal variables which may affect the perception, definition and reporting of crime. Since our focus was primarily sociological, we did not feel that there was any point in trying to investigate dimensions of personality (such as neuroticism or extraversion) which may well play some part in the perception and reporting of crime. But it seemed desirable to include some attitude questions, in part because they might have explanatory value in their own right, and in part because they might help to validate other items in our questionnaire. Thus we included Srole's anomia scale,[10] together with three attitude scales recently developed by Professor R. L. Kahn and his associates in their study of violence in the United States.[11] As it turned out, these attitudinal data did not seem, in our sample, to have much relationship to victimization; they are thus not described in detail in this book.

(2) Victims versus Non-victims

In their attempts to explain criminal behaviour, criminologists have for the most part concentrated on studying offenders, thus implicitly assuming that crime is wholly or primarily a function of the criminal's behaviour, personality or social situation, and that the victim of crime is a passive rather than an active element in it. The research strategy dictated by this assumption involves the comparison of a sample of 'criminals' (whether identified from official records, or from observation or self-report studies) with a sample of 'non-criminals,' in the hope that observed differences between the two groups will be indicative of some causally relevant factors. But it has increasingly come to be realized that the 'victim' (in a legal sense) of a criminal act may in fact play an important part in the causation of that act, in a number of ways. He may be a willing participant in the crime; or he may consciously or unconsciously incite or provoke it; at a minimum he may be placed (or may place himself) specially at risk. In what criminologists are pleased to call 'the literature,' the study of this aspect of crime is usually referred to by the inelegant name of 'victimology.'[12] Many questions concerning the transactions between criminals and their victims are of a micro-sociological kind, and are better investigated by observation or experimental methods than by social surveys. But there is nonetheless a need for basic factual information, of a kind which sample surveys can provide, concerning the incidence and distribution of criminal victimization and the attributes of victims themselves. Is there, for example, a distinguishable group of persons who seem to be 'victim-prone,' as there are persons who appear to be 'accident-prone'? What are the age, sex and social-class distributions of the victims of personal crime— and are generally held stereotypes of victims reasonably accurate? These questions—discussed in Chapter IV—are of increasing practical importance, in view of the development in recent years, in England and elsewhere, of schemes for the compensation of victims of crime.[13]

(3) Effects of Crime on the Community

For much of this volume our data on respondents' attitudes, beliefs, perceptions, etc. are considered mainly in relation to their possible effects on the reporting of crimes to the police: in other words, they are viewed as independent or intervening variables which help to produce official crime statistics. But they can be looked at in another way. The public's attitudes to crime and the criminal law, their perceptions of the frequency and seriousness of crime, their attitudes to the police, stereotypes of offenders, and the like, are themselves the consequences of social phenomena; it may be hypothesized that they are affected by—among other things—the public's direct and vicarious experience of crime and contacts with the police. In this sense, the impact of crime on the community is undoubtedly far greater than would be suggested by direct monetary losses and physical injuries resulting from crime, which are experienced to a serious degree by only a small minority.

A belief that crime is prevalent in one's immediate social environment— in the streets of one's home neighbourhood, around the fabric of one's house —can result in fear or concern about becoming a victim which in turn can lead to reorganization of one's customary way of life and one's way of looking at the world. It may be, as several American surveys had suggested, that these fears are not closely related to the *actual* risk of becoming a victim of crime.[14] Even so, they may still have important consequences for social life. Erving Goffman has pointed out the importance of the everyday assumption that the building in which one lives is free from hazards and will keep out intruders—

an assumption frequently violated, with drastic consequences, in many housing developments in the United States.[15] London is, of course, a relatively peaceful place. But this should not lead us to conclude that concern about crime is nonexistent there, or—even if ill-founded—is unimportant.

We did not feel that there was much value in asking about our survey respondents' concern about crime in general (i.e., in England as a whole); instead, we wanted to try to refer specifically to the part of the city with which respondents were most familiar, and where they presumably spent most of their time. We thus attempted to get respondents to define for us the physical boundaries of the 'neighbourhood' in which they lived, and to provide some information on their perceptions of, and attitudes to, their social environments and the people with whom they live and presumably interact. Do they feel integrated into that community, or alienated from it? Are their neighbours representative of their reference groups? How often do they go out at night—and what for? It is only against the background provided by the answers to questions like these that the impact of crime on the community can be adequately studied.

It was in part because we wanted to study questions of this kind that we deliberately chose for our London survey three contrasting areas—Brixton, Hackney and Kensington. *These areas may well not be representative of inner London, and the reader is warned against any attempt to make inferences from our data about the prevalence of crime in London as a whole.* The important thing for our purposes is that there are marked differences between those three areas, not only in recorded crime rates but in cultural and social terms: it is these differences with which we are concerned, and not the areas' typicality. But our three survey areas are by no means homogeneous within their boundaries; like all London districts, they display many variations in culture and way of life, from corner to corner and street to street. We hope to explore some of these differences in more detail in the future, drawing on Census materials and recorded crime rates as well as on our survey data. We have made a beginning on this subject, however, in Chapter VIII of the present volume. Necessarily, our work in this area is in large part methodological and exploratory in character; it is still far from clear how far questions like those just discussed can in fact be effectively studied by survey methods.

Our London survey was thus designed to provide both *individual* data on criminal victimization, perceptions of crime and attitudes to criminal justice, and—in a modest way—*ecological* data on crime rates, patterns of norms, attitudes and perceptions. Insofar as it involves a comparison of different types of urban area—whether these be police sub-divisions, Census enumeration districts, or 'natural areas' identified in some other way—research of this kind necessarily builds on, and may make a contribution to, the ecological and subcultural theories which have a long history and an important place in criminology. But it is important to note that we are *not* attempting in this book to explain why a certain area has a high actual crime rate (as measured by a victim survey). Instead, we are primarily interested in variations in the ways in which crime is perceived and dealt with by persons in different sections of

12

the community, and in the effects of this process on social life. This may not be the traditional subject of empirical research in criminology; but it is no less important for having been so long neglected.

Notes and References

1. The Measurement of Crime

1. Jeremy Bentham, 'Observations on the Hard Labour Bill.' IV, *Works* (Bowring ed.) 29.
2. See the discussion in Thorsten Sellin and Marvin E. Wolfgang, *The Measurement of Delinquency* (New York: Wiley, 1964) Chapter 2.
3. See, for example, Raymond A. Bauer (ed.), *Social Indicators* (Cambridge, Massachusetts: M.I.T. Press, 1966), especially the Preface by Bertram M. Gross and Chapter 2 by Albert D. Biderman.
4 A. M. Guerry, *Essai sur la Statistique Morale de la France* (Paris, 1833).
5. L. A. J. Quetelet, *Essai sur la developpement des facultés de l'homme, ou Physique Sociale* (Brussels, 1831). For a further discussion see Albert D. Biderman and Albert J. Reiss, Jr., 'On exploring the Dark Figure of Crime.' (1967) 374 *The Annals* 1–15, especially 2–3.
6. The literature on self-report studies of delinquency is vast. For a critical summary of research up to 1969, see Roger Hood and Richard Sparks, *Key Issues in Criminology*, (London: Weidenfeld and Nicolson; New York: McGraw–Hill, 1970) Chapters 1–2. More recent studies include Lynn MacDonald, *Delinquency and Social Class* (London: Faber, 1971); M. J. Hindelang, 'Time perceptions of self-reported delinquents.' (1973) 13 *British Journal of Criminology* 171; H. B. Gibson, S. Morrison and D. J. West, 'The confession of known offences in response to a self-reported delinquency schedule.' (1970) 10 *British Journal of Criminology* 277. The self-report technique, by providing a more accurate and precise measure of past delinquencies than is obtained from police or court records, might be expected to have a considerable impact on etiological studies based on comparisons between 'delinquents' and 'non-delinquents'—especially in view of the social-class bias known to inhere in most police records. Some impact there has been; but not much. See Travis Hirschi, *Causes of Delinquency* (Berkeley: University of California Press, 1969) especially Chapter IV. Hirschi states that in a further analysis of his data (by Irving Piliavin) the same relationships between delinquency and other attributes of his sample persist whether the measure of 'delinquency' used is a self-report one or is based on official records, but that relationships found are weaker in the latter case.
7. It seems to have been first suggested in print, in modern times, by a Finnish criminologist, Inkeri Anttila: see her paper on 'The criminological significance of unregistered criminality.' (1964) 4 *Excerpta Criminologica* 411. See, however, the Preface to Philip H. Ennis, *Criminal Victimization in the United States: A Report of a National Survey*, President's Commission on Law Enforcement and Administration of Justice, *Field Surveys II*, (Washington, D. C.: U.S. Government Printing Office, 1967) iii. (This volume will hereinafter be cited as *Field Surveys II*.) Ennis indicates that the idea of victim surveys was initially discussed by the staff of the National Opinion Research Center in 1962.
8. Philip H. Ennis, *Field Surveys II*.
9. Albert D. Biderman *et. al.*, *Report on A Pilot Study in the District of Columbia on Victimization and Attitudes toward Law Enforcement*, President's Commission on Law Enforcement and Administration of justice, *Field Surveys I*; Albert J. Reiss, Jr., *Studies in Crime and Law Enforcement in Major Metropolitan Areas*, President's Commission on Law Enforcement and Administration of Justice, *Field Surveys III*,

Vol. 1 (both Washington, D.C., U.S. Government Printing Office, 1967). These studies are hereafter cited as *Field Surveys I* and *III* respectively.

10. By mid-1975, the Census Bureau's program had included victim surveys (based on probability samples of 10,000 households including about 22,000 individuals aged 12 and over, plus 2,500 businesses) in each of the five largest American cities (New York, Chicago, Los Angeles, Detroit and Philadelphia); and in the eight cities participating in the LEAA 'high impact' crime reduction programme (Atlanta, Baltimore, Cleveland, Dallas, Denver, Newark, Portland (Oregon), and St. Louis); pilot studies were carried out in Washington, D. C., Baltimore, San Jose and Dayton. Other cities for which data on criminal victimization have been collected include Minneapolis–St. Paul and Phoenix. The cost of the LEAA-Census program is currently estimated to be rather more than $10 million a year.

11. Some of the findings of these surveys are discussed in Chapter IV, pp. 81–96.

12. Mary Durant, Margaret Thomas and H. D. Willcock, *Crime, Criminals and the Law* (London, HMSO, 1972) especially 232–253.

13. It is understood, however, that these questions were not included in the Household Surveys for 1974 and subsequent years. See below, p. 233.

14. See A. J. Reiss, Jr., in *Field Surveys III*, Vol. 1, s. ii; *Crime Against Small Business, A Report of the Small Business Administration*, Senate Document No. 91–14, 91st Congress, 1st session (Washington, D.C.: U.S. Government Printing Office April 3, 1969) especially Appendix A, 53–143, by Albert J. Reiss, Jr. As noted above, the Census Bureau—LEAA National Crime Surveys also include samples of businesses.

2. Methodological Questions

1. The full results of this study—done by Reiss in the course of the Boston and Chicago surveys for the President's Commission—are not in fact published. The study is briefly alluded to by A. J. Reiss, Jr., in *Field Surveys III*, Vol. 1 at 150, and by the same author in his paper, 'Systematic observation of natural social phenomena,' in H. L. Costner (ed.), *Sociological Methodology 1971* (San Francisco: Jossey–Bass, 1971) 3 at 8, where a somewhat different account of the findings is given.

2. In particular, the question of congruence between victims', survey researchers' and police classification of reported incidents, and the desirability of using 'personal' rather than 'household' reports. See further below, Chapter III, pp. 36 and 51; and Chapter IV, p. 81.

3. To some extent there has been a reaction from the initial (and undoubtedly excessive) enthusiasm generated by self-report studies, on precisely this ground: see, for example, Nils Christie, 'Hidden delinquency: some Scandinavian experiences,' a paper presented to the Third National Conference on Teaching and Research in Criminology, Cambridge, July 1968; R. A. Dentler in R. H. Hardt and G. E. Bodine, *Development of Self-Report Instruments in Delinquency Research* (Syracuse, New York: Youth Development Center, 1965) at 18.

3. Theoretical Issues

1. L. Wittgenstein, *Philosophical Investigations* (Oxford: Basil Blackwell, 1953), II, xi.

2. The steps included in Figure I.1 relate to the processing of *events* as *crimes*; further steps may however ensue, after either step (2) or step (4), relating to the processing of *persons* as *criminals*. Thus, if the police have been called and accept the event as a crime, they may or may not investigate to see who was responsible; they may or may not arrest an alleged offender; they may or may not prosecute him; he may or may not be convicted and sentenced. Many cases of course fail at each of these steps; and at each step there are fairly definite biases, as 'labelling' theorists have been at great pains to point out in recent years.

3. Survey methods can in theory be used to measure all *perceived* crimes of certain kinds, by asking respondents about some wider category of events which they may or may not have defined as criminal; the definition can then be done by the researcher, on the basis of the respondents' accounts of the 'facts.' For example, Albert Biderman has proposed that violent crime could be studied by asking persons about *injuries* which they may have received. See A. D. Biderman, 'A proposed measure of inter-person violence,' (Washington, D. C.: Bureau of Social Science Research, 3 June 1971); A. D. Biderman, 'When does interpersonal violence become crime?', (Washington, D.C.: Bureau of Social Science Research, 1973).

4. They can also provide part of the data necessary to study step (4) of the process, which essentially involves a comparison of the classification of types of events or situations by members of the public with the classifications adopted in practice by the police. See further below, pp. 144–146. Step (5) of the process—the recording of crimes by the police—obviously requires a different type of study: see Chapter IX, pp. 223, 232, for a brief discussion of this problem.

5. See, for example, E. O. Smigel, 'Public attitudes toward stealing as related to the size of the victim organization,' (1956) 21 *American Sociological Review* 59–67; Donald M. Horning, *Blue Collar Theft* (Unpublished Ph.D. Dissertation, University of Indiana, 1964), especially 78–100.

6. A number of colleagues have questioned this belief, with (as we now think) some justification. The original basis for it was the assumption that the interpersonal transactions typically involved in, say, assault or rape are apt to be more ambiguous—since their correct description depends on such things as intention and consent—than those involved in, say, burglary; and that the definition of violent crime depends to a greater extent on norms relating to justification, than is the case with property crime. But ambiguities can certainly arise with many forms of property crime (e.g. consumer fraud); even a damaged front door must be interpreted (and thus may be misinterpreted) as the consequence of an attempted burglary or a bit of malicious mischief. Normative variations can also occur with property crimes, e.g. in respect of what lawyers call 'claims of right.' It is also true that important theoretical issues concerning the social definition of 'crime' are raised by other types of behaviour which we did not investigate at all, such as 'white-collar' crime, political corruption and 'victimless' crime. See further below, Chapter IX, pp. 226–227.

7. B. Latané and J. M. Darley, *The Unresponsive Bystander: Why Doesn't He Help?* (New York: Appleton–Century–Crofts, 1970).

8. Thorsten Sellin and Marvin E. Wolfgang, *The Measurement of Delinquency* (New York: John Wiley and Sons, 1964).

9. Jack D. Douglas, *American Social Order: Social Rules in a Pluralistic Society* (New York: Free Press, 1971) 90–91. See also Ian Taylor, Paul Walton and Jock Young, *Critical Criminology* (London: Routledge, 1975) at 43–5, 78–80, 198ff.

10. L. Srole, 'Social integration and certain corollaries: an exploratory study.' (1956) 21 *American Sociological Review* 709–716.

11. M. Blumenthal, R. L. Kahn, F. M. Andrews and K. B. Head, *Justifying Violence: Attitudes of American men* (Institute for Social Research, University of Michigan, Ann Arbor, 1972.) Our approach to the study of norms relating to violence was in fact suggested to us by Professor Kahn, though our use of the method differed from that used in the Blumenthal study.

12. See, for example, H. Von Hentig, *The Criminal and His Victim* (New Haven: Yale University Press, 1948); M. E. Wolfgang, *Patterns in Criminal Homicide* (Philadelphia: University of Pennsylvania Press, 1958); B. Mendelsohn and W. Nagel, in (1963) 3 *Excerpta Criminologica* 239, 245; Stephen Schafer, *The Victim and his Criminal* (New York: 1968); E. Viano, 'Victimology: the study of the victim.' (1976) 1 *Victimology* 3.

13. For the present British scheme see the Annual Reports of the Criminal Injuries

Compensation Board (London, H.M.S.O.); generally, S. Schafer, *Restitution to Victims of Crime* (New York: Quadrangle Books, 1960).

14. See the studies summarized in Jennie MacIntyre, 'Surveys of public attitudes to crime.' (1967) *The Annals* 43. It may be, however, that in certain circumstances the fear of crime—or a belief that it is prevalent—may increase the risk of victimization and thus increase crime rates: for example, it may lead people to carry weapons and to over-react to relatively minor threats or provocation. See further below, Chapter IV, pp. 97–103.

15. Erving Goffman, *Relations in Public* (London: Allen Lane, The Penguin Press, 1971) 284–302; and see, for example, Lee Rainwater, 'Fear and the House-as-Haven in the lower class,' (1966) *A.I.P. Journal* 22–31.

CHAPTER II

Description of the London Survey

The purpose of this chapter is to describe, briefly and in general terms, the survey on which this book is based—the questionnaire used, the London areas where our fieldwork was done, and the samples interviewed.

1. An Overview of the Research

Our research began in mid-January 1972, and was designed to be conducted in two consecutive phases. Phase I, which lasted from January to September 1972, was devoted to questionnaire design and development, and incorporated two pretests of the questionnaire in a town in the Cambridge area. Phase II of the project, which ran from October 1972 until December 1973, consisted of the administration and analysis of a medium-sized sample survey in the inner London area.

Phase I of the project began with the construction of a skeleton questionnaire which was tested on a small sample of Cambridge residents drawn from the electoral register. Following this preliminary exploration in the field, the first version of our questionnaire was drafted and the town of Peterborough, near Cambridge, was chosen as a suitable site on which to carry out pretests of the questionnaire. The first pretest of the questionnaire was conducted in April 1972 with a random sample drawn from census enumeration districts within the central residential area of Peterborough. With six interviewers hired and trained by us, 108 residents of Peterborough were interviewed in their homes over a period of two weeks with a questionnaire which took an average of over one-and-a-half hours to complete. After analysing the results of this pretest, the questionnaire was revised and preparations were made for a second pretest to be conducted in Peterborough in July 1972. Since only two of the 108 completed interviews in the first pretest had been with non-English respondents, it was decided that the second pretest should be concentrated in and around a central area of the city which contained a fairly high concentration of immigrant families, rather than drawn from the whole of the central residential area, in order to increase the number of responses from immigrants. Accordingly, the second Peterborough sample was drawn at random from within this limited area and over a two week interviewing period 131 interviews were obtained, including a higher proportion of non-English respondents—about 20 per cent—than in the first survey.[1]

With the data gained from these two pretests, and bearing in mind our experiences in the fieldwork there, Phase II of the project began in October 1972 with a final revision of the questionnaire in preparation for its administration in London. As we have already explained, in the London survey, approximately half of our initial sample would consist of people who were known to have reported to the police that they had been the victim of a crime during the preceding year, while the remaining part of the sample would be drawn at random from the adult population. This design was necessary in order to fulfil the first major objective of our survey—namely to test the methods devised for estimating the 'dark figure' of crime by investigating whether information relating to the victimization of individuals could or would be accurately recalled and reported to a survey interviewer. Thus, in London our survey areas were based on police subdivisional boundaries, in order that known victims could be selected from official records and so that the victimization rates estimated on the basis of our survey could be compared with official police statistics for those areas.

Having selected three areas to be surveyed within London and having completed the final version of our questionnaire, the project staff moved to London in November 1972 in order to hire and train a team of interviewers who would administer our questionnaire. We employed a total of 28 interviewers—12 male and 16 female—as well as three (female) supervisors, and after three weeks of training the interviewing programme began on 1st January 1973. Over a period of one-and-a-half months, a total of 858 interviews were completed with a combination of respondents selected from police files and those randomly drawn from the electoral register. After a preliminary check of the completed questionnaires, 17 were finally excluded from the sample, mainly as a result of respondents' language difficulties. The final sample was thus reduced to 841.

2. The Questionnaire

During the early stages of the project, our questionnaire underwent considerable revision and modification on the basis of responses gained during the Peterborough pretests and reports by our interviewers about their experiences in administering the questionnaire in the field. We conducted experiments during the pretests on the ordering of sections of the questionnaire, the ordering of questions within those sections, and with different methods of administration in certain sections; and the whole questionnaire was shortened, so that on average it took just over an hour to administer.[1] In its final form, the questionnaire consisted of rigidly structured questions which allowed for both pre-coded, forced choice responses (using printed prompt cards)[2] and open-ended responses.

The first section of the questionnaire consisted of basic personal data relating to such things as the sex, race, marital status, socio-economic status and educational history of respondents.[3] In addition, the occupation of the respondent's father was obtained, in order to provide some measurement of intergenerational social mobility. Next, questions about household composition, the frequency and nature of respondents' social activities at night, and their most usual method of transportation, were asked to provide some sort of objective measure as to the amount of time, and the types of social situations in which respondents could be deemed to be 'at risk' of becoming victims of different sorts of crime; and to assess the relations between their general social habits and experiences of criminal victimization.

We wished to investigate respondents' perceptions and fears of the risk of crime specifically within their home neighbourhood areas (as subjectively defined by them), as well as within London as a whole. We thus asked whether they thought that much crime was committed in their neighbourhood; what sorts of crime were committed, and who they believed to be responsible for the different types of crimes they mentioned. We also asked respondents whether they were 'concerned' about crime in London as a whole. They were then shown eleven cards, each with a category of crime printed on it, and were asked to say whether they believed that those crimes had been increasing, decreasing or remaining constant in frequency in recent years.

The next section of our questionnaire was designed to elicit information about our respondents' past contacts with the police, their attitudes towards the effectiveness of the police system, and the manner in which the police carry out their duties. We intended that the questions in this section would be ultimately related, in the analysis of the data, to the reporting of crime incidents; but in addition we were interested to see in what ways age, ethnic origin and personal criminality affect attitudes towards the police, whether or not the respondent had been a victim. We thus asked respondents when they last had contact with the police, what the circumstances were and whether the respondents had been satisfied with the behaviour of the police on that occasion. We also asked how they felt about the work of the police in their own particular neighbourhood areas, as well as the work of the police in general.

Next, respondents were given the series of descriptions of hypothetical situations involving violence in response to provocation; they were asked to say whether they approved or disapproved of the violence, and (in some cases) to interpret the situation. A series of attitude-measuring questions, mostly of the 'Agree—Disagree' type, followed; and respondents were then asked to assess the seriousness of 33 types of offences, on a 1-to-11 point scale. This last section of the questionnaire was the only one to be completed by the respondents themselves, rather than by the interviewers.

In the penultimate section of the questionnaire, we attempted to get respondents to recall incidents of criminal victimization which had taken place in the preceding twelve months. Since it was important that the information we received be accurate both in terms of when it took place as well as what actually occured, we devoted some considerable time at the beginning of this section is attempting to get the respondents to recall the past year by a reconstruction of salient events during that period.[4]

Following this memory prompt, each respondent was asked whether a number of things, ranging from attempted theft to burglary, car theft, and assault, had happened to them during that time and if so how many times it had happened. In order to be sure of covering all possible incidents, interviewers were instructed to probe on every negative response that they received. Thus the question, 'Did anyone physically attack you or assault you, in any way, during the past year?' was followed by a probe, 'Did anyone hit you, or use any other kind of violence against you?' if the initial question received a negative response. This question was followed by another which asked, 'Did anyone *try* to attack you, or assault you, or molest you in any way?' and again this was reinforced with a probe, 'Anyone—even someone you knew? For example in an argument or quarrel?' Finally, respondents were asked, 'In the past year did anyone *threaten* you in any way with violence of any kind?' followed by the probe, 'Anyone—even someone you knew? Were you in any situation in which violence *might* have been used against you—for example, an argument or quarrel?' Thus effectively we asked as many as six questions about the possibility of respondents' having been assaulted in some way, in order to try to catch any violent incident, no matter how trivial it may have seemed to the respondent. A similar pattern was followed for questions concerning burglary, theft, car theft and damage.

Having gained as many positive responses as possible to these specific questions about victimization, interviewers were instructed to complete a crime incident form, which was separate from the main questionnaire, for every incident that had been mentioned as having taken place during the preceding twelve months. On these forms a verbatim description of what actually occurred was recorded and the date and location of the event were noted. In the case of crimes against the person, respondents were asked about the extent of any injuries they may have received and any resulting disabilities or loss of income through absence from work. For property crimes, the value of loss or damage to property, and whether any property had been recovered were noted. All victims were asked whether they were in any way related to the respondent or whether they were a friend or acquaintance.[5]

A series of questions followed, relating to whether or not the offence had been reported to the police, and reasons were obtained for both reporting and failure to report. Respondents were asked whether the experience of victimization had caused them to change their attitudes or behaviour in any way and finally they were asked to rate the gravity of the offence of which they had been a victim on an eleven point scale in the same manner which they had used in an earlier section of the questionnaire. Finally, respondents were asked the series of self-report questions inviting them to admit to crimes which they might have committed at some time in their lives.[6]

3. The London Areas

The choice of London as a location in which to conduct a survey presents any researcher with a staggering selection of contrasting areas from which to choose his subject population. The criteria upon which our own final choice was based were as follows: first, since half of our sample was to be drawn from police records of known victims, it was necessary to use police sub-divisions as sampling areas, rather than local authority ward boundaries (with which police areas do not, in general, coincide). This was also necessary if recorded crime rates were to be compared with the amounts of crime reported to us. Second, in order to ensure that a random sample of the electoral register would yield a substantial amount of victims for the purposes of comparison, it was necessary to choose police sub-divisions in which reasonably high rates of victimization might be expected, i.e. those with relatively high recorded crime rates.[1] Finally, in order to gain comprehensive information on factors associated with victimization, and differences in attitudes, definitions and perceptions of crime, we were anxious to find areas that would contrast significantly, particularly in respect of social status and ethnicity. In addition to these basic criteria, it was also felt necessary to select our three areas from within the inner London area, in order to avoid introducing other variables such as the suburban/inner-urban contrast. On the basis of these requirements, we selected one police sub-division in each of the three London boroughs of Lambeth, Hackney and Kensington.

(1) Brixton

The area selected in the borough of Lambeth is that encompassed by Metropolitan Police station area LD. This covers a large area approximately equal to the borough wards of Angell, Ferndale, Town Hall, Herne Hill and Tulse Hill, plus half of the Larkhall and Vassall wards. The area stretches from Kennington in the north to Brockwell Park in the south; the western side is bounded by Brixton Hill and Clapham Road and the east by Herne Hill and Denmark Hill (See Figure II.1). In this book we shall for convenience use the name 'Brixton' to refer to the whole of the LD subdivisional area; but in the area itself that name is commonly reserved for the centre of the subdivisional area, that is, the mainly commercial district situated around Brixton railway station. This central district and its neighbouring residential area has, since the 1950's, increasingly become one of West Indian settlement, and it now constitutes one of the oldest and most stable West Indian communities in the country. This community is settled mainly in the wards of Town Hall, Angell, Ferndale, and Vassall, but an outward movement of the West Indian population has reached Herne Hill ward and across the west side of Brixton Hill. Characteristically, the majority of these families live in overcrowded, multi-occupation dwellings, some of which were at one time the large and fashionable residences of a bygone wealthier population. Although this area can in no way be called a ghetto in the American sense, there is nonetheless within that relatively

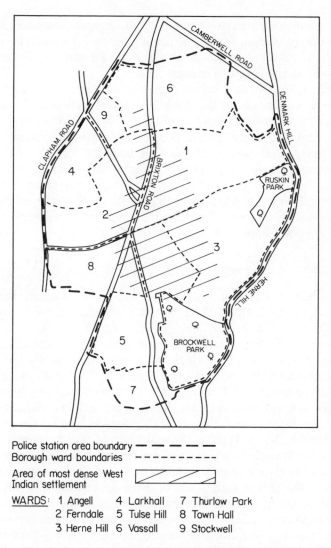

Police station area boundary — — — — — —
Borough ward boundaries — — — — — — — —
Area of most dense West
Indian settlement

WARDS: 1 Angell   4 Larkhall   7 Thurlow Park
2 Ferndale   5 Tulse Hill   8 Town Hall
3 Herne Hill 6 Vassall   9 Stockwell

Figure II.1. Police Station Area LD in the London Borough of Lambeth

confined area a high concentration (by English standards) of West Indians, mostly of Jamaican origin, whose cultural influence can readily be observed. Brixton Market, still manned mainly by white stallholders, now displays a wide range of West Indian specialties, record stores emanating the sound of 'reggae' music proliferate in the shopping area, and several pubs have a largely West Indian clientele, as well as West Indian managers.[2]

Around this central area of Brixton, particularly to the east and south, there are areas of better accommodation inhabited by middle-class whites and some more prosperous West Indians. It is interesting to note that the West Indians who have managed to move away from the central section of Brixton are—

like their white counterparts—anxious to distinguish themselves from that section of the population. Many who could objectively be said to reside within the general Brixton area prefer to describe their neighbourhoods as Camberwell, or Stockwell, Herne Hill, or Denmark Hill.[3]

In selecting Brixton as a survey area our interest was to compared the attitudes and experiences of the West Indian community with those of two others, mainly white—one working-class and one middle-class—as well as the perceptions held towards black people as potential or symbolic criminals by whites living in all three areas. We considered the borough of Lambeth to be more appropriate for this purpose than such areas as Paddington and North Kensington because it is clearly an area of settlement rather than one of transience and high mobility; it was important, given our sampling method, that we choose an area where the maximum number of residents—especially immigrants—would appear on the electoral register.

(2) Hackney

Police subdivision GH in the London borough of Hackney includes the borough wards of Chatham, Wick, Kingsmead, and Victoria, plus parts of Downs, Dalston, Lea Bridge, and Queensbridge wards. The north of the area is bounded by Lea Bridge Road and the south by Victoria Park; the west of the area is bounded by Hackney Marshes and the east goes as far as London Fields and Dalston Lane (see Figure II.2). It includes the areas of Lower Clapton and South Hackney, which are predominantly working-class residential areas, as well as the busy shopping area around Mare Street to the west. As a result of its proximity to such places as Bethnal Green, Hoxton, and Haggerston, South Hackney shares some of the traditional East End working-class atmosphere which has been characterized both in sociological studies,[4] and more notoriously in life histories of some infamous East End 'gangsters'.[5] The area is mainly one of dense council housing which has re-placed old streets of terraced houses, and although there are a number of newer high-rise estates, the many pre-war blocks that remain, in poor physical condition, present a somewhat depressing environment in which families at the lowest end of the social hierarchy reside. There had recently been some controversy, sparked by an article in a national daily newspaper,[6] referring to the Kingsmead Estate which is situated in this area, concerning the alleged unwritten policy of 'dumping' so-called 'problem' families in these old estates. This practice has been strongly criticized as an administrative expedient; it certainly appears to be in no way beneficial to the families themselves, and to serve only to make already aesthetically depressing conditions even less congenial to live in.

Although our particular area of Hackney contains a stable core of working-class white residents, the surrounding areas of Stoke Newington and Dalston have, over the past 13 years, been undergoing a steady population change. Originally areas of early Jewish settlement, the outward movement of this

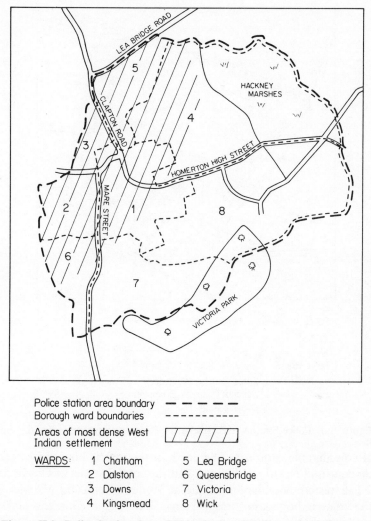

Police station area boundary — — — — —
Borough ward boundaries — — — — — — — — — —
Areas of most dense West
Indian settlement

WARDS: 1 Chatham 5 Lea Bridge
2 Dalston 6 Queensbridge
3 Downs 7 Victoria
4 Kingsmead 8 Wick

Figure II.2. Police Station Area GH in the London Borough of Hackney

community to the more prosperous suburbs has left a space in the borough which is gradually being occupied by increasing numbers of West Indian and Asian immigrants. The effect of this change, being more recent than that in Brixton, proved to be of particular interest to us because of the extent to which it appeared to have influenced the attitudes of many of our respondents towards the causes of crime and stereotypes of criminals.

(3) Kensington

Police district BK, in the borough of Kensington, covers a somewhat smaller area than those in the other two boroughs, but it is nevertheless an

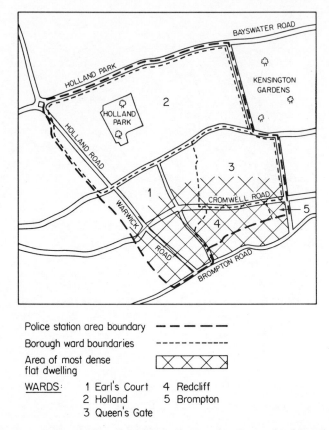

Police station area boundary — — — — —

Borough ward boundaries - - - - - - - - - - -

Area of most dense
flat dwelling

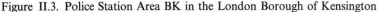

WARDS: 1 Earl's Court   4 Redcliff
          2 Holland   5 Brompton
          3 Queen's Gate

Figure II.3. Police Station Area BK in the London Borough of Kensington

area of considerable contrasts. The north of the area is bounded by Holland Park Avenue and Notting Hill Gate, and the south by part of Old Brompton Road. The western boundary is parallel to Holland Road and Warwick Road, and the eastern boundary runs through Kensington Gardens and along Queen's Gate, Earl's Court, and parts of the Redcliffe and Brompton wards. There is a striking contrast between the northern and southern parts of this area, roughly divided by the Cromwell Road. The northern two-thirds is composed of the fashionable and expensive residential areas of Kensington and South Kensington, which house wealthy upper-middle and middle-class professional people who form a distinctive community residing within a fairly small and well-defined area. This is a well established, fairly homogeneous, stable population whose life-styles and experiences we hoped would contrast strongly with those of the populations in our other two areas. The characteristics of this population are probably similar to those of other areas such as Chelsea, but we preferred Kensington to Chelsea since there is also a fairly large council housing estate situated within the Chelsea Police Sub-divisional area.

In the southern third of our area is to be found part of the Earl's Court 'bed-sitter belt'. Here the comparatively poorer physical accommodation houses a mixture of students, short-term foreign visitors and other transients. The large Victorian houses are subdivided again and again to provide minimal accommodation for short-stay tenants. The population of this area threatened to present problems of sampling for us, since not only would it be under-represented on the electoral register, but there was also a strong possibility that a substantial number of those who did appear on the register, as well as those whose addresses we obtained from police records, would have moved away from the area. We nevertheless decided to use this particular police subdivision since our main interest—for purposes of contrast with the other two areas—lay in the stable middle-class population situated in its northern part.

For purposes of comparison we were able to construct a fairly accurate picture of both the levels and types of recorded crime most prevalent within our three areas, from statistics made available by the Metropolitan Police.[7] In Table II.1 we have ranked all the Metropolitan Police divisions (not sub-

Table II.1. 21 Metropolitan Police District Divisions ranked according to recorded crime rate per 100,000 population[a]

Division		Population[a]	Number of indictable offences	Rate per 100,000
A, C & D	Westminster	233,360	48,013	20,574
B	Kensington and Chelsea	182,230	21,507	11,737
E	Camden	197,390	18,821	9,534
T	Hounslow, etc.	206,460	15,304	7,412
H	Tower Hamlets	159,200	11,714	7,358
N	Islington	194,280	12,996	6,689
F	Hammersmith	181,880	11,066	6,084
L	Lambeth	301,690	18,111	6,003
M	Southwark	253,360	14,246	5,625
G	Hackney	215,270	11,736	5,451
W	Wandsworth	297,080	13,082	4,403
X	Ealing, etc.	535,830	18,223	3,400
P	Bromley, etc.	569,470	19,324	3,393
K	Barking, etc.	637,860	21,560	3,380
Q	Brent, etc.	503,990	15,591	3,093
Y	Cheshunt, etc.	552,960	16,828	3,043
R	Bexley, etc.	433,160	13,128	3,030
S	Barnet, etc.	372,410	10,910	2,929
J	Chigwell, etc.	541,010	15,112	2,793
V	Esher, etc.	380,870	10,474	2,750
Z	Banstead, etc.	620,190	16,581	2,673
Total, Metropolitan Police District		7,840,350	354,445	4,520

[a]Population estimates from Registrar-General's Statistics, age 0 upwards.

divisions) according to overall recorded crime rates per 100,000 population. It can be seen from this table that the divisions which include our particular subdivisional areas rank in the highest ten of the 21 divisions. Kensington (B division) has the second highest recorded crime rate of all London boroughs; whilst Lambeth (L division) and Hackney (G division) rank eighth and tenth respectively.[8] These relatively high levels of recorded crime assured us—we hoped—of a sufficient number of people in our sample who would have been victims of a crime in the past year.

The pattern of recorded crime varies somewhat predictably between the three areas. Kensington has the highest proportion of burglary and theft from dwelling houses—35·8 per cent, against 29·4 per cent in Brixton and 32·7 per cent in Hackney. The proportion of offences against the person, however, is much lower in Kensington than in the other two areas: 2·1 per cent for all robbery, wounding, assault and other offences against the person, against 6·8 per cent in Brixton and 6·1 per cent in Hackney. The figures for fraud, a predominantly white-collar crime, probably reflect the differences in social class between our three areas, with Kensington having approximately twice as much as Brixton and almost three times as much as Hackney.

According to the 1971 Census, the populations of persons aged 18 years and over in our areas were 61,264 in Brixton, 46,238 in Hackney, and 54,471 in Kensington.[9] In all three areas the number of adult females is slightly greater than the number of males: females constitute 55·8 per cent of the population in Brixton, 54·2 per cent in Hackney and 55·8 per cent in Kensington. There is also a discernible difference in the age structures of the three areas. Kensington has a higher proportion of both men and women between the ages of 20 and 29, with about 40 per cent of both the male and female populations falling within this age group, as compared with about half that figure in both Brixton and Hackney. At the other end of the scale, we find that the proportions of both males and females over the age of 60 are higher in both Hackney and Brixton than in Kensington.

An analysis by marital status shows little difference between Brixton and Hackney, but again Kensington differs in that two-thirds of the total population falls into the category of 'Single, Widowed or Divorced'; the number of single, widowed or divorced females in Kensington represents some 40 per cent of the total population of that area.

Census data on the birthplaces of the enumerated populations in our three areas (see Table II.2) reflect the intended disparity between them in terms of ethnic composition. Brixton has by far the greatest number of residents giving their birthplace as the Caribbean; this is further reinforced by the proportions of residents (according to the 1971 Census) having both parents born in the New Commonwealth, while in Hackney the figure is 13·1 per cent and in Kensington it is only 4·2 per cent. It is also of interest to note that over a quarter of the enumerated population of Kensington were born outside of the UK and Commonwealth countries.

Table II.2. Birthplaces of enumerated populations in three police subdivisions, according to the 1971 Census

	Brixton %	Hackney %	Kensington %
England and Wales	69·6	82·1	53·7
Elsewhere in UK	2·4	1·6	5·2
Irish Republic	4·4	2·6	3·6
Old Commonwealth	0·3	0·1	4·7
Africa	2·5	0·8	1·6
Caribbean	11·5	6·0	0·8
India	0·7	0·8	1·9
Pakistan	0·2	0·2	0·5
Elsewhere	8·4	5·9	27·8
	100·0	100·0	100·0
All Residents	84,879	61,944	51,906

4. Selection of Samples

A primary objective of this project was to investigate the completeness and accuracy of reporting of crime incidents by persons who were known to have been victims of crime within the preceding year. It was thus necessary for us to obtain, from police records, the names and addresses of known victims whom we could interview and whose responses regarding their victimization we would be able to check against positive records. Accordingly, the names and addresses of an initial pool of known victims in 1971 and 1972, and details of the crimes in which they had been involved, were obtained from copies of crime reports at Scotland Yard.[1] The cases selected for this initial pool were chosen at random, though the sampling fractions used varied owing to the different numbers of recorded crimes in the three subdivisional areas; for example, in Hackney we initially selected all major crimes recorded in 1972, but only one in five of the minor or 'beat' crimes. Initially, therefore, we selected a sample of *crimes* rather than a sample of *victims;* some of the victims could have been involved in more than one of those crimes, though this did not in fact happen in our initial sample. It is important to note that we excluded from this initial sample those crimes in which the victim lived outside the sample area (even though the crime might have been committed, and thus recorded, there). The police record crimes in the area in which they take place, rather than the area in which the victim lives: the two are identical for residential burglary,[2] of course, but are not necessarily so for other offences. Thus our sample of cases in Hackney, for example, included only those assaults and thefts which took place in Hackney, *and* involved residents of Hackney.

In addition to the sample of known victims, we also wanted to interview random samples of the populations in our three areas, in order to estimate the incidence of victimization in the general population, and to explore perceptions and attitudes to crime which would be in some way representative of the three areas. Thus in each area a number of cases were selected at random from the electoral registers. A few of the persons selected in this way had already been chosen from crime reports; these were excluded from the electoral register sample, and were treated as 'known victims' only.[3] The electoral register is not an ideal sampling frame for our areas, especially since our survey took place only two months before the publication of the latest register; but it was necessary for us to use it (rather than some form of area sampling) because our interviewers had to be given names and addresses of the known victims in our sample. It is important to note that our interviewers did not know that any of their cases was known by us to be a victim; they were told that *all* of their cases had been drawn from the electoral register. This insured that they did not (consciously or unconsciously) bias the responses of those whom we knew to have been victims.

The cases selected in each area were thus of three types, as follows:

1. Persons selected from police reports who were recorded as victims of crimes which took place between 1 January 1972 and 31 October 1972. These cases we shall refer to as the Main Victim (MV) sample.

2. Persons selected from police reports showing them to have been victims of crime which took place between 1 October 1971 and 31 December 1971. These cases were included in the sample in order to check on the extent to which they reported incorrectly to our interviewers that their crimes had occurred during 1972, i.e. to investigate the phenomenon known as 'time telescoping'; we shall therefore refer to them as Telescope cases, or the T sample.

3. Persons chosen at random from registered electors in the three survey areas; these we shall refer to as Register cases, or the R sample.

We wished, if possible, to investigate systematically the effects of such factors as age, sex, type of crime and time, on the recall and reporting of crimes by our Main Victim sample. Accordingly, from our initial pool of Main Victim cases in each area, we selected a subset in accordance with an experimental design. In Brixton, the design consisted of four independent Latin squares based on the factors just mentioned; in Hackney and Kensington, owing to the smaller number of crimes of violence available and the less complete information recorded on the Kensington crime reports, a less elaborate randomized block design had to be used. Each design included equal numbers of victims of crimes of violence (including purse-snatching recorded as theft from the person), burglary, and theft. The Telescope cases were not chosen in accordance with a rigorous experimental design, but were selected so as to give approximately equal numbers of victims of violence, burglary and theft in each of the three months October–December 1971 in each of the three areas. Thus at the beginning of the fieldwork our target sample consisted of 144 Main Victim cases and 50 Telescope cases in each area. Replacement cases were also selected at the beginning of the fieldwork for each cell in each of the three experimental designs, and (so far as possible) for the Telescope cases, giving us a total sample of about 1,000 completed interviews, about half of which would be with known victims.

In the event, this design proved to be too ambitious, owing to the difficulty of locating both Main Victim and Telescope cases. This difficulty was especially great in the Kensington area, where no more than a quarter of the known victims could be located. In both Kensington and Hackney, the total number of known victims of recorded crimes of violence was simply too small to provide us with sufficient replacements for our Main Victim experimental designs; this was so despite the fact that in each area we collected information on *all* of the victims of recorded crimes of violence during the period January–October 1972.[4] Fortunately it was possible for us to combine the Main Victim cases interviewed in the three areas, into a randomized block design of the kind originally planned for Hackney and Kensington; and we had in any event sufficient cases in different categories of age, type of crime, etc. to carry out adequate analyses of the effects of those factors on recall and reporting.

5. Response Rates

From Table II·3 it can be seen that the overall response rate for the survey was 40·9 per cent, being 45·0 per cent for the Register sample and 35·1 per cent for the Victim and Telescope samples combined. While this rate is certainly lower than we should have liked, it is probably not abnormally low in view of the special nature of our samples, the relatively short period of fieldwork and the areas in which the survey was carried out.[1] The main reason for non-response in all three areas was that respondents were either known to have moved away, or could not be contacted by the interviewers at the designated address.[2] The proportion of respondents who had moved or who could not be contacted was especially high for Main Victim and Telescope cases in Kensington. (This was a problem which we had to some extent foreseen in Kensington with respect to the Earl's Court area, as a result of the transient nature of the population; in the event it was of much greater proportions than we had expected.) The number of refusals, however did not vary significantly between the three areas, and the overall refusal rate for the sample was only 8·9 per cent. In Hackney the percentage was slightly higher than this in both the Register and Main Victim and Telescope samples, while Kensington had consistently the lowest refusal rate of all the three areas.

In analysing our data we were concerned to investigate the direction and magnitude of any bias, especially in the MV and T samples, resulting from non-response; and in particular to discover whether the type of crime of which a respondent had been a victim would in any way influence his willingness to be interviewed or our ability to contact him. If any particular category of victim

Table II.3 Response rates for the MV, T and R samples in the three London areas[a]

Area and sample	Moved or could not be contacted		Refused		Completed		Total	
	No.	%	No.	%	No.	%	No.	%
Brixton:								
MV & T	119	43·8	25	9·2	128	47.1	272	100·0
R	170	43·1	39	9·9	185	47.0	394	100·0
Total	289	43·4	64	9·6	313	47·0	666	100·0
Hackney:								
MV and T	115	47·9	27	11·3	98	40·8	240	100·0
R	158	40·9	43	11·1	185	47·9	386	100·0
Total	273	43·6	70	11·2	277	44·2	626	100·0
Kensington:								
MV and T	257	73·0	18	5·1	77	21·9	352	100·0
R	234	51·7	34	7·5	185	40·8	453	100·0
Total	491	61·0	52	6·5	262	32·5	805	100·0
All three areas:								
MV and T	491	56·8	70	8·1	303	35·1	864	100·0
R	562	45·6	116	9·4	555	45·0	1233	100·0
Total	1053	50·2	186	8·9	858	40·9	2097	100·0

[a]This table includes 17 completed interviews subsequently excluded on grounds of language difficulties, senility, etc.: see page 17 above.

were consistently excluded from the survey, because he could not be located or refused to be interviewed, it could throw doubt on the effectiveness of the survey method for locating victims of crime in the populations. Since for Main Victim and Telescope cases we had obtained information from police records relating to sex of respondent and the type of crime of which they had been a victim, we were able to analyse response rates in relation to these two attributes. Although no clear pattern emerges from these analyses (an encouraging fact), it appears that female victims of violence tended to refuse to be interviewed more often than male victims of violence.[3] It must be borne in mind, however, that overall, in both the Register and Main Victim and Telescope samples, there was a somewhat greater tendency for women to refuse than for men. Overall, victims of theft refused less frequently than victims of either burglary or violence, but conversely they were more often unable to be contacted by interviewers. Of those respondents who were known to have moved away from the address obtained from police records, no pattern emerges in relation to any of the categories of offence.

6. Representativeness of the R Sample

Our final samples are broadly similar, in most respects in which they can be compared, to the enumerated populations in our three areas according to the 1971 Census. (Some differences would be expected, of course, since the population of registered electors is not identical with the enumerated population; it must be remembered that it is the former, and not the latter, with which we are concerned.) So far as we can judge, therefore, the relatively low overall response rate did not introduce any gross biases into our final samples. Data on age and sex are presented in Tables II.4, II.5 and II.6. It will be seen that the greatest discrepancies occur in the Kensington Register sample, where the younger age groups (18–29) are under-represented among both males and females. This is almost certainly accounted for by the nature of the population in the Earl's Court area: here there is a high concentration of young people,

Table II.4. Age and sex composition of the Brixton samples, compared with enumerated population age 18 and over in 1971 Census

	Enumerated population (%)		R sample M		F		MV and T samples M		F	
	M	F	No.	%	No.	%	No.	%	No.	%
18–19	4·1	3·7	2	2·6	3	2·8	0	—	0	—
20–29	21·9	20·4	18	23·7	21	19·8	11	16·4	12	20·3
30–39	18·6	16·0	15	19·7	18	17·0	20	29·9	13	22·0
40–49	18·3	16·7	12	15·8	18	17·0	19	28·4	15	25·4
50–59	16·9	15·7	8	10·5	13	12·3	10	14·9	8	13·6
60 +	20·1	27·6	21	27·6	33	31·1	7	10·4	11	18·6
Total	29042	32222	76	100·0	106	100·0	67	100·0	59	100·0
Per cent of total	47.4	52.6	41.8		58·2		53·3		46·7	

Table II.5. Age and sex composition of the Hackney samples, compared with enumerated population age 18 and over in 1971 Census

	Enumerated population (per cent)		R sample M		F		MV and T samples M		F	
	M	F	No.	%	No.	%	No.	%	No.	%
18–19	3·6	3·7	1	1·2	3	3·2	5	12·5	4	7·5
20–29	20·2	18·5	13	15·5	12	12·6	6	15·0	13	24·5
30–39	15·6	13·4	11	13·1	19	20·0	7	17·5	11	20·8
40–49	17·3	15·6	16	19·0	21	22·1	10	25·0	7	13·2
50–59	18·8	16·8	21	25·0	14	14·7	6	15·0	12	22·6
60 +	24·4	32·0	22	26·2	26	27·4	6	15·0	6	11·3
Total	21244	24994	84	100·0	95	100·0	40	100·0	53	100·0
Per cent of total	45·9	54·1	46·9		53·1		43·0		57·0	

Table II.6 Age and sex composition of the Kensington samples, compared with enumerated population age 18 and over in 1971 Census

	Enumerated population (per cent)		R sample M		F		MV and T samples M		F	
	M	F	No.	%	No.	%	No.	%	No.	%
18–19	3·9	5·3	4	4·9	3	2·9	3	9·1	0	—
20–29	40·4	40·2	14	17·1	28	27·5	11	33·3	22	50·0
30–39	18·3	13·0	22	26·8	12	11·8	6	18·2	12	27·2
40–49	13·3	10·9	17	20·7	18	17·6	6	18·2	4	9·1
50–59	11·3	11·0	10	12·2	13	12·7	2	6·1	2	4·5
60 +	12·7	19·7	15	18·3	28	27·5	5	15·2	4	9·1
Total	24029	30442	82	100·0	102	100·0	33	100·0	44	100·0
Per cent of total	44·1	55·9	44·6		55·4		43·4		56·6	

such as students and foreign visitors, who would not have been on the electoral register, or would have moved away from the address of enumeration before our survey was conducted. As we shall see,[1] there is some evidence that in our sample length of residence is negatively associated with criminal victimization; thus our data probably tend to understate victimization rates, especially in Kensington. But length of residence was not related, in any significant or consistent way, with any of the other behavioural or attitudinal variables on which we obtained information.

The Main Victim and Telescope samples, on the other hand, differ more markedly from the enumerated populations; these samples are drawn from the population of persons who had reported crimes to the police, and thus reflect, in part, the risk of becoming a (known) victim. As we shall see,[2] this conclusion is borne out by the patterns of reported victimization found in our R samples. Thus in general we find that among our known victims the younger and middle-aged groups tend to be over-represented (compared with the enumerated populations); those over 60 tend to be under-represented.

Notes and References

1. An Overview of the Research

1. The attempt to interview larger numbers of immigrants—in particular, West Indians— was made with a view to the London survey, where we expected a larger proportion of non-English respondents; we wanted to try to get some idea of how people from other cultures would respond to our questions. It was here that we first met with diffi- culties—encountered by most survey researchers—in interviewing people who did not speak English; and here that we decided, regretfully, to exclude such persons from the London sample.

2 The Questionnaire

1. The final version of the questionnaire is reproduced in the Appendix, pp. 237–266 below.
2. Throughout the pretests, and in the London survey, the ordering of responses on prompt cards was systematically varied. Each interviewer was given two sets of prompt cards, and was instructed to select the appropriate set of cards before commencing each interview, in accordance with a number printed on the front of the questionnaire. The order in which choices were printed was alternated both within and between the sets of cards; for example, the responses 'Strongly Agree—Agree—Disagree—Strongly Disagree' were presented in that order on approximately half of the questionnaires, and in the reverse order on the remainder. Subsequent analysis suggested that responses to such forced-choice questions may have been slightly influenced by the order in which choices were presented; but the effects of this were not consistent, and in no case did they attain statistical significance.
3. Respondents' occupations were subsequently coded according to the Registrar-General's social class scale, the Hall–Jones Scale and the North-Hatt Occupational Prestige Scale. (In the case of married women, the husband's occupation was used whether or not the wife was herself employed.) Though these three methods of rating social status are not exactly isomorphic, in no case did the use of an alternative classification affect the results of our analyses; the six-category Registrar-General's classification is thus generally used throughout the book.
4. See below, p. 37.
5. If respondents said that they did not *know* who had been responsible for the crime, they were nevertheless asked who they *thought* might have been responsible, giving age, sex, and race. This question was designed to elicit the stereotypes which our victims held as to the kind of people who they thought might have committed the offence of which they had been a victim.
6. Throughout the two Peterborough pretests and in the London survey, this section of the questionnaire was invariably administered at the very end of the interview. This was done so that in the event of a respondent taking offence at being asked questions of this nature, it would not prejudice his responses to other questions. It may be noted here that as a general rule respondents did not object to being asked questions of this kind.

3. The London Areas

1. This was, of course, the only information we had on this point. But see below, Chapter VI, pp. 157–158, for a discussion of how misleading such information can be.
2. For a fairly full description of both the history of West Indian settlement in Brixton and the physical characteristics of Brixton see Sheila Patterson, *Dark Strangers* (London: Tavistock Publications, 1963).
3. See Chapter VIII, pp. 202–203 below.
4. Notably in some of the work done by the Institute for Community Studies; for example, Michael Young and Peter Willmott, *Family and Kinship in East London* (London: Routledge and Kegan Paul, 1957), and Peter Townsend, *The Family Life of Old People* (London: Routledge and Kegan Paul, 1957).
5. A recent example full of rich descriptive information is the biography of the Kray twins: John Pearson, *The Profession of Violence: The Rise and Fall of the Kray Twins* (London: Weidenfeld and Nicolson, 1972).
6. See *The Guardian*, 8th August 1973, where a feature article was written about the Kingsmead Estate in Hackney by Peter Hildrew and Hugh Hebert.
7. We are grateful to Mr. H. D. Walton of the Metropolitan Police for making these statistics available to us.

8. Divisional crime rates have been used in Table II.1 since we do not have population data for subdivisions other than the three in which our survey was carried out.
9. Our population data for the three police subdivisional areas were obtained by aggregating 1971 Census data for all of the enumeration districts in each area.

4. Selection of Samples

1. We wish to acknowledge the considerable help which we received from Mr. I. M. Fernie and his staff at Scotland Yard, during this part of our work.
2. Though the term 'burglary' is no longer confined, in English law, to breaking into a dwellinghouse (rather than, for example, a shop or office): see the Theft Act 1968, s. 9.
3. This was a mistake, as Dr. Kauko Aromaa has since pointed out to us: such cases should have been treated as belonging to both samples. Excluding them from the R sample made our calculations of crime rates even more complicated than they were already: see below, Chapter VI, pp. 142–151.
4. An additional problem here was that a substantial number of the violent crimes recorded in our three areas involved victims residing outside the areas, who had to be excluded from the sample. We estimate that this was so far at least 10 per cent of the crimes against the person recorded in Brixton and Hackney, and for at least 15 per cent of those recorded in Kensington, where the number of tourist victims is naturally high. See further below, Chapter VI, pp. 146–147.

5. Response Rates

1. Our overall response rate may be compared with that obtained in a survey of white registered electors living in five Inner London Boroughs (including Lambeth) in 1966 on behalf of the Institute of Race Relations: of an initial sample of about 4,200 names, about 12 per cent were excluded because they had moved, a similar proportion refused and about 10 per cent could not be located after four calls, thus giving an overall rate of 66 per cent. See E. J. B. Rose and associates, *Colour and Citizenship* (London: Oxford University Press, 1969) 785.
2. Interviewers were instructed to make up to five call-backs, if necessary, before treating the case as a 'non-contact.'
3. It is possible that female victims of violence were more likely to refuse owing to the nature of the offences committed against them, or the identity of their assailants (e.g. common-law husbands); the information contained on police records which were made available to us, relating to these cases, was unfortunately too limited to permit a thorough investigation of this point.

6. Representativeness of the R Sample

1. See below, Chapter IV, pp. 86–87.
2. Below, pp. 84–85.

CHAPTER III

Accuracy of Recall and Reporting

1. Evidence on Recall and Telescoping

Retrospective surveys. in which persons are asked for information about their past experiences, have a number of different major sources of inaccuracy relating to recall. First, the respondents may simply fail to remember the events in question, or if they do remember them, they may not tell the interviewer about them, through deceit or misunderstanding. In practice it is difficult, if not impossible, to distinguish between simple memory failure and the deliberate or unconscious withholding of information; in either case, the net effect— that the event is completely lost so far as the survey researcher is concerned— is the same. The second source of inaccuracy is known as 'telescoping': it occurs when a respondent remembers and reports an event, but recalls the event as having happened either earlier or (more usually) later than in fact it did. One purpose of a survey of criminal victimization is to estimate the frequency with which certain types of crimes occur in a given time period. In such a survey, backward telescoping has the same effect as a simple failure to recall or report an incident; sample estimates of the frequency of crime will be lower than the true frequency, since some crimes which actually took place within the survey reference period will be reported as having occurred earlier. Telescoping forward has the opposite effect: it leads to events being reported as within the survey reference period when in fact they appeared earlier, thus inflating the survey estimates above their true value.

Both non-reporting and telescoping can to some extent be minimized by good questionnaire design and interviewing technique; and one objective of methodological research in this field is to discover ways of keeping these two sources of error to an acceptably low level. Some of these are fairly obvious. For example, respondents' recall of past events is almost certainly affected by the length of the time period for which they are asked to remember. Most people can recollect what they did last week; but few can recall in the same detail what they did twenty years ago. But recall and reporting may also be affected by question wording and question order, and by the energy and skill which interviewers display in asking questions and probing. If questions about experiences of victimization are asked early in the interview, the respondent may not be 'warmed up' to the subject, or he may not have obtained adequate rapport with the interviewer. On the other hand, if questions about victimization come at the end of a long interview, recall may be influenced by fatigue or boredom, either on the part of the interviewer or of the respondent. Unfortunately it was not practicable for us to investigate this in our London survey. But in the second of our pilot studies in Peterborough, we systematically varied the order of the sections in our questionnaire, so that some respondents were asked about their experience of victimization at the beginning of the interview, some in the middle, and some at the end. We found slightly lower rates of reported victimization when the questions about it came at the end of the interview, indicating that responses had to some extent been affected by fatigue. The difference was not great, and our data showed no apparent advantage in asking about victimization at the beginning of the interview rather than in the middle; and given the range of subjects on which we wanted information—and the possibility of biasing responses to questions on the police, etc.—it seemed to us best to keep the questions about respondents' experiences of victimization nearer the end of the interview in our London survey. As we have already noted,[1] however, the questionnaire was substantially shortened before being administered in London.

In one part of the pilot survey carried out in Washington, D.C. for the U.S. President's Crime Commission, the respondent was asked for details about each event immediately after he mentioned it.[2] It was evident that this produced a downward bias in the number of victimization incidents per respondent, since, as Reiss has put it, 'It soon became clear that a respondent controls the number of experiences he or she had on the basis of what they consider a sufficient amount of time they had given the interviewer.'[3] The better method—which we used in all of our surveys—is for the interviewer to ask the respondent a series of 'screening' questions about the number of time he has had his house broken into, had something stolen from him, been assaulted, etc.: and to record at that time merely the *numbers* of incidents of each type mentioned by the respondent. Details of each incident mentioned in this series of 'screening' questions can then be recorded later on a separate form (such as our crime incident form). A few of our respondents—and a few of our interviewers—did occasionally balk at spending the extra time at the end of the main interview which this method entails. But in almost every one of these cases the information was obtained by a call-back; and at any rate, this method clearly gives a better estimate of the total amount of victimization experienced by the sample, than the method of asking concurrently for details of each item mentioned.

A further source of under-reporting of crime incidents—strictly speaking a matter of sampling rather than questionnaire design—is exemplified by the U.S. national survey carried out by the National Opinion Research Center for the President's Commission, in which one member of the household was asked to give information about the experiences of victimization of all members of the household. Since the person interviewed may well know nothing of crimes committed against other members of his immediate family, it is better to ask respondents about their own experiences only, and to estimate household victimization from data on household size and composition. This method requires some re-weighting of individual responses, for those offences (such as burglary and car theft) which are in a sense committed against the whole household, and which thus might be reported by any one of its members who was interviewed. Nonetheless, it seems likely to yield more complete information on victimization than the use of 'proxy' respondents.[4]

A usual method of trying to minimize telescoping—which we followed in our own survey—is to begin with questions involving recall of past events by asking the respondent to try to think back to the beginning of the reference period (e.g. to remember what he was doing a year ago), and then to ask him about other things which he did or which happened to him during the year, to which his experiences of criminal victimization can be related. Thus section G of our London questionnaire began with the following introduction:

'I would like to ask you about some things which might have happened to you during the past year. Can you think back to what you were doing a year ago—that is the (beginning/middle/end) of (month) 1972?
Can you remember some of the things which you did in the past year—for example, did you go away on holiday? When was your birthday? Did you change your job? Were you off work at any time? Were there any deaths, births, marriages, or illnesses in your family? Any other things that you particularly remember?'

Interviewers were instructed to try and get the exact dates of any events mentioned and write them down; and if necessary, to try to get the respondent to remember, and place his events in relation to, events such as Easter Sunday, Bank Holidays and Christmas. After noting the dates mentioned by the respondent and probing his memory of other events, the interviewer was instructed to run through them quickly in chronological order, e.g. 'So your birthday was March 5th, then you went to Grimsby at the beginning of last August for two weeks, then when your children went back to school in September you were off ill with the flu for a fortnight' etc. It is fair to add, however, that this method depends not only on the memory of the respondent, but on his co-operativeness. It also depends on the interviewer's diligence and skill in establishing the reference period in the respondent's mind. Some of our own interviewers were apparently less successful at this than others.[5]

While techniques such as these may limit under-reporting and telescoping of crime incidents in a victim survey, it is in practice almost impossible to eliminate these two types of inaccuracy entirely. Thus it is important to try to learn as much as possible about their magnitude and nature. Specifically, we need to know at least the following:

(1) How much under-reporting and telescoping of crime events is likely to occur in a victim survey, and what are the optimum strategies for minimizing

under-reporting and telescoping? In particular, what is the longest time period for which suitably accurate estimates of victimization can be obtained in a retrospective survey? This question has important implications for the victim survey method, since in a full-scale programme of such surveys, the length of reference period used will be an important determinant of sample size. In general, in order to obtain the same degree of precision in population estimates of victimization, twice as large a sample will be needed if the respondents are asked about the preceding six months, than if they are asked about their experience during the preceding year; the sample will need to be twice as large again if the reference period is only three months.

(2) Do under-reporting and telescoping of crime incidents tend to occur in a reasonably random fashion, or do they appear to be systematically associated either with certain sorts of subject matter, or with attributes of the respondents (such as age, sex, social class or mobility)? If the former, they may pose no greater problem than any of the other types of random measurement error found in social science research: they may tend to mask associations (e.g. to attenuate correlation coefficients), but may introduce no further serious bias which would make statistical inference from survey results impossible. If the latter, it may to some extent be possible to correct for them, provided information on the population surveyed (e.g. on demographic attributes such as age, sex and area of residence) can be obtained for the samples and populations surveyed.

Some research on these questions has been done by students of survey methodology, in relation to other types of subject matter. Among the earliest of empirical investigations of the questions of recall and telescoping were those done in connection with the Survey of Sickness, carried out in Britain by the Social Survey during the years 1944–1952. In this survey, different samples of adults were questioned in the first fortnight of each month, about their illnesses in previous months. Reference periods of one, two and (until September 1949) three previous calender months were used. Since interviewing was carried on throughout the year, it was possible to compare the number of illnesses reported as occurring one and two months previously; differences in the reported rates in these two periods would give an indication of the extent to which non-recall and telescoping forward were affecting responses. An analysis of the results for 1947 showed that for persons aged 16 to 64, the number of new illnesses remembered two months back was only 66 per cent.[6] The deficit varied from month to month. For recurrent and continued illnesses, however, the results from two months back were much nearer to 100 per cent of the one-month rate. It may, of course, have been difficult for respondents to decide exactly when such illnesses began. Visits to the doctor are much more precisely dateable, and respondents in the Survey of Sickness were also asked about these. Commenting on the results of this part of the survey, Gray notes that 'the memory effect is not simply one of forgetting an increasing proportion of consultations as time goes by. It seems that the difference between the curves (of consultation reported in different reference periods) is affected by the way in which the actual rate is varying.'[7] It appeared that when the actual rate of consultations was falling sharply from a high level, there was a tendency for people to report more consultations when asked two months after the event, than when asked one month afterwards. Gray himself carried out an experiment in which members of a government department were asked about the amounts of sick leave and annual leave which they had taken in the preceding four and a half months; the responses were checked against departmental records of leave. About 95 per cent of those who had taken no sick leave in the four and a half month period correctly reported in the survey that they had taken none; but of the persons who had taken some leave, only about a third gave completely correct answers which placed the leave within the month in which it actually occurred. The average discrepancy between remembered and true values for the whole of the four and a half month period was very slight; though there were considerable variations in particular months, these happened almost exactly to cancel each other out when averaged over the whole of the reference period. Gray concludes that 'forgetting mainly took the form of forgetting *when* rather than forgetting completely.'[8] There was considerable telescoping both backward and forward; Gray's data suggest, however that on balance there was a tendency for respondents to report leave as having occurred in a later month than it in fact occurred. This illustrates the importance of carefully defining and re-defining the reference period for the respondent; to quote Gray again, 'It has to be remembered that it is often the event, and not when it happened, which appears important to the informant.'[9]

The potential importance of recall losses and telescoping has been demonstrated, even for fairly short reference periods, by several surveys of household expenditure. Neter and Waksberg conducted an experiment in which respondents were asked about this subject, using questionnaires with different reference periods—one month, three months and six months.[10] In addition, with the one-month and three-month questionnaires, bounded interviews were conducted. (With bounded interviews, respondents are re-interviewed on one or more occasions. The interviewer knows what items were reported by the respondent at the preceding interview, and can thus avoid recording items which have been telescoped into the latest reference period; he can also used the respondent's earlier reports to help establish the latest reference period in the respondent's mind.) The use of bounded interviews with a reference period as short as one month raises the possibility of 'conditioning' effects, e.g. that respondents will tend to become bored with the whole business and will thus report fewer items on the second and subsequent interviews.[11] After making a somewhat complicated allowance for this, however, Neter and Waksberg found strong evidence of a very high degree of forward telescoping when the results from the bounded one-month questionnaires were compared with the unbounded one-month ones. Unbounded recall yielded about 40 per cent more jobs, and 55 per cent higher expenditures, than bounded recall;

these differences were well beyond sampling errors. There was also strong evidence that the forward telescoping effect is a function of job size: the net telescoping effect for jobs of a value of under $20 was only about eight per cent, against about 28 per cent for jobs between $20 and $100 and about 56 per cent for the jobs of over $100. As with chronic illnesses, the completion date of expenditures on household repairs may be in fact somewhat fuzzy; it may not be clear, for example, whether a certain job was completed in January or February. But Neter and Waksberg's analysis of their data on do-it-yourself jobs and on purchases of materials (both of which could be given a more precise date in the interview than contracted repairs) showed very similar patterns of telescoping to those of contracted repairs, with the one-month questionnaire.

Analysis of the data from the three-month questionnaire showed further evidence of telescoping forward into the reference period. Naturally the degree of error introduced into the estimates through telescoping was less in this case than with one-month recall, since they affected only the first month of the reference period. There were, however, tremendous differences between first-month, second-month and third-month reports of jobs and household expenditures: for instance, the numbers reported for the month nearest the time of the interview were more than twice as great as the corresponding estimates based on recall for the month most distant from the time of the interview. But these differences were due to *internal* telescoping, i.e. a shifting forward in time of events within the three-month reference period; they did not affect estimates of the total volume of work done in the reference period. Again, there was evidence that forward telescoping was greater for larger expenditures.

Neter and Waksberg note that non-reporting (which they call recall loss) has at least two components; first, losses due to the respondent's inability to remember expenditures over a long time period, and second, the losses due to a 'reporting load effect' (that is, an effect due to the respondent's having to remember *more* items, as distinct from *earlier* ones) from lengthening the reference period.[12] They estimate that the effect of the second of these in their case was slight. Nonetheless, there were still substantial recall losses for jobs of lower value. For example, bounded *three*-month recall produced about 44 per cent fewer jobs of less than $10, and 40 per cent lower expenditures for such jobs, than bounded *one*-month recall. There was no evidence of such recall loss for jobs worth $50 and more. It was also found that when the reference period was increased to six months, reported expenditure in the last of those months (that is, the month immediately preceding the interview) was substantially lower than that obtained when a one-month reference period was used. In this case, therefore, there also appeared to be some recall loss due to reporting load. Neter and Waksberg conclude that 'three-month recall appears to provide as satisfactory data for large expenditures as one-month recall,' but that 'for small expenditures, on the other hand, serious under-reporting exists with three-month recall.'[13]

In their recent study of response effects in surveys, Sudman and Bradburn hypothesize—on the basis of experimental research relating to short-term memory—that non-reporting of events through failure of memory can be represented by a simple exponential function of time since the event, so that r_o, the fraction of all actual events reported, is given by

$$r_0 = ae^{-b_1 t}$$

where a is a non-time-related parameter depending on such things as the threat or social desirability of the event in question, or on the likelihood that the respondent is in fact aware that the event has occurred; b_1 is an 'omission parameter' which determines the rapidity of memory decay, and depends on such things as the event's importance or salience to the respondent, and the characteristics of the respondent and the interview; t is of course the time between the actual occurrence of the event and the interview.[14] Sudman and Bradburn also suggest that errors due to telescoping can be represented by Weber's law, which says that net absolute errors in the perception of time will be a function of the logarithm of the time period involved; thus the relative error r_t will be given by

$$r_t = \frac{\log b_2 t}{t}$$

Combining these two expressions makes it possible to specify the ratio between levels of reporting of incidents at two different time periods, which would be expected on the assumptions just mentioned; this ratio is given by

$$R_{(t_2/t_1)} = \frac{t_1}{t_2} e^{-b_1(t_2 - t_1)} \left(\frac{t_2 + \log b_2 t_2}{t_1 + \log b_2 t_1} \right)$$

Sudman and Bradburn tested this model against data from an experimental study on reporting of household expenditures,[15] which used reference periods of three, six and nine months. Though these data had some measurement problems, and though only three time periods were used in the study, the model appeared to fit reasonably well for each of the three categories of purchases (furniture and major appliances, housewares and small appliances, and auto supplies and services) included in the study.[16] This study, like Neter and Waksberg's, suggests that memory failure and telescoping tend to affect reporting of different types of events in different ways: more salient items were *less* likely to be forgotten, but *more* likely to be telescoped, whereas the reverse was true for less salient items (e.g. minor purchases).[17] Thus even if the net incidence of events (e.g. household purchases, crimes) were correctly estimated by a retrospective survey, the proportions of different *types* of those events is likely to be biased, with some over-representation of more salient events (e.g. more serious crimes) and under-representation of less salient ones (e.g. petty thefts).

In addition to failure of memory, the non-reporting of information in surveys may be due to the conscious or unconscious inhibition by respondents of their information, if it is thought to be a very shameful or socially undesirable kind.

Martin David conducted a survey in which low-income families were asked about cash payments and other assistance which they had received from local welfare authorities during the year 1959.[18] He found that only 37 per cent of his sample reported income from assistance which was within 10 per cent of the amount actually recorded in the welfare records. Only three families out of the 46 interviewed denied that they had received assistance during 1959; nonetheless, the average amount of assistance received by the sample was understated by 18 per cent. It was found that those persons who reported some welfare income gave relatively unbiased reports when the amount received was in the range of $1,500–$2,000. Negative bias in the reports increased as actual welfare income received was beyond that amount. It is of special interest that no clear relationships between demographic characteristics and response errors emerged from this admittedly small sample. Race, sex, age of the respondent, family size, and race of the interviewer appeared to have no affect on accuracy of reporting. David suggests that many of the families interviewed had neither a high level of intelligence nor good memory of their finances, nor systematic records, nor any particular motivation to report accurately on their income. In view of this, he regarded his results as quite satisfactory. It may well be, however, that some of his respondents harboured a suspicion that the interviewer was in some way connected with the welfare authorities and was checking up on them; if so, of course, the respondents might have been motivated to give more accurate reports than would otherwise have been the case.

Bias caused by the inhibition of reporting may be a consequence of the interview situation, as well as being due to the respondent himself. This question was investigated by Weiss, in a study of 549 Negro mothers who were receiving public assistance in New York City in 1966.[19] Respondents were asked, *inter alia*, about their registration and voting in the 1964 Presidential election, receipt of money from welfare, child's failure of a subject in school, and child's ever being held back to repeat a grade in school; validation data were available on all of these. Rates of error to the different questions ranged from a low of 2 per cent on the welfare questions to a high of 37 per cent on the child's failure of a subject at school. Most of the error lay in reporting more socially desirable behaviour than the facts warranted: for example, 16 per cent of the sample over-reported registration to vote and voting, whereas only 2 per cent under-reported it. Respondents who over-reported in the 'socially desirable' direction tended to be those who had lived in their neighbourhoods longer, were older, better educated, and longer work experience and were apparently oriented to middle-class values. It had been expected that respondents would give interviewers who were most unlike themselves a more biased and idealized picture, and conversely that they would more comfortably acknowledge less desirable behaviour and attributes to interviewers who were most like themselves. The data did not support this conclusion, however. When each pair of respondents and interviewers were matched on education, age and socio-economic status, the 'unlike' interviewer on each item did *not* generally receive more biased (i.e. socially desirable) responses. If anything, it appeared that status similarity, not status disparity, was associated with such bias. Weiss also investigated the question of the effect of rapport on response bias. Interviewers rated rapport at the end of the interview on a five point scale: confiding, frank, equivocal, guarded and hostile. The respondents who were rated highest in rapport were the most biased (in the direction of reporting more socially desirable behaviour). This also appeared to be true for attitudinal questions, where high rapport and similarity to the interviewer both tended to produce more socially desirable answers. This question is complicated, however, since 'social desirability' in an interview situation may have two quite distinct meanings. On the one hand, it may refer to behaviour, attitudes, etc. which are *generally* regarded as desirable or appropriate, within a particular culture or society; on the other hand, it may refer to what *the respondent believes that the interviewer regards* as a 'desirable' response. These two things may often coincide, but they need not: e.g. it may be thought generally shameful or otherwise undesirable to have been raped or assaulted, yet a particular respondent may more readily remember (or be willing to admit) to these things if it appears that such reports are what the interviewer wants to hear.

All of these studies confirm that both non-reporting (for whatever reason) and telescoping can introduce serious degrees of error into the results of retrospective surveys, especially for events (such as minor illnesses or small household expenditures) which are both relatively frequent and of low salience to most respondents. This bias may lead to large degrees of error even with fairly short reference periods; with longer reference periods, the loss due to non-reporting may be even greater—both because the respondent is asked to report about a possibly larger number of events (the 'reporting load effect'), and because earlier events are more likely to be forgotten. Conversely, non-reporting seems likely to be less of a problem with relatively infrequent events, especially ones which are some importance to the respondent; but it is with these events that forward telescoping is likely to be most serious. It is far from clear, however, just how far the results of the studies discussed in this section are directly applicable to surveys of criminal victimization. Are sicknesses more salient, on average, than crimes? Plainly much depends on the type of sickness, and the type of crime. Being robbed in the street or having one's house broken into are, in principle, more *precisely* dateable events than coming down with the 'flu or carrying out do-it-yourself work in one's home. But surveys relating to such things as sickness or unemployment are not so much concerned with the reporting of discrete *events*, as with the reporting of *states* (e.g. of ill-health), which typically last for some period of time and for that reason alone may be more readily remembered than, say, the isolated burglary, theft or assault.[20] It may also be that problems of *definition* (as opposed to recall) are more serious in the case of criminal victimization, than with such things as household purchases: buying a dishwasher is buying a dishwasher, whereas an incident involving physical violence may be conceived as anything from an argument to a case of attempted murder. Reporting of events defined as burglary may be relatively unlikely to be inhibited by respondents on the grounds of social undesirability—either generally, or in the context of the interview situation; but it may be otherwise with events defined as robbery or rape. Fortunately, some evidence is available which bears directly on the recall and reporting of criminal victimization. To this evidence we now turn.

2. The U.S. Census Bureau Pilot Studies

The completeness and accuracy of victims' recall and reporting of crime incidents was investigated in three pilot surveys carried out by the U.S. Census Bureau as part of its ongoing long-term programme of victim surveys.[1] These pilot studies use the same 'reverse record check' technique which we used in our London survey. But it is important to note that their questionnaires were structurally very different from our own. Since the main objective of the Census Bureau's research at this stage was measurement, and not explanation, they tended to ask respondents only about their experiences of victimization, and obtained little other information except basic personal data about the respondents themselves. It is also fair to point out that these three pilot studies were in large measure concerned with questionnaire development and that each resulted in substantial improvements in question design and wording; their results may thus not be indicative of those obtained by the current programme of Census Bureau surveys. The types of crime incidents covered by these pilot studies, however, were similar to those included in our own London survey.

The first of these three pre-tests was conducted in Washington, D.C. in March 1970.[2] It was designed to investigate three problems: first, to determine the most effective reference period for victim surveys; second, to measure the degree of forward telescoping; third, to explore the possibility of identifying incidents by a few broad general questions, as opposed to a series of more specific probing questions. The original design of the Washington survey called for a sample containing equal numbers of persons known to have reported incidents of assault, burglary, theft and robbery to the police. About two-thirds of these cases were selected (by Police Department staff) from crimes recorded three, six and 11 months before the interviews were carried out; the remaining third, included to investigate forward telescoping, had been recorded seven to eight months, and 13 to 14 months, before the fieldwork. The questionnaire used contained two fairly broad questions asking about any property crimes and personal crimes, respectively, plus a series of more detailed probing questions intended to jog the respondent's memory by mentioning relatively specific situations and examples. Depending upon the responses to these probing questions, incident sheets were completed for each incident mentioned.

Since the main purpose of this pretest was to determine the ability of the victims to recall criminal incidents and the dates of those incidents, questions as to other details of the crime were kept to a minimum. As a result, the completed interviews were very short—on average, they lasted only 14 minutes—and only a few took more than half an hour. It was originally intended that the respondents would not be contacted in advance and informed that they were to be interviewed. However, owing to an apparently high degree of mobility (and perhaps to the inaccuracy of addresses contained in the police records), the interviewers appear to have experienced some difficulty in locating respondents, despite the fact that they were given the address and telephone number of the victim's place of work as well as his home address. Using this information, interviewers were able to contact respondents by telephone and to schedule visits at times when they were likely to find the respondents at home. In fact, therefore, an unknown but possibly substantial proportion of the sample finally interviewed had been forewarned about the survey. Undoubtedly this minimized non-contact and did not appear to increase the refusal rate; moreover, it appears that no respondent gave any obvious sign of preparing himself for the interview. Nonetheless, some element of bias may well have been introduced; when contacted over the telephone, respondents tended to be cautious and to demand an explanation of the survey, its sponsor and its purpose. In many cases, it was necessary to reveal that their names had been obtained from the Washington Police Department records. Further, it seems clear that the interviewers themselves were aware not only that the persons whom they were interviewing had in fact been victims of crime. but also of the details of the event on which the respondents' recall was to be tested. The conditions of this pretest thus departed substantially from those of a real victim survey, and it is possible that the results obtained would have been less favourable had there been no such foreknowledge on the part of the interviewers and respondents.

Despite the pre-interview telephone contact, interviews were completed with only 326 respondents out of an initial sample of 484 (a completed interview rate of 67 per cent.)[3] Of the 226 persons who had reported incidents to the police within the reference periods (either six or twelve months before the interview, depending on the questionnaire used), 183, or 81 per cent, recalled the target incident and mentioned it to the interviewer. Predictably, the proportions recalling the target incident declined as the time between the incident and the interview increased: it was 86 per cent for those incidents occurring three months before the interview, 78 per cent for those occurring six months earlier, and only 70 per cent for those occurring eleven months earlier.[4] Recall appeared to be better for incidents of robbery (91 per cent) and burglary (88 per cent) than for theft (77 per cent) or assault (65 per cent). Accuracy of recall— as judged by respondents' reporting the incident as having occurred in the month in which it actually took place—also declined as the time between incident and interview increased. Of those recalling the target incident at all, 85 per cent gave the correct month when the incident had occurred only three months previously, compared with 77 per cent for the six-month cases and only 63 per cent for the eleven-month cases; there was little difference in this respect for different types of crimes. Of those who remembered the target crime, but were unable to locate it as having occurred in the correct month, about half reported it as having taken place in a later month (forward telescoping) and half in an earlier month (backward telescoping).

The Washington sample also included 100 respondents who had been victims of offences known to have taken place outside the reference periods of the questionnaire (either seven or eight months previously for the six-month questionnaire, and thirteen or fourteen previously for the twelve-month version). Of those respondents, no less than 19 per cent reported that the target incidents had taken place within the reference period—17 per cent for the six-month questionnaire, and 21 per cent for the twelve-month questionnaire. Clearly this represents a substantial amount of forward telescoping. It was about the same for burglary, assault and robbery, but much lower for theft, presumably because of the higher numbers simple forgetting these less salient incidents. It may also be that forward telescoping was increased by the interview procedure mentioned earlier, of contacting respondents in advance to arrange an interview.

Without more data on the attributes of the respondents in the Washington pretest, it is not possible to estimate from its results the likely amounts of non-reporting and telescoping in a random sample of the Washington population. Its main findings, however, may be summarized as follows. Suppose that a sample were drawn consisting of equal numbers of persons who were known to have been victims of crime during each of the preceding fourteen months. About one-third of these persons would not have been located by interviewers. Of the remainder, about 72 per cent would have reported that they had been victims of a crime incident within the preceding year; and about four per cent of these incidents would have been 'false positives' resulting from forward telescoping. In the case of assaults, the inaccuracy would be much greater. Nearly half of the respondents would not have been located; of those who were interviewed, about 65 per cent would have reported an incident, but to these 5 per cent would have been incorrectly reported owing to forward telescoping.

A second pretest was carried out in Baltimore, Maryland, in July 1970.[5] The questionnaire used in this survey, modified in wording and question order as a result of the Washington study, employed a six-month reference period beginning on January 1, 1970. The original sample selected from Baltimore police records included about 500 persons who were known to have reported crimes: 100 victims of burglary, 100 of larceny and about 150 of robbery and of assault. Half of these target incidents had taken place three months before the interview (that is, April 1970); the remainder had taken place about six months before the interview, in January 1970. On average, the interviews in this pretest took about 20 minutes to complete. As in Washington, interviewers were given the name, address, home telephone number, place of employment or school, business telephone number, occupation and working hours of respondents.[6]

Interviews were completed with 362 of the 527 persons in the sample, a completion rate of 69 per cent. The proportion of interviews completed varied from 78 per cent for larceny down to 63 per cent for cases of assault; as in the first pretest, over half of the non-interview cases simply could not be located. This was so for over three-quarters of the assault victims who could not be interviewed, thus confirming the earlier suggestion that such persons either tend to be more transient than victims of property crime, or are less accurately identified in police records.

The proportion of target incidents recalled and reported to interviewers in the Baltimore survey was significantly lower than in Washington, owing in part to the composition of the sample. Of 362 completed interviews, 242 respondents (or 67 per cent) recalled the target incident and mentioned it to the interviewer. In the sample as a whole, the recall rate was slightly lower for the incidents which had occurred six months before the interview, than for those which had occurred only three months earlier (64 per cent, against 69 per cent). But this was not consistently true for all types of offences: the proportion of January burglaries recalled and reported to the interviewer was actually *higher* than the proportion of burglaries which had occurred in April (89 per cent, against 82 per cent). There was a considerable variation in the reporting of target crimes of different types, however. Burglaries had the highest recall rate, with 86 per cent being reported; for robbery the figure was 76 per cent and for larceny 75 per cent. Only 36 per cent of the victims of assault, however, recalled their target incidents and reported them to the interviewers. When the assault had occurred six months previously, this figure fell to 33 per cent.

Accuracy of recall was also lower than in the Washington pretest. Of those victims who reported their offences at all, only 57 per cent were able to locate the incident within the correct month.[7] Victims of assault were also the least accurate, with 48 per cent giving the month correctly. An interesting finding was that for all types of crime except robbery, respondents who did recall the target incident were more accurate in their recollection of the crimes which occurred in January than for those occurring three months later in April. This suggests that the month of January may be a slightly more salient month in people's memories.

In this study more detailed information was collected on both incidents and respondents, which throws some light on the processes of recall. For cases of larceny, burglary and robbery, the average loss in dollars was available from police records. With the exception of robberies, this was higher for the recalled incidents than for those which were not recalled. (The dollar loss reported in the interview was the same as that in police records, however, for only one-quarter of the cases.) Victims of aggravated assault recalled the target incident to a greater degree than victims of simple assault, but the difference was not very great (41 per cent, against 33 per cent). An examination of the location of the assault did not provide any conclusive evidence on the problem of recall. Aggravated assaults taking place in dwellings were more likely to be recalled than those occurring on the streets or in taverns or other public places (50 per cent as compared with 31 per cent). On the other hand, simple assaults occurring on the street, in taverns, etc. were slightly *better* recalled than those which took place in dwellings (37 per cent, against 30 per cent).

Information was collected from respondents about the identity of the offender in assault and robbery cases (including, apparently, additional incidents other than the target incident). In 57 per cent of the cases of assault, the victim stated that the offender had been known to him (and in 22 per cent of the cases had been a relative); 41 per cent of the offenders were said to be strangers. The proportions of strangers among those responsible for incidents of robbery was exactly twice as high. Unfortunately, no information seems to have been collected from police records on the identity of offenders in the target incidents of assault and robbery. It is thus not possible to tell how far acquaintanceship or a family relationship with the offender may have affected recall in this study; in particular, it is not possible to estimate how far respondents were inhibited from reporting events which were the outcome of family disputes. As noted earlier, however, simple assaults which occurred in dwellings were slightly less likely to be recalled and/or disclosed to the interviewer than those taking place on the street or in public places; it is possible that this is because they included a number of assaults arising out of family disputes, which the respondent was reluctant to disclose in the interview situation.

On balance, therefore, the results from the Baltimore pretest were much less favourable than those from the Washington study: a full scale survey with the same rates of 'success' in recall and reporting as those found in the Baltimore pretest would recover about three-quarters of the larcenies and robberies which had been reported to the police, and about 86 per cent of the burglaries, but it would yield only about one-third of the assaults which had been reported to the police even as recently as six months ago. No data on telescoping are presented in the brief report on the Baltimore pretests; but presumably some did occur, and because of the lower recall rate for incidents actually in the six-month reference period, the amount of error introduced into population estimates by forward telescoping would have been even greater.

The third of the Census Bureau's pilot studies was carried out in San Jose, California, in January 1971.[8] This study was designed to investigate the optimum reference period for what had by now become a panel design; as we have already noted, in such a design the most important question is the extent to which respondents can place an event within a designated reference period, rather than whether they can remember the precise date of that event. The sample initially selected from police records included 620 victims of robbery, assault, rape, burglary and larceny; and—contrary to the practice in the Washington and Baltimore pretests—the interviewers in San Jose were not told that they were interviewing known victims of crime.[9] As before, screen questions about victimization were followed by more detailed questions on incident forms for each reported incident. Interviews were completed with 394 of the 620 cases—a completion rate of 63.5 per cent; as in the earlier surveys, most of the non-interview cases had moved out of the area.

Of the 394 cases in which an interview was completed, the target incident was correctly recalled (as having occurred 'within the past twelve months') by 292 respondents, or 74 per cent. Recall rates varied by type of offence from a high of 90 per cent for burglary and 81 per cent for larceny to 76 per cent for robbery, 67 per cent for rape and 48 per cent for assault. Comparison of the recall rates by actual date of occurrence of the target incident showed very little difference between recent incidents and those occurring about a year previously. This study suggests, therefore, that a reference period of twelve months is satisfactory if the purpose of the survey is merely to ascertain how many crimes occurred within that reference period.

When accuracy of recall and reporting are considered, a slightly different conclusion emerges. Of the incidents reported to the police between one and six months before the interview, 67 per cent were recalled as being within the same (six-month) time period; of those occurring within seven and 12 months before the interview, the percentage recalled was 53 per cent. It is important to note, moreover, that this 'success' rate relates to the reporting of an incident within a particular six-month period; the percentage of respondents who succeeded in placing their incidents within the correct month was much lower. While telescoping is not discussed in the report on the San Jose survey, data contained in the report [10] permit an analysis of it, by type of crime, which is summarized in Table III.1.

It will be seen from this table that of the total of 292 incidents which were reported to interviewers, 156 (or about 53 per cent) were placed correctly, within the month of occurrence; roughly 21 per cent were telescoped forward, and 17 per cent were telescoped back, while a further nine per cent could not be placed by respondents within a particular month. On average, incidents telescoped forward were reported as having occurred 2.2 months later than in fact they did; those telescoped backward, an average of 1·6 months earlier.

Table III.1. Accuracy of recall in the San Jose survey

	Burglary	Theft	Robbery	Assault	Rape	Total	Percentage of total
Recall:							
Accurate (in same month)	53	31	30	23	19	156	39·6
Telescoped forward	15	13	18	8	6	60	15·2
Telescoped backward	17	15	9	4	4	49	12·4
Not reported	10	16	19	42	15	102	25·9
Reported, date too vague to classify	9	9	4	4	1	27	6·9
Total	104	84	80	81	45	394	100·0

The results concerning the reporting of rape in this survey are of special interest, since (as the authors of the report put it) 'historically, there has been a great deal of reluctance to pose, in an interview setting, a question of the genre, "were you raped at any time during the past ... months?"'[1] In fact, the 45 rape victims interviewed in this survey produced a substantially higher reporting rate than did the 81 assault victims: 66.7 per cent against 48.1 per cent. This result does not show, of course, that the victim survey method would generally be useful in measuring the incidence of rape. Reporting of this type of offence to an interviewer is presumably inhibited to some extent by feelings of shame and embarrassment on the part of the respondent; but these feelings might well be less important if the offence had been reported to the police (as it had in all of those included in the San Jose study), than if it had not. It is also clear that reporting of rape was significantly influenced by the relationship between the victim and the alleged offender: the target incident was reported in 16 of the 19 cases (that is, 84 per cent) where the offender was a stranger, compared with only 13 of the 24 (54 per cent) where the offender was known to the victim before the incident. This was also true for offences of assault: e.g. only about 22 per cent of the simple assaults by relatives were reported to the survey interviewers, compared with 54 per cent when the assault was by a stranger. Of the cases not reported to interviewers in the San Jose pretest, two out of every three were incidents where the victim and the assailant were related or otherwise known to each other.[12]

This finding, which implies that crimes by strangers are likely to be substantially over-represented in victim surveys because of response bias, is, of course, based on a small sample: it cannot be treated as definitive, nor can great weight be put on the exact proportions of stranger *versus* non-stranger rapes and assaults reported to interviewers in the San Jose survey. Nor is the explanation of this bias clear: it may be that respondents did not report assaults by acquaintances because of feelings of shame or embarrassment, or because they did not define the incidents in question as criminal. Nonetheless, it is striking that in early reports on the National Crime Panel surveys, absolutely no mention of this probable bias was made: instead, it was baldly stated without qualification that the majority of incidents involving the threat or use of violence involved confrontations between strangers.[13] Applying even a crude correction factor based on the San Jose pretest leads, in fact, to precisely the opposite conclusion: namely, that 'stranger' assaults are a *minority* of all assaults which occur. This conclusion, is, of course consistent with the findings of previous criminological research on violence, based on police-recorded data.[14]

Data from another Census study (the 1971 Quarterly Household Survey supplement) throw further light on the extent to which telescoping may occur in surveys on victimization.[15] A sample interviewed in January 1971 were asked about incidents of victimization which had taken place during the year 1970. Respondents reported substantially greater numbers of events as occurring in the last six months of the year—nearly 80 per cent for personal crimes and

Table III.2. Comparison of bounded and unbounded recall in U.S. Census Bureau study (July 1971)

Type of victimization	Collection procedure Unbounded (1)	Bounded (2)	Procedure Ratio, (1)/(2)
Burglary	0·0448	0·0370	1·21
Household larceny	0·1091	0·0792	1·38
Auto theft	0·0090	0·0074	1·22
Robbery	0·0047	0·0025	1·88
Aggravated assault	0·0011	0·0009	1·22
Simple assault	0·0025	0·0016	1·56
Attempted assault	0·0060	0·0061	0·98
Rape	0·0002[a]	0·0002[a]	[a]
Personal larceny	0·0028	0·0012	2·33

[a]Too small to be statistically significant.

55 per cent for property crimes—than in the first half of the year. These differences are very much greater than those which would have been expected from rates in the *Uniform Crime Reports*. A further study carried out in July 1971 compared the results from bounded interviews with those from unbounded ones. This survey involved personal interviews with household respondents at each of about 18,000 designated households, seeking information on victimization for the preceding six-month period (i.e. January to June 1971). About 12,000 of these households had been interviewed in January 1971, thus bounding the July interviews; the remaining 6,000 households were new to the sample in July, and their interviews were thus unbounded. The results of the two types of interview procedure are summarized in Table III.2.

It is clear from this table that the unbounded interviews almost invariably produced higher victimization rates than the bounded ones. While in some instances the observed difference may not exceed sampling error due to the smallness of sample size, the trend is a consistent one (except for rape, for which there were too few cases, and attempted assault.) It should be borne in mind, however, that the questionnaire used in these surveys included no special efforts for attempting to get respondents to define the reference period before attempting to elicit information about victimization. It is probable that some of the observed forward telescoping could have been reduced by this method.

Other results from the NCP studies confirm the general conclusion of other surveys already discussed, concerning the lower rate of reporting when one respondent is asked to give information about victimization of all members of their household, and that screening by means of a postal questionnaire is unsatisfactory for this type of survey.[16]

It may be thought that the results of these three pilot studies are not exactly encouraging, and that they scarcely support the substantial investment in victim surveys which the current Census Bureau—L.E.A.A. programme entails. The problem of non-response encountered in all these pilot studies undoubtedly owes—as it did in our own London survey—to the sampling frame used, and the difficulty of locating named respondents; using sampling methods appropriate to mobile urban populations, this difficulty would probably disappear.[17] But it would seem that the high proportions of respondents who did not recall or report their offences to the interviewers necessarily injects a high degree of error into any population estimates of victimization from such sample surveys. The recall rates for burglary (and possibly larceny) are perhaps broadly satisfactory. But in all three of these pilot studies, only about half of the assaults included (all of which had been reported to the police) were mentioned to the survey interviewers. Plainly, this is too much error, and casts grave doubt on the validity of the National Crime Panel's findings. The three pretests also demonstrate considerable telescoping forward, though this is presumably less of a problem with bounded-interview or panel designs. Notwithstanding these results, however, the Census Bureau's studies have provided valuable information on the methodological problems of measuring crime by victim surveys, and they furnish a useful comparison to the results which we obtained under somewhat different interviewing conditions, in our London survey.

3. Results of the Present Study: The Main Victim Sample

(1) Description of the Sample and Target Incidents

Our Main Victim (MV) sample includes 241 persons who were known to have reported offences to the Metropolitan Police during the first ten months of 1972.[1] The 'target' offences which defined the MV sample, though chosen at random from those recorded by the police in our three areas, were not intended to be representative of all recorded crimes in those areas in the first ten months of 1972. Instead, as explained in the last chapter, we deliberately over-sampled offences of Violence and Burglary in an effort to complete an experimental design which would enable us to study the effects of offence type and time on recall and telescoping. For this purpose, the ten months to 31 October 1972 were divided into six equal periods, and the cases further classified by offence type and sex of respondent; the resulting distribution is shown in Table III.3.

The categories of offences in this table are admittedly not completely homogeneous; and they do not correspond exactly to the classifications used by the police. Thus our category of Violence includes offences initially classified by the police as felonious wounding, malicious wounding, assault occasioning actual bodily harm, and common assault;[2] it also includes some which the police classified as offences of robbery, and some which they had treated as thefts from the person. The robberies were confined to so-called 'mugging' or other similar personal robberies, and excluded cases in which the victim had been attacked in the course of his employment, e.g. when carrying his firm's payroll from the bank. It is often difficult, in practice, to distinguish between robbery and theft from the person; accordingly we included cases

Table III.3. Distribution of target offences by time period, sex of victim and type of offence

Type of crime and sex of victim	Time period						Total
	Jan. 1– Feb. 20	Feb. 21– Apr. 11	Apr. 12– June 1	June 2– July 22	July 23– Sept. 11	Sept. 12– Oct. 31	
Violence: Male	2	3	9	4	5	8	31 (12·9)
Violence: Female	4	4	3	7	6	1	25 (10·4)
Burglary: Male	8	9	5	10	6	9	47 (19·5)
Burglary: Female	9	10	14	12	11	5	61 (25·3)
Theft: Male	4	2	3	8	8	8	33 (13·8)
Theft: Female	6	5	9	7	9	8	44 (18·3)
Total	33	33	43	48	45	39	241
Per cent	(13·7)	(13·7)	(17·8)	(19·9)	(18·7)	(16·2)	(100·0)

failing in the latter category, when the statement of facts on the crime report indicated that the theft had been effected by using some degree of force (as in a 'purse-snatching'), as opposed to being done by stealth or deception (e.g., by a pick-pocket).

The target offences of Violence were, in objective terms, fairly serious ones; certainly they tended to be more serious than either the additional incidents of violent crime (i.e. over and above the target incident) reported by the MV sample, or the violent incidents mentioned by the R sample.[3] About 70 per cent of those reported were said by the respondents to involve some degree of physical injury (though over half of these cases resulted in nothing more than bruises, cuts or abrasions); two-thirds had involved attacks with fists or feet only, and in about one-fifth a knife or other sharp weapon had been used. About 42 per cent had required medical treatment, and 29 per cent had entailed a stay in hospital (usually for less than a week). Seven cases resulted in some permanent physical defect (e.g. the respondent had been crippled or blinded). Our category of Burglary includes some cases recorded by the police as theft in a dwelling house; particularly in Kensington, there were many such cases, and on the facts available to us from the crime reports it was often difficult to distinguish between the two types of offence. In all of the cases in our category of Burglary, however, it appeared clear from the crime report that an offender had entered the premises in question illegally in order to steal, even if he did not break in, in the strict legal sense. The category of Theft/Damage is an especially heterogeneous one. It includes some thefts from the person which did not appear to involve any element of force; it also includes thefts of, and from, motor vehicles; and it includes some offences of damage to property even of amounts of £20 or less (which are not treated as indictable offences for the purposes of the Metropolitan Police statistics).

Of the target offences against property (burglary, theft and damage) 22 per cent were cases in which the offender had been caught in the act of committing the crime—a significantly higher proportion than in the additional property incidents reported by the MV sample.[4] In 85 per cent of the burglaries, entry to the premises had definitely been forced; this too is significantly higher than in the additional offences, for a quarter of which the house was stated to have been open. According to police records, over half of these cases involved loss or damage worth over £20, with over a quarter involving £100 or more. Comparable figures for the MV sample's additional offences are not, of course, available, but on the respondent's estimate of the loss involved, the target incidents are again considerable more serious. In 40 per cent of the target cases the property had been insured; this, too, is higher than in the additional incidents reported by the MV sample.

When completing the survey crime incident forms, respondents were asked, 'Do you know who was responsible for the crime?'[5] In about 38 per cent of the reported target incidents the respondents said Yes to this question; no less than 42 per cent of this sub-group (almost all of them in Brixton and Hackney) stated that the offender was a West Indian. When asked why they had reported the target incidents, about one-third of the sample gave an answer which merely indicated some general obligation to report wrongdoing (e.g. 'It's wrong, isn't it? You have to report it.') Only five per cent explicitly mentioned claiming on insurance, and 18 per cent said they wanted to get the offender punished, or to prevent repetition of the incident. To the respondents' knowledge, only 17 per cent of the target cases had resulted in the apprehension of a suspect. Despite this, 80 per cent said that they were satisfied with what the police had done about the crime; those who were dissatisfied were split about two to one between those who thought the police had not treated the matter seriously, and those who had merely had no further information about what had been done.[6] At the end of the questions on the crime incident form, respondents were asked if they had changed their outlook or way of life as a result of the incident; 60 per cent said Yes, most of them stating that they had become more suspicious of other people, or were taking better care of their property. Respondents were also asked to rate the seriousness of the incident on a 1-to-11 scale (as they had previously done for the series of crimes in an earlier section of the main questionnaire). For the target offences the mean score given was 6·41, compared with 4·48 for the MV sample's reported additional offences.

(2) Reporting of Target Incidents

The overall results for reporting of target incidents by our MV sample are summarized in Table III.4. It will be seen from this table that over 90 per cent

Table III.4. Recall and reporting of target incidents in the MV sample[a]

	N	Percentage
Reported accurately (within month of actual occurrence)	123	51·9
Telescoped forward	51	21·5
Telescoped backward	45	19·0
Not reported	18	7·6
Total	237	100·0

[a]Excludes four cases which could not be classified.

Table III.5. Proportions of target offences reported in the three survey areas, MV sample[a]

	Reported	Not reported	Total	Per cent reported
AREA:				
Brixton	96	4	100	96·0
Hackney	62	12	74	83·8
Kensington	61	2	63	96·8
Total	219	18	237	92·4

[a]Excludes four cases which could not be classified.
$\chi^2 = 11·43$, df $= 2$, $p < 0·001$

of our MV sample definitely mentioned the target incident during their interviews. Since we had information not only on the date and type of the offence, but also (in most cases) on the time and place at which the incident was reported, the offender (where apprehended) and a description and value of the property, maching of respondents' reports and police records was seldom a problem.[7] There were four cases in which the respondent mentioned an event of the type which we knew he had reported to the police, but was too vague either about the date of the event or its nature for us to classify the case in Table III.4.[8] In at least three of these four cases we are confident that the target incident was in fact recalled; their inclusion would bring the gross 'success rate' to 92·5 per cent for the whole of the MV sample. But we cannot be sure about this; so in the rest of this analysis they are excluded.

If the recall of target incidents is considered on an 'all or nothing' basis—that is, without regard to the accuracy with which respondents placed the events in time—Table III.5 shows that our Hackney residents did significantly worse than those in Brixton or Kensington. There are also differences in reporting, across our admittedly rather heterogeneous categories of offense.[9] It should be noted that we did *not* find the much lower rates of reporting for assaults which were observed in the U.S. Census Bureau's pretests: the rate of assaults and thefts reported is almost the same, at about 89 per cent. But in our sample, offences of burglary (including some thefts in dwellings) were the most consistently reported, over 97 per cent being mentioned; this, of course, is consistent with the U.S. Census Bureau studies discussed in the preceding section, and suggests clearly that this type of crime is highly salient in the minds of most respondents.[10]

Since our MV sample was selected in accordance with an experimental design, the numbers in the sample whose offences occurred in different months of the year are slightly different from what would be expected from the monthly totals of indictable offences recorded by the Metropolitan Police in 1972. The sample also contains a much higher proportion of cases from Hackney, and correspondingly lower proportions from Brixton and Kensington, than would be expected in a random sample of all recorded crimes; finally, offences of burglary and of violence are over-represented, and offences of theft are correspondingly under-represented, in the sample compared with a total number of crimes recorded in our three areas in 1972. It might conceivably be, therefore, that our results concerning completeness and accuracy of recall would not apply to a representative sample of victims in our three areas. To investigate this, we re-weighted the sample by the month in which the offence occurred and by area and type of offence, in accordance with the statistics of all reported crimes in the three areas in 1972.[11] In fact, however, re-weighting by time period and type of offence made virtually no difference to our overall results. Reweighting by area actually produced a higher 'success' rate, both in terms of reporting of offences on an 'all-or-nothing' basis and in terms of accuracy of reporting (within the correct month). This is so primarily because Hackney, where the recall rate in our sample was the lowest, was also substantially over-represented in the sample. For the remainder of this chapter, therefore, we shall report only the unweighted sample results.

It will be seen from Table III.6 that the proportion of target incidents not reported at all to interviewers is higher in the first half of the ten-month time period in which the incidents occurred, than in the second: 12 per cent against about 4 per cent. In our sample, however, non-reporting to interviewers is not quite a monotonic function of time since the incident; there is something of a fall-off in the probability of reporting for incidents occurring before the

Table III.6. Recall and reporting of target incidents by time period, in the MV sample

	Reported	Not reported	Total	Per cent reported
Time period:				
Jan. 1–Feb. 20	29	4	33	87·5
Feb. 21–Apr. 11	29	4	33	87·9
Apr. 12–June 1	37	5	42	88·1
June 2–July 22	45	2	47	95·7
July 23–Sept. 11	42	1	43	97·7
Sept. 12–Oct. 31	37	2	39	94·9
	219	18	237	92·4

beginning of June (i.e., on average over eight months before the interviews), but not much difference between time periods either before or after that date.[12] It seems, therefore, that our date show that substantially higher—and thus more accurate—estimates of victimization would be produced by using a six-month reference period than a twelve-month one, contrary to what is suggested by the U.S. Census Bureau study in San Jose.[13]

This conclusion must be qualified, however. In assessing the efficiency of reference periods of different lengths, we must take into account not only those incidents which are lost through non-recall, but also those which are recalled by respondents but telescoped backward out of the reference period. Thus in our sample, using a twelve-month reference period, we must deduct not only those 18 respondents who did not mention their target incidents at all, but also those who telescoped them back and reported them as having occurred in 1971;[14] this gives a net 'success' rate of 89 per cent. A similar calculation for a six-month reference period gives five respondents (out of 132) who did not mention their incidents at all, one who telescoped it back into 1971, and ten who telescoped them back into the first part of 1972; this yields a net 'success' rate of 88 per cent for the shorter reference period, which is actually slightly lower than that for 12 months. It is also necessary to take into account the higher degree of inaccuracy introduced by forward telescoping when a six-month reference period is used (since the telescoped incidents

Table III.7. Reporting rates by type of offence and sex, in the MV sample[a]

	Reported	Not reported	Total	Per cent reported
Violence				
Male	26	5	31	83·9
Female	24	1	25	96·0
Total	50	6	56	89·3
Burglary				
Male	45	1	46	97·8
Female	56	3	59	94·9
Total	101	4	105	96·2
Theft				
Male	27	6	33	81·8
Female	41	2	43	95·3
Total	68	8	76	89·5
Total, all offences	219	18	237	92·4

$\chi^2 = 11·93$, df = 5, p < 0·01
(For males against females, $\chi^2 = 2·39$, df = 1, $0·10 < p < 0·20$)

[a]Excluding four cases which could not be classified

represent a higher proportion of the total); when this is done, the twelve-month period is undoubtedly more accurate.

We were unable to find more than a few attributes which discriminated in any meaningful way between those respondents who did recall and report their target incidents, and those who did not.[15] Male respondents were less likely than females to report target incidents of Violence and Theft/Damage; but they were slightly more likely to report offences of Burglary, and the overall difference between men and women is not statistically significant. Nor is there any consistent relationship with age, though the proportion not reporting among those aged 61 and over is twice as high as in the sample as a whole. There is no evidence of an association between non-reporting and race, marital status, intergenerational social mobility, or length of residence at current address; non-reporting was higher for those working part-time or not at all than for those working full-time, and for those who had held their present job less than a year, but in neither case is the difference statistically significant. Nor are there any consistent or significant associations between reporting of target incidents and any of the attitudinal or perceptual questions which we asked concerning the respondent's local neighbourhood, the prevalence of crime, safety on the streets, etc.

Bearing in mind the significantly lower reporting rate in Hackney, and the social-class composition of that area,[16] it might be expected that social class by itself would be associated with non-recall; but as Table III.8 shows, our data provide scant support for that conclusion. There are suggestions in the data that recall is associated with level of educational attainment; those who finished their secondary education before or at the school-leaving age were twice as likely *not* to report target incidents as those who left after school-leaving age, and those who had no further education were also slightly more likely to be non-reporters than those who had. These associations (neither

Table III.8. Recall and reporting of target offences, by social class, in the MV sample[a]

	Reported	Not reported	Total	Per cent reported
Registrar-General's Social Class:				
I	12	1	13	92·3
II	42	2	44	95·5
IIIa	55	1	56	98·2
IIIb	55	6	61	90·2
IV	23	4	27	85·2
V	18	2	20	90·0
Total	205	16	221	92·8

[a]Excludes 16 respondents who could not be classed by own or husband's occupation, as well as four for whom incidents could not be classified.

$$\chi^2 = 6·11, \text{df} = 5, 0·20 < p < 0·30$$

of which reached statistical significance) are consistent with the hypothesis that recall and reporting in a survey like ours are in part in part a function of the verbal fluency needed to complete a fairly long interview which sometimes required a certain amount of abstract conceptualization on the part of the respondents. This suggestion is perhaps reinforced by the finding that those respondents who were rated by the interviewers as 'somewhat cooperative' or 'not cooperative' were significantly more likely not to report target incidents than those who were rated 'very cooperative';[17] there was a similar though not significant association between the interviewer's rating of the respondent's understanding of the questions and reporting of target incidents.[18] But if there is such an effect it cannot—in our findings—be a very strong one; it appears to be heavily overlaid by the results of simple memory failure operating in a more or less random fashion across respondents.

This conclusion is supported by an inspection of the particular target incidents which were not reported at all: on the information available to us from police records there is little to distinguish them from those which were recalled and reported. Those who did not mention their target incidents were just as likely to mention additional incidents—in one case, no less than nine—as the rest of the sample. In only one case did it appear that inhibition on the part of the respondent, rather than failure of memory, was responsible for the failure to report. In this case, an elderly woman's daughter had been accused of attempting to murder her (though the charge was later reduced to assault); we discovered afterward that the daughter had been present during the interview.[19]

On balance, then, our interviewers appear to have been highly successful in getting respondents in the MV sample to recall and report target incidents of violent and property crime occurring as much as 12 months before the interview. In common with the American studies discussed earlier in this chapter, we found that offences of Burglary were most likely to be recalled and reported; but we did not find a lower recall rate for offenses of Violence than for Theft/Damage. In assessing these results it must also be borne in mind that our interviewers did not know that any of the people whom they were interviewing had in fact been victims of crime, or had reported offences to the police; *a fortiori* they did not know this for any particular respondent before the interview. In addition, since MV and T cases comprised only about a third of the total cases in the sample, it is extremely unlikely that expectations of the interviewers could have led them to probe harder in the MV cases than in the rest of the sample. Finally, the respondents themselves were not contacted by us in advance.[20]

(3) Accuracy of Reporting

The accuracy of respondents' recall is, of course, another matter. Before considering this aspect of our data it is important to note that the *precision* of the respondents' replies was often not very great. In fact, about 60 per cent could apparently give only the month in which the incident occurred, and could not—or at least did not—venture a date within the month. While our interviewers were instructed to probe in order to find out exactly when the event occurred, it is possible that some of them were not as assiduous in this respect as they might have been. Two things, however, are against this. The first is that we know that some of our interviewers did go to some lengths to try to get respondents to remember the exact dates, without success; the second is that in many cases when an exact date was ventured, it turned out to be wrong. It is doubtful, therefore, that we could have obtained a much greater degree of precision in responses, at least without substantially lengthening the interviews, and risking greater recall losses through 'fatigue.'[21]

The proportion of the sample recalling target offences as occurring within the correct month is slightly lower in the first half of the reference period than in the second; the difference is slight, however. On balance, there are a few more events telescoped forward than back; again, however, the differences are slight and almost cancel each other out. In studying the accuracy of response for reported incidents we have, of course, data on the incidents from crime incident forms as well as data on the respondents from the main questionnaires. We have, from police records, the dates on which the target offenses were reported as occurring;[22] and we have the dates of the offences given by the respondents themselves. From these two dates we calculated two different measures of the accuracy or inaccuracy of time placement. The first is simply the *algebraic* difference between the date as recorded by the police, and the date mentioned by the respondent (signed positive if the respondent's date was later, and negative if it was earlier). The second is the *absolute* difference between the two dates. Necessarily each of these measures contains a certain amount of error, since when respondents mentioned the month only we had to arbitrarily assign the incident to the middle of that month.[23] Nonetheless, these two variables give the best available measure of relative accuracy of time placement.[24]

Since the algebraic difference in actual and reported dates is a directional one, it can be interpreted as a measure of telescoping forward and back; for convenience, therefore, we shall defer discussion of it until the next section. The absolute difference in dates is, strictly speaking, a measure of inaccuracy rather than of telescoping, since a case telescoped back a month and a case telescoped forward a month both have the same value of 30. We have, therefore, two different ways of looking at the errors in time placement in our sample. The first corresponds to the tendency of events to be shifted either forward or backward in the respondents' memories; the second, to straightforward misremembering without any particular directional bias. There is little treatment in the psychological literature on memory of the possible differences in the origins of these two different sorts of partial memory failure; it might be hypothesized that telescoping forward or back is more strongly related to the salience of the target event itself (as opposed to the salience of 'landmark' events in its temporal context), whereas non-directional inaccuracy might result from, for example, a tendency of the respondent simply to guess at dates.

It would be natural to expect that the value of the absolute-difference variable would increase as the time between the target incident and the interview increased. Somewhat surprisingly, however, in our sample as a whole the association between the two things is not very great ($r = +0.138$, which is significant at just below the 5 per cent level). Inspection of the data shows that this is mainly due to the existence of a group of respondents with target incidents distributed more or less evenly throughout the year, whose recollection is generally accurate. If such cases are excluded, the relationship between the two variables is substantially increased ($r = +0.307$); nonetheless, it is far from perfect.

Very few attributes, either of the target incidents or of the respondents, are significantly associated with our measure of inaccuracy. The mean absolute difference is lowest for cases of burglary (23·63) and assault (29·31), and highest for theft from the person (96·57) and thefts from outside the house (82·5); over eleven offence types, the differences are statistically significant.[25] But there is no relationship between absolute difference and perceived seriouness of the target incident (as measured on an eleven-point scale). Nor are there significant differences between male and female respondents, nor between different social classes, areas of residence, combinations of sex and offence type (Violence, Burglary, Theft/Damage), or the total number of incidents reported. Similarly, there are no significant differences associated with attachment to a local or other neighborhood area, or with any of the measures of educational attainment (age of leaving school and having had further education). There is a slight tendency for respondents rated somewhat or not cooperative to be less accurate than those rated very cooperative, and a similar tendency in relation to the interviewers' ratings of respondents' understanding; neither attains significance, however.

Our analysis would thus appear to support the conclusion that inaccuracy of recall and reporting, like complete failure of recall and reporting, can be regarded as a more or less random phenomenon which is unlikely by itself to introduce any serious biases into estimates from victim survey data.

(4) Data on Telescoping

Our data on telescoping in the present study come from several sources. First, there are the 55 cases included in the sample who were known to have reported offences to the Metropolitan Police in the last three months of 1971. We included these cases in order to see how many would mention their incidents (in reply to the screening questions) as having occurred in the year preceding the interview. These respondents could, of course, have correctly mentioned their incidents in reply to question G14, which asked if they had ever been a victim; thus this admittedly small sample provides us with some data on recall over a maximum period of about 15 months. In addition, they give some indication of the magnitude and nature of 'external' telescoping into the twelve-month reference period which we used in our questionnaire. Secondly, of course, we have data from the reported MV cases within the reference period, and the algebraic differences between actual and reported dates for those incidents (and respondents). Thirdly, we have the distribution within the reference period of the additional cases reported by the MV and T samples, and of the incidents reported by our R samples; these can be compared with the numbers which would be expected (according to police statistics) in each month of the reference period, to see if there is any evidence of a concentration in the later months of the year. Such a concentration may in part reflect non-reporting of incidents in the earlier part of the year; but it would also be due, at least in part, to 'internal' telescoping within the reference period. We shall examine each of these in turn.

(a) The Telescope Sample. The initial pool of target offences in our telescope sample was not selected in accordance with an experimental design; but an effort was made to obtain approximately equal numbers of cases in the three broad categories of Violence, Burglary and Theft/Damage, in each of the three months October–December 1971. Non-response (mainly owing to persons who had moved or could otherwise not be traced) was a rather more serious problem with this sample than with the MV or R samples; and the resulting distribution of cases, by months and type of offense, was as shown in Table III.9. In one of these cases it was not possible for us to make a decision about matching the identity of the target incident with one of the incidents mentioned by the respondent; this case has accordingly been excluded from the subsequent analysis.

It will be seen from Table III.10 that 30 of these 54 respondents, or 55.6 per cent, recalled the target incidents, and reported them correctly (as *not* having occurred in the reference period). Ten, or 18·5 per cent, recalled them as having taken place within the reference period; these cases represent forward

Table III.9. Month of occurrence and type of offence for target offences in the T sample

	October	November	December	Total
Violence				
Male	3	2	4	9
Female	2	3	3	8
Burglary				
Male	5	4	3	18
Female	3	5	1	9
Theft				
Male	5	1	3	9
Female	2	2	4	8
Total, all offences	20	17	18	55
Per cent of Total	36·3	31·0	32·7	100·0

Table III.10. Recall and reporting of offences by the T sample[a]

	No.	Per cent
Recalled accurately (i.e. not in reference period)	30	55·6
Telescoped forward into 1972	10	18·5
Telescoped back	1	1·9
Not reported at all	13	24·1
Total	54	100·0

[a]Excludes one case too vague to classify.

external telescoping. One respondent recalled his 1971 incident as having happened more than a month earlier than in fact it did; and the remaining 13, or 24·1 per cent, did not report the target incident at all. It is not perhaps surprising that the latter group should bulk so much larger in the T sample than in the MV sample, not only because of the greater length of recall demanded but because of the much more general wording of the question which should have led to the target incident being mentioned; having come at the end of a series of much more specific questions about events in 1972, replies to this question were in addition probably affected by fatigue. Ignoring the one respondent who placed his event as having happened earlier than in fact it did, we are left with almost one in five of this group who incorrectly reported that their target incidents occurred within our survey's reference period.

Making allowance for the distribution of these cases in the three months October–December 1971, the average amount of forward telescoping for these cases is about the same as in the MV sample. Owing to the relatively small size of the T sample and the inherent vagueness of the replies which mentioned these telescoped incidents, we have not thought it worthwhile attempting to calculate the differences in actual and reported dates, as we did for the MV sample. We have, however, some data on the respondents who telescoped their incidents into the survey reference period. If anything, these show less by way of significant differences associated with inaccurate response than the data from the MV sample. Younger respondents (from 18 to 35) were more likely to project their target offences into the reference period, as were those with some further education (but *not* those who left secondary school after the school-leaving age); so were those who—on their answers to several questions in an earlier section of the questionnaire appeared to dislike or disapprove of their neighbours. But none of these differences attains statistical significance; and there is not much comfort to be gained from looking for trends. The only indication of a possible explanation for these inaccurately reported cases lies in the number of other incidents which they reported (as happening in 1972); there is a marked positive association between the number of these, and the likelihood of telescoping forward the target offense, in our T sample.[26] It is possible, therefore, that some of the target offences were telescoped because of a response set, owing to the number of other incidents which the respondents claimed to have experienced in 1972.

(b) Telescoping in the MV Sample. We have already seen[27] that about 20 per cent of the MV sample reported their target incidents as having occurred later than in fact they did, while a slightly lower proportion reported them as having occurred earlier. The average algebraic difference in days between the actual and reported dates of the target incidents for the MV sample was $+15 \cdot 75$, indicating a net forward telescoping effect for the sample as a whole. As in the earlier analysis based on the absolute difference, an attempt was made to find attributes of the target offences, and of the respondents themselves, which are associated with this measure of telescoping effect; but even fewer statistically significant or meaningful associations emerged. There is a significant difference between types of offences;[28] but there is only a weak and non-significant relationship with the seriousness score for the target incident, and no consistent relationship at all with sex of respondent, area of residence, social class or any measure of educational attainment. As with the absolute-difference variable, there is a significant positive correlation between algebraic difference and days between incident and interview. But this relationship is by no means a strong one, and is in part influenced by the fact that the algebraic difference between actual and reported dates is effectively bounded by the date of the interview. The maximum amount of telescoping forward possible for the latest target incidents in the sample is only about sixty days.

(c) Distribution of the R and the MV Additional Incidents. A final check on the amount of inaccuracy likely to occur in time placement of victimization incidents can be made by comparing the observed monthly distributions of incidents reported by the R sample,[29] and the additional incidents (that is, other than the target incidents) reported to our interviewers by the MV and T samples, with the expected monthly distributions based on the Metropolitan Police statistics for 1972. This is admittedly a crude measure of the forward telescoping effect, since our own data suggest that there will probably be a somewhat greater degree of non-reporting in the early months of the reference period than in the later months; also, the true distribution of victim incidents in our area need not necessarily be the same as that for all recorded indictable crimes in London (which is all we have monthly statistics for).[30] Nonetheless, for what the comparison is worth, it is presented at Table III.11. It will be seen that there is a significant tendency for the R sample incidents to cluster in the second half of the year—57 per cent, against about 49 per cent for all indictable offences recorded in the M.P.D. in 1972—but that no such tendency appears in the additional incidents of the MV and T samples. It may, of course, be that having reported the target offences to the police made the MV and T samples likely to recall additional incidents early in the year, or more likely to place those incidents in time throughout the year. It seems more likely, however, that the relatively greater shift in the distribution of the R sample's incidents

Table III.11. Expected and observed monthly distributions of crime incidents, MV, T and R samples

	Expected,[a] per cent	Observed[b] MV, T additional incidents		Observed[c] R incidents	
		No.	Percentage	No.	Percentage
Month:					
January	7·8	30	8·3	24	6·5
February	8·2	29	8·0	17	4·6
March	7·6	30	8·3	30	8·1
April	9·0	27	7·4	22	5·9
May	8·8	27	7·4	22	5·9
June	9·9	40	11·0	44	11·9
July·	8·3	40	11·0	39	10·5
August	8·5	21	5·8	38	10·3
September	7·8	32	8·8	31	8·4
October	8·0	25	6·9	34	9·2
November	7·7	23	6·3	30	8·1
December	8·4	39	10·7	39	10·5
Total	100·0	363	100·0	370	100·0

$$\chi^2 = 13\cdot21, \ 0\cdot20 < p < 0\cdot30 \qquad \chi^2 = 22\cdot07, \ p \simeq 0\cdot02$$

[a]Based on statistics supplied by the Metropolitan Police.
[b]Excludes 24 incidents in which respondent did not give the month in which the incident occurred.
[c]Excludes 64 incidents in which respondent did not give the month in which the incident occurred.

is due to a higher degree of recall loss in the early months; as we shall see, that sample's experience as victims of crime is in several respects different from that of our MV and T samples.[31]

4. Conclusions

The findings from this part of our research are encouraging, since they show that—at least in certain conditions of interviewing—the survey method can effectively be used to capture a high proportion of incidents of personal victimization. It must be remembered, of course, that all of the target incidents used in our reverse record check had been reported to the police; we would not expect to obtain such high rates of recall and reporting for crimes which had not been reported to the police, not only because those incidents are probably on average less serious but because the fact of having notified the police may itself make the incident more memorable to a survey respondent. As we shall see in the next chapter, our R sample did remember, and disclose to our interviewers, a very large number of incidents which they said they had not reported to the police. But it is likely, for the reason just mentioned, that even this large number represents something of an underestimate of the sample's experience of victimization of certain kinds. The slight tendency, on average, to telescope incidents forward, on the other hand, leads to an over-estimation of victimization; even if the two types of error were to offset one another completely, the result would probably be some distortion of the *pattern* of crimes experienced by the sample. Fortunately, in our data, it seems that both non-reporting (to interviewers) and telescoping are not systematically associated with particular types of respondents, but are more or less randomly distributed phenomena.

From a methodological point of view, it may be felt that our findings—satisfying as they are—stand in need of some explanation. In particular, they seem to raise an obvious question: why did we succeed in obtaining the more favourable rates of recall from our known victims of crime, than were obtained in the U.S. Census Bureau studies reviewed earlier in this chapter?

There are several possible answers to this question. First, it may be that our sample—or the population from which we selected it—simply contained a higher proportion of 'good' survey respondents than the samples used in the Washington, Baltimore and San Jose surveys. No data have been published from any of those studies on relationships between non-reporting of incidents and any attributes of respondents. But this possibility certainly cannot be ruled out.

Secondly, the sample of *incidents* on which our reverse record check was based may have differed significantly from those used in the Census Bureau research.

We have noted that the target incidents which we selected were all relatively serious, as crimes recorded in the Metropolitan Police District go. Certainly they were more serious, on average, than the MV sample's additional incidents or the R sample's incidents; and they were seen by the respondents as such. They may have been more serious, and thus more salient, than those of the Washington, Baltimore and San Jose respondents—though such data as are available do not show clearly that this was so. At any rate, we cannot conclude from our results that equally high rates of recall would be found for the more trivial kinds of victimization experience in the general population in our three survey areas in London generally.[1]

Two factors relating to questionnaire design and interviewing strategy may also be important. First, our questions about victimization came near the end of an hour or so's interviewing, most of which had been devoted to questions about various aspects of crime; our respondents thus had a much longer period of time than their counterparts in the American studies, to recall things which had happened to them. By contrast, in most of the Census Bureau's interviews the screening questions must have been asked after about ten minutes;[2] leaving aside questions of rapport, this is scarcely time for respondents to bring to mind their own experiences of crime, let alone to remember exactly when they took place. Secondly, there seems to us no doubt that the method of introducing our questions on the respondent's experiences of victimization—by asking him to 'bracket' the reference period in his own mind, and to recall 'landmark' dates within it—helped respondents not only to remember more, but to remember more accurately, than if we had not done this.

A further possibility which may help to explain the difference between our results and those of the U.S. Census Bureau researchers is related to differences in the perceived (and presumably the actual) levels of crime in the United States and England.[3] In the United States, where there is a general belief that crimes of all kinds are taking place fairly frequently, a survey respondent's own experiences may well not be as salient as they would be in an English context, where an incident involving criminal victimization may 'stand out' more clearly against the relatively crime-free background. It is true, as Biderman[4] has pointed out, that personally experienced victimization is probably not a very important problem for most people, even in the United States; thus public opinion or attitude surveys about 'the crime problem' may well give a misleading impression on the importance of that problem, and its salience for American survey respondents. Nonetheless, the point is that the *relative* difference in the (perceived or actual) levels of crime in the two countries may go some way to explaining why our respondents recalled such a high proportion of the crime incidents on which we had information.[5]

Notes and References

1. Evidence on Recall and Telescoping

1. Above, p. 17.
2. Albert D. Biderman *et. al, Field Surveys I.* In the second part of this survey (in the 13th Precinct), the method was changed, precisely because it was suspected that the method used in the first part had constricted responses to screening questions.
3. Albert J. Reiss, Jr., *Field Surveys III*, Vol. 1 at 149. See also A. D. Biderman, 'Surveys of population samples for estimating crime incidence.' (1967) *The Annals* 16 at 27–28.
4. Evidence on this question from other types of survey is general though not invariably in favour of this conclusion. See, for example, John Neter and Joseph Waksberg, *Response errors in collection of expenditure data by household interviews: an experimental study.* U.S. Department of Commerce, Bureau of the Census, Technical Paper No. 11 (Washington, D. C.: U.S. Government Printing Office 1965); Carol M. Jaeger and Jean L. Pennock, 'Consistency of response in household surveys,' (1961) 50 *Journal of American Statistical Association* 320–37; Robert Ferber, 'On the reliability of responses secured in sample surveys.' (1961) 50 *Journal of American Statistical Association* 788–810; Seymour Sudman and Norman A. Bradburn, *Response Effects in Surveys* (Chicago: Aldine, 1974) 62–63.
5. Or so we infer from variations between them in the numbers of incidents disclosed to them, and the differing degrees of accuracy of the reporting of 'target' incidents.
6. See *The Survey of Sickness*, a report of the Government Social Survey (London: H.M.S.O. 1952) 27–29.
7. Percy G. Gray, 'The memory factor in social surveys.' (1955) *Journal of American Statistical Association* 344–63, at 351.
8. Percy G. Gray, 'The memory factor in social surveys.' 357.
9. Percy G. Gray, 'The memory factor in social surveys.' 362.
10. John Neter and Joseph Waksberg, 'A study of response errors in expenditures data from household interviews.' (1964) 59 *Journal of the American Statistical Association* 17–55. See also J. Neter and J. Waksberg, 'Response errors in collection of expenditures data by household interviews: an experimental study,' U.S. Department of

Commerce, Bureau of the Census, Technical Paper No. 11 (Washington, D.C.: U.S. Government Printing Office, 1965).

11. The same thing is likely to happen in any form of panel design, of course, e.g. when respondents are asked to keep diaries of expenditure: see Robert Turner, 'Inter-week variations in expenditure recording during a two week survey of family expenditure.' (1961) 10 *Applied Statistics* 136–146. The problem of 'time-in-sample' bias is now being investigated in the National Crime Panel surveys: see Henry Woltman and John Bushery, 'A panel bias study in the National Crime Survey,' a paper presented at the meeting of the American Statistical Association, August 25–28, 1975 (Washington, D.C.: U.S. Department of Commerce, Social and Economic Statistics Division, mimeo.

12. John Neter and Joseph Waksberg, 'A study of response errors in expenditures data from household interviews.' 41–42.

13. John Neter and Joseph Waksberg, 'A study of response errors in expenditures data from household interviews.' 48.

14. Seymour Sudman and Norman M. Bradburn, *Response Effects in Surveys: A Review and Synthesis*, National Opinion Research Center Monographs in Social Research No. 16 (Chicago: Aldine, 1974) 68–80.

15. The data are reported in Seymour Sudman and Robert Ferber, *Experiments in Obtaining Consumer Expenditures in Durable Goods by Recall Procedures* (Urbana, Illinois: Survey Research Laboratory, 1970).

16. Seymour Sudman and Norman M. Bradburn, *Response Effects in Surveys: A Review and Synthesis*, 74–79.

17. Thus the parameters b_1 and b_2 are inversely related to one another; this conclusion is also supported, to some extent, by John Neter and Joseph Waksberg, 'A study of response errors in expenditures data from household interviews.' See Seymour Sudman and Norman M. Bradburn, *Response Effects in Surveys: A Review and Synthesis*. 77–79.

18. Martin David, 'The validity of income reported by a sample of families who received welfare assistance during 1959.' (1961) 57 *Journal of the American Statistical Association* 680–85.

19. Carol H. Weiss, 'Validity of welfare mothers' interview responses.' (1969) 32 *Public Opinion Quarterly* 622–33.

20. Though, as we shall see, there are certain types of criminal victimization (so-called 'series victimizations') which involve large numbers of incidents of the same type occurring over an extended period (e.g. repeated threats or assaults, or numerous incidents of theft or damage); in such cases the respondent may be *more* likely to recall that the series occurred though he may be unable to recall the precise date, or other details, of particular incidents comprising the series. See below, Chapter IV, p. 74.

2. The U. S. Census Bureau Pilot Studies

1. We are grateful to Dr. Anthony G. Turner of the Law Enforcement Assistance Administration, and to Professor Albert J. Reiss, Jr. for having made available to us the reports on these studies and on the Census Bureau's programme. With the exception of the report on the San Jose study (note 8 below) these documents are unpublished.

2. U.S. Bureau of the Census, *Victim recall pretest (Washington, D.C.): Household Survey of victims of crimes*. Unpublished report, June 10, 1970.

3. This rate ranged from a low of 55 per cent for assault cases to a high of 77 per cent for burglaries. Most of those who could not be interviewed were persons who were known to have moved, or simply could not be located (after an unspecified number of recalls); the refusal rate was only 7 per cent. The 'could not be located' category accounted for over half of the assault victims who could not be interviewed, suggesting

that victims of this type of crime may tend to be more transient than victims of burglary, theft and robbery; alternatively, they may have been less accurately identified in police records than burglary victims, whose crimes took place, by definition, in their homes.

4. In fact, however, among the 11-month cases there were five respondents who mentioned what appeared to be the crime in question, but who could not place that crime in any particular month; if these cases are counted as 'successes' then the figure for 11-month cases rises to 78 per cent, i.e. equal to that for six-month cases.

5. Linda R. Yost and Richard W. Dodge, 'Household surveys of victims of crime, Second pretest (Baltimore, Maryland),' unpublished report, November 30, 1970.

6. Persons selected for the Baltimore survey were not officially notified of their inclusion in the sample; and the introduction used by interviewers in contacting them did not reveal the real purpose for which the interview was wanted. It appears, however, that some interviews in this pretest were scheduled by telephone, in which case the interviewers 'found that a more detailed explanation was required.' As in the Washington pretest, the interviewers knew that they were interviewing persons who had been victims of crime.

7. This excludes 12 cases in which the incident was elicited by a general question at the end of the interview, or was simply mentioned in an interviewer's note, and the date of the crime was therefore not ascertained.

8. National Institute of Law Enforcement and Criminal Justice, Statistics Division, *San Jose Methods Test of Known Crime Victims.* Statistics Technical Report No. 1 (Washington, D.C.: June 1972).

9. The San Jose reverse record check was carried out in conjunction with a larger survey of victimization involving about 5,500 households and about 1,000 businesses in each of two cities (San Jose and Dayton, Ohio). For a description of this larger survey see *Crimes and Victims: A Report on the Dayton–San Jose Pilot Survey of Victimization.* U.S. Department of Justice, Law Enforcement Assistance Administration, National Criminal Justice Information and Statistics Service (Washington, D. C.: June 1974).

10. National Institute of Law Enforcement and Criminal Justice, Statistics Division, *San Jose Methods Test of Known Crime Victims.* 14–15 (Tables 4–4E).

11. National Institute of Law Enforcement and Criminal Justice, Statistics Division, *San Jose Methods Test of Known Crime Victims.* 2.

12. National Institute of Law Enforcement and Criminal Justice, Statistics Division, *The San Jose Methods Test of Known Crime Victims.* 9. In this pretest it was also found, as in the Baltimore study, that crimes defined (by the police) as aggravated assaults were more likely to be mentioned to interviewers than those defined as simple assaults.

13. See the Advance Reports on *Crime in the Nation's Five Largest Cities* (April 1974) at 2–3, and on *Crime in Eight American Cities* (July 1974) at 1–2; also *Criminal Victimization in the United States, January–June 1973* (Vol. 1, November 1974) at 2–3, and *Criminal Victimization in the United States, 1973 Advance Report* (Vol. 1, May 1975) at 2–3. (All of these reports published by the U.S. Department of Justice, Law Enforcement Assistance Administration, National Criminal Justice Information and Statistics Service.) Subsequent reports on these surveys have been more cautious, and have adverted briefly to the possibility of response bias; but they have still repeated the claim that the majority of assaults are committed by strangers. The statement was also repeated by President Ford in his message to Congress on crime on 19 June 1975: see the *L.E.A.A. Newsletter*, Vol. 5, No. 1 (June–July 1975) 1–2.

14. See, for example, Marvin Wolfgang, *Patterns in Criminal Homicide* (Philadelphia: University of Pennsylvania Press, 1958) 203 ff; Donald J. Mulvihill and Melvin M. Tumin, *Crimes of Violence*, a staff report to the U.S. National Commission on the Causes and Prevention of Violence (Washington, D.C.: U.S. Government Printing Office, 1969), Vol. 11, Chapter 5 at 207–258; F. H. McClintock, *Crimes of Violence*

(London: Macmillan, 1961) 33 ff; Menachim Amir, *Patterns of Forcible Rape* (Chicago: University of Chicago Press, 1971). Since all of these studies are based on police-recorded data, they too almost certainly under-estimate the proportion of assaults which occur between persons known or related to each other, as these crimes are also probably less likely to be reported to the police.

15. This study is described in Anthony G. Turner, 'Methodological issues in the development of the national crime survey panel: partial findings,' an unpublished paper dated December 1972.

16. Anthony G. Turner, 'Methodological issues in the development of the national crime survey panel: partial findings' at 6–8, 10–11.

17. In the San Jose report it is stated (National Institute of Law Enforcement and Criminal Justice, Statistics Division, *San Jose Methods Test of Known Crime Victims.* 6) that the response rate in a general household survey carried out in that city was 97 per cent, which is consistent with the usual level obtained by Census Bureau interviewers when the sample consists of occupied housing units rather than named individuals. See further below, Chapter IX, pp. 220–221.

3. Results of the Present Study: The Main Victim Sample

1. See above, pp. 31–32, for data on the age and sex of the final MV samples in each of these areas.

2. Of the offences classified by the police as assaults, 16 had subsequently been written off as 'no crime.' Almost invariably, however, it was clear that this had been done because the victim was unwilling to give evidence; there was no doubt that an assault had in fact occurred.

3. The R sample incidents, and the MV sample additional incidents, are discussed further in Chapter IV, pp. 74–80 below.

4. In general, throughout this book the expression 'significant' is used in its statistical sense, to indicate a difference the probability of whose occurrency by chance is small (less than 0·05, or less than one in twenty). Where appropriate, the value of statistics such as χ^2, and the associated value of p, will be given in footnotes and tables. In the present case, however, a statistically significant difference merely involves rejecting the hypothesis that the target and additional incidents represent random samples from the same population; since there is no earthly reason to accept that hypothesis in the first place, the finding will not be tricked out with statistics.

5. This question is admittedly badly worded, being ambiguous between personal acquaintance with the offender and mere knowledge (or belief) about the kind of person he was.

6. This point is discussed further in Chapter V, pp. 136–137 below.

7. But see below, pp. 144–145.

8. In two cases the respondent refused to give any details of the event; in two it was telescoped backward, and mentioned only in question G14 (which asked if the respondent had ever been the victim of a crime); no crime incident form was filled out for incidents mentioned in answer to this question.

9. It will be recalled that our MV cases were originally selected in accordance with an experimental design, so that we could study the effects on reporting of sex of victim and type of offence as well as time (i.e., from incident to interview). An analysis of variance on the final MV sample, using the six categories of victims and six equal time periods in Table III.3, showed that differences in reporting between the victim categories were statistically significant ($F = 2·91$, $p = 0·02$); the effect of time was not ($F = 1·70$, $p = 0·14$). There was no significant interaction between time and victim category.

10. This might conceivably have been due to the order of questions GI–G10, in which burglary was asked about first. In our earlier pilot studies, however, we varied the order of questions in the section, and found no significant differences in the numbers of inci-

dents mentioned with different orderings. In a personal communication, Norm Okihiro has informed us that in pre-tests for the study of residential burglary carried out by Okihiro and Dr. Irvin Waller, incidents of burglary were often vividly recalled after five or six years, though exact dates were often foggy. (The main part of the Waller–Okihiro survey used a reference period of 16–17 months.)

11. We are grateful to Mr. H. D. Walton and his staff for making these unpublished statistics available to us.

12. Thus the exponential model suggested by Sudman and Bradburn (above, p. 41) does not give a very good fit to our data. But it is apparent that for our data the value of the non-time related parameter a is very close to 1.0, and that the time-decay parameter b_1 is very small (close to 0.01); indeed, those values give a very good fit if our six time periods are collapse into three. (By comparison, fitting the Sudman–Bradburn model to the U.S. Census Bureau's pretests in Washington and Baltimore give $a = 0.92$, $b_1 = 0.025$ for the Washington sample and $a = 0.74$, $b_1 = 0.025$ for Baltimore.)

13. Above, pp. 48–49. It must be remembered that our data are not exactly comparable with those in the San Jose study: all of the target incidents in our MV sample were at least two months old, and most were at least three months old, at the time of the interviews; whereas in the San Jose study some incidents must have happened less than one month before the interview. In any case, a close reading of the National Institute of Law Enforcement and Criminal Justice, Statistics Division, *San Jose Methods Test of Known Crime Victims* report suggests that the decision to use a six-month reference period in the National Crime Panel was made independently of pretest findings, because of a desire for 'timely' data.

14. These incidents were elicited in replies to question G. 14, which asked, 'Have you, or any member of your household, *ever* been the victim of a crime?'

15. It is important to note, at this point, that our findings relate to a sample of (fairly serious) offences, all of which had been reported to the police; the evidence on reporting to interviewers might be different if we had been able to use a truly random sample of crimes (whether or not reported to the police).

16. Above, pp. 22–23.

17. $\chi^2 = 4.72$, df $= 1$, $p < 0.05$

18. There was an apparent tendency, however, for these ratings to be influenced by status disparity; almost all of our interviewers were visibly middle-class, and they tended to give lower ratings to the understanding and cooperativeness of lower-class respondents. It should also be pointed out that some of the variation between areas may be the function of variations between interviewers. Of the 30 interviewers whom we used in our London survey, 17 were able to get reports of all the target incidents in the cases which were randomly assigned to them (in some cases, of course, this was only one or two incidents). The two interviewers with the highest proportions of non-reported target incidents (three out of six, and five out of 14) had most of their MV cases in Hackney.

19. Interviewers were instructed, of course, to interview the respondent alone whenever possible. But—as in this case—this could not invariably be arranged. Unfortunately, we did not ask our interviewers to note specifically when another person was present; from the notes which they did make, however, it appears that this happened only infrequently.

20. Advance notice was had, of course, by those respondents who could not or would not give an interview on the first call on which they were contacted by the interviewer (which may not, of course, have been the first call made at their address.) Our data show that all of those interviewed after three or more calls—about half of the sample—reported their target incidents; that is, those interviewed on the first or second call included all of those who did *not* report the target incident. Unfortunately, from our interview records we do not know in all cases when the respondent was actually first

contacted; he may well have been out at the time of the earlier calls. But while it is possible that forewarning did increase recall in some cases, this would, of course, happen in a proportion of cases in any survey.

21. It was to avoid lengthening the interviews that we did not instruct interviewers to get the respondents to consult diaries or other records which they might have had, to try to date reported events more exactly (some respondents did, however, do this of their own accord.)

22. In the great majority of cases the crime reports stated that the offence had occurred on a definite day; in some cases of burglary and theft, however, a range of two or three days was given since the offence was not discovered until some time later, e.g. after a weekend or holiday. We rejected, in selecting our sample, cases in which the time interval shown on police records was greater than this, however. It may also be, of course, that in some cases the date on police records was incorrect. But this probably did not happen often, since the date of the offence was usually the same day, or the day before, the report to the police.

23. Strictly, these cases should have been randomly assigned. However, when this was done in a later analysis, it made no difference to the result.

24. Both can be treated as continuous variables on a ratio scale: the algebraic differences are approximately normally distributed though this is not, of course, true for the absolute differences.

25. $F = 2.19$, df $= 10$ and 214, $p < 0.01$.

26. $\gamma = +0.25$.

27. See above, p. 55.

28. $F = 1.80$, df $= 5$ and 203, $p < 0.05$.

29. These incidents are discussed in more detail in Chapter IV, pp. 74–80 below.

30. Since these statistics include crimes against business organizations, etc., they may well vary seasonally in a different way from individual victimization.

31. As will be evident from inspection of Table III.11, the telescoping function suggested by Sudman and Bradburn does not fit our data, either for the MV and T samples or for the R sample. While there is a slight *net* forward telescoping of incidents in the MV and T samples, there was also some backward telescoping; plainly the resulting distribution by months cannot be adequately represented by a one-parameter function of time.

4. Conclusions

1. It must also be pointed out that we carried out our interviews in January and February of 1973, and that our reference period effectively coincided almost exactly with the calendar year 1972; it may well be that beginning on January 1 is an easier period for people to place incidents accurately in, than one beginning in, say, April or August. Having pointed out this possibility we must add that there is apparently little evidence from other survey research that this is true. Why should people *not* remember a year beginning when they took their summer holidays?

2. See above, p. 45.

3. We are grateful to David Nelkin for this suggestion.

4. Albert D. Biderman, 'Surveys of populations for estimating crime incidence.' (1967) 374 *The Annals* 16.

5. After completing this part of our research, we learned of another reverse record check, conducted by Dr. J. P. S. Fiselier of the Criminolisch Instituut at the Katholieke Universiteit in Nijmegen. In a personal communication, Dr. Fiselier states that he sent a postal questionnaire to a purposive sample of 191 known victims (selected from Nijmegen police records for 1970–72). Of the 80 persons who responded, 74 per cent definitely mentioned the target incidents; 16 per cent definitely did not mention them, and in 10 per cent of the cases no decision could be made. Failure to mention the

target incident was highest for minor thefts (23 per cent) and aggressive offences (25 per cent), and lowest for higher-value thefts (10 per cent) and sexual crimes (6 per cent). As would be expected, mention of the target incident was highest for the most recent year (89 per cent), and fell to about 81 per cent for the two preceding years. As was the case in our study, about half of the incidents which were mentioned were located within the correct month of occurrence; and there was a net tendency for the remaining respondents to telescope their incidents forward rather than back. The lower overall reporting rate for target incidents in Dr. Fiselier's survey is probably to be expected, given his use of postal questionnaires rather than interviews; that apart, his findings seem in many ways similar to ours.

CHAPTER IV

Criminal Victimization in Three London Areas

1. Crime Incidents Reported by the Register Sample

This chapter and the four which follow it are based primarily on data relating to our London electoral register (R) sample. As we have shown,[1] there is reason to believe that this sample is broadly representative of the resident population aged 18 and over in the three London areas—Brixton, Hackney and Kensington—where our fieldwork was done. But the reader is warned again that these three areas were not themselves chosen at random, and that our cases, therefore, do not purport to be a representative sample of the adult population of inner London as a whole.

The R sample contained a total of 545 respondents. Of these, 244, or just under 45 per cent, reported (in answer to the series of screening questions in our questionnaire) that they had personally experienced, in the preceding twelve months, one or more incidents which appeared to them to fit the descriptions of crimes mentioned in our questions. The total number of incidents reported by the sample in response to the screening questions was approximately 582. This total is necessarily somewhat inexact, since a small number of respondents claimed to have been victims of a particular type of crime—usually relatively minor thefts or damage to property—on many different occasions during the year, but could give no closer estimate of the numbers than 'every week or two' or 'at least once a month.' In these cases, the maximum number of incidents was arbitrarily coded by our interviewers as nine, so that the resulting total is almost certainly an underestimate.

Detailed information was recorded (on the separate crime incident forms) for a total of 434 incidents. This total differs from the total number of offences as measured by replies to the screening questions, for three reasons. First, there was a small number of cases in which respondents either could not or would not give any further details at all. Secondly, there were the cases just mentioned, in which respondents could not remember details concerning numerous offences of damage or theft which they said had occurred; this category accounts for the greater part of the difference in the two totals. Thirdly, in about five per cent of the cases it was found that a single incident had in fact involved more than one of the offences mentioned in reply to the screening questions: both an assault and some damage to property, for example. In these cases the crime incident form was coded according to the principal offence involved (defined as the one carrying the heaviest maximum penalty). We found, moreover, that the classification of incidents, in terms of the *type* of crime involved, occasionally posed something of a problem. In the great majority of cases, the respondent's detailed account of the matter (as recorded by the interviewer on the crime incident form) made it possible to conclude that one or more crimes of *some* type had probably been committed.[2] But the type of crime emerging from the incident form description was not always the same as was suggested by the respondent's earlier answers to the screening question in the main questionnaire. Thus, for example, the respondent might have given an affirmative answer to question Gla, which asked, 'Did anyone try to break into your house, or try to get in without your permission?'; on the basis of this answer, he would have been classified as the victim of an attempted burglary. But the detailed account of the incident might have revealed a completed burglary (rather than just an attempt); alternatively, it might have disclosed nothing more than offence of malicious damage to property (e.g. a broken window or door)—or no crime at all—and would have been coded as such on the crime incident form. Again, the respondent might have given an affirmative answer to question G3 ('Did anyone physically attack you or assault you, in any way, during the past year?'); this answer would have led him to be counted as the victim of an assault. But further information might have shown that the offence should really be classed as one of robbery or theft from the person. We have, then, two different (and independent) classifications of the incidents mentioned, which do not always coincide. The first, based on yes or no answers to the screening questions, approximates to the respondent's own view of 'what happened';[3] the second is our own classification, based on details of the incident as disclosed later in the interview. The relations between these two classifications, and the implications of this problem for victim surveys generally, are discussed in detail in Chapter VI. The difference between the two things should be borne in mind, however, in relation to the description of the R sample's experiences in the rest of this chapter.[4]

Table IV.1, which is based on responses to the screening questions, gives the total numbers of offences of different types reported by the respondents in our three areas. For reasons which will be discussed in detail in Chapter VI, a direct comparison with the patterns of crime disclosed by police statistics is not possible. An approximate comparison can be made, however, if we exclude non-indictable offences of damage to peoperty from the survey data, and compare the rank orders of frequency for the remaining incidents with similar rankings for the police statistics of crime recorded in 1972. The results of this comparison are presented in Table IV.2; it will be seen that there is only moderate agreement in each area,[5] even if a generous allowance is made for possible differences in classification. In particular, there are many more

Table IV.1. Incidents reported as having occurred within the preceding year, in three survey areas (based on responses to screening questions)

Type of crime:	Brixton No.	Brixton Per-centage	Area Hackney No.	Hackney Per-centage	Kensington No.	Kensington Per-centage	Total No.	Total Per-centage
Assaults	15	7·3	13	8·5	7	3·1	35	6·0
Attempted and Threatened Assault	25	12·1	16	10·5	30	13·5	71	12·2
Theft from Person	16	7·8	13	8·5	15	6·7	44	7·6
Burglary and Attempts	11	5·3	20	13·1	29	13·0	60	10·3
Theft in Dwelling	13	6·3	7	4·6	12	5·4	32	5·5
Thefts of, or from Motor Vehicles	39	18·9	23	15·0	36	16·1	98	16·8
Other Thefts	64	31·1	33	21·6	85	38·1	182	31·3
Damage to property	23	11·2	28	18·5	9	4·0	60	10·3
Total, all types	206	100·0	153	100·0	223	100·0	582	100·0

Table IV.2. Rank orders of frequency of selected offences in survey and police data, by area

	Brixton Survey	Brixton Police	Hackney Survey	Hackney Police	Kensington Survey	Kensington Police
Burglary	5	2	3	2	3	2
Thefts in dwellings	3	4	4	5	4	3
Assaults	2	5	2	4	2	5
Thefts of and from motor vehicles	4	3	5	3	5	4
Other theft	1	1	1	1	1	1

incidents in the broad category of crimes against the person—assaults and attempted assaults, robberies and thefts from the person—than would be expected from the police statistics. Such cases account for over one-quarter of all the incidents reported in our three sample areas combined, though according to police statistics they accounted for less than five per cent of the indictable crimes recorded in the three areas combined in 1972.

An examination of the details of these offences of 'violence' (as recorded in the crime incident forms) shows, however, that many of them were very trivial by any reasonable standard, and that the amount of serious violent crime experienced by our sample was extremely small. Of the 83 incidents classified (by us) as involving offences of assault or robbery, no less than 48—or 58 per cent—involved only attempted or threatened violence, rather than the actual use of it. None of the eleven robberies involved anything described by the respondents[6] as physical injury; the same was true of the 25 incidents of theft from the person (mostly purse-snatchings). Of the 35 actual assaults—as distinct from the merely attempted or threatened ones—11 cases, or just under one-third, were said to involve physical injury; but in only two of these was the injury more serious than bruises, abrasions or cuts. Only four cases involved the use of a weapon other than the offender's fists or feet; two of these involved bottles, one an umbrella and one a broom. There was no case reported in the entire sample involving the use of a knife or other weapon carried by the offender, though there were several in which knives were produced as threats.[7] Only seven of the sample required medical attention as a result of violent crime, and of these only three were required to stay in hospital over one day. Four respondents lost time from work as a result of their injuries (in the case of one victim of robbery, the period was over six months); but only two persons stated that they had suffered any kind of permanent disability as a result of violent crime committed against them in the survey period. No victim of violent crime in our R sample had applied for compensation from the Criminal Injuries Compensation Board.

It is clear, then, that the number of incidents involving the threat or use of violence (in some sense of that term) was much greater than would be expected from police statistics for our three areas for 1972; but that these incidents were far less serious, on average, than those experienced by victims of recorded violent crime.[8]

The offences against property reported by our R sample also contained many cases which appeared to be of a fairly trivial kind. Of a total of 353 incidents, there were 55 (or 15·6 per cent) which were attempts only. About one-quarter of the completed offences of theft or damage involved property worth less than £1, and another quarter involved amounts between £1 and £5. (These figures are considerably influenced by the fact that over 40 per cent of the reported thefts outside the house involved bottles of milk stolen from doorsteps.) Only 33 of the reported incidents—or 11·3 per cent of those where there was any property loss—were said to involve sums of over £50. For offenses of burglary and car theft the reported values were naturally higher: 27·5 per cent and 84.6 per cent respectively, were alleged to involve items worth £50 or more. For these offences, of course, we have only our respondents' statements as to the value and type of property stolen or damaged; and as we have seen,[9] in the MV sample there were often considerable discrepancies between the victims' estimates of the value of property and the amounts recorded by the police. For this reason, the property values reported by the R sample have been grouped within fairly broad categories. As Table IV.3 shows, however, the distribution of cases within these categories is generally similar to that which would be expected from the statistics of recorded offences of burglary, theft in a dwelling house, theft from the person and theft from a motor vehicle in England and Wales as a whole;[10] in no case is the difference statistically significant.

In just over ten per cent of the cases involving property loss, it was stated that some or all of the property was subsequently recovered. This figure is

Table IV.3. Reported values of property stolen or damaged, compared with all recorded offences in England and Wales in 1971

Value in £:	No.	Burglary Sample Percentage	All rec. Percentage	No.	Theft in dwelling Sample Percentage	All rec. Percentage
Less than 1	3	10·3	27·2	1	5·3	11·6
1–5	5	17·2	14·3	4	21·1	15·6
5–10	4	13·8	11·6	3	15·8	16·9
10–100	11	37·9	34·8	11	57·9	48·4
100 and over	6	20·6	12·1	0	—	7·5
	29	100·0	100·0	19	100·0	100·0

Value in £:	No.	Theft from person Sample Percentage	All rec. Percentage	No.	Thefts from vehicles Sample Percentage	All rec. Percentage
Less than 1	3	15·8	15·8	5	19·2	16·2
1–5	3	15·8	25·2	6	23·0	16·4
5–10	4	21·1	19·5	7	26·9	14·2
10–100	9	47·3	34·6	8	30·8	47·7
100 and over	0	—	4·9	0	—	5·5
	19	100·0	100·0	26	100·0	100·0

considerably influenced by the rate of recovery of stolen motor vehicles, however, over 70 per cent of which were eventually returned to their owners;[11] if these cases are excluded, the recovery rate (for property taken in burglary, robbery and other theft) falls to about six per cent. In the 265 incidents involving actual theft of or damage to property, the property in 81 cases, (or 30·6 per cent) was said to have been covered by insurance; though if we exclude those cases in which all of the property involved was recovered, our data show that insurance claims had only been made in 16·3 per cent of the remainder.[12] As might be expected, almost 90 per cent of the property offences reported by our sample were not discovered until some time afterwards; the proportion was slightly lower for thefts from the person and burglaries, but the differences were not statistically significant. It is difficult for us to compare the modes of entry reportedly used in the burglaries in our sample with figures collected by the Metropolitan Police for 1972, owing to doubts about the classification of these offences (particularly in Kensington, where the category 'theft in a dwelling house' is very frequently used by the police); all we can say is that the pattern in our sample is similar to that suggested by police figures, with about 40 per cent involving forcing a door, a similar proportion involving entry through a door left unlocked, and the remainder being effected by other means (e.g. forcing a window, or picking the lock).

Table IV.1 also shows that there are few marked differences, at least within fairly broad categories, between the patterns of crime incidents reported in our three sample areas.[13] In particular, there are broadly similar proportions of assaults, thefts from the person and thefts of and from motor vehicles, in all three areas; and the proportion of burglaries and thefts in dwelling houses reported by Hackney residents is very similar to that reported in Kensington. Again, however, an examination of the available details of the incidents reveals a different picture, and shows more variation between areas than the table suggests. Predictably, the value of property stolen or damaged is substantially higher in Kensington than in the other two areas: for example, 16 per cent of the Kensington cases for which we have data involved amounts of £50 or more, against 11 per cent in Brixton and less than seven per cent in Hackney.

Conversely, it is clear that the assaults reported by our Kensington respondents were on average much less serious than those reported in the other two areas. Over 80 per cent of the Kensington cases in fact involved only *threats* of violence or attempted assaults, rather than actual assaults or wounings; this proportion is twice as high as in either of the other two areas. Moreover, though the numbers involved are too small for statistical analysis, it is clear from those cases for which crime incident forms were completed that the degree of violence used in the completed assaults in Kensington was much less than used elsewhere: for example, only three per cent were said by the respondents to have resulted in any physical injury,[14] compared with 14 per cent in Brixton and 19 per cent in Hackney. Perhaps the clearest evidence of the comparative triviality of these incidents, however, lies in the respondents' subjective perceptions of their seriousness, as expressed in the score (on a scale from 1 to 11) which respondents were asked to give when completing the crime incident forms. For the cases classified by us as assaults (including threats and attempts) the mean scores given were 5·8 in Brixton, 5·6 in Hackney and only 2·9 in Kensington; over half of the assault incidents reported by the Kensington respondents were scored either 1 or 2.[15] This was so, despite the fact that a slightly *higher* proportion of the Kensington cases involved strangers (as opposed to family members or acquaintances) than in the other two areas.

It appears, then, that our Kensington residents were nearly as likely as those living in Brixton and Hackney to report having experienced situations in which (as they saw it) violence *might* have been used against them; but that these situations were much less likely to lead to an actual assault in Kensington than in the other two areas. There would seem to be two possible explanations for this difference. On the one hand, it may simply reflect inter-area differences in the definition of situations and in the reporting of those situations to our interviewers. On this hypothesis, the true ratios of threatened or attempted assault to actual assault would have been much the same in Hackney and Brixton as in Kensington (roughly four to one); the much lower observed ratios (1·67 to 1 in Brixton, and 1·2 to 1 in Hackney) would be the result of response bias. In other words, when asked, 'In the past year, did anyone threaten you in any way with violence of any kind?' the Brixton and Hackney residents might often have failed to recall such events, or have thought them not worth mentioning; whereas the Kensington respondents would have given more complete and accurate accounts of their experiences, down to the merest of shaken fists. On the other hand, our data may in part reflect real differences in the ways in which potentially violent situations tend to be dealt with in the three survey areas. It may be that our Kensington residents were simply better at ignoring threatening situations, at talking their way out of them, or at walking (or running) away from them; or that those who threatened them were less determined and less likely to turn their words into action. The norms governing behaviour in public places—in bus queues, pubs and cafes, for example—are observably different in Kensington from those applying in Hackney and in certain areas of Brixton; and it might well be that the higher proportion of threats mentioned in Kensington is a consequence of personal and social constraints on the use of violence which are stronger in a mainly middle-class area like Kensington than in the other areas.[16]

Unfortunately, our data on these crime incidents are insufficient to enable us to throw much light on this question one way or the other: we have, after all, only the respondents' versions of the incidents, and these were often recorded by our interviewers in fairly brief terms. An examination of the incidents involving assault and threats of violence in the three areas does suggest, however, that our Kensington respondents may have been somewhat less prone to behave in ways likely to precipitate actual violence in situations where it might have arisen, than respondents with similar experiences in the other two areas. There are several cases in Kensington in which (on the description of the facts available to us) it seems clear that the respondent avoided trouble by physically removing himself from the situation; no such case was reported in either Brixton or Hackney. In those two areas, a more commonly reported response to a threat of violence was by some form of self-help, as the following two incidents illustrate:

'Three of those [black] guys came up to me in the street [Railton Road, Brixton] at night. They tried to attack me but I hit them and they went off.'

'A man I knew came into my house [in Brixton] and started to make a fight . . . . he started to attack my wife. I cut him with a knife, and my wife phoned the police. He hit me with a bottle, and jumped out of the window.'

But our cases are too few in number, and too briefly described, to permit any firm conclusions on this point; and the possibility of response bias—either in the non-reporting of threatened violence in Brixton and Hackney, or in terms of differences in the ways in which the incidents were described by the respondents in three areas[17]—certainly cannot be ruled out completely.

After they had replied to the specific screening questions which asked about particular types of crime, respondents were asked the general question, 'In the past year, did anything else happen to you which you think might have involved a crime of any kind?' Coming at the end of a fairly lengthy series of specific questions, this catch-all did not produce much extra victimization: only 27 respondents (or five per cent of the sample) gave affirmative replies, and of these only one person reported more than one extra incident. We had hoped that respondents might, in answering this question, mention types of incidents (such as fraud and sexual offences) about which we had not specifically asked. A few did so; but the remainder mentioned a miscellany including motoring offenses and drug offences, and about a third of these were clearly incidents in which the respondent himself had committed the offence rather than being a victim of it. Respondents were also asked (unless they lived alone) if any of the things mentioned by the interviewer had happened to anyone else in their household during the past year. Just under one-sixth of the sample gave an affirmative answer to this question. But there was no association between size of household and number of incidents reported in answer to this question; and the victimization rate (that is, the number of incidents reported per household member) was much lower for other household members than for the respondents themselves—0·64 incidents per person, against 1·06 for the respondents. These findings confirm the results of other studies[18] on the under-reporting of victimization incidents by proxy respondents. Finally, respondents were asked if any of the things mentioned by the interviewer had *ever* happened to them or any member of their families—not just in the past year, but at any time. To this question, the majority of the sample replied in the affirmative; but it is nonetheless interesting that 105 respondents, or just under a fifth of the sample, gave a negative answer—thus asserting that they had never been victims of a crime of any kind. How far this finding owes to these respondents' good fortunes, and how far to their bad memories, is, of course, something about which we can only speculate.[19]

In summary, then, our respondents reported substantial numbers of incidents which appeared to involve crimes committed against them. But many of these incidents were manifestly not of a serious kind; as we shall see in the next chapters, many were not reported to the police, and would probably not have been treated by the police as crimes even if they had been reported.

2. Demographic Variables in Relation to Victimization

We now turn to an examination of differences in the experience of survey-reported victimization among different groups—broadly defined, in terms of demographic attributes—within our sample. (Unless otherwise indicated, our victimization data discussed in this section are derived from responses to the screening questions.) In reviewing our data we shall where possible compare our findings with those of victim syrveys carried out elsewhere, for which results are available to us. For methodological reasons, none of these other surveys is exactly comparable to our own, nor are they exactly comparable with each other. But at a very general level, several consistent findings do emerge which, taken together, may help to clarify the patterns of criminal victimization among different groups of the population.

(a) *Urban and Rural Areas.* Several studies, in the United States and elsewhere, have reported findings based on samples from cities of different sizes, or from both urban and rural areas. Almost without exception, all of these studies have found much higher rates of victimization reported by residents of inner city areas than by those living in suburban or rural areas. Thus, in the U.S. national survey conducted in 1966 by NORC,[1] it was found that central metropolitan areas had violent crime rates which were about five times higher than those of smaller cities and rural areas, and property crime rates which were twice as high. There were considerable variations in different areas of the country, however, and for selected types of crimes the pattern was different: for example, offences of fraud and theft appeared to be somewhat more prevalent in suburban parts of metropolitan areas than in the central areas. A similar survey carried out in Maricopa County (Phoenix) Arizona in 1968–69 also found higher rates for all serious (Part I) crimes in the inner city area, compared with suburban and outlying parts of the county; the pattern was different for less serious (Part II) offences, however, some types of which—including petty larceny, consumer fraud and sex offences other than rape—were more frequently reported by respondents in the outer city area.[2]

Reynolds *et al.* carried out surveys of victimization in a central city area and a suburban community in Minnesota in 1971, which produced similar findings. Estimated rates of victimization in the central city area were 7·5 times those for the suburban community for serious Part I offences, and four times as great for Part II offences.[3] Finally, it is reported by Wolf and Hauge that surveys in Finland, Denmark, Sweden and Norway have all found that the risk of becoming a victim of criminal violence is greater for residents of the capital cities than for persons living elsewhere in those countries.[4] To some extent, then, picture typically revealed by official statistics—of higher crime rates in central urban areas than in suburban and rural areas[5]—is confirmed by the findings of victim surveys. The magnitude of the difference, however, is not necessarily the same as official statistics suggest; and there are variations between different types of crime, with property offences being more evenly distributed in relation to urbanization than crimes of violence.

Our R Sample was, of course, drawn exclusively from Inner London areas. In two earlier pilot surveys, however, we interviewed samples of adults in Peterborough, an English provincial city with a population of about 94,000. In each of those pilot surveys we found that 37 per cent of the sample reported one or more crime incidents which had happened within the preceding year; the comparable figure for our three London areas combined was 45 per cent. This is not as great a difference as that reported in some of the other surveys just cited; and it may owe in part to the lesser efficiency of our questionnaire and interviewing procedures in the Peterborough surveys, which were mainly concerned with questionnaire development. Against this, Peterborough is not in any sense a rural area; it is a London overspill town with extensive industrial development. Moreover, our surveys in Peterborough were deliberately concentrated in the central area of that city. In the light of these facts, a gross victimization rate nearly one-fifth lower than that found in the inner London sample may be taken to represent a substantial difference: there is every reason to believe that even lower rates would have been found in smaller towns and truly rural areas.

(b) Sex Ratios. Combining together all of the types of offences included in our survey, a slightly higher proportion of males reported one or more incidents in the preceding year than did females—48·8 per cent against 42·6 per cent. The difference in gross victimization rates only manages to attain statistical significance in our sample, however, in the case of crimes of violence (assaults, robbery and thefts from the person combined); as Table IV.4 shows, the proportion reporting one or more such incidents was almost twice as high for males as for females.[6] For burglary, and for thefts other than from the person, the pattern is reversed, with slightly greater proportions of female respondents reporting incidents: these differences are not statistically significant, however.

Other victim surveys for which results have been published to date show broadly similar results. Thus, for example, in the current National Crime Panel surveys in the United States, both the national panel and 26 city-level surveys show higher victimization rates for males than for females, for all types of personal violence (except, of course, rape).[7] In those surveys, males also have higher rates of reported victimization through 'personal larceny *without* contact;' though females have higher rates of 'personal larceny *with* contact,' a category which—like our category of 'theft from the person'—very often involves purse-snatching.

In Reynolds's surveys in Minnesota, higher estimated rates of victimization were found for males than for females, for all of the broad categories of crime (Part I, Part II, property and personal offences), for both the central city and suburban communities; the differences were much greater among central city residents, however.[8] In all four of the Scandinavian surveys, it was found that males were consistently more at risk of violent victimization than females; this difference was especially marked for the more serious types of violent

Table IV.4. Reporting of incidents involving offences of violence, by males and females

| | | Number reported | | | |
		None	1	2 or more	Total
Males	No.	201	32	9	242
	Percentage	83·1	13·2	3.7	100·0
Females	No.	274	22	7	303
	Percentage	90·4	7·3	2·3	100·0
Total	No.	475	54	16	545
	Percentage	87·2	9·9	2·9	100·0

$$\chi^2 = 6·58, \text{df} = 2, p = 0·04$$

crime (i.e. those involving actual assault as opposed to threats or attempts at violence.)[9]

(c) Age. For all types of offence, our data show significant negative associations between age and the probability of reporting victimization: that is, younger respondents were more likely to report one or more incidents than older ones. The relationship is not quite a monotonic one, for any category of offence; nor is it an especially strong one, however measured. (Sample correlation coefficients between age and number of offences reported are -0.17 for all offences of violence, and -0.21 for all types of offence combined.) In particular, respondents under 21 report rather less victimization than those in their twenties. It will be remembered[10] that—especially in Kensington—the youngest age-groups are somewhat under-represented in our sample, in comparison to their numbers in the enumerated population; re-weighting our sample results in accordance with Census data would thus further weaken the relationship between age and victimization. However, it may also be that our under-21 respondents are somewhat unrepresentative; there certainly seems no good theoretical reason why they should report less violence or theft (but more burglary) than those aged 21–25. What is clear is that among the older respondents in our sample—especially those aged over 50—the probability of reporting victimization falls sharply. Among those aged over 60, less than 4 per cent reported any type of offence of violence, and only 23 per cent reported an offence of any kind; the corresponding percentages for persons aged under 60 were 16 per cent of violent offences, and 53 per cent for all types of crime combined. When the sample is grouped into five-year intervals according to age, the highest risks of victimization are found among those aged 26–30 for crimes of violence, and those aged 31–35 for property offences.

Again, similar results have been found by other researchers. A very detailed examination of this question was carried out by Reynolds *et al.*, who interviewed respondents down to the age of eight in the central city area, and down to 10 in the suburban community.[11] In general, the estimated rates of victimization reported in this survey decline steadily with age, for Part I and II offences, personal and property crimes. There were a few cases in which the estimated rates for respondents aged 20–29 were greater than those of respondents aged 19 and under; for males this was so for Part I crime in the suburbs and property offences in the suburban community; for females it was so for Part I crimes, all property offences and all personal offences, in the central city. But in no case were estimated rates for those aged over 29 greater than for those aged 29 and under. Moreover, the rates for those under 20 were in some cases strikingly high, in comparison with older age-groups: in the case of offences against the person, for males in the central city area, the 18–19 age group's rate was 5·9 times as high as that of respondents in their twenties. In the U.S. National Crime Panel surveys, very much the same picture is found: the highest rates of personal victimization (robbery, assault and theft) are generally exhibited by the 16–19 age group, with rates declining monotonically with age thereafter.

Table IV.5. Reported incidents involving offences of violence (including thefts from the person) by race[a]

| | | Number of incidents | | | |
		None	1	2 or more	Total
Whites	No.	438	41	12	491
	Percentage	89.2	8·4	2·4	100·0
Blacks	No.	30	11	4	45
	Percentage	66·7	24·4	8·9	100·0
Total	No.	468	52	16	536
	Percentage	87·3	9·7	3·0	100·0

[a]Excludes eight Oriental and Indian respondents, and one with race not known.

The same pattern holds for burglary and thefts from households, in relation to age of the head of the household.[12] The Scandinavian surveys—which were concerned only with violence—show the same result so far as age-specific victimization rates are concerned.[13]

(d) Race. Non-whites accounted for just under 10 per cent of our R sample; most of these respondents were West Indians, living in Brixton and Hackney. For all property offences except burglary, non-whites were more likely to report victimization than whites, though the differences did not reach statistical significance. As Table IV.5 shows, however, black[14] respondents were significantly more likely to report victimization involving some form of offence against the person. One in three of the black respondents reported one or more such incidents, compared with one in ten of the whites. At first sight this may seem to confirm the findings of almost all of the American victim surveys—and studies based on American police statistics—which suggest that blacks in the United States tend to have higher victimization rates than whites.[15] Any such cross-national racial comparison must be made with extreme caution, however. The social conditions of the West Indian communities in Brixton and Hackney are different from those of urban blacks in the United States, and the cultures of the two groups are also different: these cultural differences may well lead to different definitions of crime (for example, of 'assault' and other terms connoting interpersonal violence) which would make straightforward comparisons of victimization or crime rates virtually meaningless. (This point is discussed more fully below.) In any case, there is no theoretical ground, so far as we are aware, for asserting that race as such is an important determinant of participation in crime, either as an offender or as a victim. It is also important to note that in our sample—as in most if not all other studies which have investigated the question—the great majority of reported offences are intra-racial rather than inter-racial: most black victims are attacked by black offenders, most white victims by white offenders.[16]

(e) Social Class. We found no consistent or statistically significant differences in the reporting to interviewers of either offences against the person, or burglary, among respondents of different social classes.[17] In the case of thefts—both personal and household—there was a tendency for persons in the higher classes to be more likely to report incidents; but the difference did not attain statistical significance. This is in general, the finding of other surveys to date as well. In the U.S. National Crime Panel surveys, there is a slight tendency for persons with lower family income to report more personal victimization, and for those in higher income groups to report more property victimization: but this tendency is not marked, and is by no means consistent.[18] A lack of association between victimization and income was observed by Reynolds *et al.* in the Minnesota suburban community, though among central city respondents in this survey, higher estimated rates of victimization involving offences against the person were found among lower income respondents.[19] In the Maricopa County survey, there were similarly contradictory findings; *all* of the aggravated assaults were reported by respondents with incomes of $6,000 or more, whereas simple assaults were reported six times more frequently by respondents with incomes below $6,000. Burglary rates were higher among the lower-income respondents, whereas Part I thefts (of over $500) were more frequent among those with higher incomes; for Part II thefts there was not much difference.[20] Finally, in all four of the Scandinavian surveys it was found that the risk of becoming the victim of a crime of violence—or, more strictly, the probability of mentioning one or more acts of violence to the interviewer—was greater for middle and high status groups than for low status ones.[21]

(f) Other Variables. There were a few other attributes which distinguished between the victims and non-victims in our R sample in a statistically significant and apparently meaningful way; most of these, however, could be explained in terms of the variables just discussed. For example, there were slightly higher rates of reported personal and household victimization among those who were working (either full or part time) than among those who were not; this merely reflects the much lower rates of reporting among those who were old enough to have retired, and disappears when age is controlled for. Two things should be mentioned, however, not only for their substantive significance but as indicators of possible sample bias. First, the small number of respondents (in all three of our samples) who at the time of the survey said they had been living at the same address for less than a year were significantly more likely to report offences of burglary and theft (though not of violence) than those who had been in residence for a year or longer. Since our sample was drawn from electoral registers, one-year in-migrants were almost certainly under-represented in it; true victimization rates in our areas are therefore probably higher than our data suggest.[22] Secondly, we asked respondents how many nights a week, on average, they went out. Responses to this question were significantly related to the reporting of victimization of all types: those who

said they went out five nights a week or more were two and a half times as likely to report some victimization as those who said they went out less than once a month or never. Those who are seldom at home in the evening are, of course, less likely to be contacted by interviewers; the result again is that our sample estimates of victimization are likely to be biased, and to understate the true rates.[23]

It also remains to be considered how far the differences in reporting of victimization are likely to be real, and how far they may be due to some form of response bias leading to over-reporting or under-reporting of incidents by selected groups in the population. Plainly there is little reason to accept this as an explanation of the urban–rural (or suburban–central city) differences. But where many other attributes are concerned, the possibility of response biases is not so easily dismissed. In the case of racial differences, for example, the probable direction of any response biases which may exist (e.g. under-reporting of certain types of assaults by blacks) would mean that the true difference in victimization rates between blacks and whites is, if anything, greater than survey findings suggest. The general finding that females are at least as likely as males to report victimization involving property offences may be due, as Biderman has suggested,[24] to the fact that crimes such as burglary are offences against the 'hearth and home', which is still thought of as the special preserve of the female; women may be more likely to regard themselves as victims of such offences (and also more likely to know about them) than men. (There is, as it happens, no support for this suggestion in our data: married women were only very slightly more likely to report incidents of burglary or theft than married men. Moreover, the latter are slightly more likely to report such incidents than single men or those who were divorced, separated or widowed; this does not suggest masculine ignorance of (or unwillingness to report) what may be regarded as 'household' offences.) In the case of age differentials, it seems reasonable to suppose that the very marked drop in reporting of incidents found in most surveys among respondents in the oldest age-group, is due in some part to generalized under-reporting by those respondents.[25] As we shall see, however,[26] there is reason to believe that this finding largely reflects the more limited social interaction of this age group; it will be remembered that there was no consistent or significant association, in our MV sample, between age and the reporting of target incidents or accuracy of time placement.[27]

Several researchers have suggested that the apparent absence of social-class differentials in the reporting of violent victimization is due to response bias, either in terms of a generalized under-reporting to interviewers by lower-class persons, or of differential definitions of 'violence' leading higher-class respondents to report more (or relatively more) trivial incidents.[28] Bearing in mind the inter-area differences in our sample in patterns of reported violent offences, discussed above,[29] and the social-class composition of our three survey areas, we might expect—on this hypothesis of response bias—differences in the proportions of incidents involving attempted, threatened or otherwise very minor violence in different social classes in our sample: and this is in fact the case. Of the 33 incidents involving assaults reported by respondents in social classes I and II, under a quarter involved actual violence (in the sense of kicks, blows, etc.), with the remainder being mere threats or attempts; among respondents in social classes IV and V, the proportion of similar incidents involving actual violence is over four-tenths.

We have already argued that this difference may in part be a real one, reflecting different characteristic strategies for dealing with interactions involving potential violence.[30] It will also be recalled that there was little suggestion in the data relating to our MV sample that under-reporting and inaccurate reporting were more common among lower-class respondents.[31] However, the possibility of response bias here should not be lightly dismissed. In the current National Crime Panel studies in the United States, for example, the majority of assaults reported by white respondents, and those of higher family income, have been simple assaults or attempts; the majority reported by blacks and lower-income respondents, on the other hand, have been aggravated assaults (or completed crimes, as distinct from merely attempted ones).[32] Comparison of the *absolute* rates of aggravated and completed assaults for these different groups strongly suggests that the observed differences in patterns of violent victimization in the different racial and income groups are largely the product of response bias, rather than being a reflection of the groups' actual experiences. This finding—if confirmed by further research—would itself be of considerable theoretical importance: too little is now known about different social groups' definitions of various forms of criminal behaviour.[33] It would, however, considerably complicate the *measurement* of those forms of criminal behaviour by means of victim surveys.

3. The Distribution of Reported Victimization

So far, we have tended to consider reported victimization on an all-or-nothing basis, and thus, to classify persons simply as victims (if they reported any incident in the preceding year) or non-victims. But in any given time period, some persons will not be victims at all; some will be victims of one crime only; some will be victims of more than one crime. Data relating to our R sample's experience on this point are presented in Table IV.6; it will be seen that in all three of our sample areas a minority of respondents reported that they had been victims on more than one occasion during the preceding year.

It is conceivable, of course, that this should happen purely by chance; and the first step in investigating the phenomenon of 'multiple victimization' revealed by Table IV.6 is to see whether or not it occurs in our sample more frequently than would be expected if victimization were the result of a purely random process. Suppose that we have a sample of n persons who between them have a total of v incidents of victimization in a single time period (such as a year); thus, the average number of incidents for the sample as a whole is $v/n = \lambda$ incidents per year. Suppose further that the probability of victimization

Table IV.6. Distribution of victimization incidents by sample area (based on responses to screening questions)

| Number of incidents: | Area | | | | | | | |
| | Brixton | | Hackney | | Kensington | | All areas | |
	No.	Percentage	No.	Percentage	No.	Percentage	No.	Percentage
None	101	55·5	104	58·1	93	50·5	298	54·7
1	40	22·0	40	22·3	40	21·7	120	22·0
2	13	7·1	11	6·1	32	17·4	56	10·3
3	14	7·7	18	10·1	8	4·3	40	7·3
4	6	3·3	2	1·1	3	1·6	11	2·0
5	2	1·1	3	1·7	1	0·5	6	1·1
6 or more	6	3·3	1	0·6	7	3·8	14	2·6
Total	182	100·0	179	100·0	184	100·0	545	100·0
Total no. of incidents:	208	—	151	—	223	—	582	—

is the same for all members of the sample (and thus, identical to the sample mean λ); and that events of victimization are independent in the sense that the occurrence of one event does not alter the probability of a further occurrence, for that sample member or any other. Incidents of victimization thus occur randomly, with a given mean rate of occurrence for the sample as a whole. In that case the probability that an individual experiences exactly k incidents ($k = 0, 1, 2\ldots$) during the time period is given by the Poisson distribution

$$p(k, \lambda) = e^{-\lambda} \frac{\lambda^k}{k!} \qquad (1)$$

Evidently it follows from this equation that the probability of *not* becoming a victim in that time period (i.e. the probability of exactly zero events) is given simply by

$$p(0, \lambda) = e^{-\lambda} \qquad (1.1)$$

There are numerous physical and biological processes which conform to the simple model given by equation (1): the behaviour of chromosomes in organic cells, the disintegration of radioactive substances, the dialling of wrong numbers, the arrival of calls at a telephone switchboard—these and many other phenomena involving essentially random processes occurring in nature have been found to conform to the Poisson distribution.[1] As Coleman[2] has pointed out, however, the importance of the Poisson process in relation to social phenomena does not lie in its empirical fit to social data, but in the assumptions on which the distribution is based and the fact that these may be reasonable assumptions about the processes underlying the phenomena. In fact, there are probably more social phenomena which do *not* conform to

Table IV.7. Observed frequencies of victimization, compared with expected numbers based on a Poisson distribution

Area and Type of Crime:		Numbers of incidents 0	1	2	3	4	5+	χ^2	p
Brixton: Violence	(Obs.)	158	18	3	1	0	2		
	(Exp.)	144	33	4	—	—	—	9·14	< 0·01
Property	(Obs.)	108	40	14	11	5	3		
	(Exp.)	81	65	26	7	1	—	50·97	< 0·001
Hackney: Violence	(Obs.)	158	17	2	2	0	0		
	(Exp.)	154	24	2	—	—	—	4·58	0·02
Property	(Obs.)	116	33	13	13	1	3		
	(Exp.)	90	62	21	5	1	—	45·38	< 0·001
Kensington: Violence	(Obs.)	159	19	5	0	0	1		
	(Exp.)	150	30	3	—	—	—	6·97	< 0·01
Property	(Obs.)	103	44	20	7	3	6		
	(Exp.)	72	67	31	10	2	—	41·18	< 0·001

the Poisson distribution than there are which do. In these cases, however, we are at least able to reject a rational hypothesis which *might* have accounted for our observations; and the ways in which the data deviate from expectation based on the Poisson formula may suggest alternative hypotheses which do account for what we have observed.

Table IV.7 gives the observed numbers of respondents in our three survey areas who reported different numbers of victimization incidents involving violence (of all kinds) and property offences in each area, and also gives the expected numbers calculated by means of the Poisson distribution. The values of χ^2 and the resulting levels of significance for each comparison are also shown.[3] It will be seen that in each case, the differences between observed and expected values are statistically highly significant; the hypothesis represented by the Poisson formula can clearly be rejected for both types of offence in all three survey areas. We found the same results in both of our pilot surveys in Peterborough: and very similar findings have been produced by several other surveys of criminal victimization. In Aromaa's study of violent crime in Finland,[4] and Wolf's similar survey in Denmark,[5] the distribution of violent incidents differed significantly from what would be expected from a Poisson process; the same is true for the distribution of Part I and Part II offences, and personal and property crimes, reported by respondents in Reynold's surveys in Minnesota.[6] A similar pattern was also found in the Maricopa county survey, and in the U.S. national survey conducted by NORC.[7] In all of these studies, the nature of the deviation from expectation was similar, and resembled that shown by Table IV.7 for our Register sample: that is, there were more respondents reporting *no* incidents of victimization, and correspondingly more reporting more than one incident, than the Poisson distribution predicts.

It turns out, then, that the distribution of incidents of criminal victimization resembles that of industrial injuries, automobile accidents, convictions for crimes of violence, and many other social phenomena for which the assumptions underlying the Poisson distribution have been shown to be invalid.[8] Clearly there may be a number of different possible explanations, in any of these cases, for the greater-than-expected numbers of cases in which several incidents have occurred. Two of these, however, have received considerable attention from statisticians concerned with studying biological and social data; both involve simple modifications of the basic assumptions of the Poisson process, in order to generate expected distributions which differ from the Poisson in the same ways as our data.

The first of these models involves the assumption that the happening of an event alters the probability of its subsequently happening again, thus producing something akin to a 'contagion' effect. In the present case, for example, the fact that a person had been the victim of one crime would increase the probability of his becoming the victim of a second; a second victimization would increase the probability of a third, etc.[9] Intuitively, this does not seem particularly likely; though it might conceivably be that, for example, a man who was assaulted once would begin carrying a weapon, take lessons in self-defence and the like, become more paranoid or more belligerent and thus increase the probability of being assaulted a second time. Or again, a burglar who visits a house once may discover that it contains many things worth stealing and has no burglar alarm; he may decide to burgle it again, or may tell other burglars about it, either of which would increase the probability of its being burgled a second time.[10] But the notion of this kind of 'contagion' effect does not seem very plausible in relation to most types of victimization, and in particular would seem ill-suited to explaining the excess victimization of persons who claim to have suffered from a large number of incidents involving different *types* of crime (for example, burglary, assault, and theft).

The second modification of the Poisson model, however, is one which does seem reasonable as a hypothesis in relation to victimization. It involves the assumption of *heterogeneity* rather than of contagion. On this assumption, the population consists of a number of sub-groups each of which is characterized by a different degree of 'proneness' to the phenomenon in question. Within each sub-group incidents are assumed to be distributed according to a Poisson process; and the attribute of 'proneness' is itself distributed in the population according to the Poisson or some similar formula. This heterogeneous Poisson model was first explored by Greenwood and Yule, in their investigation of the frequency of multiple accidents in a factory.[11] Greenwood and Yule reasoned that the distribution of 'proneness' in the population would be skewed rather than normal; they assumed a Pearson Type III distribution,

Table IV.8. Expected values for k incidents of burglary according to two theoretical distributions, and observed values (three survey areas combined)

Number of incidents	Simple Poisson	Expected values Heterogeneous Poisson	Observed
	$\lambda = 0 \cdot 1688$	$r = 0 \cdot 119, c = 0 \cdot 703$	
None	459·82	490·50	482
1	78·15	34·27	50
2	6·65	11·26	8
3	·38	4·67	1
4 or more	0	2·97	4

though they remarked that 'the choice of skew curves is arbitrary.'[12] On this assumption, the probability of k events is given by the successive terms of

$$P_k = \left(\frac{c}{c+1}\right)^r \left(1 + \frac{r}{c+1} + \frac{r\,(r+1)}{2!(c+1)^2} + \frac{r\,(r+1)\,(r+2)}{3!\,(c+1)^3} + \cdots\right)$$

The mean and variance of this distribution are $\mu = r/c$ and $\sigma^2 = r(c+1)/c^2$, and the values of r and c are accordingly easy to estimate from the sample mean and variance.[13] As an illustration of the application of this heterogeneous Poisson model to our data, expected values for burglaries calculated according to equation (2) are shown in Table IV.8, together with expected values for a simple Poisson process and the numbers actually observed. It will be seen that the fit of the heterogeneous model is by no means perfect,[14] but it is a great deal better than that of the simple Poisson process, which comes nowhere near to the pattern of burglary victimization actually observed.

Unfortunately, it is not possible, using our data, to carry out an empirical test of the contagious Poisson model. Though this model begins with wholly different assumptions from those of the Greenwood–Yule distribution based on heterogeneity, it has been shown by Feller[15] that the two distributions are in fact identical, and generate the same expected values. Over-time data would be needed in order to see whether or not 'contagion' (in the sense of an increasing probability of victimization) existed. As we have already noted however, this model seems an inappropriate one on theoretical grounds in the case of most types of criminal victimization.[16]

In the heterogeneous model discussed above, the distribution of the hypothesized attribute of 'proneness' to victimization was derived in an *a priori* fashion, according to a particular mathematical model (such as the negative binominal used by Greenwood and Yule). An alternative approach, however, has been suggested by Coleman:[17] this is to establish the distribution of 'proneness' empirically, by examining the variations in victimization rates displayed by different sub-groups within the sample. In other words, the sample can be divided into sub-groups on the basis of some attribute or combination of attributes, such that each sub-group has a different mean rate of victimization; the hypothesis would then be that the numbers of incidents occurring *within* each sub-group were distributed randomly in accordance with the simple Poisson model. By fitting separate distributions to each sub-group in this way, it should be possible to get some indication of the effects of different attributes or independent variables on extreme proneness to victimization.

We experimented at some length with this approach, trying various demographic and attitudinal variables both singly and in combination. Unfortunately, however, we did not succeed in isolating any attribute or combination of attributes which even came close to accounting for the greater-than-expected numbers of 'multiple victimization' cases found in the sample.[18] In order to do this, at least two things are necessary. The first is that the sub-groups defined by the attribute (for example, males versus females, or different social classes) should have mean rates of victimization which are significantly different from each other, and thus from the sample as a whole; the second is that the mean and variance for each sub-group should be approximately equal (otherwise the distribution of incidents within that sub-group cannot be represented by the simple Poisson process.) Quite a few attributes (not all of them theoretically meaningful ones) fulfilled the first of these conditions; but none managed to fulfil both the first and the second. Inevitably there was at least one sub-group for which it was clear that the number of 'multiple victims' was much greater than would be expected according to the simple Poisson model;[19] moreover, these sub-groups tended to be ones for which no straightforward theoretical explanation was apparent. As an illustration, the means and variances for offences of violence among different age-groups are set out in Table IV.9. It will be seen that there are substantial differences between the means of the nine groups in the table, with respondents in their late twenties reporting over eight times as many incidents, on average, as those ages 46 and over. Thus, even allowing for the substantial standard error of these means, there is evidently heterogeneity in the sample according to age.[20] The data suggest that in the

Table IV.9. Mean rates and variances, of victimization for violent offences, for different age-groups

Age group	Mean	Variance	N
Under 21	0·231	0·345	26
21–25	0·304	0·361	56
26–30	0·604	2·590	53
31–35	0·349	1·566	43
36–40	0·200	0·204	50
41–45	0·155	0·204	58
46–50	0·077	0·073	39
51–55	0·071	0·067	84
61 and over	0·059	0·115	136
Total sample	0·195	0·532	545

age groups between 36 and 60, which have lower rates of victimization, the number of 'multiple victims' may be no more than would be expected purely by chance: and a comparison of the observed distributions for these age-groups with expected values according to the Poisson model confirms that this is in fact the case. But a comparison of the means and variances for the other age-groups shows that for each of them the simple Poisson model clearly would not fit; in particular, among the groups with the highest apparent 'proneness' (those aged from 26 to 35) there is still considerable within-group heterogeniety.

Further analysis shows that in the 26–30 and 31–35 age-groups it is the female respondents who account for almost all of the excessive variance in reported incidents of violence. The figures are as follows:

	Mean	Variance	N
Age 26–30:			
Male	0·500	0·660	26
Female	0·700	4·524	27
Age 31–35:			
Male	0·278	0·212	18
Female	0·400	2·583	25

It appears, moreover, that this is due almost entirely to the extremely high numbers of incidents (in one case, 18) reported by a few West Indian female respondents; if these cases are excluded from the analysis on the ground that they are atypical,[21] the amount of multiple victimization observed in the sample in different categories of age, sex and race is not much greater than would be expected purely by chance. Owing to the small numbers of cases and incidents involved, and the consequent unreliability of the sample means as estimators of Poisson transition rates, the results of this analysis must obviously be treated with extreme caution. Nonetheless, this approach can be of considerable heuristic value, since it may make it possible to identify particular sub-groups defined by attributes associated with relatively high rates of multiple victimization; there may well be causal processes affecting these sub-groups which do not apply to the rest of the sample, which may well be obscured by an overall comparison of victims and non-victims, in the sample as a whole.

In this section we have considered only a few of the possible simple models which might be used to explain the observed distributions of reported incidents of victimization in our sample. There is a need for substantive theory—or at least for some reasonable hypotheses—to justify such models, if their application to cross-sectional data is not to degenerate into mere simple-minded curve-fitting; and we shall consider some such hypotheses in the next section. A few further possibilities, however, may be briefly mentioned at this point. First, it is plainly conceivable that there is a proportion of the population for whom—because they take special precautions against crime, or for some other reason—the probability of becoming a victim is very near to zero; and that the incidents which do occur are distributed among the remainder of the population according to a simple Poisson model (or a heterogeneous one). If we designate this 'immune' group by n_1, and the remainder of the sample by n_2, so that $n_1 + n_2 = N$, and writing f_0 for the observed number of cases with no incidents of victimization, and p_0 for the (simple) Poisson probability of no events in the n_2 sample members who are *not* 'immune', then

$$f_0 = n_1 + n_2 p_0 = n_1 + (N - n_1)p_0 \tag{3.1}$$

$$p_0 = \frac{f_0 - n_1}{N - n_1} \tag{3.11}$$

But $p_0 = e^{-\lambda}$ for the simple Poisson process, where λ is the transition rate for the n_2 'non-immune' cases. Thus,

$$e^{-\lambda} = \frac{f_0 - n_1}{N - n_1} \tag{3.12}$$

$$\lambda = \ln \frac{f_0 - n_1}{N - n_1} \tag{3.13}$$

Since there are two unknowns here—the size of the 'immune' group n_1 and the transition rate λ for the 'non-immune' group n_2—this model cannot be fitted without some further assumptions about one or other of the two parameters. It turns out, however, that in order to achieve even an approximately good fit to our data the hypothesized 'immune' group must be assumed to account for about two-thirds of the sample; this seems implausibly large, bearing in mind that only about a fifth of the sample reported that they had never been victims of an offence of any kind at any time in their lives.[22]

A second, and possible more realistic, assumption would be that the population is composed of two sub-groups, the first of which is subject to either a simple or a heterogeneous Poisson process, and the second of which is subject to a 'negative contagious' Poisson process. That is, in the second group the occurrence of one event would reduce the probability of a second occurring, the occurrence of a second would reduce still further the probability of a third, and so on.[23] This is what we would expect to happen if some of those who had been victims were led to take special precautions, or changed their way of life, as a result; e.g., if they installed (and remembered to use) stronger locks after a burglary, or if they ceased to go out at night alone after having been robbed or assaulted in the street.[24] A complication involved in the application of this model is that a precaution-taking effect induced by some forms of victimization presumably tends to 'wear off' in time; as the event recedes in time, people once again forget to lock their doors, or resume going out alone at night. Unfortunately with cross-sectional data it is not possible to investigate this possibility; over-time data would be needed, to see if such a 'negative contagion' existed and were related to precaution taking.[25]

Before leaving this subject, we must mention one further possible explanation

for the greater-than-expected numbers of cases of 'multiple victimization':
namely, response bias in the reporting of more than one incident. As we have
already seen, many of the incidents reported by our R sample were of a relatively
trivial kind; this is also true of many things mentioned by those who said they
had been victims on several occasions. Now, it may be that these respondents'
experience was really not all that unusual, but that they remembered, and reported to our interviewers, many such things which other respondents simply forgot
or neglected to mention. Two things must be said about this possibility,
however. The first is that it would not, even if true, much improve the fit between
expected values on the hypothesis of a Poisson process, and observed values,
in our sample. The precise effect of this kind of bias depends to some extent
on how it is supposed to be distributed among the sample members: in particular, whether those who are supposed not to have mentioned many incidents
which in fact occurred to them are mostly assumed to be found among those
who reported at least one incident, or among those who reported none at all.
But in either case, though the effect of such a bias would be to reduce artificially
the sample mean (and thus the estimated transition rate governing the Poisson
process), it would not materially affect the goodness of fit between observed
and expected distributions. Put the other way around, if we suppose that the
true incidence of multiple victimization is greater than our data suggest (because
of some non-reporting of large numbers of incidents), this would mean that the
expected numbers of multiple victims would be increased; but the *observed*
numbers would also increase, and the Poisson distribution would still not fit.[26]

The second point is that those persons in our sample who reported more than
one incident showed no tendency to report increasingly trivial incidents, at least
as measured by their own evaluation on a 1-to-11 point scale. This is not conclusive, of course, since it may very well be that most of the incidents reported
by our multiple victims were *in fact* more trivial, on average, than those of
persons reporting only one;[27] those who suffered several incidents during the
preceding year may on the account have regarded them as less serious, even
though by an objective standard they were not.[28] But an examination of the
substance of reported incidents on which we have data does not suggest that
this is so; nor, as just mentioned, does a comparison of the seriousness scores
given by respondents to the first, second, third, etc. incidents reported. The data
are as follows:

Table IV.10. Mean seriousness scores on a scale of 1 to 11,
given to (chronologically) first and subsequent incidents reported
(based on crime incident forms)

Incident:	Mean score	N
First	4·39	232
Second	4·22	116
Third	4·94	55
Fourth	4·71	17
Fifth and higher	5·33	8

We conclude, then, that while response bias in the form of under-reporting of large numbers of 'series' incidents may have distorted our findings to some extent, it is unlikely to have materially affected the disproportionate numbers of multiple victims observed in the sample, compared with expectation based on the hypothesis of a Poisson distribution.[29]

4. Explaining the Distribution of Victimization

The excess amount of 'multiple victimization' disclosed by our survey and others has a number of important implications. From a purely statistical point of view, it means that the victimization *rate* (e.g. the number of victimizations per 1,000 persons or households) may be very misleading as an indicator of the *risk* of victimization or as a summary descriptor of a group's victimization experience. By definition, such a rate is an average, for a group defined by a particular attribute or attributes; but since the numerator used to calculate this rate includes all of the incidents befalling 'multiple victims', the rate will be much too high for most of the group, and much too low for the unfortunate minority.[1] Indeed, any statistics measuring the *incidence* of victimization (such as the victimization rate) may be fundamentally misleading in a more general way. It may be that a more appropriate measure would be one of *prevalence* (e. g. the percentages of the population victimized on one, two, etc. occasions in a given time period). A wife regularly beaten by her husband, a child robbed of his lunch money every day on the way to school, may more appropriately be conceived of as suffering from a chronic condition, rather than as victims of a number of discrete incidents. This may be especially important in the case of some victims of so-called 'series' offences, i.e. those cases in which the respondent states that several crimes were committed against him in a certain time period, but in which he cannot remember precise details of each of the incidents. As we shall see in Chapter VI,[2] such cases raise formidable problems for comparisons of survey estimates of victimization rates and police statistics.

From an explanatory point of view, the phenomenon of 'multiple victimization' raises equally important issues. In the preceding section of this chapter, we explored a number of very simple models which might have been consistent with the observed excess, in our sample, of 'multiple victimization.' The failure of these models to fit our data is not perhaps surprising. Indeed, it might be argued that it would be surprising if they did fit: if, for example, some simple combination of attributes (such as age, sex and expressed attitudes) could be used to partition our sample into sub-groups with different mean rates of victimization and a simple Poisson distribution of incidents within sub-groups. Little is known from any previous research about the complex determinants of 'multiple victimization.' But even at a commonsense level, there are some situations in which it seems very likely: the wife who continues to live with a drunkard who beats her, or the shopkeeper who regularly takes cheques from customers without asking for identification, would be examples. Our data did not permit us to identify such cases in our sample, with any degree of certainty;[3] had we been able to do so, it is conceivable that the remaining cases of 'multiple victimization' would have been no more numerous than the simple Poisson distribution predicts.[4]

Let us, therefore, raise a fundamental question: *why* do some people become victims of crime, while others do not? More generally, what factors determine the distribution of crimes in physical and social space, and so influence the likelihood of a particular person's being assaulted or robbed, or having his house burgled?

For many years, the first of these questions was virtually neglected by criminologists; if they considered it at all, they generally assumed that it should be answered wholly by reference to the attributes of offenders rather than of the victims themselves. In fact, the question was usually formulated as 'Why do crimes take place?'—and put this way, the question encourages concentration on the offender and consequent neglect of the role of the victim. Thus, it was generally assumed, for example, that crimes of violence came about because certain persons were prone to use violence, and found themselves in situations in which the use of violent behaviour was facilitated or encouraged; in such situations they committed crimes against persons who—so far as their role in the explanation of crimes was concerned—might just have happened to be standing there at the time. The criminal was thus conceived of as the active element in the situation, and the victim as a wholly passive one.

The second question—which concerns the epidemiology of crime—has received much more attention, from the earliest studies of the French demographers in the last century to the 'ecological' studies of this one. Even here, however, attention has generally been focused on offenders or offences, rather than on victims; it seems to have been generally assumed that the attributes and behaviour of victims could in some sense be 'averaged out' in the course of explaining the observed distribution of crimes and criminals. In practice, this amounted to assuming that the probability of becoming a victim of crime is the same for all members of the population, and that criminals choose their victims at random.

As we have been in the preceding two sections, this assumption cannot be sustained. Plainly there is *some* element of chance or randomness in the selection of victims, in the sense that offenders do not always select as targets any particular members of the population, or of sub-sets of the population characterized by certain attributes. But the selection of victims is almost never a *purely* random process; and the risk of becoming a victim varies considerably for different types of crime.[5] Broadly speaking there are three different ways in which this may come about.

First, the victim may act in such a way as to precipitate—or at least strongly encourage—the behaviour of the offender. It was this to which von Hentig was referring when he wrote that there may be cases in which 'the two distinct categories (of perpetrator and victim) merge. There are cases in which they are reversed, and in the long chain of causative forces the victim assumes the role of a determinant.'[6] Thus, homicide and other crimes of violence, for example, are often the outcome of quarrels or arguments in which the offender reacts to provocation in the form of insults or attack by the victim; it is characteristic of such crimes, of course, that they tend to take place between persons who are known or related to one another, or who have associated together for some time prior to the crime.[7]

Secondly, even if the victim does not take anything which could be called an active part in the crime, he may nonetheless offer a specially great opportunity or inducement to its commission. He may deliberately, negligently or unconsciously place himself at special risk of crime. Thus, persons who leave property in unlocked cars thereby increase the probability that it will be stolen; shopkeepers who regularly carry their takings down dark streets to the bank may find themselves the victims of street robberies; persons who cash cheques without asking for adequate information may find themselves accepting forged or stolen cheques. Here, as with victim-precipitation, the probability of victimization is greater for some people than for others; but it is important to distinguish between the two cases, since with victim-precipitation it is the victim's behaviour in interaction with the offender which matters, whereas the creation of special risks is (if anything) associated with the attributes or usual behaviour of the victim rather than with some features of a bilateral transaction with the offender.

Thirdly, it may be that certain persons—by virtue of their appearance or behaviour, or their place in a social system—are more likely than others to be victims of criminal behaviour, even though they themselves do not act in any way such as to bring this about. This point is perhaps more clearly put negatively: there are some persons who lack those attributes which provide the opportunities which are (logically) necessary conditions for crime. Thus, in order to be a victim of rape, it is necessary to be a woman; in order to have one's car stolen it is necessary to own a car; in order to be a victim of vandalism one must possess some property which can be damaged. In the last resort, what matters may simply be propinquity: a man who never goes out of his house will never get robbed in the street.

Though these three categories may be analytically distinct, the borderlines between them are naturally not clearcut ones. Moreover, while these three types of 'proneness' relate to *persons*, it may in some cases be more appropriate to regard them (or at least the last two) as inhering in particular physical areas or locales to which persons go, or in particular social situations in which they find themselves. The relative importance of each category no doubt differs, for different types of crime; in particular, victim-precipitation (as we have defined it) is probably much less important in relation to property offences (excluding robbery) than to offences against the person.

There are limits to the contribution which victims' accounts, obtained in a survey like ours, can make to the understanding of these problems. Earlier in this chapter we discussed some findings from our own survey, and speculated that our respondents may have tended to use different strategies in coping with situations involving potential violence. But we stressed that our respondents' accounts of the incidents in question were of doubtful validity, and were in any case incomplete; in our opinion such retrospective and one-sided accounts of violent interaction must always be of limited value, at least unless very special interviewing techniques are used. We have, however, some other data which bear on the question of the question of our victims' involvement in crimes committed against them, which we summarize here.

(a) Self-reported Crime and Victimization. To what extent are the victims of crimes themselves offenders? It seems reasonable to suppose that a willingness to use illegal violence would be likely to result in a greater involvement in situations where violence is used against one; those who get into fights sometimes lose.[8] Again, it is perhaps conceivable that those who engage in theft are less likely to protect their own property from theft; alternatively, if they associate with other thieves, and if there is no honour among them, then their likelihood of being victims of theft may be increased.

In order to explore these possibilities, and to study the possible relations between our respondents' involvement in criminal behaviour and their other attitudes (e.g. to the police), we included at the end of our questionnaire a section in which respondents were asked to state whether they had committed any of a series of illegal acts. So far as we are aware, this is the first time that such a study has been carried out on a random sample of the adult population. In order to maintain some degree of confidentiality, and to try to induce respondents to answer truthfully, they were not asked for details concerning any illegal acts they admitted having committed; nor where they asked to say whether they had ever committed any particular one of the set of illegal acts which we asked about. Instead, they were given three cards, each of which contained brief descriptions of six illegal acts; they were then asked to say how many of the acts on each card they had committed once, and how many they had committed more than once. The descriptions on the three cards were as follows:[9]

First Card: Property Offences
I have stolen money or property from another person
I have stolen from work
I have had something that I knew was stolen
I have taken something from a shop without paying for it
I have taken another person's car or motorbike without their permission
I have got into someone's house without their permission and stolen
something

Second Card: Motoring and 'Public Order' Offences
I have driven a car over the speed limit
I have driven a car without a licence
I have driven a car after having had too much to drink

I have deliberately damaged some other person's property
I have deliberately damaged public property
I have been drunk and disorderly

Third Card: Offences against the Person
I have hit another person with my fist during a quarrel or argument
I have hit another person with a weapon during a quarrel or argument
I have taken something from another person by using violence
I have threatened another person with violence
I have been in a fight with more than one other person
I have tried to kill another person

This technique is, of course, far from ideal; in retrospect, we feel we might have been a bit more adventurous, and might have asked about each of these (or other) items separately, since our interviewers met with very few refusals to answer during this part of the questionnaire.[10] Obviously, the validity of the responses which we obtained is also open to question; without further evidence, we cannot assume that our data reflect the respondents' actual involvement in crime. In analysing the data, we calculated an index score for each respondent on each set of items (property, public order and violence), by adding three times the number of things he admitted doing 'more than once' to the number of things he admitted doing only once.[11] These three indexes were in turn added together to produce an overall self-reported crime index. The maximum range of the individual indexes is thus from zero to eighteen; for the overall index it is from zero to 54. The highest score reported in our sample was 18 for a single set of items, and 42 for the overall index. Since these indexes, however much error they may contain, have some claim to be interval-level measures of our sample's self-reported criminality, we have used the raw scores for most of our analysis.[12] For some purposes, however, the scores were grouped into five broad categories; for convenience, it is in this form that the data will mostly be presented here.

Overall, 63 per cent of the sample said that they had committed one or more of the 18 offences they were asked about. A significantly higher proportion of Kensington respondents—76 per cent—reported committing one or more illegal acts; the proportions in Brixton and Hackney were 56 per cent and 57 per cent, respectively. This is largely influenced, however, by responses to the 'public order' and motoring card; for the violent offences the proportion reporting one or more was highest in Brixton, though the differences for these offences and the property crimes were not statistically significant. With the exception of the (possibly atypical) respondents under 21, there are significant, and generally consistent, negative associations between self-reporting and age, for all three sets of offences;[13] overall, 86 per cent of those in their twenties reported having committed one or more offences, compared with only a third of those aged over 60. Whites were somewhat more likely to report having committed all three types of offences, though the differences were not

Table IV.11. Self-reporting of violent offences and reported incidents of violent victimization[a]

Self-reported violent crimes		Reported incidents as victim of violence			
		None	1	2 or more	Total
None	No.	354	31	3	388
	Percentage	91·2	8·0	0·8	100·0
1 or 2	No.	46	4	7	57
	Percentage	80·7	7·0	12·3	100·0
3 or 4	No.	48	8	2	58
	Percentage	82·8	13·8	3·4	100·0
5 to 8	No.	11	8	0	19
	Percentage	57·9	42·1	—	100·0
9 or more	No.	15	2	4	21
	Percentage	71·4	9·5	19·1	100·0
Total	No.	474	53	16	543
	Percentage	87·3	9·8	2·9	100·0

$$\chi^2 = 72·2, p < 0·001, \gamma = 0·43$$

[a]Excludes two cases for which self-report data not available.

statistically significant; as would be expected, males were significantly more likely to say they had committed offences of all kinds, though somewhat surprisingly the difference between males and females is rather less marked for the violent offences than for the others. There were no significant differences in self-reporting—nor any particular trends—in relation to social class on the Registrar-general's scale, for either property or violent offences; the upper-class respondents reported significantly more 'public order' offences, but this is evidently related to the motoring offences on that list, and to the pattern of car ownership.

When these self-report data are examined in relation to reported victimization, only one significant association clearly emerges: this is between self-reporting of violent crime, and reporting of violent victimization. The association holds for males and for females, and for both white and black respondents (being much stronger for the latter than for the sample as a whole): controlling for age reduces it only slightly.[14] The data are summarized in Table IV.11.

The hypothesis of an association between committing violent acts, and being a victim of violence, is thus supported by our data.[15] Even allowing for their questionable validity and obvious imprecision, our self-report data also help to explain the observed differences in reported violent victimization in relation to age and sex. Thus, males, and younger respondents, were more likely to report that they had committed one of the violent acts which we asked about; and they are also more likely to report being victims of violent crime. But the self-report data do not completely account for the age and sex differences: that is, the observed relationships between those attributes and violent victimization are only slightly reduced, if self-reported offences are controlled for. Moreover, self-reported violent crime does not explain the racial difference in violent victimization observed in our sample, since our black respondents were slightly *less* likely to report having committed one or more of the six violent acts than were whites, whereas they had a higher rate of violent victimization. It is possible, however, that this result may be due to sampling or response bias,[16] and we must repeat that not too close an analogy should be drawn in social or cultural terms between the West Indian respondents in our sample and blacks in the United States. For example, the subcultural tradition of carrying knives or other weapons, often said to exist among young black males in the United States, is apparently much less marked among West Indians in London.[17] In any case, as we have seen, even among our black respondents there was a strong association between self-reporting of violence and violent victimization.

(b) Interaction Patterns and Victimization. Our self-report data suggest, then, that the notion of victim-precipitation may have had some application in relation to the offences of violence reported by our sample. But it is plain that victim-precipitation cannot account for more than a minority of those offences; and it is of no importance whatever in relation to the (much more numerous) reported offences against property. It remains to consider, then, the other ways in which victims may in part determine the distribution of crime, through the creation of special risks and more generally through the differential distribution of opportunities for crime. A number of rather miscellaneous findings in our survey bear on these points, though we must admit that our data do not go as far as we would like toward an adequate explanation.

To consider first the provision of special risk: in every developed society there are certain jobs (more precisely, certain occupational roles) in which—because of the nature of the work involved—the risks of criminal victimization are abnormally great. It seems clear, for example, that policemen, security guards, and night-club 'bouncers' are more likely to be physically attacked in the course of their work than are ministers of religion, academics or lighthouse keepers. In coding the incidents reported by our R sample, we were careful to exclude those in which the respondent's employer, rather than the respondent himself, was the victim: this was the case in a few thefts and robberies reported by salespeople in shops, for example. But there were a number of other cases, among the incidents for which we have data, in which the offence was committed against the respondent himself, but during the course of his employment: this was true of about 25 per cent of the offences of violence, and 11 per cent of the offences against property.[18] The proportion of respondents involved in these 'job-connected' crimes was less than this, since several respondents mentioned a number of incidents of this kind. Examples include a hotel chef who had several fights with waiters in the hotel, and a nurse who on several occasions had been attacked by patients brought into the hospital where she worked.[19] Some element of special risk-creation was also evident in the property offences reported by our respondents: in 23 per cent of the burglaries and thefts from dwelling houses for which we have data, it was stated that the house or flat had been left unlocked.[20] Parenthetically, it may be noted that there was only a moderate ($\gamma = 0\cdot21$) relationship between the number of rooms in the respondent's house or flat, and reporting of burglary or other property offences. The position is complicated, however, by the different types of accommodation (private houses, council houses, flats or lodgings) in the three survey areas; a more accurate specification of the types of property at risk in each area might well show clearer differences in the risks of crime associated with each.

In general, it may be hypothesized that the distribution of opportunities for being a victim of a crime of violence (and, to a lesser extent, of theft) is very largely a function of the amount and intensity of contact between potential victims and potential offenders; and that this in turn is a function of the patterns of social interaction in which each group engages. Thus, in common with many other researchers, we found that a substantial fraction of the assaults reported by our respondents—47 per cent—involved family members or acquaintances rather than strangers;[21] if we were to standardize these three rates by the average rates of contact with family members, acquaintances and strangers which our respondents had, we would certainly find that the chance of being assaulted by a family member or an acquaintance was many times greater than the chance of being assaulted by a stranger.[22]

We have some evidence of a fairly general kind on this point. As we have already noted, we asked our respondents how often, on average, they went out in the evenings; there was a significant association between the answers to this question, and the reporting of incidents involving violence and theft (there was a weaker association in the case of burglary). The data for offences of violence are presented in Table IV.12. Further analysis shows that this very largely explains the low rates of victimization among the older members of our sample; those over 60 reported going out much less frequently on average, and in particular a much larger proportion of them said they never went out in the evenings at all.[23]

Of course, the risk of victimization depends not only on the frequency with which people interact, but on the type of interaction and its location: some places are safer than others. We hypothesized that there would be differences in victimization between those who went out mainly to public places (such as cinemas, or pubs and clubs in the West End of London), and those who went out mainly to visit friends or family members in their own homes, with those who went out to 'semi-public' places (e.g. to work, or to their own neighbourhood local pub) falling in between. Accordingly, after asking about nights out, interviewers asked 'For what sort of things?' and coded responses into the categories just mentioned. In the event, this hypothesis was not upheld; there are no systematic differences in the reporting of incidents involving violence or theft according to type of usual activity. Almost certainly, however,

Table IV.12. Average number of nights a week out, and reporting of incidents involving violent victimization[a]

Average no. of nights out per week:		Reported incidents			
		None	1	2 or more	Total
Every night	No.	21	3	3	27
	Percentage	77·8	11·1	11·1	100·0
5–6	No.	37	6	4	47
	Percentage	78·7	12·8	8·5	100·0
3–4	No.	97	14	2	113
	Percentage	85·8	12·4	1·8	100·0
1–2	No.	174	23	4	201
	Percentage	86·6	11·4	2·0	100·0
Less than 1	No.	78	7	1	86
	Percentage	90·7	8·1	1·2	100·0
Never	No.	59	1	1	61
	Percentage	96.7	1·6	1·6	100·0
Total	No.	466	54	15	535
	Percentage	87·1	10·1	2·9	100·0

$$\chi^2 = 21·54, p < 0·02, \gamma = +0·29$$

[a]Excludes ten cases for which data on going out not available.

this is a consequence of the crudeness of the measures we used; a better classification of activities and locales might well have revealed such differences in risk.[24]

The analysis of differential opportunities for victimization has important implications in view of the widely-held stereotype of 'the victim' of crime (particularly violent crime) as being typically a respectable elderly person— usually female—who is attacked by a younger person (usually a male) and who, far from provoking the crime, is completely passive and defenceless against it. We do not deny that such cases occasionally take place. But it is clear from our own data, and that of other surveys, that the victims of crime—in particular of offences against the person—are very much more likely to be young persons; males; and persons who lead reasonably active social lives.[25] Further, they are much more likely to be attacked by a friend, acquaintance or family member than by a stranger; and in many cases they will have provoked or specially induced the crime by their own actions.

There is also a need, for explanatory purposes, for much more survey data on interaction patterns in relation to victimization. At a descriptive level, such data are needed for an accurate standardization of crime rates in relation to opportunities for crime.[26] But they are also essential for an understanding of the epidemiology of crime, and thus, for an understanding of crime itself. Naturally, data on victims will not by themselves provide a complete explanation of epidemiological patterns, any more than will data on offenders; it is no doubt largely for this reason that we had very little success in our attempts to predict victimization using the data which we have collected.[27] But the analysis of differential opportunities and risks of victimization is a necessary first step in the analysis of the patterns which criminal behaviour tends to take. In one sense it may be sociologically trivial to point out that a man who does not have a car cannot be a victim of car theft, or that one who does not go out of his house cannot be robbed in the street. In another sense, however, it is not: since these 'opportunity' variables are not randomly distributed in the population, but are a consequence of the culture and social structure of the community. Moreover, the opportunity structure is not static, but instead may change markedly over time: a change in opportunities may thus lead to a change in the amount of crime committed.[28] Opportunity thus provides one of the necessary intervening variables in any cultural or structural explanation of crime.

Notes and References

1. Crime Incidents Reported by the Register Sample

1. Above, pp. 31–32.
2. The total number of incident forms actually completed was 489. Of these, 55—or 11·2 per cent—were judged by the two senior researchers (a teacher of criminal law and a barrister, respectively) not to involve crimes of any kind, and were accordingly excluded from the analysis. (In these cases the incident was also excluded from the responses to the screening questions.) Our criterion for excluding such cases was that the stated facts, if true, would not have amounted to any offence against the criminal law against the respondent, in the preceding year; we did not exclude cases merely because they would probably not have been regarded as crimes by the police. In this respect our procedure differed from that followed in the U.S. national survey conducted by NORC (see Philip H. Ennis, *Field Surveys II* at 88–93). See further below, pp. 144–145.
3. Though it must be remembered that these responses may in some part be a function of question order. Since respondents did not know what further screening questions they were to be asked, they may have mentioned (for example) a theft from the person when asked whether they had been attacked or assaulted, since this question came before the one about thefts from the person.
4. It must also be remembered that either or both of our classifications may differ from that which might be made by a police officer investigating the incident, who would often form a final judgment on the basis of other evidence; and that *none* of these classifications necessarily gives a correct description of what (if anything) actually happened.
5. The value of Kendall's τ is -0.2 for Brixton, and $+0.4$ for Hackney and Kensington; neither of these is significant.
6. I.e., in response to the open-ended question, 'Were you physically injured in any way?' Interviewers did not probe negative answers to this question, which may in any case have led some respondents not to report bruises or other minor injuries. It should be added that the respondent was the only person attacked or threatened in 82 per cent of the 108 incidents involving assault, robbery or theft from the person. In only one of the remaining 19 cases was it stated that one or more of the other persons involved had been injured at all.
7. In English criminal law there is not, strictly speaking, an offence of 'attempted assault'; broadly speaking, any 'putting in fear' constitutes an assault, and an attempt to inflict injury could be an attempted *battery*. However, for convenience we shall use the term

'attempted assault' to refer to those cases in which (according to our respondents) an attempt of some sort was made to inflict physical violence; we used it in our screening questions, and respondents had no difficulty in understanding it.

8. The statistics published by the Metropolitan Police do not permit a precise comparison with our survey data in this respect. But an earlier study of recorded indictable crimes of violence in the whole of the Metropolitan Police District found very much higher proportions of cases involving weapons, and resulting in some degree of physical injury to the victim: see F. H. McClintock, *Crimes of Violence* (London: Macmillan, 1963) 48–55. We do not know, of course, what proportion of the violent offences in our sample would have been regarded by the police as indictable ones.

9. Above, p. 54.

10. Corresponding statistics for the Metropolitan Police District are not available. Table IV.3 is based on the Criminal Statistics for 1971 (Cmnd. 5020, Appendix 1 (b), p. iii), since the statistics for 1972 are grouped in a different (and less informative) way as a result of the decision in that year that the police should no longer record thefts of a value of less than £5 as 'crimes known to the police.'

11. In a number of these cases, however, property which had been *in* the car or motorbike was not recovered; and in others, the vehicle itself sustained some damage. Unfortunately, we did not systematically record these extra offences, and so can give no indication of the proportion of all vehicle thefts in which other property loss or damage was sustained.

12. In another four per cent, the respondent stated that he intended to make a claim, but had not yet done so.

13. This table, of course, gives no indication of the *rates* of reported offences of different types; it merely shows relative frequencies, which need to be related to the populations at risk in the three sample areas. This is done in Chapter VI: see below, pp. 151–156.

14. See note 6 on p. 106.

15. It may be that this result is influenced to some extent by general differences between the three groups' general evaluations of violent crime: see Chapter VII, pp. 000–00. below. Even when allowance is made for this, however, it is clear that the Kensington cases were less serious than those reported in Brixton or Hackney, and were seen by the respondents themselves as being so. Note again that the term 'assault' is not used in it strict legal sense.

16. For some further evidence on this point see below, Chapter VII, pp. 181–190.

17. Our data do not suggest the existence of response bias owing to either the sex or the experience of the interviewers. It may well be, however, that some respondents were inclined to give misleadingly non-violent accounts of their own behaviour in the incidents which they reported to the interviewers, or were inclined to exaggerate their own belligerence.

18. Above, p. 37.

19. Those who denied ever having been victims did not differ significantly from the rest of the sample in terms of age, sex, race, or area of residence; each of which—as we shall see in the next section—discriminates to some extent between victims and non-victims in the most recent year. There was a barely significant tendency for them to be more common among lower-class respondents and the less educated; and a tendency—though not a significant one—for them not to go out at night even as often as once a week. They were also more likely to have been rated by our interviewers as having 'fair' or 'poor' understanding of the questionnaire. Some form of response bias does, therefore, seem likely.

2. Demographic Variables in Relation to Victimization

1. Philip H. Ennis, *Field Surveys II* at 23–30. Data on this point from the series of surveys currently being carried out by the U.S. Census Bureau (see above, pp. 2, 13) have not at present been published.

2. *Criminal Victimization in Maricopa County* (Berkeley, California: Institute for Local Self-government, June 1969, mimeo) 11–13.
3. Paul Davidson Reynolds *et al.*, *Victimization in a Metropolitan Region: Comparison of a Central City Area and a Suburban Community* (Minneapolis, Minnesota: Minnesota Center for Sociological Research, October, 1973, mimeo.) III-73–III-78. The comparison is somewhat complicated, since different reference periods were used in the central city and suburban questionnaires.
4. Preben Wolf and Ragnar Hauge, 'Criminal violence in three Scandinavian countries.' Unpublished draft (forthcoming in Vol. 5 of *Scandinavian Studies in Criminology*). We are grateful to Dr. Wolf for supplying this paper to us; it actually contains data on all four Nordic countries.
5. For England, see F. H. McClintock and N. H. Avison, *Crime in England and Wales* (London: Heinemann, 1968) 138; and for a discussion of American studies, see Judith A. Wilks, 'Ecological Correlates of Crime and Delinquency,' in The President's Commission Task Force Report on *Crime and its Assessment* (Washington, D.C.: U.S. Government Printing Office, 1967) 138.
6. If thefts from the person—most of which involved purse-snatching—are excluded from this comparison, the ratio of male to female victims of violence naturally becomes even greater.
7. See the following reports published by the U.S. Department of Justice, Law Enforcement Assistance Administration, National Criminal Justice Information and Statistics Service: *Criminal Victimization in the United States*, 1973 Advance Report at 14–15 (Tables 3 and 4); *Criminal Victimization in the Nation's Five Largest Cities*, at 91–100 (Tables 15a-16e); *Crime in Eight American Cities*, Table 3 for each city; *Criminal Victimization Surveys in Thirteen American Cities*, Table 3 for each city. See also *Crimes and Victims: A Report on the Dayton–San Jose Pilot Survey of Victimization* at 80–81. The 1966 NORC national survey is methodologically worthless on this point, since for some reason all victimization reported in that survey was assigned to the characteristics of the head of the household no matter who the victim was.
8. Paul Davidson Reynolds *et al.*, *Victimization in a Metropolitan Region: Comparison of a Central City Area and a Suburban Community*. III-52.
9. Preben Wolf and Ragnar Hauge, 'Criminal violence in three Scandinavian countries.' 8.
10. Above, pp. 31–32.
11. Paul Davidson Reynolds *et al.*, *Victimization in a Metropolitan Region: Comparison of a Central City Area and a Suburban Community*. III-52–III-60. Separate questionnaires were used for respondents aged under 15, for those aged 15–20 who were still living at home and for those aged 20 and over. The age-groups used in the analysis are 19 and under; 20–29; 30–49; and 50 and over.
12. Cf. the references cited in note 7 above; and note that the 1966 NORC survey cannot be relied upon here, for the reason given in that note.
13. Preben Wolf and Ragnar Hauge, 'Criminal violence in three Scandinavian countries.' 8.
14. In general, throughout this book we use the term 'black' to refer to the West Indians and Africans in our sample, and will exclude the small number of culturally quite different Oriental and Indian respondents from comparisons relating to race.
15. This conclusion is generally though not invariably supported by all of the National Crime Panel survey results published up to the time of writing: cf. the references cited in note 7 above.
16. Of the 83 offences of assault and robbery for which we have data on this point, 67 involved white victims; 48 of these (or 71·6 per cent) were said by the respondents to have involved white offenders. Similarly, of the 16 incidents reported by black respondents 11 (or 68·8 per cent) involved black offenders. These data must be treated with extreme caution, since in many cases the respondents said they did not *know* who the

offender was; moreover, there was some evidence that white respondents in Brixton and Hackney had stereotyped conceptions concerning the race of offenders in their areas. A similar suspicion also surrounds the N.C.P. data on this point, since the validity of victims' identifications of offenders is at present unknown.

17. This was so for both the Registrar-General's classifications and the Hall–Jones scale. For all types of incidents combined, the association nearly reaches significance ($p \simeq 0.08$, $\gamma = +0.13$ over the Registrar-General's classification).

18. Cf. the references cited in note 7 on p. 108 above.

19. Paul Davidson Reynolds *et al.*, *Victimization in a Metropolitan Region: Comparison of a Central City Area and a Suburban Community.* III-54–55, III-61. A Finnish survey on property victimization found higher rates in higher income groups: see Kauko Aroma and Seppa Leppa, *Omaisuuskikosten Yksitouhrien Tarkastelva* (A survey on individual victims of property crimes), Helsinki: Kriminologien Tutkimoslaitos, Sarja M (1973) 25 (Table 12d).

20. Institute for Local Self-government, *Criminal Victimization in Maricopa County.* 32–34; the authors suggest that the difference may be due to 'the less serious definition taken by lower income groups regarding personal conflict, and the greater tendency among lower-income groups to resort to physical and verbal means to settle personal disputes.

21. Preben Wolf and Ragnar Hauge, 'Criminal violence in three Scandinavian countries.' 8. In common with our own findings, however, all of these surveys except the Finnish ones show higher rates of the more serious forms of violence—involving at least light blows, as opposed to threatening, pushing or shoving—in lower-class groups. In the Finnish data, inter-class differences diminish when only the more serious offences are considered, but they do not disappear completely.

22. This is especially likely to be true in Kensington.

23. A well-known method of compensating for this problem, due to Politz and Simmons, involves stratifying respondents in accordance with the number of evenings (out of the preceding week) on which they say they were at home, and then re-weighting each stratum's responses by the reciprocal of the probability of their being contacted; for example, for those out every night except the night of the interview, responses would be weighted by 6. See A. Politz and W. Simmons, 'An attempt to get at the "not at homes" in a sample without callbacks. II,' (1949) 44 *Journal of the American Statistical Association* 9–31. This method entails that interviews be evenly spread through the fieldwork period, and that each potential respondent receives only one call; these conditions were not fulfilled in our survey, since interviewers were instructed to make up to five call-backs before treating the case as 'no contact,' and were thus more likely to contact eventually those who were out frequently. Applying the Politz-Simmons weighting method to our data suggests, however, that the proportion of the population in the three areas reporting some victimization could easily exceed 50 per cent, compared with the 45 per cent observed.

24. Albert D. Biderman, *Field Surveys I* at 57.

25. In our R sample, the proportion of respondents over 60 who said they had *never* been the victim of any offense was substantially higher than the proportion of respondents below that age (28 per cent, against 16 per cent). However, the older respondents would have been most at risk of victimization in earlier years, when crime rates may generally have been lower.

26. See pp. 104–105.

27. See above, Chapter III, p. 58. As our MV sample shows, victims of *recorded* violent crime tend to be younger than would be expected given the age distribution of the enumerated population.

28. E.g., Preben Wolf and Ragnar Hauge, 'Criminal violence in three Scandinavian countries'. 9.

29. Above, pp. 78–80.

30. Above, pp. 78–80. It may also be, as Dr. Kauko Aromaa has pointed out to us, that the difference is a real one in a different sense, at least for certain sorts of incidents: it may be, for example, that certain kinds of 'urban street violence' typically involve relatively well-to-do persons being disturbed by strangers of somewhat lower status, e.g., being asked for money or a cigarette; sometimes such situations may develop into something which is later seen by the person being 'panhandled' as an attempted or threatened assault.
31. Above, Chapter III, pp. 58–59.
32. Cf. the references cited in note 7 on p. 108 above.
33. We discuss this problem further in Chapter VII, pp. 190–193 below.

3 The Distribution of Reported Victimization

1. See, for example, W. Feller, *An Introduction to Probability Theory and its Applications* (New York: Wiley, 1968) 156–164.
2. James S. Coleman, *Introduction to Mathematical Sociology* (New York: The Free Press, 1964) 291.
3. Cells with small expected frequencies have been combined as necessary in order to carry out the χ^2 tests. An extra degree of freedom must be subtracted in each case, since an extra parameter has been estimated from the sample data; and a one-tailed test of significance is used since the alternative to the null hypothesis is directional, viz. it is that there will be more extreme cases of victimization than expected. Since the mean and variance of the Poisson distribution are identical, the alternative hypothesis is that the sample variance is significantly higher than its mean. In this case a more powerful test of significance than χ^2 is available, since in a sample of size N from a Poisson population, $(N-1) S^2/M$ is distributed as χ^2 with $N-1$ degrees of freedom. See E.S. Keeping, *Introduction to Statistical Inference* (Princeton, N. J.: Van Nostrand, 1962) 254.
4. Kauko Aromaa, *Arkipäivan Väkivaltaa Suomessa* (Everyday Violence in Finland), Kriminologinen Tutkimuslaitos, Sarja M:11 (Helsinki 1971) 8–11.
5. Preben Wolf, *Vold I Danmark og Finland 1970/1971. En sammenligning af voldsofre.* Projekt Noxa. Forskningsrapport nr. 1, Nordisk Samarbejdsrad for Kriminologi 1971/72 (Copenhagen: mimeo.) Appendix C (by Karin Zedeler).
6. Paul Davidson Reynolds et al., *Victimization in a Metropolitan Region: Comparison of a Central City Area and a Suburban Community.* III-11–III-30. Reynolds claims in fact that the distributions of events in his sample *do* correspond—the fit is said to be 'from "fairly good" to extraordinary'—to expected values derived from a Poisson process; this conclusion is apparently based on his inspection of graphs of obseived and expected values presented on pp. III-17 to III-27 of his report. Observably, however, the fit between the two sets of graphed values is not in fact particularly good; as stated in the text above, there is in each case an excess of cases reporting no incidents, and of cases reporting high numbers of incidents, compared with Poisson expectation. A reanalysis of the data presented on p. III-13 of Reynolds' report, and a calculation of expected numbers using the Poisson distribution, shows that the differences are statistically highly significant for all four of the categories of crime considered by Reynolds, for both adults and dependent youths in his sample.
7. Institute for Local Self-government, *Criminal Victimization in Maricopa County.* 30; Philip H. Ennis, *Field Surveys II* at 40. Both of these surveys use the household, rather than the individual as the basic unit when considering multiple victimization; however, in neither survey are the data standardized for household size, so the results must be treated with reserve. Moreover, in neither of the surveys is the exact total number of incidents reported given; households with four or more incidents are grouped together, so that it is impossible to calculate exact mean rates. Using a

conservative average of five incidents for the 'four or more' category yields a very great excess of multiple victimizations, compared with Poisson expectation, however.

8. See, for example, A. G. Arbous and J. E. Kerrich, 'Accident statistics and the concept of accident proneness.' (1951) 7 *Biometrics* 340–90; G. D. Mellinger *et al.*, 'A mathematical model with applications to the study of accident repeatedness among children.' (1965) 60 *Journal of the American Statistical Association* 1046; R. A. Carr-Hill, *The Violent Offender: Illusion or Reality*, Oxford University Penal Research Unit Occasional Paper No. 1 (Oxford: Basil Blackwell, 1971).

9. See the discussion in James S. Coleman, *Introduction to Mathematical Sociology* (New York: Free Press, 1964) at 299–307. In its simplest form this distribution depends on two parameters: the first, say α, represents the probability of a first event, and the second, say β, represents the amount by which α is incremented for subsequent transitions to two, three, etc. events. Coleman shows that the probability of k events on these assumptions is given by the successive terms of

$$p_k = \frac{\alpha(\alpha + \beta)...(\alpha + \{k - 1\}\beta)\,e^{-\alpha}(1 - e^{-\beta})^k}{k!\,\beta^k}$$

The values of the parameters α and β are given by $\alpha = \hat{\mu}^2\beta/(\hat{\sigma}^2 - \hat{\mu})$ and $\beta = \ln(\hat{\sigma}^2/\hat{\mu})$ where $\hat{\mu}$ and $\hat{\sigma}^2$ are sample estimates of the mean and variance of the distribution.

10. This possibility was actually mentioned to us by one or two of our respondents who had been victims of burglary; so far as we could discover, however, they had no evidence for it.

11. M. Greenwood and G. Udny Yule, 'An inquiry into the nature of frequency distributions representative of multiple happenings with particular reference to the occurrence of multiple attacks of disease or repeated accidents.' (1920) 83 *Journal of the Royal Statistical Society*, 255–279, at 273–77. See also, F. Thorndike, 'Applications of Poisson's Probability Summation.' (1926) 5 *Bell Syst. J.* 604–24.

12. M. Greenwood and G. Udny Yule, 'An inquiry into the nature of frequency distributions representative of multiple happenings with particular reference to the occurrence of multiple attacks of disease or repeated accidents.' 274. Other investigators have assumed proneness to be distributed according to Beta and Poisson distributions; the theoretical rationale for preferring any one of these is not always clear, and the similarity of the results obtained from different distributions gives force to Greenwood and Yule's remark. Mathematical tractability is probably as important as anything else in dictating the choice, given the vagueness of theories in this area.

13. But it is not so easy to give a straightforward interpretation of the *meaning* of the parameters r and c, analogous to the interpretation of α and β in Coleman's formulation of the contagion model (cf. note 9 above).

14. $\chi^2 = 11\cdot55$, df $= 3$, p $< 0\cdot01$.

15. William Feller, 'On a general class of "contagious" distributions.' (1943) 14 *Ann. Math. Statist.* 389–400.

16. The 'contagious' model presented by Coleman has been shown to give a reasonably good fit to victimization data collected by Aromaa in Finland and Wolf in Denmark: see the references cited in notes 4 and 5 on p. 110 above. Aromaa interprets his findings on the assumption of heterogeneity, however; as explained in the text, either set of assumptions leads to the same expected values.

17. Janes S. Coleman, *Introduction to Mathematical Sociology*. 379.

18. The same approach was tried, using Finnish data on violent victimization, by Dr. Kauko Aromaa; he too had little success. See his paper on 'Victimization to violence: some results of a Finnish survey,' (1973) 1 *Int. J. of Criminology and Penology* 245.

19. No better luck was had with fitting the Greenwood–Yule model in this method. In

112

any case, of course, this model still assumes some randomly distributed residual heterogeneity within the sub-groups, which is precisely the assumption we are trying to avoid by sub-dividing the sample into groups characterized by different observed victimization rates.

20. The analysis of variance gives $F = 3.665$, which is highly significant, $p < 0.001$. The sample product-moment correlation coefficient between age and violent victimization, however, is only -0.018, owing to the curvilinear nature of the relationship.

21. This is not necessarily the arbitrary procedure which it might seem. Perhaps the most famous application of the Poisson distribution to empirical data is that done by Bortkewitsch, who analysed the numbers of deaths due to kicks by a horse in ten Prussian army corps over a period of 20 years. There were in fact fourteen corps, but Bortkewitsch excluded four of these precisely because they had abnormally high numbers of deaths: cf. Coleman, *Introduction to Mathematical Sociology* 291. Of course, it is preferable to have some theoretical rationale for excluding such very extreme cases, and it is a matter of nice judgement how extreme they must be to qualify as atypical. This general issue is discussed in greater detail in the next section, pp. 97–106.

22. Cf. above, pp. 80–81. As Dr. Kauko Aromaa has pointed out to us, however, such an 'immunity' model might be consistent with the data over a shorter period of time, for example, one or six months.

23. In the notation employed by Coleman (cf. note 9 on p. 111 above) the transition rate for those who have not yet been victims would be α; the transition rate for those having been victims once would be $\alpha - \beta$; and so on until it reached zero.

24. On our sample's stated changes in their ways of life and outlooks following reported incidents, see below, pp. 208–211. In the Washington pilot study it was found that respondents reporting more than one incident more often reported taking precautionary measures than those reporting one or none: see A. D. Biderman in *Field Surveys I* at 49.

25. In fact, of course, 'negative contagion,' 'immunity' and 'victimization—proneness' are by no means mutually exclusive: nor is it necessarily true that any one of the three inheres in *persons* (as distinct from places or activities).

26. As an illustration of this, we may take the reporting of all property offences (including damage), and suppose that (1) the true proportion of very extreme cases—reporting five or more incidents—is twice that found in the sample, owing to response bias; and (2) that the bias is randomly distributed among the rest of the sample members. Then the value of $(N-1)s^2/M$—indicative of the extent of deviation from the Poisson predicted values—is actually increased. It is however possible that another type of response bias influenced our results: namely the non-reporting of incidents by one-time victims. Our reverse record check does not suggest that this was marked; but it might have occurred a sufficient extent in the R sample to help produce the distribution of incidents which we found.

27. Unfortunately, our information on this point (from crime incident forms) was not sufficient to enable us to examine this point satisfactorily. No trend was apparent, when broad categories of offence (assault, burglary, etc.) were considered; but, of course, that does not prove very much.

28. This point is discussed in greater detail in Chapter VII, pp. 190–191.

29. Though data on our crime incident forms are incomplete, they suggest that *objective* measures of seriousness are also unrelated to numbers of victimizations; no trends appear. The existence of 'series' victims considerably complicates this matter, however.

4. Explaining the Distribution of Victimization

1. We are indebted, on this point, to discussions with Maurice E. B. Owens, and to an unpublished paper by him.
2. Below, pp. 142–151. Albert Biderman has suggested to us that incidents reported by

certain 'chronic' victims be referred to as 'serial' victimization, to distinguish them from 'series' victimization which involves causally discrete incidents; an incidence measure might be appropriate for the latter cases, but a prevalence measure would be needed for the former.

3. Though see above, p. 94, on the experiences of a small number of West Indian female respondents in our sample.

4. We have benefited here and elsewhere from discussions with Albert J. Reiss, Jr., Albert Biderman, Steven Fienberg and David Seidman.

5. To say that there is an element of chance or randomness in the selection of victims does not, of course, imply that some crimes are 'undetermined' (whatever that might mean), or that no explanation of them can be given. Further, it must be remembered that the simple Poisson model starts with the assumption that the transition rate λ is the same for all members of the population (and in a sample is equal to the observed mean); the model states that *if* this assumption is met, a certain number of 'multiple victims' may be expected purely by chance. What we have shown in the preceding section is that the assumption of a single transition rate is almost certainly invalid. But it does not follow that the multiple victims observed in a sample *are in fact* the result of chance rather than of some specific causal processes operating in those cases, even if their number is no greater than the Poisson formula predicts; this is a separate matter.

6. Hans von Hentig, *The Criminal and his Victim* (New Haven: Yale University Press, 1948) 384.

7. For data on victim–offender relationships in homicide and other recorded crimes of violence, see Marvin E. Wolfgang, *Patterns in Criminal Homicide* (Philadelphia: University of Pennsylvania Press, 1958) Chapter 14; Donald J. Mulvihill and Melvin M. Tumin, *Crimes of Violence*, Vol. 11 of the staff reports submitted to the National Commission on the Causes and Prevention of Violence (Washington, D.C.: U.S. Government Printing Office, 1969), Chapter 5; E. Gibson and S. Klein, *Murder 1957–1968*, Home Office Research Studies No. 3, (London: HMSO); F. H. Mc-Clintock, *Crimes of Violence* (London: MacMillan, 1963) 36–45; K. Svalastoga, 'Homicide and social contact in Denmark,' (1956) 62 *American Journal of Sociology* 37–41; D. J. Pittman and W. F. Handy, 'Patterns in criminal aggravated assault.' (1964) 55 *Journal of Criminal Law, Criminology and Political Science* 462–70; Menachim Amir, *Patterns in Forcible Rape* (Chicago: University of Chicago Press, 1971); Lynn A. Curtis, 'Victim-precipitation and violent crime.' (1974) 21 *Social Problems* 594; Saverio Siciliano, *L'omicidio: Studio su un'indagine criminologica compiuta in Danimarca*. Cedam Casa Editrice Dott. Antonio Milani (Padova, 1965). We are grateful to Dr. Preben Wolf for the last of these references.

8. Some evidence for this proposition comes from a survey carried out for the U.S. National Commission on the Causes and Prevention of Violence in 1969. A total of 1,176 adults and 496 teenagers were asked a series of questions about their approval of violence in specific situations, and were also asked whether they had used certain types of violence against others, and had had violence used against them. Strong inter-item associations ($\lambda = 0.84$ for adults, and 0.82 for teenagers) were reported between responses to the questions about the use of violence and experience as a victim of it. See David L. Lange, Robert K. Baker and Sandra J. Ball, *Mass Media and Violence*, Vol. XI of the staff reports to the National Commission (Washington, D.C.: U.S. Government Printing Office, 1969) 362.

9. The order of items on each card was varied, as was the order in which the cards were presented; in neither case was there any evidence of order effect.

10. In particular, it would have been interesting to separate out motoring and drunkenness offences, to see whether an admitted propensity to drink was associated with other crimes and/or with victimization.

11. The weighting of three for the 'more than once' responses is, of course, entirely arbitrary.

Different weightings were experimented with, but they made very little difference to the observed relationships between self-reported crime and other items.

12. Sample means and standard deviations are as follows:

	Mean	S.D.
Property offences	1·29	2·75
'Public order' and motoring	1·91	2·83
Violent offences	1·09	2·44

The intercorrelations between the three indices are: property–public order, + 0·36; property–violence, + 0·42; and public order–violence, + 0·34.

13. The sample product-moment correlations between age and index scores are − 0·27 for the property offences, − 0·31 for the 'public order' and motoring offences, − 0·25 for the violent offences, and − 0·37 overall.

14. The zero-order product-moment correlations between violent victimization and self-reported violence are as follows: Males, 0·17; females, 0·22; whites, 0·21; blacks, 0·32. The corresponding first-order partials are 0·12, 0·19, 0·18 and 0·25; all of these are significant at $p < 0.001$.

15. As might be expected, the incidents of victimization mentioned by persons who reported committing one or more violent acts were more likely to involve strangers (as opposed to family members or acquaintances) than those reported by respondents who said they had not committed any violent acts.

16. Since our sample contained only persons aged 18 and over, it contained no black adolescents; it thus excluded a group whose experience of crime (both as offenders and as victims) may be very different from that of the older generation of West Indians, almost all of whom were not born in England. It should be noted at this point that all of our interviewers were white.

17. This is at any rate what we were told by police in both Brixton and Hackney. On the U.S. see, for example, Leroy G. Schultz, 'Why the Negro carries weapons.' (1962) 53 *Journal of Criminal Law, Criminology and Police Science* 477–83. In the Washington pilot survey it was found that respondents who said they usually carried a weapon of some sort when they went out reported victimization in greater proportion than those who did not; these respondents were not necessarily all black, of course. See A.D. Biderman *et al.*, *Field Surveys I* at 54–55.

18. Based on data in the crime incident forms.

19. There was no policeman or security guard in our R sample. But in our earlier interviewing in Peterborough we had two policemen. each of whom reported several cases in which they had been assaulted or threatened by prisoners; and the most serious case of violence reported to us in those pilot surveys (in which the respondent had had his skull fractured by a gang who attacked him) was reported by a night-club bouncer.

20. American readers may also regard the practice of having milk delivered to one's door as creating a special risk of theft; certainly it led to a considerable number of thefts of bottles of milk in our sample. But it does not seem reasonable to regard it as creating an abnormal risk of theft for the members of our sample; it merely creates an opportunity which has long since ceased to exist in many American cities.

21. If anything, response bias may make this an under-estimate of the frequency of assaults by other family members. It is also important to note that over half of these assaults occurred in the respondent's home or some other private place; only a quarter took place on the streets, in the respondent's area or elsewhere.

22. Cf. K. Svalastoga, 'Homicide and social contact in Denmark,' at 40–41.

23. As Dr. Desmond Ellis has pointed out to us, alcohol use can be an important factor here in several different ways. For example, young people who drink, especially in groups, may become belligerent (thus raising their probability of involvement in

assaults); whereas older people who drink may become more vulnerable (to mugging,
etc.). Unfortunately, such limited data as we have on our sample's drinking behaviour
do not support either of these hypotheses; we are inclined to believe, however, that
both are true.

24. We also asked respondents how they usually travelled when they went out at night,
on the assumption that those who went on foot or by public transport would be more
at risk than those who drove in their own cars or went by taxi. Here too, however,
there was no difference; if anything those who used their own cars reported more
victimization, both violence and theft. But this may be due to class-linked variations
in car ownership.

25. Two further instances may be given. We asked respondents to define their home
'neighbourhoods,' i.e., the physical space around their homes with which they were
familiar, to which they were attached and where they felt 'at home.' (These data are
discussed in Chapter VIII, below, pp. 200–204.) In our pilot studies in Peterborough
we attempted to plot the responses to this question on a map; and we found that several
elderly respondents claimed that they only knew about, and only ever ventured into,
an area comprising the sidewalk on one side of the street for a length of a few city
blocks—e.g., the distance from their house or flat to the nearest group of shops.
Such an attenuated social existence clearly provides virtually no opportunities for
crime (or anything else). In London this way of life is probably less common; but
there are many elderly working-class people in areas like the ones where we interviewed
who have never been to Piccadilly Circus. Secondly, the female victims of the much-
publicized wave of robbery and purse-snatching which occurred in Brixton late in
1972 were almost invariably white. This was so because West Indian women—middle-
aged ones, at any rate—very rarely go out in the evenings to pubs, clubs and the like,
and are thus very seldom alone on the streets at night.

26. We discuss this point in more detail in Chapter IX, pp. 230, 235.

27. Of the many regression analyses which we carried out, the best gives R^2 of about 0·12
(age, self-reported violence, race and nights out, for violence against males).

28. Only a handful of studies pay any attention to this point, which is admittedly compli-
cated. See, for some discussion, A. J. Reiss, Jr., in *Field Surveys III* at 10–12, 18–23;
Leslie T. Wilkins, *Social Deviance* (London: Tavistock, 1964) 53—5; K. Svalastoga,
'Homicide and social contact in Denmark'; Leroy C. Gould, 'The changing structure
of property crime in an affluent society,' (1969) *Social Forces* 50–59; J. E. Price,
'A test of the accuracy of crime statistics', (1966) 14 *Social Problems* 214–21.

CHAPTER V

Attitudes to the Police and the Reporting of Victimization

1. The Decision to Call the Police

Much has been written about the reasons why persons who believe that a crime has been committed against them may decide *not* to tell the police about that crime.[1] The reasons usually mentioned are of several different kinds. First, there are reasons which are broadly 'utilitarian' in character, in the sense that they relate to the victim's perception of the probable costs and benefits of notifying the police. Thus, a (self-defined) victim of crime may believe that the police will not come if he calls them, or that they will be unwilling or unable to do anything useful about the situation; these beliefs in turn may rest either on his general views of police efficiency, or on the facts of the particular situation. The victim may not report a crime if he thinks it will involve him in further costs (e.g. through having to appear in court); or he may feel that an investigation of the crime will put him in a shameful or otherwise undesirable position, e.g. if it results in disclosing his own illegal or immoral behaviour. If he knows (or thinks he knows) the offender, he may refrain from reporting because he feels that to call in the police would be an unnecessarily harsh step; alternatively, he may feel that the offender would probably be 'let off' by the police or the courts; or he may just not want to 'get involved'.[2]

Related to these factors, but independent of them, is the victim's estimate of the benefits—in terms of compensation, satisfaction, freedom from future victimization, or whatever—which he may gain from calling the police. In part, no doubt, these benefits are of a pragmatic or prudential kind: the victim may hope to get his property back, or help to rid his neighbourhood or the community at large of a potential source of future trouble. But they may also derive from a more general sense of moral obligation: a feeling that it is 'right' to notify the police when the law has been broken. In either case, it seems reasonable to hypothesize that the victim's estimate of the 'seriousness' of the incident is what is important here: however weak the reasons *against* reporting may be, the victim will presumably not notify the police if he regards the incident as too trivial to bother about.[3]

Finally, it may also be that the reporting of offences to the police is to some extent influenced by the victim's attitudes to the law, the police and the system of social control generally. Thus, those who are strongly 'pro-authority' may go out of their way to report even trivial offences committed against them; *per contra*, those who think that the law is an ass, or that all coppers are bastards, may prefer to suffer in silence—at least up to a point. Both moral and prudential considerations, however, are presumably tempered by the victim's perception of the other possible courses of action open to him, and their probable outcomes. For example, if he can collect on his insurance without reporting stolen property to the police, or if he can persuade some friends to beat up a man who has assaulted him, the victim may prefer not to call in the police; it may be otherwise if he has no insurance, or no muscular friends.

We could not, of course, investigate all of these possible reasons for non-reporting of offences to the police. But we have four kinds of evidence which bear on this question so far as our R sample is concerned. First, we can compare those respondents who said that they had been victims of crime in the preceding year and who (said that they) had notified the police, with those respondents who had been victims but had *not* notified the police. Secondly, we can compare those *incidents* which were allegedly reported with those which were not, in respect of such things as type of crime, value of property stolen, and so forth, to see if there are any differences. Thirdly, we asked those respondents who said they had reported incidents to the police, why they had done so; and fourthly, we asked those who said they had not reported incidents why they had not done so. These last data are, of course, available only for those incidents for which crime incident forms were completed.

We tried all four of these approaches. All four pose considerable problems of analysis and interpretation, however. In particular, a problem arises in respect of the substantial minority of our sample who said that they had been victims of crime on more than one occasion during the preceding year, since the data on respondents and on incidents were basically treated as two separate data sets. It will be recalled that our procedure in respect of these 'multiple victims' was to associate data relating to their incidents with data relating to the respondents themselves, taking the incidents in random order;[4] this was necessary in order to enable us to investigate possible interactions between characteristics of the respondents and of the incidents. But this procedure, though adequate for many purposes, introduces a certain amount of error into estimates of the variable with which we are here concerned (viz. reporting behaviour), since a 'multiple victim' may have notified the police about some of the things which happened to him, but not about others. In analysing data relating to the respondents themselves, therefore, we used two measures of this variable. The first was whether or not the respondent notified the police about the 'first' incident for which a crime incident form was completed; for the majority of those who said they had been victims, this was the only incident involved, and for the 'multiple victims' it was the first of the (randomly ordered) incidents for which we had data. Secondly, we used the percentage of incidents mentioned, which according to the respondent had been reported to the police; for those with only one incident this was, of course, either 100 or zero. A further possibility would be to associate with each incident form, data relating to the respondent concerned; theoretically this would make possible a more precise analysis of the effects of expressed attitudes and other attributes of the respondents on the reporting of incidents to the police. But apart from the computational problems involved, this procedure is somewhat artificial (since it involves over-weighting of those respondents who were 'multiple victims'); and the analyses which we carried out did not suggest that it would be particularly likely to be profitable, so far as the explanation of reporting behaviour is concerned.

In fact, our data on the respondents themselves were of very little use in predicting whether crime incidents would be reported to the police. There was a slight general tendency for females to be more likely to say they had reported incidents to the police than males; otherwise there were no significant differences in reporting behaviour relating to any demographic attribute, or to social class, either overall or for particular types of offence. Furthermore, neither expressed concern about crime in London or in the respondent's own area, nor a belief that crime was prevalent in the area, appeared to make any difference to a willingness to call the police; and—somewhat surprisingly, perhaps—there was only a moderate tendency for those who admitted to violent or property offences themselves (on our self-report questions) to be less likely to have notified the police about incidents involving offences which they believed to have been committed against them in the preceding year (see Table V.1).

In the sample as a whole, there was a slight tendency for those who said they had not reported their first (and for the majority the only) incident to the police to be critical of the police in their own local area, and to say that the police would not respond immediately in any emergency; moreover, those who said they had not reported their incidents to the police were somewhat more likely to say that they were dissatisfied with what the police had done on the occasion of their last contact *other than* one involving an incident of alleged victimization. In Brixton and Hackney these differences are more marked. Thus in Brixton, some 40 per cent of those victims who failed to notify the police said they were not satisfied with the job the police did in their own area, compared with only 18 per cent of those who did notify the police; in Hackney the comparable figures are 21 per cent and 15 per cent. In Kensington, on the other hand, those who *did* report their incidents to the police were *more* likely to express dissatisfaction with the police in that area. Moreover, when we look at other indicators of attitudes to the police in relation to alleged reporting or non-reporting of incidents involving victimization, we find no significant associations. As we shall see in the next section, self-reported criminality (especially that involving violent or conventional property crime) was related, in our sample, to certain expressed negative attitudes to the police. It may thus be the respondents' own criminality, rather than their attitudes to the

Table V.1. Self-reported crime and reporting of own incidents to the police, by those reporting one or more incidents of victimization

Number of offences said to have been committed:	Whether reported 'first' incident to police					
		Yes		No		Total
Property offences	No.	Percentage	No.	Percentage	No.	Percentage
None	52	38·5	83	61·5	135	100·0
One or two	8	29·6	19	70·4	27	100·0
Three	9	23·1	30	76·9	39	100·0
Four or more	7	25·0	21	75·0	28	100·0
Totals	76	33·2	153	66·8	229	100·0

$\chi^2 = 4\cdot53$, df $= 3$, $0\cdot30 > p > 0\cdot20$

Violent offences	No.	Percentage	No.	Percentage	No.	Percentage
None	53	36·8	91	63·2	144	100·0
One or two	11	34·4	21	65·6	32	100·0
Three	8	24·2	25	75·8	33	100·0
Four or more	4	21·1	15	78·9	19	100·0
Totals	76	33·3	152	66·7	228	100·0

$\chi^2 = 3\cdot65$, df $= 3$, $p \simeq 0\cdot30$

police, which led to non-reporting; unfortunately we cannot disentangle these relationships in our data. But in any case, in our sample, the relationships between expressed general attitudes to the police and the non-reporting of incidents are not at all strong.

We found only one other attitudinal variable which had any clear relationship to the reporting of incidents to the police, and the significance of this variable is unfortunately not at all easy to assess. At one stage in our questionnaire, we put a number of hypothetical situations to our respondents, asking them whether they thought that the majority of their neighbours, and they themselves, would approve or disapprove of acts of violence used in response to certain sorts of provocation.[5] We then compared the respondents' own expressed attitudes in each hypothetical case with those which they said their neighbours held. In the majority of cases, the two responses were concordant: e.g. if the respondent himself said he strongly approved of the violence used, he also said that his neighbours would strongly approve. A small sub-set of our sample, however, consistently expressed *more* approval of the violence described than they imputed to their neighbours; a somewhat larger minority of the sample were *less* approving than they thought their neighbours would be. Both of these groups differed significantly from the generally concordant members of the sample, in respect of their reporting of incidents to the police. Those who were generally more likely to approve of the hypothetical acts of violence were somewhat *more* likely to have notified the police about their own victimization; conversely, those less approving of violence than their neighbours were *less* likely to have called the police about things which had allegedly happened to them.

In view of the possibility of response bias, and the comparatively small numbers involved, this finding must be treated with considerable care. A possible explanation, however, is that those who tended to express approval of using violence (in retaliation to provocation) were expressing a general attitude favourable to the punishment of 'wrongdoing,' which carried over to their own notification of the police; and that those less likely to regard the hypothetical violent responses to provocation as justified were generally less likely to feel that 'something needed to be done' about the incidents alleged to have happened to them.[6]

Our mainly negative findings should not, of course, be taken as showing that general attitudes to crime and the criminal justice system, or beliefs concerning the prevalence or seriousness of crime, play no part at all in determining the decision to call the police. It does seem, however, that the most important factors influencing that decision are primarily 'incident-specific,' and depend much more on the features of the particular situation than on the characteristics of the victims themselves or their general attitudes or beliefs. Thus, in general, completed crimes were more likely to be reported than attempts; assaults which caused some degree of physical injury were more likely to be reported, and for property crimes reporting increased, the greater the value of the property said to be involved. These facts are consistent with the hypothesis that notifying the police is mainly a function of the objective seriousness of the incident, in commonsense terms. This finding also emerges from victim surveys done elsewhere. Thus in both the U.S. national survey, conducted by NORC in 1966, and the Washington pilot study by Biderman *et al.*, it was found that higher proportions of more serious (Part I) incidents were said to have been reported to the police than of less serious (Part II) ones; in the national survey the proportion reported was higher for completed crimes than for attempts in the case of offences against the person, though this was not so for property crimes.[7] Reynolds *et al.*, in their surveys in Minnesota, found a similar result.[8] The same picture is revealed by most of the city-level surveys done to date by the U. S. Census Bureau, as part of the National Crime Panel: for example, aggravated assaults are more likely to be reported to the police than simple assaults, completed crimes more likely to be reported than attempts, burglaries (especially those involving forcible entry) more likely than thefts in dwelling houses.[9]

Reynolds also found that a significant factor affecting the decision to call the police was the relationship between the victim and the offender; in not one of the incidents reported by his samples, in which the offender was said to be a close friend or family member, was the incident reported to the police.[10] This was certainly not so in our sample, however: in fact, incidents involving family members of acquaintances (mainly in assaults) were slightly *more* likely to have led to the police being called than incidents involving strangers, though the difference was not statistically significant.[11] The explanation of this may be, however, that in many cases involving friends or family members the victim called the police primarily in order to have the dispute stopped, rather than with a view to initiating a prosecution. The fact that stolen property had been insured was significantly associated, in our sample, with reporting to the police of thefts other than burglaries and thefts in dwellings. For the latter offences, though there was a slight association between being insured and reporting, it was not a statistically significant one. A possible explanation of this is that in the case of burglaries, the symbolic significance of intrusion into the household had also affected the decision to call the police, even in cases where little or no property was stolen.

We also asked our respondents to give a subjective assessment of the 'seriousness' of the incidents they mentioned, by means of a score on a 1-to-11 point scale; and these assessments were also related to the reporting of incidents to the police. For all types of incidents combined, the mean score given to those which were reported to the police was 5·4; for those not reported it was 4·0. This difference is statistically significant.[12] It is possible, of course, that in giving these retrospective assessments of 'seriousness' our respondents were to some extent influenced by whether or not they had called the police at the time of the incident; having failed to do this might well have led them to discount the gravity of the incident during the interview by giving it a lower score. It is interesting to note that the difference in seriousness scores (between reported and non-reported incidents) did not appear in the case of burglaries; and it may be that for these offences; at least, our respondents' retrospective assessments of the seriousness of these incidents differed from the ones which they made (on whatever grounds) at the time of the incidents, which presumably influenced their decisions to call the police.

The seriousness scores given by our respondents were in fact the variable most strongly associated with the reporting to the police of those incidents for which we had crime incident forms.[13] Since these scores in general reflected the objective seriousness of the incidents, in terms of such things as the value of property stolen and degree of physical injury caused, their association with reporting behaviour is, of course, to be expected. But in the case of property offences there was an interesting interaction between subjective and objective valuations. At an earlier stage in the interviews, our respondents had been given similar seriousness scores (from 1 to 11) to each of a series of 33 briefly described hypothetical incidents. As we shall see in a later chapter,[14] there was general agreement between respondents in different social classes, in the scores given to offences involving violence; but there was a general tendency for respondents in the lower social classes to give higher scores to property offences, indicating that they regarded them as relatively more serious than the middle-class respondents did.

The average scores given to the hypothetical incidents were also positively associated with the average scores given to the respondents' own incidents of victimization. It might be expected, therefore, that our working-class respondents would be more likely to have notified the police about incidents involving property crimes committed against them. This was not the case, however; there was no difference in the proportions of property offences reported to the police, between social classes. Further analysis shows that this is due to the fact that the working-class respondents' incidents were on average *objectively* less serious, in terms of the value of property involved, than those suffered by middle-class respondents; the two valuations tended to offset each other, leaving no overall difference in the proportions of property offences reported to the police. The data are set out in Table V.2.

Owing to small numbers, even with several categories collapsed, the interrelationships in this rather complicated table do not reach statistical significance; but several trends are evident.[15] First, it will be seen that overall, the proportions of these property incidents reported to the police are virtually the same in the two social-class groups: 32·3 per cent for classes I–IIIA and 31·3 per cent for classes IIIB–V. Next, it will be seen that the proportions reported to the police increase, for both social-class groups, as the value of property stolen increases; for all cases included in the table, the proportions reported to the police are 13·7 per cent for thefts of less than £5, 35·7 per cent for thefts of £5 up to £20, and 69 per cent for thefts of £20 or more. It will also be seen that in general, within categories of property value, incidents given a high seriousness score (5 or more) are more likely to have been reported to the police than those given a low score (1 to 4): this does not hold for lower-class respondents' reporting of medium and high-value offences, but the numbers are very small in each case. Over the table as a whole, incidents given seriousness scores of 5 or more are about twice as likely to have been reported to the police as those given scores of 1 to 4: 45·2 per cent against 23·5 per cent. Finally, within each category of property value, respondents in the low social class group consistently gave higher seriousness scores to their incidents than did respondents in the higher social classes: for low- and medium-value thefts, they were more than twice as likely to have given a score of 5 to more. But while just over half of the thefts from respondents in the high social-class category involved £5 or more, this was true for only about 43 per cent of the thefts from lower-class respondents: this tends to offset the effect of higher seriousness scores on reporting, so that the proportions reported are virtually the same overall in the two social-class groups.

Further evidence of the influence of perceived seriousness on reporting comes from the reasons given by those respondents who did *not* report offences, for their failure to do so; the commonest reason—given in 57 per cent of these cases—was simply that the incident was 'not sufficiently serious.' It is true that this answer, like the seriousness score, was given retrospectively; and it may be that some respondents said that the incident was 'not serious' in part *because* they had not notified the police. Moreover, since it was not practicable for our interviewers to probe the answers to this question, we cannot say exactly what the respondents meant by 'not serious' here; but in general it can be

Table V.2. Reporting of property offences to the police, by social class, value of property and seriousness score

123

Value:	Under £5						£5 up to £20						£20 or more						Total
Seriousness score:	1–4		5 +		Total		1–4		5 +		Total		1–4		5 +		Total		Total no. of incidents
Social class:	Rptd	Not Rptd	Rptd	Not Rptd	Rptd	Not Rptd	Rptd	Not Rptd	Rptd	Not Rptd	Rptd	Not Rptd	Rptd	Not Rptd	Rptd	Not Rptd	Rptd	Not Rptd	
High (I, II, IIIA)	5	34	3	7	8	41	4	15	2	4	6	19	6	5	12	2	18	7	99
Low /IIIB, IV, V	2	25	3	16	·5	41	4	3	5	5	9	8	3	0	8	6	11	6	80
Totals	7	59	6	23	13	82	8	18	7	9	15	27	9	5	20	8	29	13	179

Percentages based on above table:

	Under £5						£5 up to £20						£20 or more						Total percentage reported
	Rptd	Not Rptd	Rptd	Not Rptd	Rptd	Not Rptd	Rptd	Not Rptd	Rptd	Not Rptd	Rptd	Not Rptd	Rptd	Not Rptd	Rptd	Not Rptd	Rptd	Not Rptd	
High social class	13	87	30	70	16	84	21	79	33	67	24	76	55	45	86	14	72	28	32·3
Low social class	7	93	16	84	11	89	57	43	50	50	53	47	100	0	57	43	65	35	31·3
Total	11	89	21	79	14	86	31	69	44	56	36	64	64	36	71	29	69	31	31·8

Percentages within categories of value, *and* of totals:

	Under £5 1–4	Under £5 5 +	Under £5 Total	£5 up to £20 1–4	£5 up to £20 5 +	£5 up to £20 Total	£20 or more 1–4	£20 or more 5 +	£20 or more Total	Total
High social class	79·6	20·4	49·5	76·0	24·0	25·3	44·0	56·0	25·3	100·0
Low social class	58·7	41·3	57·5	41·2	58·8	21·3	17·6	82·4	21·3	100·0

said that their replies, like the scores, were reasonably consistent with the objective factors mentioned earlier concerning degree of physical injury, value of property and the like. The second commonest reason given for not reporting—that the police would be unable to do anything useful about the matter—was given in 21 per cent of the cases. Our data on attitudes to the police (discussed in the next section) suggest that these responses related mainly to the facts of the particular incident, rather than to a general belief that the police were imcompetent; in only three cases did the respondent state that he did not report an incident because he thought that the police would not come. Eleven incidents were described as being a private matter rather than something for the police to deal with.[16]

A slightly different picture emerges if we look at the reasons given for reporting those incidents which *were* said to have been reported to the police. For all types of incidents combined, in over a fifth of the cases the respondent gave as his reason a feeling of obligation to report the matter (e.g. statements of the form 'You have to do it,' etc.). It may well be, of course, that this was not in fact the primary motive for reporting in these cases; it may merely be the way in which our respondents justified their actions, *ex post facto*, to our interviewers.[17] Moreover, the element of perceived benefits was by no means lacking; in over a third of the incidents involving property loss, a desire to get the property back was mentioned as the reason for reporting. 'In order to get the offender punished' was mentioned in 11 per cent of the cases; in a slightly greater proportion, preventing a repetition of the incident (not necessarily reprisals) was mentioned.

2. Attitudes to the Police

It appears, then, that among our respondents the decision to call the police as a result of victimization was largely influenced by the seriousness (in both the subjectively perceived and objective terms) of the particular incident. It is, however, reasonable to suppose that another factor which might influence such a decision would be the victim's view of the police. It might be, for example, that a person who had faith in the ability of the police to act usefully upon information given would be more likely to report an incident than one who felt otherwise. Or a person who believed that the police might be prejudiced against him, on the grounds of age or colour, might be less likely to report an incident than someone who considered the police to be free from such forms of discrimination, (or at least unlikely to discriminate against him).

It was not within the scope of this project to explore in detail how attitudes to, and beliefs about, the police develop. It seems safe to assume that indirect sources—such as reports in the press and television programmes about the police—play a substantial part in the formation of such beliefs. But in addition, actual contact with the police—as a result of a previous incident of victimization or for some other reason—might well have some impact on attitudes to the police, and thus on the decision whether or not to invoke police action. We feel that our respondents' views of the police are of some interest in their own right, independently of their possible effects on the reporting of crime; in this section, therefore, we shall summarize our data on attitudes to the police among the R sample as a whole.

In all three of our survey areas, and among all groups of people, we found the general opinion of the police to be high. When respondents were asked the question 'What sort of job do you think the police do in general?' 83 per cent of the sample said that it was either 'very good' or 'good;' 15 per cent thought it 'fair' and only 2 per cent of the sample said that the police did a 'poor' job in general. There was surprisingly little variation in response between areas on this question, which suggests that, whatever the differences in police–public relations between our three survey areas, the overall image of the police is extremely favourable.

Those 93 respondents who said that they thought the job which the police did in general was only 'fair' or 'poor' were asked 'In what ways do you think that the police could do better?' Of these respondents, 22 per cent thought simply that there should be more policemen, mostly on the beat. This opinion— which may merely express a certain nostalgia for 'the good old days,' and may not even reflect a belief that more men on the beat would be more effective in in any sense—was expressed more strongly in Brixton and Hackney than it was in Kensington, and particularly by respondents aged over 50. A further 14 per cent said in effect that they thought the police should spend more time attending to crime, and another 18 per cent—that is, about three per cent of the whole R sample—simply made statements about the police that were derogatory or abusive in tone or content but were otherwise unclassifiable.[1]

We did find some differences between areas in responses to the more specifically-focused question, 'Are you satisfied with the job that the police are doing in this neighbourhood?' In Brixton, some 30 per cent of respondents said that they were *not* satisfied with the job that their *local* police did, compared with only 17 per cent in Kensington and 15 per cent in Hackney who felt this way. Again, the main source of dissatisfaction in all three areas seemed to lie mainly in a feeling that there were not enough police patrolling in the area— 41 per cent of those dissatisfied with the local police in Brixton gave this reason, 42 per cent in Hackney and 43 per cent in Kensington. The next most commonly expressed cause of dissatisfaction was a belief that the police were in some way incompetent, or were not doing all they *could* do; 24 per cent in Brixton, 21 per cent in Hackney and 13 per cent in Kensington of those dissatisfied with the local police gave this response.

Neither age, sex nor social class of the respondent had any significant effect on attitudes to the work of the police in general; on the other hand, having a close friend or relative who belonged to the police force did seem to be associated to a slight (but not statistically significant) degree with a more favourable attitude to the police both in the home neighbourhood and in general.

Respondents were asked, 'How often do you see a policeman in this neighbourhood?' Over the whole sample, 45 per cent said more than once a

Table V.3. 'How often do you see a policeman in this neighbourhood?' by satisfaction
with the local police, in three areas

How often sees a policeman		Brixton			Hackney			Kensington		
		Yes	No	Total	Yes	No	Total	Yes	No	Total
Every day	No.	61	10	71	63	7	70	85	7	92
	Percentage	85·9	14·1	100·0	90·0	10·0	100·0	92·4	7·6	100·0
At last once a week	No.	37	16	53	46	11	57	31	13	44
	Percentage	69·8	30·2	100·0	80·7	19·3	100·0	70·5	29·5	100·0
Less than once a week	No.	18	22	40	25	5	30	23	8	31
	Percentage	45·0	55·0	100·0	83·3	16·7	100·0	74·2	25·8	100·0
Never	No.	5	3	8	4	1	5	2	2	4
	Percentage	62·5	37·5	100·0	80·0	20·0	100·0	50·0	50·0	100·0

Whether satisfied with the local police

$\chi^2 = 20\cdot81$, df $= 3$, $p < 0\cdot001$ $\chi^2 = 2\cdot38$, df $= 3$,NS $\chi^2 = 15\cdot03$, df $= 3$, $p < 0\cdot01$

week; 21 per cent said less than once a week; and only 14 per cent said that they *never* saw a policeman in the neighbourhood. Comparing areas, we find that respondents in Kensington were more likely than those in the other two areas to say that they saw a policeman 'every day.'[2] At the other extreme, respondents in Brixton tended to say that they saw a policeman less often than respondents in the other two areas. There is an association, over the whole sample, between satisfaction with the police in the local neighbourhood and the frequency with which respondents said that they saw a policeman there. This is particularly true for Brixton and Kensington, where the association reached statistical significance. (See Table V.3.)

We have seen that in response to questions about dissatisfaction with local police, a large proportion of respondents felt that there are not enough men on the beat; Table V.3 reinforces the view that dissatisfaction may often be the result of the police not being as visible as they were before they were motorized. Although, logically, if the police are mobile they can cover more ground in the course of a day, and can make their way to a trouble spot more quickly than by foot or bicycle, it seems that for many respondents being able to *see* the local 'bobby on the beat' produces a greater feeling of security and reassurance that the police are around if needed.[3]

We also found that expressed dissatisfaction with the local police was to some extent associated with the feeling that there is a lot of crime in the local neighbourhood. Although this association only reaches statistical significance in Brixton, the same trend can also be discerned in both Hackney and Kensington. (See Table V.4.) Similarly, we found that those respondents who said that people were not safe on their neighbourhood streets after dark tended to express greater dissatisfaction with the local police.[4]

When asked the question, 'Are there any things which you think the police

Table V.4. Satisfaction with local police, and beliefs about crime being committed in local area

Area, and Amount of crime in local area:	Satisfied with local police					
	No.	Yes Percentage	No.	No Percentage	No.	Total Percentage
Brixton:[a]						
Quite a lot, a great deal	60	58·9	42	41·1	102	100·0
Not much, very little, none	53	85·5	9	14·5	62	100·0
Total	113	68·9	51	31·1	164	100·0
Hackney:[b]						
Quite a lot, a great deal	60	78·9	16	21·1	76	100·0
Not much, very little, none	75	90·4	8	9·6	84	100·0
Total	135	84·9	24	15·1	159	100·0
Kensington:[c]						
Quite a lot, a great deal	57	77·0	17	23·0	74	100·0
Not much, very little, none	74	86·0	12	14·0	86	100·0
Total	131	81·9	29	18·1	160	100·0

Excludes 63 respondents giving 'Don't know' answers to one or both questions

[a] $\chi^2 = 11·6$, df $= 1$, $p < 0·001$.
[b] $\chi^2 = 3·2$, df $= 1$, $0·05 < p < 0·10$.
[c] $\chi^2 = 1·6$, df $= 1$, n.s.

should be spending more time on?' 62 per cent of the sample thought that there were; we found no significant differences between areas on this question. Those respondents who thought there were things which the police could spend more time on were asked what sorts of things they had in mind. The answers to this question were divided between those who mentioned offences and those who mentioned non-criminal matters. Of those who mentioned crimes of some kind, the most frequent responses overall were simply 'serious crimes' (21 per cent); vandalism (14 per cent); and traffic offences (11 per cent).[5] Between areas, we found that respondents were concerned about different kinds of offences, although the differences did not reach statistical significance (see Table V.5). We can see from this table that respondents in Hackney show a concern about vandalism that is not shared to the same extent in either Brixton or Kensington, and that a need for more police time to be spent on 'mugging' is felt more keenly in Brixton than in the other two areas. We found that the white population tended to be more concerned about 'serious crimes', mugging and violence

Table V.5. Types of offences on which the police should be spending more time, by area

Types of offence mentioned:	Brixton		Hackney		Kensington	
	No.	Percentage	No.	Percentage	No.	Percentage
Vandalism	5	12·5	11	22·5	4	7·7
Mugging	5	12·5	3	6·1	3	5·8
Violence	3	7·5	5	10·2	6	11·5
Serious crimes	4	10·0	8	16·3	17	32·7
Burglary	4	10·0	4	8·2	4	7·7
Drugs	1	2·5	2	4·1	1	1·9
Traffic offences	5	12·5	6	12·2	5	9·6
Other	13	32·5	10	20·4	12	23·1
Total	40	100·0	49	100·0	52	100·0

Table V.6. Other matters which the police should be spending more time on

Non-criminal matters	Brixton		Hackney		Kensington	
	No.	Percentage	No.	Percentage	No.	Percentage
More police on the beat	40	54·8	32	57·1	19	33·3
Crime prevention	12	16·4	14	25·0	16	28·1
Road safety	2	2·7	2	3·6	2	3·5
Public relations	13	17·8	2	3·6	17	29·8
Other	6	8·2	6	10·7	3	5·3
Total	73	100·0	56	100·0	57	100·0

than black respondents; women were twice as concerned as men about vandalism and men were more concerned about 'serious crimes' than women.

Among those respondents who thought that the police should be spending more time on matters other than particular types of crime, we again find certain differences in response between areas (see Table V.6).

We see here again a common feeling that there should be more men on the beat, although this is mentioned more frequently in Brixton and Hackney than in Kensington. In Kensington, by contrast, there is a fairly strong feeling that police–public relations should be improved. This concern in Kensington probably indicates that police–public relations is a more middle-class concept, rather than that relations with the police are especially bad in that area. This view is indeed upheld if we look at responses to this question by social class; only one person in social class V (in the whole sample) mentioned police–public relations. On the other hand, we find that when these responses are examined by race, black respondents show a greater concern for improved police–public relations—29 per cent of black respondents mentioned this compared with only 16 per cent of white respondents. Thus, an alternative explanation may be that the concern in (mainly white) Kensington for improved police–public relations is an expression of middle-class 'liberalism' which takes note of the need for the police to maintain good relations with the black population, and which is not necessarily felt by the whites who actually live in racially mixed communities.

We also found that the desire for more men on the beat is stronger among those respondents aged over 50, while a feeling that public relations should be improved in concentrated mainly among those under 40. A desire for more men on the beat is also felt more commonly among those lower down the social scale.

Respondents who said that there were things which the police should be spending more time on were asked, 'Why do you think that the police are not spending enough time on these things?' About half of these respondents attributed the failure to a 'lack of resources,' reflecting an appreciation of the problems facing the police force which would gratify the police themselves. Twelve per cent thought that the police spent too much time on (unspecified) 'irrelevancies' and eleven per cent thought that too much time was spent on traffic control. Only three per cent suggested that the police were 'lazy' and only five people thought that the police were restricted in their activities by the law. Between classes, although we find a consensus on the lack of resources hampering the police, there is a tendency for those lower down the social scale to think that the police spend too much time in cars and thus do not *see* crime going on; this reflects their relatively greater concern (compared with those higher up the scale) that there are not enough men on the beat. In answer to the question, 'If you called the police in an emergency, do you think that they would respond immediately?' some 92 per cent of the sample answered yes; there were no significant variations in response by area, race, sex, age or social class.

Concerning the problem of beliefs about police discrimination, we asked respondents, 'Do you think that in general the police are fair in dealing with people?'; 86 per cent of the sample thought that the police were fair. Of the minority who dissented from this view, there were no significant differences between respondents by sex or area, although a slightly higher proportion of respondents in Brixton thought the police were unfair (17 per cent compared with 11 per cent in Hackney and 14 per cent in Kensington). There were, however, some differences in answers to this question by age, race and social class. For one thing, it was clearly the younger age groups who tended to say that they thought the police to be unfair; thus, 46 per cent of those who thought the police were 'generally unfair' were under 30, and only 13 per cent were in the 51-plus age groups. We also found that black respondents were more likely than whites to say that they thought the police were unfair. Over the whole sample, 26 per cent of blacks said that they thought the police were unfair, compared with 13 per cent of whites.[6] This finding was particularly marked in Brixton where 35 per cent of blacks thought the police were unfair compared with 13 per cent of whites in that area.[7]

Those respondents who said that they thought that the police were unfair in their dealings with people were then asked, 'In what ways are they unfair?'

We received an assortment of replies to this question, to the effect that the police were arbitrary or authoritarian, or that they favoured the rich, or that they were prejudiced against the young or blacks;[8] there was, however, no significant pattern of response to this question either between areas or different groups.

Respondents were then asked if they had ever been to a demonstration where the police had been present; if so, whether they had approved of the way in which the police behaved; if not, whether they approved of the way the police generally behaved at demonstrations. The responses to these questions showed interesting differences by area. Not many people in either Brixton or Hackney had ever attended a demonstration, and of those who had the majority said they approved of the action that the police had taken on that occasion. In Brixton, of those who had never attended a demonstration, 24 per cent of blacks, but only 5 per cent of whites said that they generally *disapproved* of police behaviour at demonstrations; since they were manifestly not based on personal experience these responses must be interpreted as expressing further 'anti-police' feeling owing to other reasons. In Hackney, comparatively few people had ever been present at a demonstration, but the vast majority said they approved of police behaviour at demonstrations. In Kensington, however, almost half of the sample said that they *had* been present at a demonstration (though in what capacity we do not know): the majority of these approved of police behaviour, as did the majority of those who had never been to a demonstration.

Respondents were then asked, 'Do you think that the police ever behave differently towards different kinds of demonstrators—for example, students, trade unionists?'—and 41 per cent of the total sample said that they thought the police did. This feeling was especially marked among the 21–30 age groups, where 63 per cent overall thought that the police behaved differently to different kinds of demonstrators. In addition, respondents in Brixton and Hackney who said that they thought that the police behaved differently tended to be from the higher social classes, suggesting (with the Kensington results) that those higher up the social scale tend to perceive more variation in police behaviour, or at least have a tendency to say this.[9]

We asked respondents when they last had contact with the police, and found that in Brixton and Hackney the majority of respondents' most recent contact had been more than six months previous to the time of the interview, while in Kensington a greater proportion of respondents had been in recent contact with the police—less than 6 months previously—than in the other two areas. In Brixton 12·5 per cent said that they had never had any contact with the police; in Hackney 15 per cent, and in Kensington 11·5 per cent gave this response. In Brixton 23 per cent of black respondents said that they had never been in contact with the police, compared with 11 per cent of whites; in Hackney there was no difference between blacks and whites on this point, though in Hackney those blacks who said that they had been in contact with the police had had more recent contact than the whites in that area. In all

Table V.7. Type of last police contact

Type of contact:	Brixton		Hackney		Kensington	
	No.	Percentage	No.	Percentage	No.	Percentage
Road accident	8	5·2	10	6·7	5	3·1
Respondent contacted police, non-criminal matter	26	17·0	20	13·3	50	31·4
Respondent contacted police, criminal matter	53	34·6	56	37·3	53	33·3
Police contacted respondent, non-criminal matter	11	7·2	13	8·7	9	5·7
Police contacted respondent, criminal matter (e.g. as witness)	22	14·4	22	14·7	23	14·5
Police arrested respondent	13	8·5	9	6·0	6	3·8
Police suspected respondent of crime	3	2·0	6	4·0	6	3·8
Other	17	11·1	14	9·2	7	4·4
Totals	153	100·0	150	100·0	159	100·0

three areas, a greater proportion of women than men claimed never to have had any contact with the police; and older people in all three areas claimed, predictably, not to have had any contact with the police for a long time. Perhaps surprisingly, we find that those higher up the social scale seem to have had more recent contact with the police than those in classes IV and V, and that respondents in the higher social classes are less likely to claim that they had no contact with the police; whether these are real differences, or the result of response bias, is not clear. In all three areas, the most common reason for the most recent police contact was that the respondent contacted the police concerning a crime of some sort. As we see from Table V.7, this was common to all three areas, although there was some variation between areas for other causes of contact with the police.

Respondents in Kensington were far more likely to have contacted the police about a non-criminal matter;[10] on the other hand, even when this is taken into account, they were less likely than respondents in either Brixton or Hackney to have been arrested[11] during their last contact with the police.

Apart from those who claimed never to have had any contact with the police, respondents were asked whether they were 'satisfied' with what the police had done on the occasion of their most recent police contact. The majority of respondents in all three areas claimed to have been satisfied with what the police had done, the greatest dissension being in Hackney where 20 per cent said that they were either 'not satisfied' or were 'very dissatisfied' (compared with 16 per cent in Brixton and 15 per cent in Kensington who gave these

Table V.8. Satisfaction with last police contact, and satisfaction with local police

Satisfaction with last police contact:		Satisfied with local police								
		Brixton			Hackney			Kensington		
		Yes	No	Total	Yes	No	Total	Yes	No	Total
Very satisfied	No.	31	7	38	32	5	37	29	5	34
	Percentages	81·6	18·4	100·0	86·5	13·5	100·0	85·3	14·7	100·0
Satisfied	No.	37	18	55	50	5	55	56	10	66
	Percentages	67·3	32·7	100·0	90·9	9·1	100·0	84·8	15·2	100·0
Not satisfied	No.	11	9	20	13	6	19	12	7	19
	Percentages	55·0	45·0	100·0	68·4	31·6	100·0	63·2	36·8	100·0
Very dissatisfied	No.	2	3	5	5	1	6	6	3	9
	Percentages	40·0	60·0	100·0	83·3	16·7	100·0	66·7	33·3	100·0

$$\chi^2 = 6\cdot63 \qquad \chi^2 = 5\cdot82 \qquad \chi^2 = 6\cdot03$$
$$df = 3 \qquad\qquad df = 3 \qquad\qquad df = 3$$
$$p < 0\cdot10 \qquad 0\cdot20 > p > 0\cdot10 \qquad 0\cdot20 > p > 0\cdot10$$

responses). In Brixton and Hackney this dissatisfaction was most keenly felt among younger respondents (those under 35), while in Kensington it was spread among both older and younger respondents.

If we relate our respondents' expressed feelings about their most recent police contacts with their other attitudes to the police, we find that in Brixton there is some evidence of an association between dissatisfaction with last police contact, and general dissatisfaction with the local police. As we see from Table V.8, the association is not as clear in Hackney and Kensington, but nevertheless a similar tendency can be detected in those areas.

It is not clear which is cause and which is effect here, even if we discount response bias toward 'consistency.' On the one hand, it may be that the expressed dissatisfaction with what the police did on the occasion of the respondents' most recent contact is merely a further indication of generally felt dissatisfaction with the police; alternatively, it may be that our respondents' views concerning their most recent contacts really influenced their answers to the more general question. Unfortunately we did not ask the reasons for our respondents' dissatisfaction on the occasion of the most recent incident. But in any case it would be necessary to have over-time data (e.g. from a panel study) to investigate this important question properly.

We have already seen[12] that self-reported criminality was related, in our sample, to a failure to report incidents involving alleged victimization to the police. There are also some interesting relationships which emerge from our data, between self-reported crime (of all types combined) and expressed attitudes to the police. To begin with, as Table V.9 shows, there is a significant tendency for those who admitted one or more offences to say that they had had some personal contact with the police; the number claiming never to have had such contact diminishes steadily as the number of offences admitted increases. There is, moreover, a slight but not consistent tendency for the last contact to have been more recent, the more self-reported offences were admitted.

Table V·9. Self-reported criminality and most recent contact with the police.[a]

Number of offences admitted:	Last police contact													Total	
	Within one month		1–3 months		3–6 months		6 months– 1 yr		1 yr or more		Never			Total	
	No.	Percentage	No.	Percentage	No.	Percentage	No.	Percentage	No.	Percentage	No.	Percentage	No.	Percentage	
None	21	10·6	18	9·0	15	7·5	14	7·0	88	44·2	43	21·6	199	100·0	
One	16	12·5	13	10·2	12	9·4	12	9·4	62	48·4	13	10·2	128	100·0	
Two	20	26·7	7	9·3	8	10·7	12	16·0	22	29·3	6	8·0	75	100·0	
Three or more	24	18·9	18	14·2	16	12·6	18	14·2	44	34·7	7	5·5	127	100·0	
Total	81	15·3	56	10·6	51	9·6	56	10·6	216	40·8	69	13·1	529	100·0	

(For the whole table, $\chi^2 = 46\cdot47$, df $= 15$, $p < 0\cdot001$; comparing those who said they had contact with those who said they had *never* had contact with the police, $\chi^2 = 21\cdot85$, df $= 3$, $p < 0\cdot001$)

[a] Excludes 14 cases not answering question about police contact, and two for whom self-report data not available.

We also found differences in the *nature* of last police contacts, of those who admitted committing offences and those who did not. For respondents who admitted having committed offences, the last contact with the police was more likely to have been an arrest than for those who said that they had never committed any offences; and as the number of offences admitted increases, so does the likelihood that the last contact would have been an arrest. Only 10 per cent of those who said they were arrested during the last contact with the police denied ever having committed any of the offences which we asked about. Moreover, as the number of offences admitted increases, so does the likelihood that the last police contact was police-initiated. We also found that the level of satisfaction with the last police contact is lower among those respondents who admitted criminality, and that expressed dissatisfaction increases with the number of offences committed. Satisfaction with the local police also decreases as admitted criminality increases, and the reasons given for such dissatisfaction also vary with criminality. General 'anti-police' statements were far more common among those respondents who admitted criminality—indeed, there were none among respondents who claimed never to have committed any offences—and the feeling that the police were incompetent was frequently expressed among those respondents who admitted criminality. There was a significant difference in attitudes to the job that the police do in general, between those respondents who denied committing any offences and those who admitted one or more offences; only 14 per cent of those who denied any criminality thought that the job the police did in general was only 'fair' or 'poor'. Again, general 'anti-police' statements were more commonly given by those admitting criminality as a reason for dissatisfaction with the police in general. Respondents who admitted criminality were less likely than those who did not, to say that the police would respond if called in an emergency; and they were also significantly more likely to think that the police were unfair in dealing with people (see Table V.10).

Table V.10. 'Are the police generally fair in their dealings with people?' by admitted criminality of respondents[a]

Number of offences said to have been Committed once or more than once:	Are the police generally fair?					
	Yes		No		Total	
	No.	Percentage	No.	Percentage	No.	Percentage
None	178	94·7	10	5·3	188	100·0
One	100	83·3	20	16·7	120	100·0
Two	62	79·5	16	20·5	78	100·0
Three	35	85·4	6	14·6	41	100·0
Four	26	76·5	8	23·5	34	100·0
Five	11	68·8	5	31·3	16	100·0
Six or more	33	82·5	7	17·5	40	100·0
Total	445	86·1	72	13·9	517	100·0

$$\chi^2 = 22.22, \text{df} = 6, p < 0.01$$

[a]Excludes 28 respondents for whom data on police fairness not available.

Among those respondents who admitted committing offences, the feeling that the police are not fair in dealing with people stems from a feeling that they are 'arbitrary' or 'authoritarian' in manner, more commonly than among those who denied criminality. These findings hold true for all categories of offence (i.e. property, public order and violence) although respondents who admitted committing offences in the violence category tended, if anything, to be slightly more critical of the police than in the other two categories.

In summary, then, we see that the great majority of our sample expressed a high degree of satisfaction both with the police in their own local areas and in general. There was a tendency for younger respondents and blacks (particularly in Brixton) to be more critical of the police, and to say that the police were not fair in dealing with people; and for those who admitted to having committed a number of crimes themselves to express disapproval of the police in different ways. There is also an indication that many people regret the tendency of the police to patrol in cars, and that they would prefer to see more men on the beat; this feeling was expressed even by people who generally approved of the job that the police do.

3. Victimization and Attitudes to the Police

The experience of victimization—regardless of whether or not the crime was reported—is associated to some extent, in our R sample, with expressed dissatisfaction with the local police (see Table V.11).

This finding is reinforced by responses to other questions about the police. Thus, those respondents who had been victims during the year were more likely than non-victims to think that the police in general did only a 'fair' or 'poor' job, and this tendency also increases as the number of incidents of victimization increases. Victims as a whole were also significantly more likely than non-victims to think that the police are unfair in their dealing with people (see Table V.12).

Table V.11. Satisfaction with local police, by number of incidents of victimization during the preceding year[a]

Number of incidents	Satisfied with local police		Dissatisfied with local police		Total	
	No.	Percentage	No.	Percentage	No.	Percentage
None	235	83·6	46	16·4	281	100·0
One	79	75·2	26	24·8	105	100·0
Two	37	69·8	16	30·2	53	100·0
Three	30	78·9	8	21·1	38	100·0
Four or more	22	71·0	9	29·0	31	100·0
Totals	403	79·3	105	20·7	508	100·0

$$\chi^2 = 8·49, df = 4, 0·10 > p > 0·05$$

[a]Excludes 37 respondents for whom data on satisfaction not available.

Table V.12. Are the police fair in their dealings with people, by number of incidents of victimization during the preceding year[a]

| | Are the police generally fair? | | | | | |
| | Yes | | No | | Total | |
Number of incidents:	No.	Percentage	No.	Percentage	No.	Percentage
None	256	91·1	25	8·9	281	100·0
One	90	79·6	23	20·4	113	100·0
Two	46	82·1	10	17·9	56	100·0
Three	30	78·9	8	21·1	38	100·0
Four or more	24	80·0	6	20·0	30	100·0
Totals	446	86·1	72	13·9	518	100·0

$$\chi^2 = 13{\cdot}10, df = 4, 0{\cdot}02 > p > 0{\cdot}01$$

[a]Excludes 27 cases for whom data on fairness not available.

Victims were more likely than non-victims to think that the police should be spending more time on (unspecified) 'serious' crimes, and they were also more likely to think that the police should spend more time on police-public relations. Finally, victims were less likely than non-victims to attribute a failure on the part of the police to do these things to a lack of resources, and more likely than non-victims to think that the police spent too much time on irrelevant matters.

The data—sketchy as they admittedly are—raise a number of interesting and important questions. It may, of course, be that our respondents' attitudes to the police, and their experiences of victimization, are wholly independent; or that they are both consequences of some other factor (such as the respondents' own criminality, which as we have seen was related to violent victimization[1] as well as to expressed dissatisfaction with the police). It does not seem wholly unreasonable to assume, however, that *one* response to the experience of being a victim of crime may be the feeling—whether justified or not—that the incident might never have occurred if the police had been doing a better job in terms of crime prevention.

It may also be that victims tended to feel dissatisfied, to some extent, as a result of the action that the police took when an incident was reported to them. To investigate this, we asked those victims who said they had notified the police, 'Were you satisfied with what the police did?' Just over three-fourths of the respondents who were asked this question gave an affirmative answer to it. Dissatisfaction was greatest in Hackney, where 30 per cent of those who reported the incident said they were *not* satisfied with what the police had done, compared with 24 per cent in Brixton and 20 per cent in Kensington. The main cause for complaint mentioned was a belief that the police had not taken the matter seriously; in some form or another, this response was given by 41 per cent of those who were dissatisfied. Seven per cent said that the police had not believed them, and the same proportion were dissatisfied because the police had not made an arrest or recovered stolen property; ten per cent gave other reasons. We are unable to say, of course, how far these statements were justified; at best they represent the respondents' retrospective perceptions, and they may have little or nothing to do with the objective facts concerning the actions taken by the police. Almost certainly they are based on very limited information about the action actually taken; and this itself was a substantial reason given for dissatisfaction with what the police had done. Of 131 respondents who said they had reported a crime, no less than 28 per cent said they were dissatisfied simply because they had not subsequently heard anything more from the police about the incident in question.[2] Only seven people claimed (rightly or wrongly) to know whether the offender had been prosecuted; only five said they knew whether he had been found guilty; and of these only three said they knew what sentences had been imposed on offenders found guilty.

Those victims who said they were dissatisfied with what the police had done about reported incidents were also more likely to express general dissatisfaction with the police, both in their local area and in general; they were more likely to make general 'anti-police' statements and to say that the police should pay more attention to crime; and they were *less* likely to say that the police would respond immediately if called in an emergency. Again, it is difficult to know what interpretation to put on these associations. It may be that the respondents' statements about the way in which the police dealt with their reported incidents merely reflect a desire to be consistent with their general attitudes to the police (which they had expressed much earlier in the interview); or it may be that those who felt dissatisfied with the police on other grounds were more likely to be critical of what was done about their particular incidents. It may also be, however, that to some extent the respondents' general attitudes to the police were adversely influenced by their perceptions of what the police did about their own particular incident.

This raises a further possibility, namely that a person who reports an incident to the police and is dissatisfied (for whatever reason) with what is done, may be less likely to report incidents which occur in the future. We examined, in chronological order, the incidents mentioned by those respondents who said they had been victims on more than one occasion during the year, to see if there was any evidence that this might have happened; unfortunately, the number of 'multiple victims' who had reported offences was too small to permit us to draw any conclusions one way or the other. In any case, however, a retrospective survey can provide only limited information on this point; as with many other questions raised by our inquiry, panel data would be needed to investigate the issue properly.

The implications of this possibility are considerable, however. Those persons who report crimes to the police seem more likely to be dissatisfied (rightly or wrongly) with what the police do, if the incident is not cleared up; and in most jurisdictions (including London) the great majority of offences against property are, of course, not cleared up. If this kind of dissatisfaction leads victims of crime to be less likely to report subsequent incidents, then the 'dark figure' of unrecorded crime will automatically increase. Conceivably this in turn could raise the 'clear-up' rate, not only by reducing the number of crimes known to the police but by giving them more time and manpower to investigate those crimes which were reported. But this might not, by itself, raise the level of reporting again, since those who (because of dissatisfaction over one incident) had decided not to report subsequent ones would have no direct way of finding out, through personal experience, of any increases in the efficiency of the police in detecting crime which might have occurred.

Notes and References

1. The Decision to Call the Police

1. For discussions of this problem see Roger Hood and Richard Sparks, *Key Issues in Criminology*, Chapters 1–2, especially 32–37; F. H. McClintock, 'The dark figure,' in 5 *Collected Studies in Criminological Research* (Strasbourg: Council of Europe, 1971).
2. This last factor is even more important, of course, in the case of those who see or hear what they believe amounts to a crime being committed against someone else. Cf. Bibb Latané and J. F. Darley, *The Unresponsive Bystander: Why Doesn't He Help?* (New York: Appleton-Century-Crofts, 1970), for a discussion of this problem, and experimental evidence on the situational determinants of 'helping' in such cases.
3. The *nature* of the benefits to be gained by calling the police will also vary, however: it may be, as we have already noted, that the victim does not in fact want the offender to be caught and prosecuted, but merely wants a particular ongoing dispute settled. See further below, pp. 158–159.
4. See above, pp. 74–75. In fact, for computational reasons, we only added data relating to a maximum of four incidents per respondent to the main data files in the computer; the fifth and subsequent incidents of the few respondents with more than four crime incident forms were analysed separately, by hand. It is also important to note that the 'first' incident associated with each multiple victim was not necessarily *chronologically* his first of the reference period. Where necessary, however,—see above, pp. 96–97— we carried out a separate analysis of these respondents' incidents, in which the incidents were examined in chronological order.
5. These hypothetical situations are described, and our findings more fully discussed in Chapter VII: below, pp. 169–180.
6. Since in the sample as a whole, the numbers expressing more approval of the violence were very small, another possible explanation of the difference in reporting behaviour may be that those generally concordant with what they saw as their neighbours' views felt better integrated with their neighbours and society, and thus, more likely to call in the police when things happened to them. This possibility receives no support from any of our other data, however: for example, neither Srole's anomia scale, nor any of the questions which we asked our respondents about their attitudes to their local neighbourhood, were associated in any statistically significant or meaningful way with reporting behaviour.
7. See Philip H. Ennis, *Field Surveys II* at 42–43; cf. Biderman in *Field Surveys I* at 151–53; and see also *Criminal Victimization in Maricopa County* at 47.
8. Paul Davidson Reynolds *et al.*, *Victimization in a Metropolitan Region: Comparison of a Central City Area and a Suburban Community*. VI-13.
9. See the National Crime Panel report, *Criminal Victimization in the Nation's Five*

Largest Cities, at 27, 36, 40, 61–67; U.S. Department of Justice, Law Enforcement Assistance Administration, National Criminal Justice Information and Statistics Service, *Criminal Victimization Surveys in Thirteen American Cities*, Table 6 for each city; and for an analysis of U.S. national panel data see Wesley G. Skogan, 'Citizen reporting of crime: some national panel data,' (1976) 13 *Criminology* 535.

10. Reynolds, *Victimization in a Metropolitan Region* VI 13.

11. The same result emerges from the National Crime Panel surveys: cf. the references cited in note 9. In those surveys, moreover, there have been no consistent or significant differences in reporting of offences between blacks and whites, or males and females; the only demographic variable which has been found to be related to reporting is age, with victims aged 12–19 (a group not included in our sample) being much *less* likely to have notified the police.

12. By the Mann–Whitney U test, $p < 0.01$; $N = 129$ and 291 respectively.

13. A large number of stepwise regression analyses were carried out in an effort to predict reporting (either of 'first' incidents or of the percentage reported), using various combinations of variables relating to both respondents and to incidents. In none of these, however, were we able to obtain multiple regression coefficients of more than 0.36 (equivalent to explaining about 13 per cent of the variance in reporting behavior). Combining seriousness scores, the somewhat mysterious attitudinal variable derived from our hypothetical situations involving violence, and the index of self-reported violent crime gave a multiple R of 0.32 (with 'first' incidents).

14. Below, Chapter VII, pp. 181–190.

15. A hierarchical log–linear analysis of the in Table V.2 showed no evidence of three-factor (or higher) interactions; the model described in the text (associations between social class, objective and subjective value and reporting) gave a good fit ($\chi^2 = 10.28$, $G^2 = 11.33$, df $= 10$, $p = 0.42$), and deleting any one those effects reduced the goodness of fit though not by much. For this type of analysis, invented by Leo Goodman, see Yvonne M. Bishop, S. E. Fienberg and Paul W. Holland, *Discrete Multivariate Analysis* (Cambridge, Massachusetts: M.I.T. Press, 1974); an excellent discussion is J. A. Davis, 'Hierarchical models for significance tests in multivariate contingency tables: an exegesis of Goodman's recent papers,' *Sociological Methodology 1975* (San Francisco, Jossey-Bass, 1976) 189–231. The computing method we used is described in Shelby Haberman, *The Analysis of Frequency Data* (Chicago: University of Chicago Press, 1974) Chapter 3.

16. Those who said they did not notify the police were asked if they had taken any other action; 70 per cent said no. But about 13 per cent said that they had told some other official (e.g. a caretaker in a block of flats) about the incident; an equal number of incidents had allegedly been dealt with by some form of self-help.

17. This question also could not be probed as fully as it should have been; in particular, we only got the *first* reason mentioned, though there is, of course, no reason to suppose that the decision to report was influenced by one factor only.

2. Attitudes to the Police

1. For example, a white male aged 22 in Hackney gave this response: 'I know a lot who are bent and take bribes'; and in Kensington a white female aged 40 thought that 'they are power mad maniacs—they victimize people.'

2. This response in Kensington may well be a result of the very large number of foreign legations in that area, which generally have policemen on duty outside the buildings.

3. Cf. the Royal Commission on the Police, *Final Report*. Cmnd. 1728 of 1964 (London: H.M.S.O.' 1964); Maureen Cain, *Society and the Policeman's Role* (London: Routledge, 1974) at 241–246.

4. Our respondents' perceptions of the levels of crime in their neighbourhoods, and

their expressed fears of crime, are dealt with at length in Chapter VIII below, pp. 204–210.

5. These responses reflect the general concerns about the types of local crime most prevalent in neighbourhood areas, which we discuss in more detail in Chapter VIII below, pp. 204–205.

6. It must be remembered that our sample did not contain any respondents under 18, and in particular included no black adolescents; almost all of the immigrants in the sample were first-generation immigrants. It is quite likely that if the younger members of the immigrant community—whose problems concerning schools, employment and crime are generally agreed to be considerable, especially in areas such as Brixton— had been included, we would have had a rather less favourable picture of attitudes to the police.

7. It must be pointed out, however, that this expressed animosity to the police in Brixton was not necessarily directed toward the police from that local station. Immediately before, and during, our fieldwork a special force (known as the Special Patrol Group) had been operating in the Brixton area. This force, which operates under the central control of New Scotland Yard, is primarily used to carry out 'saturation policing' of different areas in the Metropolitan Police District where particular crime problems are thought to be present. In Brixton it had been alleged by a local community newspaper (whether rightly or wrongly) that the S.P.G. had been involved in the eviction of squatters and the harrassment of some of the West Indian community; these allegations had been fairly widely publicized, and may have affected some of our respondents' answers to our questions.

8. Of the 10 respondents who gave 'colour prejudice' as their answer, six were middle-class women from Kensington, and none was from Brixton.

9. Of those respondents who said that they thought the police did behave differently to certain kinds of demonstrators, 28 per cent thought they behaved differently to students, 15 per cent thought they behaved differently to immigrants and 13 per cent thought they behaved differently towards people who 'provoked' them; only 5 per cent of the sample thought that the police behaved differently towards trade unionists, and 4 per cent thought that 'radical leftwingers' received different treatment. Black respondents were more likely than whites to think that the police behaved differently to different kinds of demonstrators, and although the number was small they were also more likely to mention immigrants as a group which received different treatment at demonstrations. These findings, however, should be treated with extreme caution since the wording of this question might well have had the effect of 'leading' respondents. In retrospect, we feel that the question invited a positive response from respondents and also planted the idea that there were certain identifiable groups which might be treated differently by the police. It is quite possible that had we not given the examples in the question our responses would have been very different.

10. Again, we cannot rule out the possibility of response bias here: our Kensington respondents (who were mainly middle-class) may simply have remembered, and mentioned, contacts not involving crime which respondents in the other two areas failed to mention. To some extent, however, our findings here probably reflect real differences between social classes in the nature of contacts with the police. If anything, our data probably understate the extent to which contacts between the police and the public involve non-criminal matters; several American studies suggest that these contacts are by far more numerous than those involving complaints of crime, and the same is probably true in England. Cf. E. Cumming, I. Cumming and L. Edell, 'The policeman as philosopher, guide and friend,' (1964) 12 *Social Problems* 276–86; J. P. Martin and Gail Wilson, *The Police: A Study in Manpower* (London: Heinemann, 1969), at 155–159: Maureen Cain, *Society and the Policeman's Role* at 36, 54–60.

11. We do not know, of course, how many of those who said they had been 'arrested' had really experienced an arrest in the strict legal sense of that term; they might merely have been contacted by the police about a crime and then given a summons, or asked

to 'help with enquiries.' But even in its popular sense, the term 'arrest' connotes being charged with or accused of a crime; and it is in this sense that these responses should probably therefore be understood.
12. Above, pp. 118–119.

3. Victimization and Attitudes to the Police

1. See above, Chapter IV, pp. 102–103.
2. This appears to be one of those games which the police cannot win. We were informed by senior officers in the Metropolitan Police that until a few years ago it was standard practice for an officer to call back on persons who had reported crimes even if the offender had not been apprehended, in order to let them know that the matter was still being investigated. Shortage of manpower led to this practice being abandoned; but it also seems to have been counterproductive public-relationswise, since the victims not infrequently complained that the police ought to be getting on with the job rather than wasting time telling them that no progress had been made.

CHAPTER VI

Estimating the Incidence and Prevalence of Crime

1. Problems of Comparing Police and Survey Data

Surveys of criminal victimization were originally conceived of as providing an alternative to police statistics as a measure of crime rates.[1] Since victim surveys obtain information about crime directly from members of the public, they hold the promise of measuring not only the 'dark figure' of crime which is never reported to the police, but of overcoming well-known problems associated with the recording by police of crimes which are reported to them. The amount of error introduced into police figures by under-reporting—and, at least in some jurisdictions, by police recording practices—is widely (and probably rightly) believed to be very great; thus victim surveys, whatever their limitations, have seemed to many criminologists likely to provide a more accurate picture of the amount of crime actually committed in the community. The fact that most of the victim surveys carried out to date have produced evidence of much greater volumes of crime than corresponding police statistics seems to have been taken to show the survey's method superiority—and, by implication, to confirm the belief that police statistics are of little value for measuring anything—except perhaps, the working of the processes by which the statistics themselves are produced.

Making an accurate and realistic comparison of survey data and police statistics of crime, however, is a fairly complicated matter; this is especially true if the comparison is intended to throw any light on the processes by which the official statistics of crime are constructed. It is, of course, possible to estimate population crime rates from sample survey data, and to compare those rates with rates based on the total numbers of crimes recorded in the police statistics. Numerous adjustments to both survey data and police statistics are needed, however, if accurate comparisons between the two are to be made. These adjustments are especially important when considering surveys carried out in relatively small urban areas (like the London police subdivisions in the present study). In this section, we describe the main problems involved in such adjustments, and in making realistic comparisons of survey rates and police statistics.[2]

(a) Crimes against Individual Victims. Our victim survey questionnaire asked about only (some of) those events which involved crimes against individual victims in their personal capacities; we did not attempt to measure crimes committed against business or other organizations, and we excluded any incidents reported to us in which it appeared that the respondent himself was not, legally speaking, the victim. Police statistics, on the other hand, do include crimes committed against organizations. In addition, of course, the police statistics include some crimes which are 'victimless'—such as handling stolen property and possessing drugs—and some crimes in which there is not necessarily a personal victim, such as dangerous driving and certain conspiracies; these offences obviously cannot be reported by respondents in a survey of individuals. The police statistics of known crime must accordingly be deflated[3] by removing crimes against businesses, and victimless crimes, from their totals. Fortunately, the statistics collected by the Metropolitan Police[4] make it possible to do this fairly accurately, for certain types of crime. The police statistics for burglaries, for example, distinguish between residential and non-residential buildings; among thefts, shoplifting and thefts by employees are also shown separately, as are such 'victimless' crimes as handling stolen property and unlawful possession. Sexual offences and fraud, which we did not specifically ask our respondents about, are also shown separately.[5] Thus, a proper comparison with our data would only include, in the police statistics, the recorded numbers of burglaries in dwellings; woundings, assaults and other offences against the person; and thefts from the person and from dwellings. There is a fairly large category of miscellaneous thefts, however, including robberies, thefts of and from motor vehicles, and unauthorized taking of vehicles, for which we cannot be so confident that the victims are persons rather than organizations. In the absence of hard data on this subject for our areas, we have deflated the police statistics of known crimes for these categories by five per cent, to allow conservatively for recorded crimes where the victim was not an individual person. The net result of this set of adjustments is to reduce the statistics of recorded crimes in 1972 by about a third in Brixton and Hackney, and nearly 40 per cent in Kensington.

(b) Indictable versus Non-indictable Crimes. A somewhat different adjustment is needed to take account of the fact that the Metropolitan Police statistics of crime known do not, in general, include non-indictable offences (that is, those not triable by a jury). This is also true for the statistics published annually by the Home Office, for all police forces in England and Wales: these statistics only include the number of *persons prosecuted* for non-indictable offences, which is, of course, much smaller than the number of *offences* recorded. Fortunately, it is clear that many of the property offences reported by our sample would probably (if reported to the police) have been regarded by them as indictable ones: this seems likely to be true for all of the burglaries, and most of the thefts. But assaults are another matter: many of the ones mentioned by our sample, would probably have been treated as merely non-indictable, if

indeed they had been regarded as crimes at all.[6] We cannot, of course, make any kind of precise adjustment to allow for this; as a rough approximation, however, we have deflated our survey data by removing 90 per cent of the cases which involved only threatened or attempted assault: this reduces the survey rates by about 11 per cent overall (slightly more in Kensington, slightly less in Hackney) As a result of the Criminal Damage Act 1971, many offences of damage which were previously non-indictable became indictable for the first time; but the police still do not record as 'crimes known' offences of damage where the property is worth less than £20.[7] We must thus remove over half of the offences of damage reported by our sample, as they would not have been included in the police statistics. This entails a further reduction of about 7 per cent overall in the total number of incidents reported by our sample. Finally, the Theft Act 1968 made many offences of 'taking and driving away a motor vehicle' (which had previously been non-indictable) into indictable offences of theft or unauthorized taking of motor vehicles, which means that they were included in the police figures for 1972.[8]

(c) Classification of Incidents. A much more difficult problem arises with respect to the classification of our sample incidents by type of crime. As we have already noted[9] our own classification of the incidents (on the basis of information in the crime incident forms) differed in some cases from that suggested by the original responses to the screening questions. But we have no way of knowing how the police would have classified those incidents if they had been reported to them, or how they tended to classify similar incidents which were reported to them and recorded in 1972. It may well be, for example, that some 'walk-in thefts' in dwellings (i.e. those where there was no evidence of breaking into the premises[10]) are recorded as burglaries in Brixton or Hackney, but would be recorded as thefts in dwelling houses in Kensington; this at any rate is our impression from studying crime reports for the three areas.[11] Again, the borderline between robbery and theft from the person is inherently a fuzzy one, especially where purse-snatchings are concerned; and the borderlines dividing assault from attempted robbery, indecent assault and disorderly conduct are similarly imprecise.

It was not practicable for us to follow up those incidents which our R sample respondents said they reported to the police in order to see how the incidents were recorded (or if they were recorded at all), and to compare the police classification with our own. We have, however, been able to carry out a similar exercise using the 'target' incidents reported to the police by our MV and T samples.[12] For these cases, we had the police classification (from crime reports); we also had the respondents' statements as recorded by interviewers on the survey crime incident forms, for the 214 cases for which these had been completed. Accordingly, we gave copies of the crime incident forms for these cases to a law student, and asked him to say in each case what crimes, if any, had been committed in each case, assuming the facts given by the respondents to be correct.[13] We then compared his classification with that contained in the

Table VI.1. Comparison of researcher's and police classification of MV and T sample 'target' incidents[a]

Researcher's Classification:	Police Classification						
	Assault, Wound-ing	Robbery	Burglary	Theft of M/V	Damage	Other Theft	Total
Assault, Wounding	31	1	1	—	1	—	34
Robbery	—	12	—	—	—	4	16
Burglary	—	—	92	—	2	4	98
Theft M/V	—	—	—	25	—	1	26
Damage	—	—	2	—	6	—	8
Other theft	—	—	—	1	—	31	32
Total	31	13	95	26	9	40	214

[a]Based on crime incident forms, excluding cases (mostly in the T sample) where the incident was reported as *not* having happened in 1972; crime incident forms were not completed in those cases.

police report (which he had not seen); the results of this comparison are shown in Table VI.1.

It will be seen from this table that our law student assistant classified the incidents, on the basis of the description in the crime incident forms, in the same way as the police did in the crime reports, for the majority of cases;[14] the two classifications are concordant in 85 per cent of the 214 cases. But there are distinct variations by type of offence; a quarter of the crimes classified by our assistant as robberies or damage to property, and a tenth of those he classified as assaults, were recorded in a different category by the police. To some extent these differences may reflect differences in the facts as stated to the police officer filing the crime report. Moreover, the categories in Table VI.1. are obviously broad ones, and any attempt to make a finer analysis leads immediately to a much greater rate of discordant classification. A classification of crimes of personal violence as common assault, assault occasioning actual bodily harm,[15] malicious wounding[16] or felonious wounding[17] was concordant in only 32 per cent of the cases. In most of the cases where there was a difference, it arose because the police had prosecuted for a lesser offence than our law student assistant thought was disclosed by the statement of facts; indeed, a third of the discrepant assault and wounding cases were ones in which the offence had been written off (for statistical purposes) as 'no crime' by the police, usually because the complainant was unwilling to prosecute. These were almost invariably family disputes.

There is another reason why the broad classifications used in Table VI.1. disguise the extent to which there may be disagreement in classification of offences if finer classifications are used. Our law student assistant found that even on the very brief statements of facts contained in the crime incident forms, it was usually possible to conclude that more than one offence appeared to have been committed: this was so in 75 per cent of the cases, the mean number of offences being 2·4 per incident form. For example, an offence recorded by the police as a burglary might also involve theft, criminal damage, forcible entry and (if more than one offender was thought to be involved) conspiracy to trespass. Again, a robbery might also involve an assault and carrying an offensive weapon. Usually it was clear, in our sample of incidents, what would probably be regarded as the 'principal offence' by the police, both for statistical purposes and in prosecuting: but there is obviously still much room for differences in classification, given the number of possible headings under which the case could be recorded. Moreover, there were many cases in which either of two alternative charges—e.g. theft of a motor vehicle, and unlawful taking of a motor vehicle—could have been recorded; the only remedy for this situation is to combine such categories, when comparing police and survey statistics.

For estimation purposes, a further adjustment to our survey data which might appear to be necessary would be a deflation to exclude that proportion of assaults arising from family disputes and the like, which might be treated as 'no crime' if they had been reported to the police (e.g. because of the victim's unwillingness to testify). Since many such cases are at least initially recorded as crimes, however, and since we have no clear criterion (other than relationship between victim and offender) for identifying cases unlikely to be recorded, we have not made such an adjustment. We have, however, excluded just over fifteen per cent of those incidents of assault, theft and damage which were mentioned in response to screening questions but for which crime incident forms were not completed. This is somewhat higher than the proportion of incidents for which we did have crime incident forms, in which we judged that no crime had been committed.[18]

(d) Residents Victimized Elsewhere. In Chapter IV, when discussing our respondents' experiences as victims of crime, we included all of the incidents which they reported to our interviewers, regardless of where the incidents took place. But for the purpose of comparing survey data with police statistics, we must exclude from our sample of incidents those which took place outside the area, which would not have been recorded in the police statistics in the respondent's area of residence if they had been reported to the police. This problem does not arise, of course, for burglaries and thefts from dwelling houses, but it entails that we must deflate our survey estimates for all other types of crime, in particular for assaults, robbery and theft from the person. It appears (from our crime incident forms) that no less than 15 per cent of these offences occurred outside the respondents' areas of residence— in a very few cases, the incidents were said to have happened outside England. Similarly, we estimate that about a quarter of the thefts of and from motor vehicles, and about 10 per cent of other thefts, occurred outside the respondents' home areas (i.e. the police subdivisional areas). It appeared that there was some overlap between these 'out of area' cases and the incidents previously excluded as probably non-indictable or non-recordable (for example, because they only

involved the threat of assault); making allowance for this, we deflated our survey estimates for assault, robbery and theft from the person by another 10 per cent, and the figures for motor vehicle thefts and other thefts by 20 and five per cent respectively. This resulted in a further deflation of the survey estimates by approximately 10 per cent overall; again the effect is greatest in Kensington.

(e) Non-residents Victimized in Area. The converse of the last adjustment involves a deflation of the police statistics in order to exclude those cases involving persons who were not residents of the area but who were victims of assaults or thefts which they reported to the police in the area.[19] Unfortunately, we do not know exactly what proportions of the crimes recorded in our three survey areas in 1972 involved non-residents; the best estimates we can make are 10 per cent in Brixton and Hackney, and at least 17 per cent in Kensington.[20] These estimates are supported to some extent by the 1971 Census data, which show that non-resident visitors to the area made up about 15 per cent of the total enumerated population in Kensington, compared with only 1 per cent in Hackney and $1\frac{1}{2}$ per cent in Brixton. Making this adjustment, then, involves a further deflation of the police statistics of about 6 per cent over the three areas taken together.

Both this adjustment and the preceding one, of course, become less important the larger the areas surveyed: in the case of a national sample, it would only be necessary to adjust for survey-reported crimes committed against respondents when out of the country, and for recorded crimes committed against foreign visitors. In our sample, the number of reported incidents which occurred outside Greater London appears to be extremely small; except in areas like Kensington, with high tourist populations, the number of recorded crimes against non-Londoners is probably also fairly small.

(f) Response Bias. The number of incidents reported by our R sample is no doubt influenced to some extent both by non-recall or non-reporting of things which happened to them in 1972, and by the telescoping forward into the survey reference period of some things which actually happened to them in the preceding year. It will be recalled[21] that in analysing the reporting of incidents by our MV sample we found that about 8 per cent of the 'target' crimes were not reported to our interviewers; and that among incidents which were reported, in the MV, T and R samples, there was evidence of a rather greater amount of forward telescoping. Given the relatively less serious nature of the R sample's reported incidents, it is reasonable to assume that recall losses in that sample were greater than in the MV sample; if so, then the losses from non-recall and the gains from forward telescoping should approximately balance out. This, at any rate, is the assumption we have made. But it must be remembered that even if the total *number* of incidents is unaffected by the net effects of non-recall and forward telescoping, the *pattern* of victimization

probably will not be. More salient events (such as burglary) are probably more likely to be remembered and telescoped forward, and thus over-estimated; less salient ones (like minor theft and assault) are probably under-estimated.

(g) Excluding Recorded Offences Against Persons Under 18. Oue sample excluded persons under 18; but the police statistics include crimes committed against persons under that age, and must accordingly be deflated in order to make our data comparable in this respect. Unfortunately, we have no information of any kind on the number of crimes which would need to be excluded on this account. Presumable the number is negligible in the case of burglary; but we do not feel that we can make this assumption in the case of any other type of offence included in our survey. Accordingly, we have deflated the police statistics for all offences other than burglary by 5 per cent, taking into account the probability of some overlap between recorded crimes excluded on this account and those excluded because they were committed against non-residents.

(h) Persons Not on the the Electoral Register. In all three of our survey areas, but probably especially in Kensington, the indictable offences recorded by the police include some crimes committed against residents over 18 who are not on the electoral register, which, therefore, could not have been reported to our interviewers. Strictly speaking, these cases should be excluded. But we only have data (from the 1971 Census) on the total resident populations of our areas; we do not know the proportions of registered electors in each area. We have, therefore, not deflated the police figures. This amounts to assuming that the experience of victimization among non-electors is the same as that of electors (as estimated from our sample); and in view of the negative association which we found between length of residence and reported incidents, this assumption is undoubtedly a conservative one, especially in relation to Kensington.

(i) In-migration and Out-migration. A further adjustment to the population base used in computing estimated survey rates is strictly speaking necessary, in order to take account of persons who migrated into and out of our survey areas during the year. We saw in Chapter IV[22] that persons who said they had resided at their survey addresses for less than a year reported more incidents than those who had been resident for a year or more. In addition, however, including such persons in the population base (i.e. the denominator used in calculating rates from survey data) will lead to a biased estimate, unless a correction is made to allow for the fact that they were at risk for less than a year. The adjustment involves either increasing the estimated numbers of offences reported by this group, or decreasing the population base; algebraically, of course, the two procedures come to exactly the same thing. An adjustment must be made in the opposite direction, however, for persons who migrated out of our survey areas during the year 1972 (and who thus were not at risk of being included in the police statistics for the entire year). Each of these

adjustment involves more complications than are warranted by our data; we have chosen to assume, therefore, that the effects of in-migration and out-migration effectively cancelled each other out, in our areas in 1972.

(j) Household Offences and Multiple Victims. A final adjustment to the survey data is needed in order to take account of those offences in which more than one adult resident in the area was involved as a victim. Offences such as burglary, which may be regarded as being committed against the entire house-hold, clearly fall into this category. Asked, 'Did anyone break into *your* house in the past year?' any member of the household—including, for example, a child over 18 still living at home—would almost certainly have answered 'yes.' A burglary of a household containing three adults would thus have three chances of being included in our sample, compared with one chance for a burglary of a single-person household. Offences of damage to the fabric of the house must be treated in the same way. It is less easy to decide what other offences would be likely to be regarded by all household members as having been committed against them. Theft of the family car, however, is probably in this category. Though our interviewers asked if the respondents themselves owned a car—and if so, whether it was stolen—we know that in some cases wives answered 'yes' to these questions even though the car was in fact owned by their husband. A similar adjustment must be made in these cases. A close approximation to the necessary adjustment here involves dividing the numbers of incidents involving burglary, car theft, and damage to the house, which were reported by respondents in households containing more than one adult, by the average number of persons over 18 residing in those households. In our sample, this figure for the sample as a whole is 2·74 for burglary (27 incidents); 3·42 for car theft (9 incidents) and 2·72 for damage to the dwelling house (12 incidents); there are slight differences between the areas. The net result of the adjustment is to reduce the numbers of incidents reported by the sample by about 5 per cent in Brixton, 3 per cent in Hackney and 7 per cent in Kensington.

Thefts of property other than cars—even motorbikes and motor scooters—can probably be regarded as 'individual' offences. But the same problem of adjustment could have arisen with a few of the assaults included in our sample, in which more than one adult resident of the area—e.g. a husband and wife—got attacked; such incidents might have been reported by any of those involved in them, and to that extent are over-represented. In fact, as it happens, our data—from the crime incident forms—suggest that this happened in only a few cases; most of these would have been excluded on other grounds, such as having taken place outside the survey area or involving threats of violence only. Accordingly, we have not made any adjustment to the numbers of assaults reported by our sample.

The net result of all of these adjustments is to deflate considerably both the numbers of incidents reported by our sample, and the numbers included in the police statistics. (The effects of the adjustments on the totals for each area are summarized in Table VI.2.) After making the adjustments, we are left

Table VI.2. Summary of adjustments to police statistics and survey data, in the three survey areas

Police Statistics	Brixton	Hackney	Kensington
Total indictable offences recorded:	5,858	2,837	8,041
Deduct:			
Crimes not against individual victims:[a]	− 1,885	− 931	− 3,101
Estimated crimes against non-residents:[b]	− 274	− 130	− 378
Estimate for victims under 18 (net):[c]	− 112	− 59	− 92
Remainder:	3,587	1,717	4,469

Survey data (from screening questions)			
Total incidents reported:	206	153	223
Deduct:			
Estimated non-indictable assaults reported:[d]	− 22	− 14	− 27
Estimated 'non-crimes':[e]	− 8	− 6	− 9
Estimated damage < £20:	− 15	− 20	− 3
Estimated incidents not in area (net):[f]	− 18	− 10	− 20
Adjustment for offences against households of more than one person:[g]	− 10	− 5	− 14
Remainder:	133	98	150

Notes:
[a]Burglary in non-residential buildings, going equipped to steal, theft from meters and machines, shoplifting, theft by employees, other thefts in non-residential buildings, handling stolen goods, fraud, and 5 per cent of all other offences.
[b]10 per cent of assaults and thefts in Brixton and Hackney, 17 per cent in Kensington.
[c]5 per cent of all offences except burglary and theft in dwellings.
[d]90 per cent of all threatened or attempted assaults reported.
[e]Fifteen per cent of survey-reported assaults, theft and damage offences for which crime incident forms were not obtained.
[f]10 per cent of reported robbery, assault and theft from the person; 20 per cent of thefts of and from motor vehicles; 5 per cent of other thefts.
[g]Burglaries, damage to house and car thefts reported by households containing more than one person, divided by average numbers of persons 18 and over in those households.

with an estimate of the numbers of crimes committed against the population from which our sample was drawn. These figures obviously do not represent the total experience of criminal victimization in our sample; nor do they represent the total volume of crime in the three survey areas, or the workload of the police. They do provide a basis for estimating the 'dark figure' of unrecorded crime in the three areas, at least so far as that figure involves crimes (of the kinds about which we asked) committed against adult registered electors. To this comparison we now turn.

2. Estimates of Crime in the Three Areas

The adjustments to our survey data carried out in the last section provide the numerator for calculating victimization rates for our sample; these rates can then be applied to the resident adult populations of the three areas[1] in order to produce an estimate of the total volume of crime of the kinds included in our survey, which in turn can be compared with the numbers of similar kinds of crimes recorded in the police statistics. But before doing this, a *caveat* is in order concerning the probable precision of our sample estimates.

Table VI.3 gives the original (i.e., unadjusted) sample means, and the associated standard errors and 95 per cent confidence intervals,[2] for broad groups of offences in each of our three survey areas. It will be seen that these sample means, though generally fairly large relative to their standard errors, are nonetheless subject (like any such sample estimates) to a certain amount of variability owing to sampling fluctuations; at the 95 per cent level of confidence, the unadjusted mean number of offences per person, for the populations of the three areas combined, could be as high as 1·25 or as low as 0·89. Unfortunately, we cannot calculate standard errors for the adjusted survey data, that is, after deflating the data to take account of non-indictable offences, offences out of the area, and so forth. This is so because the adjustments could not always be made by excluding specific incidents mentioned in response to the screening questions; our information on where the incident took place and the value of property involved came from the crime incident forms, which as we have pointed out do not exactly tally on a one-to-one basis with the responses to the screening questions. For this reason, we do not know the true variances of the adjusted distributions. The most reasonable assumption we can make

Table VI.3. Unadjusted sample means and 95 per cent confidence intervals, for reported incidents in the three survey areas

| | Brixton | | Hackney | | Kensington | |
	Sample mean	1·96 ± S.E.	Sample mean	1·96 ± S.E.	Sample mean	1·96 ± S.E.
Assaults and	0·220	± 0·132	0·162	± 0·068	0·201	± 0·104
Thefts from person	0·088	± 0·060	0·073	± 0·041	0·082	± 0·040
Burglary	0·060	± 0·035	0·112	± 0·060	0·158	± 0·076
Theft in dwellings	0·071	± 0·089	0·039	± 0·036	0·065	± 0·047
Thefts of and from motor vehicles	0·214	± 0·124	0·128	± 0·058	0·196	± 0·072
Other thefts	0·352	± 0·151	0·184	± 0·089	0·462	± 0·221
Damage to property	0·129	± 0·063	0·156	± 0·118	0·049	± 0·040
All incidents	1·132	± 0·338	0·855	± 0·211	1·212	± 0·358

in the circumstances is that the adjustments do not alter the shapes of the distributions, so that they reduce the sample variances by amounts which are proportionate to the reductions in the sample means. But since the standard error of the mean is proportionate to the square root of the variance, rather than to the variance itself, our adjustments do not lead even on this assumption to the same reductions in the standard errors. The result is that the confidence intervals for population estimates based on the adjusted data are probably even wider than Table VI.3 indicates, and must accordingly be treated with considerable caution.[3] Even using unadjusted data, the confidence intervals for certain subgroups of offences in particular areas are fairly large, and our estimates correspondingly become dangerously susceptible to sampling fluctuations; for example, in the case of actual assaults (as distinct from threatened or attempted assault) the mean for the Kensington sample is 0·038, which is less than 1·96 times the associated standard error of 0·032.

With that warning, we present in Table VI.4 a comparison of the survey-estimated numbers of crimes in each of the three areas, and the (adjusted) numbers of crimes of the same kinds recorded by the police in each area in 1972. The table also gives the ratio of the survey estimates to the adjusted numbers recorded by the police. It will be seen from this table that for every type of crime, in all three areas, the numbers estimated on the basis of our survey data are very substantially in excess of the numbers recorded by the police: for all types of offences in the table, and for all three areas combined, the ratio of survey-estimated to recorded crime is no less than 11·1 to 1. The ratio is less in the case of burglaries—for the sample as a whole, it is 4·2 to 1—but in the case of offences against the person (assaults, robbery and theft

Table VI.4. Comparison of survey-estimated crimes in 1972, and adjusted numbers of crimes recorded by police, in three areas[a]

	Brixton			Hackney			Kensington		
	Survey	Police	Ratio	Survey	Police	Ratio	Survey	Police	Ratio
Assaults, robbery and theft from person	8,700	509	17·2	5,900	188	31·3	4,900	164	29·9
Burglary, theft in dwellings	6,000	1,224	4·9	6,100	611	10·1	7,215	2,800	2·6
Thefts of and from motor vehicles	9,400	1,222	7·7	4,600	720	6·4	5,400	964	5·6
Other thefts	18,800	468	40·2	7,200	135	53·1	19,800	347	57.2
Other crimes (including damage of £20 and over)	1,700	164	10·3	1,300	63	20·3	1,300	177	7·3
Totals	44,700	3,587	12·5	25,100	1,717	14.6	38,700	4,469	8·6
Estimated population aged 18 +	61,176			45,848			47,415		

[a]Survey estimates rounded to nearest hundred; ratios calculated before rounding.

from the person combined), and of other thefts, the disparity between the two sets of figures is enormous by any criterion (about 22:1 and 48:1 respectively). In other words, if our survey-based estimates are accepted as showing the amounts of indictable crime against individual victims in the three areas in 1972, then less than *one-tenth* of those crimes covered by our survey which could have been recorded in the police statistics in our areas in 1972 were actually recorded there. For offences against the person and miscellaneous thefts, the proportion is only about two to four per cent. Even for burglary and thefts in dwelling houses, the figure is only about 24 per cent.

At first sight, this may seem wildly implausible: can it really be that the volume of indictable crime against individuals in these three areas was over eleven times greater than the police statistics suggest? We think, however, that if anything, our findings understate the true position. In every case, the adjustments which we made to our own data, and to the police statistics, were conservative ones; in the case of the survey data, they resulted in a reduction of the numbers of crime reported by our sample of over 35 per cent. The majority of the assaults not excluded were ones which involved the actual use of violence, and not merely the threat of it; and in excluding offences of damage involving less than £20 we have if anything erred on the high side, since we are bearing in mind that such incidents are under-represented in the cases for which we have crime incident forms. Similarly, our adjustments to the police statistics are if anything conservative; for example, we did not deflate the recorded statistics of burglaries or thefts in dwellings, though many of these (especially in Kensington) may have involved non-residents or persons under eighteen. The allowance made in Kensington for non-residents, and the corresponding population base used for estimating rates from survey data in that area, are also likely to understate the ratios between survey-estimated and recorded crime rates.[4]

Given the magnitude of the differences between our survey estimates and the police figures, moreover, it should be clear that only the most drastic of adjustments—for which we have absolutely no justification—would be able to bring the two sets of figures even approximately into line. Even if we were to assume, for example, that owing to sampling fluctuations our survey-estimated rates are at the lower limit of the 95 per cent confidence interval, the ratio of survey estimated to recorded crime is still nearly 9 to 1; and the opposite assumption of the upper limit (which is equally defensible) yields a ratio of over 14 to 1.

Even allowing for considerable error and imprecision in our estimates, then, it is clear that the differences between the survey-estimated amounts of crime in the three areas, and the comparable police statistics, are of a very substantial magnitude; if anything, they are even greater than the overall ratio of 11·1 to 1 which Table VI.4 suggests. In our view, this is only to be expected. The two sets of figures are, after all, representative of different things: more precisely, they represent the outcomes of entirely different stages of the processes involved in the construction of criminal statistics. What our survey estimates reflect, however imperfectly, is the volume of certain kinds of acts perceived as having been committed against residents of our three survey areas in 1972, which *could have been* recorded in the statistics *if* they had been reported to the police, re-defined by them as crimes, and written down. As we shall see in the next sections, there is evidence—from a number of victim surveys—that both non-reporting *to* the police and non-recording *by* the police have an important part to play in producing the differences between survey estimates and police statistics.

Two further points should be made, however, before we turn to the issue of explaining the differences between survey-estimated and recorded crime. The first is that, in contrast to some American studies,[5] there is no more than a moderate agreement in our study in the rank orders of survey and police figures. Even when there is some agreement at a rank-order level, the relative magnitudes involved are generally very different, and the patterns of crime against individuals in the three areas look very different if one considers survey data rather than police statistics. Percentage distributions of the survey and police figures for the three areas are given in Table VI.5. It will be seen that, for instance, burglary and thefts involving motor vehicles together account for over two-thirds of the police-recorded crime against individual residents in Brixton, and over three-fourths in Hackney; yet in each area those two offences account for only 35 to 40 per cent of the adjusted numbers reported in the survey. Similarly, in Kensington burglary and thefts involving vehicles account for over 80 per cent of recorded crimes; but they account for only about a third of the survey reported incidents.

The second point relates to the consequences of a very large 'dark figure' of unrecorded crime, such as that shown by our findings in this section, for the interpretation of official crime statistics. If our findings are even approximately correct—and we have argued that they are, if anything, an understatement of the difference between survey-estimated and recorded crime—then for many types of crime, only a very small fraction of the incidents which occur

Table VI.5. Percentage distributions of survey estimates and recorded crime, in three areas

| | Brixton | | Hackney | | Kensington | |
	Survey	Police	Survey	Police	Survey	Police
Assaults, robbery and theft/person	19·5	14·2	23·5	10·9	12·7	3·0
Burglary, theft in dwellings	13·5	34·1	24·5	35·6	18·7	63·0
Thefts of and from motor vehicles	21·1	34·1	18·4	41·9	14·0	21·6
Other thefts	42·1	13·0	28·6	7·9	51·3	7·8
Other offences	3·8	4·6	5·1	3·7	3·3	4·0
Totals	100·0	100·0	100·0	100·0	100·0	100·0

in any year will find their way into the official statistics. It follows that those statistics are extremely susceptible to the effects of small changes in the proportions of incidents perceived, defined as crime, reported to the police and recorded. Even in the case of burglary and thefts in dwelling houses, where the ratio of survey to police estimates suggests that the 'dark figure' in our three survey areas is relatively low, it still appears that only about one offence in five is recorded. Thus, a 5 per cent increase in the *proportion* recorded would by itself result in over a 20 per cent increase in the *numbers* recorded, which is more than enough to give the impression of a 'crime wave'. In the case of assaults and other thefts, the effect would be even more drastic: on our findings, a 5 per cent increase in the proportion of such offences recorded would at least treble their numbers in the police statistics, even if the total volume of offences actually committed remained unchanged.[6]

3. Reporting and Recording of Crime Incidents

It will be recalled from the preceding chapter that in each case where a crime incident form was completed, respondents were asked if the incident had been reported to the police. There are several problems involved in applying this information to the estimates made in this chapter. For one thing, we must make allowance for the fact that we do not have crime incident forms for all of the offences mentioned in response to the screening questions, and that the ones which we do have are in some cases classified slightly differently. For another, we can make only very approximate adjustments in our data on the reporting of crime incidents to take account of the adjustments made to the screening question responses (e.g. to exclude offences of damage to property worth under £20, and cases involving only threatened assault). This is, however, the only information which we have on this question; and in this section we shall use it, therefore, to make a tentative investigation of non-reporting as a source of the 'dark figure' of unrecorded crime in our three survey areas.

Overall, in just over 30 per cent of the cases for which we have crime incident forms the respondent stated that the police had been notified about the offence; the proportion was slightly higher in Kensington and slightly lower in Brixton, but the differences are not statistically significant.[2] As we saw in the last chapter, completed crimes were more likely to have been reported than attempts; assaults which were said to involve physical injury were more likely to have been reported than those which did not; and for property offences the proportions reported generally increased with the reported value of the property involved. Making the best allowance we can for these and other factors—e.g. the location of the offence—we estimate that the police might have been notified in about 30 per cent of the assaults and thefts from the person which occurred in our three areas combined; about half of the burglaries and thefts in dwellings; about 35 per cent of the thefts of and from motor vehicles; less than 20 per cent of the other thefts; and about 30 per cent of the other offences (including damage of over £20). There is, however, some evidence of variation between areas, by type of offence. For all types combined, we estimate that the percentages reported to the police are probably of the order of 34 in Brixton and Hackney, and 40 in Kensington.

It should be emphasized—in case anyone is in any doubt about the matter—that these estimates are only very approximate ones. We feel that, if anything, they err on the low side (that is, that they exaggerate the relative contribution of non-reporting to the police, to the total volume of unrecorded crime); but there is really no way of estimating the margin of error which they may contain. For what they are worth, however, we can apply these rates to the survey-estimated total of crimes against individual resident victims, as given in the last section; the result is a rough estimate of the number of the cases in which (according to our sample's responses) the police were in some way or another notified about what they—the respondents—considered to be something worth calling the police about. That is, they give a rough indication of the extent to which the gap disclosed in the last section, between our survey estimates and the numbers recorded by the police, is due to the fact that the victims of those crimes did not report the matter to the police. The remaining share of the 'dark figure'—that is, the difference between the survey estimated numbers of incidents reported to the police, and the numbers recorded by them—can then be taken as an indication of the relative importance of (1) re-definition of a reported situation by the police as one not involving a (re-cordable) crime; together with (2) the non-recording, for whatever reason, of those incidents which have been defined by the police as involving (re-cordable) crimes.

The results of this analysis are shown in Table VI.6. The rows of this table show—as percentages of the survey-estimated totals for each of five categories of crime, in each area—the estimated numbers reported and the numbers recorded; and the numbers recorded as percentages of the estimated numbers reported. The first two columns can be thought of as giving estimates of the conditional probabilities that an incident defined by a would-be victim as a crime 'survives' the successive stages of reporting and recording; the third column, which is the product of the first two, gives the (unconditional) pro-bability of the incident reaching the statistics. It will be seen that, in the three areas combined, about 35 per cent of the survey-estimated crime appeared to have been reported to the police; but that of these apparently reported incidents, only about a third appear to have been recorded in the police statistics. To put the matter the other way around: of every eight crimes which we estimate were committed against residents in the three areas, it appears that about five were *not* reported to the police; of those which apparently were reported, about two-thirds did not get into the police statistics. The table suggests that *non-reporting* was highest for thefts and other offences (including damage), and lowest for burglary and thefts in dwellings; and that *non-recording* of reported incidents was highest in the category of assaults and thefts from the person, and lowest for burglaries and thefts from dwellings.[3]

Though little emphasis should be put on the absolute magnitudes involved,

Table VI.6. Estimated numbers of incidents reported to police, and recorded crimes, as percentages of survey-estimated totals; and recorded crimes as percentages of estimated numbers reported, in the three London areas

Area and type of crime:	Percent estimated reported to police	Recorded as percent of estimated reported	Recorded as percent of estimated total
Brixton			
Assault, theft/person	30	17	5
Burglary, theft/dwelling	38	48	18
Thefts of and from MV	45	28	12
Other thefts	20	42	8
Other	25	49	12
Total, all types	34	31	11
Hackney			
Assault, theft/person	33	9	3
Burglary, theft/dwelling	55	17	10
Theft of and from MV	30	49	15
Other thefts	15	44	7
Other	25	18	4
Total, all types	35	22	8
Kensington			
Assault, theft/person	25	12	3
Burglary, theft/dwelling	60	55	33
Theft of and from MV	35	43	15
Other thefts	30	24	7
Other	40	69	27
Total, all types	40	43	17

it also seems clear from Table VI.6 that there are differences between our three survey areas in the relative contributions of non-reporting and non-recording. Thus, our data suggest that the proportion of incidents reported to the police by victims is lowest in Brixton, and highest in Kensington; the proportion of reported incidents which become recorded as crimes also appears to be highest in Kensington, but appears substantially lower in Hackney than in Brixton. As we have already seen, this means that the police statistics present different patterns of crime in the three areas, from those which emerge from our survey estimates. It also means, however, that the relative *rates* of crime also differ. Thus, according to our survey estimates, Brixton and Kensington appear to have about the same overall crime rates (within the categories included in the survey); but owing to the higher proportions of survey-estimated incidents which are apparently reported and recorded in Kensington, the *recorded* crime rate in Brixton is only about three-fifths of that found in Kensington. In the case of Hackney, the survey-estimated rate is about five-sixths that for Kensington; but the *recorded* crime rate in Hackney is even lower, being only about four-tenths that of Kensington.[4]

4. On Explaining the 'Dark Figure'

The finding that non-reporting by victims does not by itself explain the whole volume of unrecorded crime also emerges clearly from victim surveys done in the United States.[1] Several of those studies also reveal differences—like those suggested by Table VI.6—in the relative contributions of non-reporting and non-recording for different types of offence. In the U.S. national survey conducted by NORC, for example, it appeared that non-reporting by victims accounted for almost all of the difference between survey estimates and police statistics for robbery; for forcible rape, however, non-recording of reported incidents seemed to have been the more important factor.[2]

It is important to emphasize that the evidence from these surveys—like ours—is entirely indirect and inferential. We did not, of course, directly investigate the treatment by the police of incidents reported to them; because of sampling considerations, a victim survey is an inefficient method of carrying out that type of investigation. Since findings like those reported in the preceding section are likely to emerge from any victim survey, however, and since those findings raise some important methodological points about this kind of research, a brief discussion is in order.

It is often alleged that the 'readjustment' by the police of crime statistics, for organizational or political ends, is widespread; and there are certainly well-documented cases in the United States in which this appears to have happened.[3]

Such practices are no doubt less common in England, owing to the greater degree of standardization which governs the recording of offences. This is not to say that they are non-existent; in particular, given the still widespread but wholly misleading interpretation of the 'clear-up' rates as an index of police efficiency, it would be surprising indeed if the British police, like their counterparts all over the world, did not occasionally find it convenient to refrain from recording offences which have little apparent likelihood of ever being cleared up.[4]

But is it important to emphasize that there may be many good reasons why an incident reported to the police, which is alleged to involve a crime, may not be recorded as a crime in those police statistics which are ultimately published.[5] To begin with, the incident may not in fact involve any kind of crime; it may be nothing more than a civil wrong or a bit of immoral behaviour which the 'victim' wrongly assumes that the police are empowered to deal with. Second, it may be that the incident, though one which apparently involves a crime, is one for which the available evidence is minimal or non-existent; as we have already noted,[6] some things which were reported to our interviewers as burglaries or thefts in dwellings, but which did not involve clear evidence of 'breaking' or trespassory entry, may well come into this category. Or again, it may be that the investigating officer does not believe the complainant's story, or that he uncovers other evidence supporting quite a different version of the facts—which, if accepted, would entail that no crime had in fact been committed.

Third, it may be that the incident is satisfactorily resolved by the policeman answering the call, and that prosecution (and recording of the incident as a crime, for statistical purposes) would be pointless; many cases involving assaults between family members or neighbours, or landlords and tenants, must surely fall into this category. As we have already noted, it may well be that when calling the police in such an incident, the 'victim' did not really want the matter to lead to prosecution (and *a fortiori* did not care about its being recorded in police statistics of crime), but merely wanted the dispute settled on the spot.[7]

Fourth, and perhaps most important, it may be that after having reported an offence to the police, the injured party will subsequently ask to have the charge dropped—or will refuse to give evidence against the offender, so that there would be no chance of a successful prosecution. In such a case, the incident may in the first instance have been treated as a crime, and a crime report completed by the officer dealing with the case; subsequently, however, the incident would have been written off as 'no crime', and would not have been included in the published statistics.[8] This kind of situation is apparently not at all uncommon, especially where domestic or other 'non-stranger' assaults are concerned. We were informed, in fact, that of all crimes initially recorded in our three survey areas, 'no crime' cases accounted for about 28 per cent in Brixton, 28 per cent in Hackney, and 18 per cent in Kensington.[9]

Finally, even if an incident is accepted as one involving a crime, recorded on a crime report and not subsequently written off as 'no crime,' it may nonetheless be of a kind which is not meant to be included in the published statistics of 'crimes known' (according to the rules which govern the preparation of those statistics). Examples (in England) would be thefts of property valued at less than £5, non-indictable crimes generally, and assaults contrary to s. 42 of the Offences Against the Person Act 1861.[10] Similar limitations, of course, relate to the collection of other 'official' statistics of crime, e.g. the *Uniform Crime Reports* in the United States.[11]

Too little is known about the nature of the complex transactions which may take place between members of the public and the police when an apparent offence is reported. But Black has argued, on the basis of an observational study of such transactions in three American cities, that complainants' attitudes are a strong determinant of the use by the police of discretion to prosecute: in particular, if a complainant in his study did not want the matter pursued, the police did not pursue it.[12] It is also likely that police officers' practice in this respect is influenced to some extent by their perceptions of the expectations of the local community; almost certainly, therefore, their handling of reported incidents will vary, according to cultural differences in that community. The treatment of reported incidents in a largely middle-class area like Kensington

160

may well differ for this reason from the treatment of comparable incidents in a mainly lower-class area like Hackney, or in certain parts of Brixton: the 'no crime' percentages just quoted certainly suggest that this is so.

Further research on these matters is badly needed in England, not so much for the light it would throw on police record-keeping practices, as for an understanding of the decision-making processes involved in the handling of crime incidents by both the police and the public.[13] The findings discussed in this chapter certainly suggest, however imprecisely, that there is plenty of scope for such research. They also emphasize the importance of interpreting official criminal statistics as the outcome of a series of social processes and organizational activities; and the extreme dangers of uncritically assuming that the statistics automatically reflect—even approximately—the amounts and types of criminal behaviour which do in fact take place.[14]

Notes and References

1. Problems of Comparing Police and Survey Data

1. Cf. Philip H. Ennis in *Field Surveys II* at 2; Inkeri Anttila, 'The criminological significance of unregistered criminality.' (1964) 4 *Excerpta Criminologica* 413–14.
2. For thoroughgoing analyses of analogous problems in relation to the President's Commission surveys, and police statistics in the United States, see A. J. Reiss, Jr., in *Field Surveys III* (1) at 153–171; A. D. Biderman in *Field Surveys I* at 63–100; Albert D. Biderman and Albert J. Reiss, Jr., 'On exploring the "dark figure" of crime.' (1967) *Ann. Am. Acad. of Polit. and Soc. Sci.* 1. In a national survey, such as the NORC survey done for the President's Commission or the ongoing LEAA-Census surveys, many of the problems discussed in this section are mitigated. But substantial adjustments to both police and survey data are still needed: see, for example, the discussion by Philip H. Ennis in *Field Surveys II* at 85–95. Considering that comparison with police statistics provided much of the animus of the LEAA-Census surveys, it is ironic that reports from those surveys to date carry a sort of government health warning to the effect that such comparisons are inappropriate because of 'substantial differences in coverage between the survey and police statistics': see, for example, *Criminal Victimization in the United States, 1973 Advance Report* (May 1975) at vi.
3. Throughout this chapter we shall use the terms 'inflation' and 'deflation' to refer to increases and decreases, respectively, of either police or survey data in order to make them more truly comparable.
4. It must be pointed out that the published statistics of crime in London—governed by Home Office instructions which are intended to be followed by all police forces in England and Wales, and not just the Metropolitan Police—are not necessarily identical with what is recorded operationally and collated internally by the police themselves. The unpublished statistics made available to us for the purposes of our research also differ in some respects from those published by the Home Office: see, in particular, note 8 on p. 161 below. We are grateful to Deputy Assistant Commissioner H. D. Walton and Mr. T. C. Jones of the Metropolitan Police, for much information on this and other points.
5. Though it may well be that some of the assaults reported by our R sample would have been recorded by the police as sexual offences, and that some of the thefts would have been recorded as frauds. The inaccuracy introduced on this account is probably negligible.

6. In particular, some assaults are treated (for statistical purposes) as 'no crime' because the complainant is unwilling to give evidence: see above, pp. 159–160. In other cases, however, the assault may be regarded as coming under s.42 of the Offences Against the Person Act 1861: Home Office instructions say that such cases *must not* be counted in the statistical returns of 'crimes known.'

7. Again, data on offences of damage to property worth less than £20 are collected by the police; but the figures were not included in the statistics made available to us, nor are they now included in published statistics.

8. We had expected that we would have to make another adjustment, owing to a change in police recording practice introduced at the beginning of 1972: Home Office instructions provide that thefts (other than motor vehicle thefts) of property worth less than £5 in value are no longer recorded as 'crimes known.' At a national level, this change resulted in a substantial amount of phony decriminalization, since there were no less than 328,257 such offences known to the police in England and Wales in 1972; including those offences in the published statistics for that year would have raised the number of 'crimes known' by about 24 per cent. But we learned that thefts worth less than £5 had *not* been excluded from the Metropolitan Police statistics which we used; thus, a deflation of our survey estimates—which would have involved removing about two-thirds of all thefts reported by our R sample—was not necessary.

9. Above, p. 75.

10. Since the Theft Act 1968, 'breaking' is no longer an element of burglary, which merely requires trespassory entry. The distinction is still retained for statistical purposes, however.

11. The difference in recording practice, if indeed there is one, may owe to the existence in Kensington (but not the other two areas) of large numbers of rooming houses; the trespassory entry needed for burglary would often be difficult to prove in cases of theft from rooms in such premises.

12. Above, Chapter III, pp. 52–54.

13. We are grateful to Mr. Philip Dann for his assistance with this part of the research.

14. For a similar result, see the U.S. Department of Justice, LEAA report on the *San Jose Methods Test of Known Crime Victims*, at 9–11, 13.

15. Offences Against the Person Act 1861, s. 47.

16. Offences Against the Person Act 1861, s. 20

17. Offences Against the Person Act 1861, s. 18.

18. See above, p. 106.

19. The practice in such cases is for the crime to be written off in the sub-division of residence as 'No Crime,' and for a report to be entered in the sub-division in which the offence occurred, and where the investigation of it will usually be centred.

20. These estimates are based mainly on the numbers of crime reports which we had to exclude when selecting the 'target' incidents for our MV and T samples; in the case of Kensington—where the number of tourist victims is naturally high—we feel that the figure of 17 per cent is probably extremely conservative. Sellin and Wolfgang cite a Dutch study carried out some years ago, of resident and non-resident *offenders* found guilty of crimes in Amsterdam, and residents of Amsterdam found guilty of offences elsewhere: briefly, this study suggested that about 92 per cent of all offences against the person in Amsterdam in the years considered (1923–27) were committed by residents, and that 92 per cent of offences against the person by residents were committed in that city; and that resident offenders committed 87 per cent of their property offences in the city, and 84 per cent of the city's property offences were committed by residents. See the discussion in T. Sellin and M. E. Wolfgang, *The Measurement of Delinquency* (New York: John Wiley and Sons, 1964) 52–54.

21. See above, Chapter III, pp. 54–57.

22. Above, p. 86.

2. Estimates of Crime in the Three Areas

1. In each area, the populations used are the numbers of opersons aged 18 and over who are ordinarily residents in the area, as enumerated in the 1971 Census. Gross figures for each of the police sub-divisional areas were obtained by aggregating the numbers for all of the enumeration districts in each area. As explained in the last section, we are forced to make the assumption (which is probably conservative) that our estimates based on a sample of registered electors are also applicable to adult residents of the three areas who are not on the electoral register. Furthermore, in assuming that in-migration and out-migration during 1972 effectively cancelled each other out, we have neglected the slight decline in population which probably took place during 1972 in Inner London as a whole (at least if recent experience is any guide); this, too, makes our survey-estimated crime rates conservative. Against this, we have made no allowance for possible under-enumeration in the Census data; for certain groups—for example, immigrants in Brixton and Hackney, and some of the transient population in Kensington—this might be as much as 5 per cent, thus leading to a slight inflation of estimated crime rates. Since we are mainly interested in comparing two different rates (based on survey data and police statistics respectively), rather than in absolute magnitudes, and since the population base used in calculating the two rates is the same, these errors do not matter; they are probably very small in any case.

2. In these calculations respondents in each area have been treated as comprising an independent simple random sample; the standard errors have accordingly been calculated by the formula $\sqrt{(\hat{\sigma}^2/N)}$; and the 95 per cent confidence intervals are given by ± 1.96 times the standard error. These intervals give the limits within which—with a 95 per cent probability—the population means probably lie.

3. There is some reason to think, in fact, that our assumption here may be a conservative one: our data suggest that many of the cases removed in the course of our adjustments were reported by 'multiple victims' (including those victims of so-called 'series' offences, especially of damage and petty theft and assault, for which precise details could not be recalled). To the extent that this were true, the proportionate reduction in the sample variances would be greater than the proportionate reduction in the means, and we could place correspondingly narrower confidence intervals around our estimates (subject to the statistical point made in the text).

    We must also warn the reader again that victimization *rates*, like those discussed in this chapter, are a very misleading indicator of the *risk* of victimization in the population, owing to the phenomenon of 'multiple victimization' (see above, Chapter IV, pp. 88–96): a relatively small proportion of the population accounts for a much higher-than-average amount of victimization in a given time period, whereas the majority are not victimized at all. It is precisely this variability which accounts, of course, for the relatively large unadjusted standard errors shown in Table VI.3: at least as much as the relative rarity of criminal victimization, it means that very large samples are needed for this kind of survey.

4. The figure of 17 per cent for crimes recorded involving 'non-residents' was based on cases where the crime reports involved a person with an address elsewhere in London, or one staying at what we knew to be a non-residential hotel. But—especially in the Earl's Court area—there are many such hotels and lodging houses which have ordinary addresses, and are not *called* hotels; persons in that type of accommodation would have appeared to us to be residents. The population figures for the three areas are based on the enumerated populations aged 18 and over, less the estimated number of persons aged 18 and over who on Census night were visitors not resident in the local authority area (which means deducting tourists and others in hotels of the type just mentioned): in Kensington this means a reduction of 12·9 per cent. In any case, as we pointed out in the preceding section, the assumption that the experience of crime of tourists (and others in the Kensington area who do not live there, for example, people

dining or shopping there) is the same as that of residents, is almost certainly a very conservative one.

5. See, for example, Philip H. Ennis in *Field Surveys II* at 8–9.

6. It must be remembered that the official *Criminal Statistics* do not now clearly distinguish between different degrees of seriousness (in terms of harm, injury or property loss) in respect of indictable offences known to the police. In particular, in the category of 'violence against the person' the large group of offences designated 'other wounding, etc.' (Home Office classification number 8) includes assaults occasioning actual bodily harm (contrary to s.47 of the Offences Against the Person Act 1861). This group of crimes accounted for most of the indictable offences of violence, and had the highest rate of increase in the decade 1955–1965: see F. H. McClintock and N. H. Avison, *Crime in England and Wales*, (London: Heinemann, 1968) 38. In English law, however, 'actual bodily harm' need not be at all serious; it has been said judicially that it 'includes any hurt or injury calculated to interfere with the health or comfort of the prosecutor.' (*R.v.Miller* [1954] 2 Q.B. 282, *per* Lynskey J. at 292, quoting a statement formerly contained in *Archbold*.) There is, thus, considerable scope for including in this category of 'indictable offences known to the police' very trivial crimes of assault like many of those reported by our sample. It will also be remembered that our analysis of MV target incidents suggested that many of the assaults in that sample apparently could, on the facts stated in the crime reports, have been classified as woundings (see above, pp. 52–53). The heterogeneity of many existing categories in the *Criminal Statistics* was recognized by the Departmental Committee on the Criminal Statistics, in its report (Cmnd. 3448 of 1967), paras. 37, 128–129.

3. Reporting and Recording of Crime Incidents

1. A separate but related point is that because of 'multiple victimization' (discussed in Chapter IV, pp. 88–96 above), a relatively small proportion of the sample provides a large share of the information on crime incidents, including information on reporting. In particular, it will be recalled that in the case of 'series' victimization (where the respondent claimed to have been a victim on many occasions but could not or would not give details of individual incidents), the screening response was coded as a maximum of 9; on balance, we feel that the resulting totals are almost certainly an underestimate. But the pattern of reporting to the police might conceivably have been different, if victimization had been more evenly spread among our respondents: unpublished data from the LEAA-Census surveys in the U.S. suggest that 'series' victimization is less likely to be reported to the police than individual (or individually remembered) incidents of the same type.

2. It is important to note that in about a third of these cases it was stated that someone other than the respondent (e.g. a neighbour or another family member) had notified the police. In a very small number of cases it was said that the offence had not been reported because the police themselves had discovered it, or had been called by someone else and were already there when the respondent discovered the crime. Cases in which an apparent offence comes to the notice of the police because of their own patrolling or crime-prevention activities ought strictly speaking to be excluded from an analysis of reporting since to include them exaggerates the proportion of apparent offences which are reported to the police by victims or other persons; we have not excluded them, since in the cases for which we have crime reports their number appears to be fairly small. In each of our areas, however, there had from time to time been some special crime squads composed of constables and sergeants drawn from the uniform branch, whose job it was to patrol the streets of the area in plain clothes in order to try to detect housebreaking, shoplifting, thefts from motor vehicles and the like; this is in any case the usual work of temporary (i.e. probationary) detective

constables in the Metropolitan Police. Data from several American studies, however, suggest that such 'police-detected' offences are more common with less serious types of time, in particular 'victimless' ones. See, for example, Donald J. Black, 'Production of crime rates.' (1970) 35 *Am. Sociol. Rev.* 733, at 736; Donald J. Black and Albert J. Reiss, Jr., 'Police control of juveniles.' (1970) 35 *Am. Sociol Rev.* 36, at 55; Thorsten Sellin and Marvin E. Wolfgang, *The Measurement of Delinquency*, Chapter II; Jerome H. Skolnick, *Justice Without Trial* (New York: John Wiley & Sons, 1966), Chapters 6–8 *passim*. In two of our three areas—as in the rest of the M.P.D., and indeed most urban police forces everywhere—the majority of *arrests* for indictable offences are made by uniform officers, rather than the C.I.D.; in 1972, according to the police statistics, the proportions were 59 per cent in B Division (which includes Kensington), 53 per cent in L Division (Brixton), and 48 per cent in G Division (Hackney). Cf. Maureen Cain, *Society and the Policeman's Role* (London: Routledge, 1973) 68; similar data for Washington, D. C. are presented in A. J. Reiss, Jr., *The Police and the Public* (New Haven, Connecticut: Yale University Press, 1971) 110. It is probable, however, that most of these arrests result from calls to the police by victims, rather than from discovery of incidents while patrolling.

3. However, even in the case of burglary, for which our data are probably best, the discrepancy between survey-estimated crime and the amount recorded in the police statistics cannot be entirely explained by non-reporting by victims. It will be recalled that we made no adjustments to the police data for this offence, and we adjusted our survey data only to take into account households with more than one person; moreover, it is likely (except perhaps in Kensington) that the classification of the incidents was more reliable than for other types. (Crime incident forms were available for the great majority of incidents of this kind mentioned.) The percentages allegedly reported to the police were 45 per cent in Brixton, 70 per cent in Hackney and 73 per cent in Kensington; comparison of the resulting estimates with the numbers actually recorded in each area suggests that the proportion of reported incidents which reached the statistics were only 55 per cent in Brixton, 15 per cent in Hackney and 28 per cent in Kensington. For Kensington, the survey-estimated number of burglaries reported to the police is twice the number of recorded burglaries and thefts from dwelling houses combined. One clue to the difference may lie in the fact that in about a third of the incidents which we classified as burglary, no property was said to have been taken; in the M.P.D. as a whole, the proportion is less than 10 per cent. We are grateful to Mr. T. C. Jones for this information.

4. For a similar finding in three police districts in Washington, D. C. see Albert D. Biderman, *Field Surveys I* at 96–100.

4. On Explaining the 'Dark Figure'

1. See Philip H. Ennis, *Field Surveys II* at 7–13; A. J. Reiss, Jr., in *Field Surveys III* (1) at 159–71; A. D. Biderman in *Field Surveys I* at 109–113; Paul Davidson Reynolds *et al.*, *Victimization in a Metropolitan Region: Comparison of a Central City Area and a Suburban Community*. Chapter IV. In the 26 city-level surveys so far conducted as part of the LEAA-Census programme, there is a striking degree of similarity in the proportions of incidents of any given type which are said to have been reported to the police; but there are wide variations between several of those cities in crime rates calculated from police data in the *Uniform Crime Reports*, which cannot be explained by corresponding differences in survey-estimated crime rates. (Unpublished data show, for example, that in the case of aggravated assault, the correlation between survey-estimated and police-recorded rates is *minus* 0.61). Many things clearly may enter into the explanation of these discrepancies; but variations in reporting by victims to the police does not seem to be one of them.

2. Philip H. Ennis, *Field Surveys II* at 8, 12 (comparison of Tables 1 and 4).

3. For example, until 1949 the police in Chicago (population about three million) recorded several times as many robberies as the police in New York (population about 7½ million); in 1949 the Federal Bureau of Investigation stopped publishing the New York figures because it no longer believed them. In 1950 New York changed its reporting system; recorded robberies rose by 400 per cent and recorded burglaries by 1,300 per cent. Development of the Uniform Crime Reporting system in the United States has led to many such paper increases in recorded crime. In part, however, changes in recording systems have also been a concomitant of increased professionalism among American police forces. See, for example, the discussion in *The Challenge of Crime in a Free Society*, the report of the President's Commission on Law Enforcement and Administration of Justice (Washington, D.C.: U.S. Government Printing Office, 1967) 25–27. See also David Seidman and M. Couzens, 'Getting the crime rate down: political pressures and crime reporting.' (1974) 8 *Law and Society Review* 457.

4. For example, in a study of thefts from gas and electricity pre-payment meters in England, Hotson compared the numbers of such thefts known to gas and electricity boards, and estimates of the numbers they reported to the police, with the numbers recorded in the statistics: he found that only about a third of the offences committed had been reported, and that of the reported ones, only about half had been recorded. Hotson—who was a Detective Superintendent in the Mid-Anglia Constabulary—comments that 'A lot of this kind of "hidden crime," it seems, can be found in the police station.' B. E. Hotson, *Thefts from pre-payment meters* (Cambridge: Institute of Criminology, 1968 (mimeo.)) 9. The 'clear-up' rate is a misleading indicator of efficiency, since it does not in general reflect either the amount or the nature of the work which may go into clearing up crimes. In fact, a substantial proportion of those recorded crimes which are cleared up become cleared through being admitted by an offender who has been arrested and charged with *another* offence, and 'taken into consideration': see, for example, F. H. McClintock and N. H. Avison, *Crime in England and Wales* (Chapter 4, esp. 104); Maureen Cain, *Society and the Policeman's Role* 52–53; and cf. J. H. Skolnick, *Justice Without Trial*, Chapter 8.

5. As distinct from statistics kept internally for operational purposes: it is probable that in most police forces incidents reported to the police will find their way into some sort of operational records, e.g. of telephone calls. Of the incidents which were said by our sample to have been reported to the police, 57 per cent were said to have been reported either in person or by telephone to the local station; only about 10 per cent were said to have been reported by '999' calls, and only two cases were reported to constables on the beat or in cars. This does not suggest that the police were often called while the incident was, so to speak, still in progress. But the 'local station' category may include some incidents which were in fact '999' calls, since these would have been dealt with by officers from the local station.

6. Above, p. 164.

7. Above, pp. 120–121. Especially in poorer urban areas, police officers often find themselves called in to referee such disputes, and in some places they not unreasonably come to regard with suspicion certain sorts of complaints which are made to them; many such 'calls for help', if not downright malicious, are merely the latest manifestations of long-standing neighbourhood grievances. See the discussion in Jonathan Rubinstein, *City Police* (New York: Farrar, Strauss and Giroux, 1973).

8. It will be recalled that in selecting the 'target' crimes for our MVT sample (above, at p. 70) we included a number of assaults of this kind; statements on the crime reports, and the information which we received from the victims, left us in no doubt that in such cases a crime (sometimes an indictable crime) had in fact occurred. In those circumstances it may at first sight seem paradoxical to find the incident written off as 'No crime—common assault only.' But this merely means: No crime *for statistical purposes*; the victim or complaint is still free to pursue the matter in the courts by means of a summons, if he (or, more likely, she) wishes to do so.

166

9. Information supplied by Mr. T. C. Jones, Statistical Advisor to the Metropolitan Police.
10. Above, p. 161.
11. See, for a discussion of U.C.R. reporting and recording procedures, *Crime and its Impact—an Assessment*, Task Force Report of the President's Commission on Law Enforcement and Administration (Washington, D.C.: U.S. Government Printing Office, 1967) Appendix E.
12. Donald J. Black, 'Production of Crime rates,' at 738–40. See also, A. J. Reiss, Jr., *The Police and the Public* at 72–83; cf. J. Rubinstein, *City Police* at 204, 325–327.
13. For a valuable discussion of variations of 'styles of policing' in an urban and a rural force in England, see Maureen Cain, *Society and the Policeman's Role*, especially Chapters 3, 4, 6, 7; and cf. John R. Lambert, *Crime, Police and Race Relations* (London: Oxford University Press for the Institute of Race Relations, 1970) Chapters 4, 5; and Michael Banton, *The Policeman in the Community* (London: Tavistock, 1964) Chapters 4–5. The American literature on this subject is by comparison vast: for an overview see Hood and Sparks, *Key Issues in Criminology* at 70–78, and references there cited.
14. Cf. Stanton Wheeler, 'Criminal statistics; a reformulation of the problem'. (1967) 58 *Journal of Criminal Law, Criminology and Police Science* 317; John I. Kitsuse and Aaron Cicourel, 'A note on the uses of official statistics'. (1963) 11 *Social Problems* 131. It is not necessary to assume, however—as Kitsuse and Cicourel seem to do—that the statistics of crime are *purely* a consequence of the actions of the system of social control.

CHAPTER VII

Definitions of Criminal Behaviour and Attitudes to Crime

1. Introduction

So far, we have seen that there is evidence of a very large 'dark figure' of unrecorded crime in the three London areas from which our R sample was drawn; and that the difference between our survey estimates of crime in the three areas, and the numbers of crimes in the police statistics, is due largely (though by no means entirely) to the victims' decisions not to report the incident to the police. It also appears that non-reporting to police of incidents which are believed to involve some sort of crime is largely influenced by the victim's view of the incident itself and the context in which it occurs, rather than by generally negative attitudes to the police.

It is reasonable to assume, however, that the significance for the victim, of an incident involving a crime committed against him, will depend to *some* extent on the general attitudes and beliefs which he holds about crime or deviance. That is, it seems a reasonable hypothesis that the would-be victim's interpretation of a particular incident or event—his inclination to see it as an event of such-and-such a kind, and as more or less 'serious'—is at least not wholly independent of the more general pattern of attitudes, values, norms and beliefs which he holds about different sorts of crime. It also seems a reasonable hypothesis that these attitudes, beliefs, etc. are in turn not wholly idiosyncratic or individual, but—like other aspects of culture—are to a large extent shared among the members of different social groups. In a pluralistic or culturally heterogeneous society, therefore, we should expect a certain amount of patterned variation in attitudes to crime. And unless we take the heroic step of assuming that individuals' behaviour in particular cases is not influenced at all by their general attitudes, we should expect that different social groups will tend to respond in different ways to situations in which crimes are committed against them.

We saw, in the last chapter, that there were very few marked associations between our respondents' expressed general attitudes and beliefs concerning crime, and their reporting to the police of incidents committed against them. But the patterned variation of those attitudes and beliefs is important notwithstanding this, since it may result in systematic differences in victims' *perceptions* of incidents, and in their tendency to define those incidents as ones in which crimes have been committed against them. Thus, a group which accepts that the use of physical violence is a permissible response to insults or verbal abuse will not regard the use of force in such situations as reprehensible; members of the group might say, if asked, that no crime (or 'no *real* crime') had been committed at all. But the same kind of incident might be generally condemned in another group which had different norms or values. Similarly, a group might take the view that certain forms of illegal behaviour (speeding, possessing marijuana, pilfering from workplaces) were not really immoral, or caused only minimal harm to anyone; even if they conceded that such acts were technically crimes, they would not really *mean* the same thing by that statement as a group which regarded such acts as sinful or socially harmful. The two groups' perceptions of crime would be different, even if their experience of crime were in an objective sense the same.

The question, then, is this: to what extent are there variations within groups like those represented by our sample, in perceptions, definitions and attitudes concerning different forms of criminal behaviour? For example, do sex-roles lead men to take different views of violent or sexual crime from those taken by women? Do immigrant communities—such as the West Indians in Brixton and Hackney—have different norms concerning the use of physical force, or the sanctity of property, from those of the indigenous English? Does 'social class'—that ambiguous concept which apparently affects so much else in contemporary English society—also mark differences in cultural variables which may affect reactions to crime and deviance? To what extent is there consensus in these matters, and where does conflict begin?

Obviously, we could not hope to investigate all of the possibly relevant attitudes, values and beliefs in a single survey; it is far from clear, *a priori*, just which of those things is relevant, or how each should be conceptualized or operationally defined. Accordingly, we chose two areas—norms concerning the use of violence, and assessments of the relative seriousness of different types of crime—which may be related to the disapproval of 'violence' in various forms—in a first attempt to map similarities and differences in the communities from which our sample was drawn.

This part of our study was frankly exploratory in nature, and is reported in this chapter as much for its possible methodological interest as for its substantive findings. There are undoubtedly limitations to the usefulness of victim surveys in studying such things; and as with most of the other topics investigated in our survey, a full understanding of the processes and structures of perception and definition of crime is likely to come only when over-time or panel data are available to show the changes (if any) which may be associated with different levels of crime or experience as a victim. But it is necessary to begin somewhere; and in this area of sociological theory—with its abundance of speculation, and paucity of data of any kind—any beginning seems better than none.

It is important to note, moreover, that the problems discussed in this chapter have important implications for the victim survey method as well as for the explanation of societal reaction to crime. For one thing, as we saw in earlier chapter,[1] perceived seriousness of an incident might affect both the chance that an incident will be recalled by a respondent, and reported to a survey interviewer—and also affect the accuracy with which the incident will be described and placed in time. For another, an incident which is defined by a respondent in some terms which do not entail that the incident involved a crime (or an 'attack', for example), will probably not be mentioned at all by the respondent when he is asked about that type of crime. The incident may thus be lost entirely, so far as the survey is concerned. To the extent that there is differential definition of certain types of incidents among different sub-groups in the population, there will accordingly be definite biases in the survey findings. We have already seen that there is some evidence of this kind of bias, in the reporting of assaults among different social classes in our survey and others.[2]

2. Norms and the Definition of 'Violence'

The first step in the process of societal reaction to crime or deviant behaviour is the *perception* of some behaviour or its consequences by the victim (if there is one) or some third party, and the *classification* of that behaviour or its consequences in terms which entail that the act was illegal or morally wrong. Someone must *see* A's fist collide with B's nose; and they must see this *as* an 'assault,' thus bringing the situation within the scope of a general term defined by a legal or moral rule.

This part of the process is problematic in several different ways. To begin with, the behaviour and its situation may be ambiguous, in the sense that there may be genuine doubt as to the correct description of 'what happened' at the most basic level. A bumps into B: was this done deliberately, intentionally, purposefully, carelessly, accidentally, or 'accidentally on purpose?'[1] This kind of ambiguity is most important in the case of violent and sexual crimes, where the interpretation of the situation crucially depends on intention, consent, and the knowledge or beliefs of the actors. Direct evidence of these (e.g. a statement of intent) is often not available, and a decision as to the correct description of the situation may thus have to be based on inferences aided by commonsense presumptions (such as that a man usually intends the natural and probable consequences of his acts). Experiments in the social psychology of perception have shown that there may be considerable variation in the interpretations of such situations, though it seems that not much is known at the present time about the cultural determinants of that variation in relation to situations involving criminal or deviant behaviour.[2]

Secondly, there may be variations, of several kinds, in the rules accepted by different social groups. For example, the members of an immigrant group may adhere to rules which conflict with those of the law or the dominant culture in their host country, as when traditions of vendetta or revenge are imported into cultures which have rules against such behaviour.[3] Normative differences of this kind—whether imported into a society or generated from within it—have usually been regarded as a central element (if not the defining characteristic) of a criminal or deviant subculture: the members of such a subculture are usually assumed to accept different rules from those of the dominant culture, whether or not their values are the same. Alternatively, the members of a subculture may accept the dominant culture's rules, but may interpret or apply those rules in a different way; or the subculture may legitimize other forms of social behaviour (e.g. certain forms of racial discrimination) which in turn lead to criminal behaviour.[4] In any case, even where there is normative consensus, the rules may be stated in ways which are vague: a term like 'assault' or 'theft' may have clear application in most cases, but there will inevitably be borderline cases where its use is more doubtful.

Finally, it is a feature of many legal and moral rules that they expressly allow for exceptions, so that what is normally proscribed may be permissible in certain circumstances. The rules defining violent crime are an important illustration of this last point. All systems of criminal law, and most social moralities, contain rules prohibiting certain forms of interpersonal physical force (blows, kicks, attacks with weapons). At the same time, most legal and moral codes explicitly provide that the use of force is permissible or even mandatory in cases of self-defence, the defence of other persons, or (in some cases) the protection of property.[5] Furthermore, the criminal law (like common morality) takes account of provocation by the victim of a violent crime, in assessing the culpability of the offender. Thus, provocation may be a defence to a charge of murder, and may reduce it to manslaughter;[6] in the case of wounding, assault and other crimes of violence not resulting in death, provocation is commonly taken into account as a mitigating factor in sentencing even though it may not completely absolve the offender from responsibility.[7] It is typical of legal rules relating to provocation, self-defence and the like, that they do not precisely define what will suffice for a defence, but leave this to be decided by juries in particular cases as a 'question of fact;' obviously, in everyday life as in the criminal courts, different people may draw the line in different places when assessing the 'reasonableness' or adequacy of provocation or threats.

There is a further complication concerning the assessment of provocation, since in cases of this kind the responsibility of the offender may be reduced for two quite different reasons. As English lawyers used to recognize (and American lawyers still do), a defence to a criminal charge may involve either a *justification* or an *excuse*. Briefly, to excuse a bit of misbehaviour is to admit that it was wrong, but to claim that the actor lacked the knowledge, self-control or opportunity to avoid doing it, so that the act was not fully voluntary or intentional. To justify the act, by contrast, is to say that special circumstances (such as a need to defend oneself) made permissible an act which would normally be wrongful. Thus, if A hits B, the result may be that B loses his temper and retaliates; B might try to *excuse* the behaviour by saying that he was 'uncontrollably angry,' 'in a panic,' etc. Alternatively, it may be claimed that A's blow gave B a *right* to hit back (by analogy, presumably, with self-defence); in this case B would try to *justify* his act, and would not necessarily claim that it was less than fully voluntary.[8] No doubt both of these moral conceptions may apply, even in a single case. But it is important to distinguish between them, since justification—which entails that the act of violence was permitted or even required—is *prima facie* a much stronger defence to a charge of wrongful violence than is an excuse.

Clearly, then, there is a good deal of scope for variation among different social groups in their interpretation and application of norms prohibiting acts of violence. They may well draw the line in different places, so far as excuses are concerned; they may differ in their views concerning circumstances which justify violence. We may hypothesize that one consequence of these differences would be a variation in responses to violence: those who tended to excuse provoked violence (on the ground that it was a 'natural' response in the circumstances), and *a fortiori* those who tended to justify it, would be less likely to disapprove of it or call the police about it. In addition, of course, the members of a group which often tended to justify acts of violence might well be more likely to commit such acts themselves.

In order to investigate our respondents' views on these matters, we asked a series of questions about their reactions to, and their interpretations of, a number of hypothetical incidents involving the use of physical violence by one person against another, in circumstances which might have been seen as affording some degree of justification or excuse.[9] Both the degree of provocation, and the degree of violence used, were varied within the three settings in which the hypothetical incidents took place. Thus, for example, in the first case[10] the situation was first described in the following terms:

Two men, of about the same age and size, are sitting in a cafe or restaurant, and they begin to have an argument. The first man loudly and repeatedly insults the second man. The second man hits the first man with his fists, and knocks him down.

After asking the respondents' views about the second man's behaviour, the case was varied as follows:

Now let us suppose that the first man, instead of just insulting the second man, also hits him. The second man then hits the first man with his fists, as before, knocking him down.

In the next case, respondents were asked to consider a situation in which a man living in their neighbourhood returned home late at night to find a stranger leaving his house. It was said that the stranger was not carrying anything; but that when the householder approached, the stranger started to run away. The householder then hit the stranger with his fists, knocking him unconscious. This situation was then varied so that the stranger was seen leaving the house, carrying what appeared to be some of the householder's property; when he tried to run away the householder picked up a brick or other object and hit the stranger with it, knocking him unconscious. Next, respondents were asked to suppose that the householder, awakened at night by a noise in his house, found an intruder in the kitchen; the householder picked up a blunt instrument and struck the intruder with it, causing him serious injuries.

The final situation was first described as follows:

Suppose that a man living here in this neighbourhood has been spreading malicious rumours about another man in the neighbourhood, such as that he has been stealing from his employer or that he has been having an affair with another man's wife. Although these things are not true, many people might believe that they are. The second man finds out what the first man has been saying about him; and after several days' thought, goes to the house of the first man and hits him with his fists, knocking him down.

The case was then varied by saying that the second man, still using his fists, had caused 'serious injuries' to the man who had spread the malicious rumours. Table VII.1 summarizes these seven hypothetical cases, and compares the amounts and kinds of provocation and the violence used in each:

In each of these seven cases, respondents were first asked to say what they thought that 'most people in this neighbourhood' would feel about the violent behaviour described: the forced-choice responses were Strongly Approve,

Table VII.1. Summary of hypothetical cases involving provocation and violent response

		Provocation	Response
Argument in cafe	1st case	Insult only	Knocks down with fists
	2nd case	Insult and blow with fist	Knocks down with fists
Household intruder	1st case	Stranger seen leaving house	Knocks unconscious with fist
	2nd case	Stranger carrying property out of house	Hits with brick, causes serious injuries
	3rd case	Stranger found in house	Hits with blunt instrument, causes serious injuries
Malicious rumours	1st case	Maliciously spreading false rumours	Hits with fists, knocks down
	2nd case	Maliciously spreading false rumours	Hits with fists, causes serious injuries

Approve, Indifferent, Disapprove, Strongly Disapprove.[11] They were then asked, 'How would you yourself feel about it?' We had hoped, by asking the questions in this fashion, to identify those respondents who did not agree with the views which they believed that their neighbours would express, and who— so far as violent behaviour was concerned—did not regard their neighbours as representing their normative reference group.[12] Depending on the situation, between 20 and 30 per cent of the sample did give different answers when asked about their own views, compared with what they said that most of their neighbours would feel; in almost half of these cases, the differences were well-marked (i.e. the 'self' response was two or more steps away from the 'neighbour' response). Moreover, as we have already noted,[13] a tendency to express different views from those imputed to one's neighbours was one of the few things found to be consistently related to non-reporting of incidents of victimization to the police: those who generally agreed with the views they imputed to their neighbours, were also more likely to say that they had notified the police about incidents committed against them.

Nonetheless, the *validity* of our findings on this point is open to question, not least because there was a general tendency for those who said they differed from their neighbours to present themselves as *less* approving than their neighbours of the violence described. It may be, therefore, that when telling our interviewers what they thought the neighbours felt, these respondents were (either consciously or unconsciously) giving their own views of the situation; and that when they subseqently were asked for their own views, they gave what they regarded as a socially desirable response, i.e. one expressing less approval, or more disapproval, than imputed to the neighbours. An analysis of the successive pairs of responses by age, sex, class and other variables partly confirms this view: women and middle-class persons tended to give less approving answers to the 'self' questions, and it is precisely such respondents who might be expected, *a priori*, to regard disapproval of violence as the socially desirable response. Not all of the differences between 'neighbour' and 'self' responses are consistent with this view, however; and the associations which we found between approval of violence and other attributes generally hold whether the 'neighbour' or the 'self' answers are used.

Table VII.2 summarizes the responses to the seven hypothetical cases, in terms of the percentages of the respondents who gave 'Approve' or 'Strongly Approve' answers to the 'neighbour' and 'self' questions respectively.[14] It will be seen from this table that over the sample as a whole, the findings are generally consistent with what would be expected from common-sense assumptions concerning norms relating to violence. The percentage approving was highest in the case involving an intruder actually found in the house at night (even though the householder was said to have reacted in this case by causing 'serious injuries' with a blunt instrument). The next highest percentage approving was in respect of the second variant of the case involving an altercation in a cafe, where the provocation had been a blow as well as insults and abuse. There was less approval for the serious injuries caused to an apparent burglar outside the house, than to one found inside it; and there was still less approval in the cases involving the deliberate attack on the spreader of malicious rumours, especially when the slandered man caused 'serious injuries' rather than merely knocking the other man down.[15] It will also be noticed that there is virtually no difference in the percentages approving of the violent behaviour in the first case involving a household intruder (in which the stranger was seen leaving the house, but without any property), and the second (in which he was apparently carrying some of the householder's belongings). It may be that the first situation, as described, was a rather ambiguous one.[16] On the other hand, in the second case *both* the provocation *and* the retaliation were increased: the stranger was said to have been carrying property, but he was also said to have been hit with a brick and given serious injuries, rather than merely being knocked unconscious with fists. Since respondents' views of these situations were presumably influenced both by the provocation and the response, the similar degree of approval in the two situations is perhaps to be expected.

We had thought that it might be possible for us to construct, from some subset of the responses relating to these hypothetical situations, a Guttman scale which would enable us to classify our respondents in terms of their general readiness to approve of violent reactions to provocative situations. Several attempts at scalogram analysis, however, showed that this was not the case: it was not possible to arrange any meaningful selection of situations on such a continuum, using either the 'neighbour' or the 'self' responses.[17] It seems likely that this was so because the seven situations involved variations in both

Table VII.2. Summary of responses to hypothetical situations: percentages 'Approving' or 'Strongly Approving' of violent behaviour

	Percent Approved or Strongly Approved		
	Neighbours	Self	N^a
Argument in cafe— insults only	39	36	525
Argument in cafe— blow with fist	60	54	526
Household intruder— outside, no property; blow with fist	54	43	528
Household intruder— outside, property taken; serious injuries caused	57	42	532
Household intruder— found in house, serious injuries caused	76	62	518
Malicious rumours— knocked down with fists	46	32	521
Malicious rumours— serious injuries caused	20	13	520

$^a N$ is for 'self'-responses; it varies because of 'Don't know' answers. The N's for 'neighbour' responses are lower for the same reason, though they are in all cases about 500.

the provocation and the violence, each of which was evaluated in different ways by different sub-groups within our sample. On the other hand, the inter-correlations between our sample's responses showed—and factor analysis confirmed—that the sample's view of the seven situations could not be explained by any simple combination of factors relating to the seriousness of the provocation and the degree of violent response. The correlations between all seven items are positive, using either 'self' or 'neighbour' responses; but the only ones of any size are those between responses relating to violence within the same locale (viz. the cafe, the household or the rumour-spreading). It seems clear, therefore, that our sample's views were highly 'situation-specific' and that they assessed the use of violence in the three different contexts according to different standards.

It also seems clear, however, that the sample's apparent readiness to approve the use of violence—even of a fairly severe kind, e.g. causing serious injuries with a brick or blunt instrument—was in part a function of their acceptance of a normative system akin to that of the criminal law, which makes such violence permissible (or at least forgiveable) in circumstances involving provocation or threats to person or property. It is of interest to compare our findings on this point with those of a recent American survey reported by Baker and Ball.[18] In this survey, which was also designed to investigate norms relating to violence, respondents were first asked if they thought there were certain role-relationships (e.g. parent–child, husband–wife, policeman–adult male citizen) in which they might approve of various degrees of violence being used; they were then asked about specific circumstances (e.g. resisting arrest, attacking another person) in which they might approve. A major finding of this survey was that there was general approval of the use of serious violence (choking, shooting, etc.) only by the police or other legally constituted authorities. But the majority of the sample only approved of the use of such violence, even by the police, in circumstances where this was legally approved, e.g. when the policeman's life was threatened or when someone was directly hindering the law enforcement process.[19] The only role-relationship in the Baker and Ball study which was directly comparable to those involved in our own hypothetical cases—namely, violence between two adult males—produced findings broadly similar to ours. A slight majority of the sample said they might approve of one man punching another, and among these respondents there was almost unanimous approval in the case of a burglary, and only slightly less approval if the prevention of violence against a woman was involved. The more serious level of violence—choking—was generally approved only if one man had knocked the other down and was trying to rob him, or had broken into his house.

Inspection of Table VII.2 will show, however, that there was far from complete agreement within our sample on the assessment of any of the seven situations; and further analysis showed that there were some interesting differences in approval or disapproval of the violence used in the hypothetical situations among different sub-groups of the sample, even if allowance is made for the possibility of response bias mentioned earlier. To begin with, there was

Table VII.3. Percent 'Approve' or 'Strongly Approve' responses, by number of self-reported violent acts

		None	1–2	3–4	5–8	9+	N^a
		\multicolumn{5}{c}{Self-reported violent acts}	
Cafe argument	(1)—Neighbour	38	39	38	44	60	518
	—Self	32	38	43	47	57	525
	(2)—Neighbour	57	67	61	72	65	516
	—Self	51	55	61	63	77	524
House intruder	(1)—Neighbour	50	65	52	70	86	523
	—Self	40	48	38	42	95	525
	(2)—Neighbour	57	49	65	59	63	530
	—Self	43	33	47	22	38	530
	(3)—Neighbour	76	74	80	70	75	508
	—Self	61	55	69	69	71	517
Rumour-spreading	(1)—Neighbour	42	55	51	56	65	510
	—Self	29	33	44	39	52	520
	(2)—Neighbour	18	25	31	18	30	508
	—Self	12	19	22	15	19	520

[a]See note to Table VII.2; N's in this table also exclude those respondents not answering the self-report questions.

a slight but consistent tendency for older respondents to be less approving of the violence, especially in the two variants of the case involving an argument in a cafe. There were no consistent differences between the views expressed by males and females. But there was also a tendency for working-class respondents to be readier to approve of the violent behaviour described; again, this was especially so in the cafe cases. Black respondents were generally *less* likely than whites to approve of the violence described, though the differences were significant only in the rumour-spreading cases. And as Table VII.3 shows, there was a generally consistent association between approval of the hypothetical violence, and self-reporting of violent crimes.

Even here, however—and the same thing was true for social class and other attributes—there is a higher degree of consensus on the three cases involving an intruder into the household, than with the other situations.[20] Finally—chiefly, but not entirely, it appears, as a result of differences in the social-class composition of the three survey areas—there were marked differences between Brixton and Hackney on the one hand, and Kensington on the other. Especially in the cafe-argument and rumour-spreading cases, our Kensington residents were markedly less likely to approve of the violence described (that is, they were less likely to *say* that they approved of it) than those living in the other two areas.

We also attempted to learn something of our respondents' reasons for their expressed approval or disapproval in the three hypothetical situations, and in particular to explore the distinction discussed earlier between justification and excuse. Accordingly, after asking for their own views of four of the situations,[21] we asked them to say what they thought the man who had used the violence was *feeling* in that situation. Responses to this question were recorded verbatim by the interviewers, and were subsequently coded so as to distinguish (1) those which mentioned anger, fear, or some other emotion, from (2) those which referred, either explicitly or implicitly, to a norm or rule making the violence permissible (e.g..by the use of phrases such as 'he had a right to,' 'he was just protecting himself,' 'he's entitled to protect his property,' etc.)

In retrospect, it must be admitted that the wording of this question is far from ideal; by asking respondents to interpret the hypothetical actor's *feelings*— rather than, say, his reasons or motives—we undoubtedly encouraged them to reply in terms of emotional states, and minimized the chance that they would mention or refer to a norm or rule relating to the justification of violence in the circumstances described. Certainly we cannot conclude, from a respondent's failure to mention such a norm in reply to our question, that he would necessarily deny the existence of such a norm, or its application to the situation described. Nor does it necessarily follow, of course, from the respondent's statement that *the hypothetical actor* believed himself justified, that *the respondent himself* would accept or act on such a rule in a similar situation: indeed, some of those who gave a justificatory interpretation of the actor's 'feelings' also said that they disapproved of the violence described, which implies that they did not regard it as completely justified.[22] On the other hand, the responses to our questions can probably be taken as indicating the *minimum* of support for such norms which existed among different sub-groups in our samples; they do enable us at least to identify those persons who explicitly referred to a justificatory norm of some sort in interpreting the situations, and who may thus have been more likely to recognize—or even accept—such norms.

In analysing these data we have combined all cases in which we judged that the respondent mentioned some element of justification, even though in a small number of these anger or some other emotion was also mentioned; these cases may be compared with those in which *only* some form of emotional response (of which anger was by far the most common) was mentioned.[23] The results, for the sample as a whole, are summarized in Table VIII.4. It will be seen from this table that in the sample as a whole there is very little support for any notion of justification in the first cafe-argument case (in which, it will be remembered, the blow was said to have been struck as a result of insults and abuse only); and there is only slightly more support for the deliberate blows inflicted by the man who had been slandered. About a third of the sample, however, gave replies to our question which indicated some recognition of a justificatory norm in both of the cases involving a household intruder. With respect to these two cases, it is perhaps somewhat surprising that the proportion mentioning some kind of justification is slightly higher in the case where the intruder was described as being outside the house, than where he was actually found inside it; this is largely due, however, to the fact that a much larger number of respondents mentioned 'fear' in response to the latter question than to the former.

Table VII.4. Responses to questions concerning the feelings of man using violence (four hypothetical situations), and percentages approving or strongly approving of the violent behaviour

	Justification	Emotion only	Total
Cafe argument—first case:			
No.	27	429	456
Per cent	6	94	100
Per cent Approving or Strongly Approving[a]	52	37	38
Household intruder—first case:			
No.	163	305	468
Per cent	35	65	100
Per cent Approving or Strongly Approving[a]	49	42	45
Household intruder—third case:			
No.	154	340	494
Per cent	31	69	100
Per cent Approving or Strongly Approving[a]	77	57	62
Malicious rumours—first case:			
No.	51	392	443
Per cent	12	88	100
Per cent Approving or Strongly Approving[a]	39	31	32

[a]Based on 'self' responses; excluding 'don't know' responses, 'revenge' and 'other' interpretations.

As Table VII.4 shows, there was also a general tendency for those interpreting the situation in terms of some form of justification to be more likely to approve of the violent behaviour described. This difference is statistically significant only in the third household intruder case; but its presence in all four of the cases in consistent with the view that the notion of justification—of acting in support of a *right* to use violence in certain situations—is regarded as a stronger ground for the use of what would normally be improper behaviour, than is an emotional response such as anger or fear.

There were also some differences within the sample in the tendency to give a justificatory interpretation of the first three situations. Black respondents were significantly more likely than whites to see the householder's actions in terms of rights, in both of the cases where this question was asked; they were also twice as likely to express this view about the cafe-argument case, though this difference did not reach statistical significance. There were even more marked differences between respondents in different social classes on this point, with those in classes III–V being about twice as likely to mention some kind of justification for the violence as those in classes I and II, except in the case involving the man who spread rumours. Again, there were differences between the three survey areas: Kensington residents were much less likely to give a justificatory interpretation than those living in Brixton or Hackney, except for the rumour-spreading case where there was no difference.

There is some evidence, then, that a proportion of our sample recognized a normative justification for the use of force against an intruder into one's household. But there was little, if any, indication of such justification for violence in response to mere verbal provocation (as in the cafe and rumour-spreading cases). Nonetheless, it will be recalled that a substantial minority of the sample indicated their approval of the action of the man who had been insulted in the cafe, and that over half of the sample approved when the provocation was described as including a blow as well as verbal abuse. Presumably the numbers regarding such a blow as justified (by analogy with self-defence) would also have been higher in the second situation. The cafe-argument case, however, also raises an issue of public order: it involves a kind of violent behaviour which by virtue of its situation might turn out to involve more than just the two original participants.[24] This in turn raises the question of how such incidents should be dealt with by those who witness them. Should the police be called, and if so, how should *they* deal with the situation? To explore this issue, we asked the following question about each of the hypothetical cafe-argument cases:

Suppose a policeman had come in then and witnessed the whole scene. What should the policeman do?

The forced-choice answers were: arrest the first man and take him to court; arrest the second man and take him to court; arrest both men and take them to court; stop the fight but take neither man to court; do nothing at all.

In the first situation, where the provocation was in words only, a majority of the sample said that the policeman should stop the fight but make no arrest; just over a quarter of our respondents said the policeman should make an arrest, and of these the majority said that *both* men should be arrested. In the second case, where the provocation consisted of a blow as well as insults, the proportion wanting the policeman to make an arrest rose to half; of these the majority still said that both men should be arrested, though a quarter would have wanted the policeman to arrest only the man who had started the incident and landed the first blow. Even in this case, however, it is to interest that the sample was evenly divided, as to whether the policeman should take positive action or merely stop the fight without arresting either participant. In both cases those who had disapproved of the violent response were more likely to say that the policeman should make an arrest, than those who approved; but the differences were very slight, and were in neither case statistically significant. There was a significant tendency for older respondents to say that there

Table VII.5. What should policeman do in first and second cafe argument cases, by area[a]

	Arrest one or both men		Stop fight but not arrest		Total	
	No.	Percentage	No.	Percentage	No.	Percentage
First case:						
Brixton	54	30·0	126	70·0	180	100·0
Hackney	53	30·1	123	69·9	176	100·0
Kensington	34	18·8	147	81·2	181	100·0
Total	141	26·3	396	73·7	537	100·0

$$\chi^2 = 7·87, \text{df} = 2, p < 0·02$$

	Arrest one or both men		Stop fight but not arrest		Total	
Second case:						
Brixton	95	53·1	84	46·9	179	100·0
Hackney	87	49·4	89	50·6	176	100·0
Kensington	75	41·2	107	58·8	182	100·0
Total	257	47·9	280	52·1	537	100·0

$$\chi^2 = 5·35, \text{df} = 2, 0·10 > p > 0·05$$

[a]Excludes eight respondents giving 'Don't know' answers.

should be an arrest, in both cases; in the first, the proportion of those aged over 60 who were in favour of arrest was twice that among respondents aged 30 and under. There was also a general tendency for respondents in the higher social classes to say that the policeman should stop the fight but *not* make an arrest. (This may have been because the middle-class respondents had a rather 'sympathetic' image of the sort of person who they thought would be likely to get into such a situation—i.e. 'good chaps' like themselves, a bit under the influence. Or it may just be your average liberal tender-mindedness.) The results by area are summarized in Table VII.5; again it will be seen that there are marked differences between Brixton and Hackney, on the one hand, and Kensington on the other.

Clearly the findings described in this section must be treated as no more than suggestive. We do not claim to have *demonstrated* the existence of sub-cultural variation in respect of norms relating to violence, e.g. in respect to immigrants or among persons of different social classes. The differences which we found in expressed attitudes to, and interpretation of, our hypothetical situations are by no means large ones; and they may to a large extent reflect no more than different styles of answering hypothetical questions. Much more research will be necessary, in order to identify and map different normative patterns relating to violence or other forms of crime and deviance.

It they should turn out to be valid, however, our findings would have some important implications both for the investigation of the processes of societal reaction to deviant or criminal violence, and for the victim survey method. So far as they go, our data confirm the familiar suggestion that violent behaviour (in situations like the hypothetical ones we asked about) is more likely to be seen as justified, and less likely to be disapproved of, in predominantly lower-class communities like Brixton and Hackney (and among some immigrant groups) than in a mainly middle-class community like Kensington. It might thus be expected that the incidence of such acts would be greater in the former areas.[25] But even if the incidence were the same, it might be still expected that a lower proportion of such acts would have been defined as 'assault,' 'affray,' or otherwise unacceptable violence, in areas such as Brixton and Hackney. Conversely, it may be residents in an area like Kensington would be readier to regard such acts as 'criminal', and would perhaps apply that label to actions which would be tolerated or approved of elsewhere. As we have already noted,[26] this may in part explain the qualitative differences in the assaults reported to our interviewers, and the higher proportion of attempts and threats mentioned by the Kensington respondents. We have no data on the reporting of such incidents to the police, except in relation to assaults allegedly committed against the respondents themselves; different considerations may obviously apply to breaches of public order (like our hypothetical case involving an argument or fight in a cafe), and it may well be that residents in a middle-class area would be readier to call the police in such cases than those in lower-class neighbourhoods. But our data do suggest that our Kensington residents would be less likely to insist that the police arrest (and prosecute) the offenders in such situations; since there is reason to believe that the police take some account of complainants' wishes and expectations in such cases,[27] this would suggest that the police would be more likely, *ceteris paribus*, to deal with such cases informally in a middle-class area than in a lower-class one. This would seem especially likely to be true if—because of a greater tendency on the part of the middle-class residents to perceive and define such behaviour as criminal—the incidents to which the police were called were on average less serious (in terms of injuries inflicted, etc.) in the middle-class area. It would be interesting to study this question by comparing the incidents of this kind to which the police were called, in contrasting areas, in order to see (1) if the incidents themselves differed in number and type, in accordance with our predictions; and (2) if the police showed a greater tendency to deal with such incidents informally, in middle-class neighbourhoods; and (3) if this were so, *why* it was so. Statistics of *recorded* crime can, of course, throw no light whatever on these questions.

3. The 'Seriousness' of Crimes

As we saw in Chapter V, one of the most important reasons given by our respondents for their failure to notify the police about incidents apparently involving crimes committed against them was that they felt that the incident was not serious enough to warrant reporting. But people notoriously differ in their views of the seriousness of things; and one might reasonably expect to find patterned variation in assessments of the relative gravity of different types of crime, just as one might expect to find patterned variation in norms.

In order to investigate this possibility, we made use of a rating technique similar to that suggested by Sellin and Wolfgang in their book *The Measurement of Delinquency* (1964). Briefly, this technique consists of giving respondents a set of short descriptions of crimes, and asking them to give each incident a score—from 1 to 11—which reflects their view of its seriousness. By comparing the scores given to different types of offences (e.g. violent versus property crimes) some idea can hopefully be gained of the criteria by which scores have been assigned; in addition, comparison of the scores given by different groups of respondents to similar items may throw some light on between-group variations in perceptions of seriousness. In the 12 years since Sellin and Wolfgang's study was first published, it has been replicated—more or less faithfully—by a number of researchers in different countries;[1] it has also been subjected to considerable criticism.[2] Many of these criticisms have related to the *objective* of Sellin and Wolfgang's research, which was the construction of a weighted index of delinquency which would reflect both the seriousness and the frequency of recorded delinquent acts. For the most part, these criticisms seem to us to be well-founded: they are not relevant to our research, however, since the object of our study was quite different. But the Sellin–Wolfgang study has also been criticized on methodological grounds; and for this reason it is important to emphasize that our procedures differed in several respects from theirs.

On the basis of experience gained in our pilot studies, we selected a set of 33 descriptions of illegal acts to be rated by respondents in our London survey. Each of the descriptions set out, in one or two sentences, the bare facts of an offence (for example, 'The offender breaks into a person's house and steals property worth £10.') Each description was printed on a separate 3 × 5 inch slip of paper, accompanied by a row of numbers ranging from 1 to 11; the format of these slips is illustrated in Figure VII.1. After receiving instructions from the interviewer, the respondent was handed a set of the slips and a pencil, and was told to score each crime by circling the number which he thought indicated how serious he thought the crime was. (This was the only part of the questionnaire which was physically completed by the respondent himself.) Respondents were told that they could check back and change any scores if they wished; and after scoring all of the 33 crimes—or as many as they could—they were invited again to check back to make sure they were satisfied with the scores they had given, though as a matter of fact very few did so.[3]

The offender breaks into a person's house and steals property worth £10.

1	2	3	4	5	6	7	8	9	10	11
LEAST SERIOUS					AVERAGE					MOST SERIOUS

Figure VII.1. Example of the slips used for rating seriousness of offences

The resulting scores were affected by (at least) three different types of response bias. First, as happened with the hypothetical situations discussed in the preceding section of this chapter, some respondents appeared to our interviewers to have difficulty in understanding or completing this section, while others complained that they could not give realistic ratings without fuller details of the incidents described. Since the scores given by these respondents did not differ in any clear or consistent fashion from those given by the rest of the sample, however, we have not excluded them. Secondly, despite our instructions to the contrary, a number or respondents (about seven per cent of the sample) insisted on giving all 33 of the offences the maximum score of 11—presumably on the ground that all transgressions of the law are equally serious. Whether or not this is a defensible basis for moral judgement, it is not the one which we asked our respondents to use;[4] we have accordingly excluded these respondents from the final analysis, though in fact their effect on the results was barely perceptible. Thirdly, it is possible that some bias was introduced through the order in which the offences were presented to the respondents; for example, it is possible that an offence of theft might have been given a different score when rated after a violent offence than when rated after a motoring offence. In order to guard against 'order effects' of this kind, interviewers were instructed to shuffle the slips before giving them to the respondent, so as to vary (if not completely randomize) the order in which the crimes were rated. This does not completely remove the possibility of bias, of course, since each respondent necessarily scored the cases in *some* order; it does, however, reduce the possibility to such biases affecting the scores for the whole sample or any substantial sub-set of it.[5]

Strictly speaking, of course, the 1-to-11 scores resulting from this kind of procedure—sometimes called a 'category scale'—yield only an ordinal level of measurement; that is, they reflect the respondents' rank-ordering of crimes rather than their measurement on an interval or ratio scale. We have no way of knowing, for any respondent, whether the difference between a score of 1 and a score of 2 is the same as the difference between a score of (say) 9 and a score of 10; nor is a score of 10 equal to twice one of 5; nor can we be sure that the difference between any consecutive pair of scores is the same for any one respondent as for another.[6] For this reason we have, for the most part, used non-parametric statistics in our analysis of between-group variations in scores.[7] It seems reasonable to assume, however, that for each respondent scores the 1-to-11 point scale reflected *some* sort of underlying continuum roughly corresponding to *some* concept of seriousness; for this reason we shall in what follows refer to our data as scores rather than as ranks.

Bearing in mind these limitations of the data, let us first consider the assessments of relative seriousness, within the sample as a whole,[8] for the 33 offences. The mean scores for each offence are set out in Table VII.6, in which the offences have been grouped within broad categories. It will be seen that, in general, the rank order of mean scores corresponds fairly closely to what would be expected from the legal category of the offence, the degree of injury caused

Table VII.6. Mean seriousness scores for 33 offences[a]

	Mean score	S.D.	Rank of mean score
Attack with blunt weapon causing death	10·67	0·90	1
Attack with knife causing death	10·64	1·01	2
Rape and beating, serious injuries	10·12	1·15	3
Attack with knife, serious injuries	9·52	1·51	4
Rape, no other injuries inflicted	8·98	2·03	6
Assault on police officer-serious injury	8·84	2·01	8
Attack, blunt weapon—minor injury	8·02	2·06	10
Assault on police officer—minor injury	7·79	2·32	12
Attack with fists—minor injury	6·71	2·37	18
Robbery of £25 + serious injury	8·96	1·81	7
Robbery of £25 + minor injuries	8·00	2·09	11
Robbery of £25 with no injuries	7·34	2·21	15
Burglary + assault, nothing stolen	7·53	2·17	13
Burglary + theft of £10 cash	5·42	2·60	27
Burglary + theft of £10 in property	5·35	2·49	29
Burglary—nothing taken	5·03	2·45	30
Obtaining £1,000 by fraud	7·37	2·72	14
Obtaining £100 by forged cheques	6·60	2·66	19
Embezzlement of £100	6·57	2·65	20
Theft of £100 property from car	6·49	2·47	21
Theft of £100 materials from work	6·25	2·53	22
Theft of £10 from wallet	6·10	2·61	23
Theft of £10 by employee from shop till	5·40	2·65	28
Theft of £10 property from car	4·94	2·36	31
Theft of £10 materials from work	4·91	2·55	32
Theft of goods worth £10 from shop	4·83	2·47	33
Reckless driving causing injury	8·58	2·02	9
Reckless driving, £100 property damage	6·83	2·46	17
Sale of marijuana to person aged 15	9·13	2·41	5
Sale of marijuana to adult	7·08	3·45	16
Causing £50 damage to private property	6·04	2·53	24
Causing £50 damage to public property	5·47	2·51	26
Buying property known to be stolen	5·73	2·95	25

[a]Excluding 28 respondents who scored all items 11; remaining N's range from 492 to 517 owing to missing data. Note that because of sampling errors differences between adjacent scores may not be statistically significant. Standard errors of means would range from 0·04 to 0·13 if the total sample were a simple random one; since it is not, a safe estimate of standard errors is twice those amounts.

and/or the value of property involved. Thus, the two cases involving attacks which resulted in death have the highest mean scores; cases described as involving serious injuries have higher mean scores than similar cases causing only minor injuries,[9] which in turn have higher mean scores than those in which no injuries to a person were caused; among offences against property the case involving £1,000 has a higher mean score than those involving £100, which in turn have higher means than those involving only £10;[10] burglary which included an assault on the householder was scored higher than burglary involving the theft of cash or goods worth £10, which in turn was scored higher than a burglary in which the offender, caught in the act, left the house without taking anything. The only jarring note among these agreeably rational results concerns the mean scores for selling marijuana; sale to a 15-year-old received a higher score, on average, than rape; even sale of marijuana to an adult was scored higher than an attack causing minor injuries or causing £100 worth of damage to property through reckless driving. It is possible that this resulted from a general ignorance among our sample as to the nature of marijuana; on the other hand, it is broadly consistent with some contemporary judicial views as to the seriousness of 'pushing' even soft drugs.[11]

This kind of broad concordance between the mean scores given by our sample, and the seriousness attached by the law to various kinds of crimes, has been found by most other researchers who have attempted to ascertain the views of the public (or some section of it) on the seriousness of crime. Though a precise comparison with Sellin and Wolfgang's work is not possible, owing to the differences in our methodology and in the offences rated, inspection of the raw scale scores for the 141 offences originally included in their study reveals much the same patterns as were observed in our sample;[12] the same is true for the replication of Sellin and Wolfgang's research by Akman and Normandeau in Canada.[13] At a minimum, these findings suggest that this method of measuring the public's views of seriousness works reasonably well; moreover, they suggest that public opinion—as measured by the views of our sample as a whole—is in general agreement with the norms of the criminal law.

Further evidence on this point comes from two other recent surveys. The first was carried out in England, by Durant et al., as part of a study of public attitudes to crime, criminals and the law. Respondents in this survey were asked to classify eighteen descriptions of crimes, according to whether they thought the offences were 'serious' or 'not serious.' The percentages classified as 'serious' ranged from 99 in the case of murder and armed robbery down to 10 in the case of vagrancy.[14] More recently, Rossi and his colleagues conducted a survey in Baltimore, in which a sample of 200 persons (stratified by sex and race) were asked to rate a total of 140 offences on a scale from one (least serious) to nine (most serious). It was found that crimes against persons tended to receive very high seriousness ratings, as did drug selling; crimes against property involving no personal injury or threat were rated significantly lower; and that such things as public drunkenness, 'white-collar' crimes and refusing to pay parking fines were rated lowest of all.[15]

While it is true that there is agreement, over our sample as a whole, in the evaluation of injury, value of property and the like, it is also true that there are important differences *within* the sample, and that consensus in scoring the 33 offences is by no means complete. In particular, comparison of the mean scores and standard deviations in Table VII.6 shows that there is considerable variation within the sample in respect of many of the property offences. There is more agreement in respect of the offences involving injury to persons (assault, wounding and robbery);[16] even here, however, there is by no means complete agreement as to relative seriousness.

This issue was not investigated by Sellin and Wolfgang, or by Akman and Normandeau in their Canadian replication. In both of these studies, however, the rating groups consisted of samples of university students, policemen and judges, who were chosen precisely because they were thought to represent the middle-class value system from which the 'principal cultural themes of legal prescriptions and sanctions' come.[17] It has been vigorously argued by Rose that this choice of raters is inappropriate, even for the purposes of constructing a crime index of the kind Sellin and Wolfgang were aiming at.[18] Whether or not this is so, it is clear that the original Sellin–Wolfgang study can say nothing about possible value dissensus in the general population. Sellin and Wolfgang found no significant differences between the scores given by their three groups—students, policemen and judges;[19] given a priori likelihood of the three groups' values being similar, however, this is scarcely surprising. Wolfgang has subsequently defended his choice of a rating population composed of representatives of 'the normative structure of the dominant middle class' by asserting that 'this kind of phenomenon [i.e. the assessment of the relative seriousness of crime] is not appropriately democratized. . . . There exists now no conventional metric for criminal offences, but there are sets of observers who possess conventional wisdom and professional experience in the study and administration of criminal law enforcement and justice.'[20] Even if one were to accept this point, however, it would seem important to know how much divergence there was between the 'conventional wisdom' of this relatively privileged and powerful group, and the views of the rest of the population. To what extent does the 'normative structure of the dominant middle class' differ from that of the rest of society?

Durant et al., in their examination of this question, found few differences in the proportions rating offences as 'serious' in different groups in their sample. In particular, there were few differences in respect of the seven violent crimes included in the study, in part because over 93 per cent of the sample as a whole thought those crimes (with the exception of manslaughter) were 'serious.' There was, however, a tendency for most offences to be regarded as 'serious' by a higher proportion of those with higher education; the only exceptions to this were being drunk and disorderly, vagrancy and fighting (common assault). While there were few consistent or marked differences according to social class, it was found that the higher managerial and professional group (Registrar-General's class I) were more likely to rate stealing without violence as serious, and that unskilled workers were least likely to take this view. There was no consistent variation according to age.[21]

Rossi et al., in their study in Baltimore, found evidence of relatively high consensus between major sub-groups in their sample, in terms of correlations between mean scores on the 140 offences rated: these correlations were $+0.94$

for blacks versus whites, and + 0·89 for males versus females and for those with high school or more education versus those who had not finished high school. The subgroup least in agreement with the rest of the sample was that consisting of black males aged under 45 with less than high school education: and it appeared that for this group the main area of disagreement centred on crimes against the person in which the victim and offender were described as acquainted.[22]

In the case of offences against property, a considerable volume of recent theoretical writing, and a certain amount of empirical research, suggest that we should expect to find social-class differences of precisely the kind found by Durant *et al.*: that is, we should expect to find that middle-class persons—who, after all, tend to have more property—would regard theft as relatively more serious than did working-class persons. Douglas, for example, has argued that middle-and upper-class groups, who control the power of state legislatures, use the legal definitions of crimes in an attempt to control the kinds of things lower-class individuals commit against them, in particular, property crimes and certain acts of violence.[23] In a similar vein, Quinney has argued that the State 'arose to protect and promote the interests of the dominant economic class, the class that owns and controls the means of production', and that it 'continues as a device for holding down the exploited class, the class that labours, for the benefit of the dominant class.'[24] He adds that 'laws institutionalize and legitimize the existing property relations.[25] Taylor, Walton and Young go further, and suggest that criminal statistics [*sc.* statistics of theft by lower-class persons] 'can be used as examination [*sic*] of the extent of compliance in industrial society (in quite the same way, for example, as it is possible to use statistics on strikes as an index of dissensus in direct class relations at the work-place). In particular, the criminal statistics can be read as a measure of the credibility of a propertied society at particular periods in its development—the extent to which the distribution of property is latently accepted or rejected amongst certain sections of the working population.'[26] At an empirical level, Moorhouse and Chamberlain, in a survey of tenants in two council estates, found a substantial group who expressed attitudes to property which were contrary to the 'dominant' views in capitalist society.[27]

Our own findings were very different. To begin with, there was a general tendency for older respondents in our sample to give higher scores: the differcences were statistically significant[28] for two of the 13 violent offences (including robbery), and for 15 of the 20 other offences. There was also a tendency for non-white respondents (i.e. both West Indians and Asians) to give higher scores to offences against property than did white respondents; the difference was statistically significant for 14 of the 20 property offences. There was also a well-marked general tendency for scores on the offences against property to be negatively associated with social class (on the Registrar–General's classification); that is, lower-class respondents tended to give *higher* scores to property crimes than did upper class ones. The differences are statistically significant for 14 of the 20 offences against property; there was no such trend—

indeed, there were no consistent differences—for offences against the person. Largely in consequence of this, there were significant differences between our three areas, with Brixton and Hackney respondents giving higher mean scores than those from Kensington, to 19 of the 33 offences. Finally, there was a general tendency—statistically significant for about two-thirds of the offences, again mainly those against property—for the number of illegal acts admitted to on the self-report questions to be negatively associated with seriousness scores.

It is important not to exaggerate the magnitude of these differences. Table VII.7 shows the mean scores given to the 33 offences, by respondents in different social classes; while the rank orders of these mean scores differ to some extent, the table shows that there is still a substantial amount of agreement between different social classes.[29] Even between classes I and V, the rank correlation of the order of mean scores is 0·706, which is certainly highly significant.[30] Moreover, the *meaning* of the differences shown in Table VII.7 is in fact far from clear. What can be said is that, for lower-class respondents, there tends to be *less difference* between scores given to offences of violence, and scores given to offences against property, than is the case for upper-class respondents; in other words, relative to the generally similar scores which they gave to violent offences, the lower-class respondents gave higher scores to property crimes than the middle-class ones did.

This finding must obviously be treated with great caution, on methodological grounds.[31] Even if it is accepted as valid, it may no doubt be explained away— as most findings can—on the ground that it is merely a manifestation of 'false consciousness.' What our data definitely do *not* reveal is 'a good deal of dissent among working-class people from the dominant values, ideas and legal codes which seek to legitimate the institution of private property.'[32] If anything, they suggest that persons with relatively little wealth and property are more likely to take a dim view of their property being stolen, than those who have more to lose, and who can thus better afford to lose it.

We also examined the seriousness scores in relation to the respondents' experiences of victimization (as revealed by responses to the screening questions), in the expectation that those who had been victims on one or more occasions within the past year would tend to give higher scores, especially to those offences of the same type as the ones which they had experienced. This expectation did not prove to be quite correct; there were very few statistically significant differences in mean seriousness scores between those who said they had been victims on one or more occasions, and those who said they had not. There was, however, an interesting pattern which was generally present in relation to all types of victimization: the mean scores tended to be distributed in a curvilinear fashion, with the highest (mean) scores being given both by those who said they had not been victims at all, and by those who said they had been victims on more than one occasion. Those who said they had been victims on only one occasion tended to give lower scores than either of the other two groups. This suggests that having been a victim of some sort of crime on one

Table VII.7. Mean seriousness scores for 33 offences, by Registrar-General's social class[a]

Incident number	Social class					
	I	II	IIIa	IIIb	IV	V
N^b =	30	102	130	142	63	46
1 [d]	4·91	5·20	4·58	5·82	6·23	6·03
2 [d]	5·80	6·18	6·55	7·58	6·92	7·52
3 [d]	5·43	5·11	4·77	6·01	5·36	5·57
4 [d]	5·44	5·31	4·77	6·40	6·11	5·89
5 [c]	10·71	10·73	10·62	10·70	10·63	10·72
6 [c]	7·46	7·34	7·23	7·05	7·62	7·36
7	4·63	4·70	4·65	5·30	5·32	4·97
8 [c]	8·54	8·21	8·01	8·00	7·68	7·52
9 [c]	8·50	8·82	9·12	9·08	8·81	7·93
10 [c]	6·86	6·80	6·81	6·73	6·87	5·86
11	7·77	7·47	7·49	7·79	7·29	7·55
12 [c]	9·66	9·52	9·39	9·60	9·69	9·38
13 [d]	5·40	5·00	4·34	5·55	4·65	5·21
14	6·24	6·30	6·09	7·04	6·41	6·86
15 [d]	7·77	8·63	9·00	9·74	9·78	9·72
16 [d]	5·21	5·50	5·86	6·82	6·66	6·54
17 [c]	8·00	8·03	7·64	8·22	8·13	8·43
18 [d]	5·13	5·67	5·52	6·48	6·87	6·46
19	4·40	4·64	4·50	5·08	5·34	5·00
20 [d]	4·66	5·04	5·20	5·88	6·00	5·72
21	5·71	5·98	5·86	6·53	6·60	6·31
22 [cd]	8·15	8·09	8·32	9·20	8·40	8·97
23 [cd]	9·60	10·05	10·04	10·43	10·13	10·24
24 [d]	5·53	6·32	5·88	7·06	7·24	7·17
25 [d]	5·46	5·06	6·09	7·00	7·08	6·97
26 [d]	4·97	5·37	4·54	5·84	6·18	5·96
27 [c]	8·88	8·88	8·72	9·27	9·13	9·35
28	4·49	4·61	4·35	5·12	5·00	5·21
29 [cd]	8·31	8·44	8·85	9·08	9·14	9·62
30 [d]	4·30	6·48	7·17	8·09	7·76	8·52
31 [c]	10·69	10·65	10·75	10·72	10·70	10·93
32 [c]	7·91	7·67	7·66	7·87	7·89	8·10
33 [d]	6·60	6·90	7·14	7·77	7·39	8·76

[a] The order indicated by these numbers corresponds to that in which they are listed in the questionnaire (Appendix, p. 253 below); it was not the order in which items were typically presented to respondents (see p. 183 of the text). Brief descriptions of the offences are given in Table VII.6 on p. 184 above.

[b] Excludes 28 respondents who scored all items 11; remaining N's vary slightly owing to missing data, and those shown in this row are maximum numbers in each class.

[c] Indicates an offence involving violence against the person.

[d] Indicates inter-class differences statistically significant at the 5 per cent level or better by the Kruskal–Wallis test.

(fairly recent) occasion may lead people to take a less serious view of crime in general than that generated by the stereotypes held by non-victims: they may, in effect, feel that 'It happened to me, and it's not really so serious as people think [and as I used to think myself].' But repeated victimization may tend to lead to a revision of this attitude, and a feeling that crime really is a serious matter after all.[33]

There was some evidence of an association between expressed concern about crime, and a belief that it was prevalent in one's neighbourhood, and higher seriousness scores; the differences were statistically significant, for a substantial number of crimes, in relation to responses to questions about whether or not the neighbourhood streets were safe at night, whether there was 'a great deal' or 'quite a lot' of crime in the neighbourhood, and in relation to an index based on beliefs about the increase or decrease of crime of various kinds in London as a whole. But as we shall see in the next chapter,[34] the relationships between these expressed beliefs and the respondents' own experiences of crime were not particularly strong ones; and they occasionally displayed the same curvilinear form in relation to reported victimization as that shown by the seriousness scores.

We saw in Chapter V that there was an association between the scores which respondents gave to their own incidents of victimization, and the reporting of those incidents to the police; this association interacted with the objective value of property stolen, and provided a possible explanation of the overall similarity in reporting of property victimization in different classes.[35] It might thus be thought that there would be an association between reporting one's own incidents to the police, and the seriousness scores given to the hypothetical crimes discussed in this section. In fact, however, there was no such direct relationship in our sample: product-moment correlations between mean seriousness scores and percentage of own incidents reported to the police were near zero ($+0.0008$ for the 13 violent crimes, and $+0.053$ for the 20 property crimes). There were moderately strong correlations, however, between mean scores on the hypothetical incidents, and mean scores on the respondent's own incidents ($+0.244$ for the violent crimes, and 0.546 for the property crimes); and there was also a moderate positive correlation ($+0.246$) between the mean score on the respondent's own incidents, and the percentage of those incidents in which he said he had notified the police. Thus, it may be that, for those respondents who were victims on one or more occasions, the perception of the seriousness of those incidents was influenced to some extent by a general tendency to give higher seriousness scores to the 33 hypothetical offences; and that their view of the particular incident in turn tended to influence the decision to call the police.

4. Methodological Implications

The two concepts discussed in this chapter have some important methodological implications for the measurement of crime through survey methods. Both differences in the definition of situations, and differences in the perception of 'seriousness,' may bias responses to questions about victimization.

It is clear that variations in the definition of situations may influence the pattern of survey responses. We tried, through the use of hypothetical incidents, to measure variations in the definition of assault; but there are many other areas where—depending on the factual substance of the incident, its context and the parties to it—we might well expect patterned variation in the classification of incidents as 'crime.' Thus, what some may consider theft may be regarded by others as mere 'pilfering' or 'perks of the job'; what one person regards as seduction may be seen by another as rape. Clearly, if a survey respondent defines a situation in a way which entails that it is *not* a crime, he is less likely to mention it to an interviewer who is asking him about 'criminal' victimization; he may remember the incident perfectly well, and may even remember exactly when it occurred, but he will not regard it as something which the interviewer is interested in hearing about.[1] We saw in this chapter that our middle-class respondents were more likely to disapprove of violence in the hypothetical situations, and were somewhat less likely to give justificatory interpretations of those situations; this may well explain the finding, discussed in Chapter IV,[2] that our middle-class respondents reported a higher number of merely threatened or attempted assaults than did our working-class respondents. Theoretically, if such consistent biases could be identified, and related to other attributes such as race, sex, age or social class, it would be possible to correct survey responses concerning victimization by making ratio adjustments (just as is often done, for example, to correct for non-response). At the present time, however, neither our data nor anyone else's (so far as we know) would permit anything so ambitious.[3]

Variations in the perception of 'seriousness' may also be a cause of response bias in the measurement of victimization, for a quite different reason. We saw in Chapter III[4] that incidents which were regarded as relatively unserious were still likely to be placed accurately in time by our MV sample. But there is still reason to think that relatively trivial incidents are also more likely simply to be forgotten, or for other reasons not mentioned to interviewers.

This might not matter so much if non-recall (or telescoping) due to differential assessments of seriousness were reasonably uniform in the surveyed population. But where there is patterned variation—as there appears to be in our sample, in respect of the evaluation of property offences in different social classes—the issue of response bias may be more of a problem.

Notes and References

1. Introduction

1. Above, Chapter III, p. 40.
2. See above, Chapter IV, pp. 79–80.

2. Norms and the Definition of 'Violence'

1. Cf. J. L. Austin, 'A plea for excuses,' in his *Collected Papers* (edited by J. O. Urmson and G. L. Warnock: Oxford University Press, 1961) 123, at 128–9; J. L. Austin, notes

on 'Three ways of spilling ink,' in Carl J. Freidrich (ed.) *Responsibility: Nomos III* (New York: Liberal Arts Press, 1960) 305.

2. Most of the psychological research in what social psychologists call 'perception' seems to be concerned with contextual or situational determinants of perception (often of the *physical* properties of things or persons, rather than with actions) and with possible sources of *individual* variation in the perception of, or response to, rule-breaking situations. There is also a good deal of experimental research in the area of 'person perception' which would seem to us more relevant if only it were less inconclusive. One of the few studies attempting to explore cross-cultural differences in this general area is Marshall H. Segal, Donald T. Campbell and Melville J. Herskovits, *The Influence of Culture on Visual Perception* (Indianapolis: Babbs-Merrill, 1966). Much research on differential socialization, of course, deals with this subject though (so far as we are aware) more usually with the causes of such differences than with their consequences.

3. Cf. Thorsten Sellin, *Culture Conflict and Crime* (New York: Social Science Research Council, 1933); and the discussion in Donald R. Cressey, 'Culture conflict, differential association and normative conflict,' in M. E. Wolfgang (ed.) *Crime and Culture: Essays in Honour of Thorsten Sellin* (New York and London: John Wiley and Sons, 1968) 43.

4. Cf. Marvin E. Wolfgang and Franco Ferracuti, *The Subculture of Violence* (London: Tavistock, 1967), esp. Chapter 3. It has recently been argued that homicide rates in the United States can in part be explained by the existence, and subsequent diffusion through migration, of a Southern 'regional culture of violence': see R. D. Gastil, 'Homicide and a regional culture of violence,' (1971) 36 *American Sociological Review*, 412–427. See also Gresham M. Sykes and David Matza, 'Techniques of neutralization,' (1957) 22 *American Sociological Review*, 664.

5. For England, see now the Criminal Law Act 1967, s.3; *R.v.Duffy* [1967] 1 Q.B. 63, [1966] 1 All. E. R. 62 is an example. Only such force as is 'reasonable in the circumstances' may be used, however. Until the 1967 Act, it appeared to be the law that a man might kill one who unlawfully sought to dispossess him of his home: *R.v.Hussey* (1924) 18 *Cr. App. R.* 160.

6. Homicide Act 1957, s.3; this section continues the common law provision that the provocation must have been such as would make a 'reasonable' man do as the accused did, though it now makes clear that words, as well as deeds, may suffice. The killing must also have been done in the heat of passion, i.e., there must have been no 'cooling time' in which the offender could reasonably have been expected to regain his self-control: *R.v.Hayward* (1833) 6 C. & P. 157.

7. *R.v.Cunningham* [1959] 1 Q.B. 288, [1958] 3 All E.R. 711; and cf. the discussion in D. A. Thomas, *Principles of Sentencing* (London: Heinemann, 1970) 94–100.

8. See J. L. Austin, 'A plea for excuses,' at 124–5; Marvin B. Scott and Stanford M. Lyman, 'Accounts, deviance and social order,' in Jack D. Douglas (ed.) *Deviance and Respectability* (New York and London: Basic Books, 1970) 89, at 93–4; Marvin Scott and Stanford M. Lyman, 'Accounts.' (1968) 33 *American Sociological Review* 46–62. A legal example of the difference concerns murder by one who finds his spouse committing adultery. In England, this has been held to be manslaughter (i.e., to be excusable on the ground of loss of self-control) since Blackstone's day: see 4 *Commentaries* 192; *R.v.Maddy* (1792) T. Raym. 212. It appears, however, that (at least until fairly recently) the penal codes of Texas and New Mexico provided that a man's killing of someone who had committed adultery with his spouse was *justifiable* and not merely excusable: see Jerome Michael and Herbert Wechsler, *Criminal Law and its Administration* (Chicago: Foundation Press, 1940) 1283–84n.

9. For the exact wording of these cases and the accompanying questions, see Section D of the questionnaire in the Appendix, pp. 246–249 below. The items finally used in the London survey were selected from a much larger number tried in pilot studies; they

were in fact those which (in the pilot samples) showed the least evidence of consensus among respondents.

10. In the interview itself, the first situation described involved a cyclist hitting a motorist who had knocked the cyclist off his bicycle. This case was used as a 'warm-up,' to familiarize respondents with this type of question; we have, therefore, excluded responses to it from our analysis.

11. As usual, the prompt cards used to present these responses were systematically varied, half beginning with 'Strongly Approve' and the remainder beginning with 'Strongly Disapprove.' There was a slight, though consistent, tendency for respondents to bias their responses toward the items near the top of the list (e.g. to approve when the responses began with 'Strongly Approve'); but this was in no case statistically significant.

12. Two other kinds of response bias, neither very serious, were noted in relation to this part of our questionnaire. Our interviewers were asked to record, at the end of the questionnaire, any items which the respondent appeared to have difficulty answering. Analysis of these impressions showed that there were in fact two distinct groups for whom this appeared to be true. First, 42 respondents (or about 8 per cent of the sample) were said by the interviewers to have had general difficulty in understanding the questions or the procedure for answering. Another 22 (for about 4 per cent) complained—perhaps not unreasonably—that the situations were described in too simplistic a fashion, and that they could not really give an adequate answer without knowing more about the situation. As might be expected, these 'quibblers' tended to be middle-class, and to have had some further education (i.e. beyond secondary school); they tended—when they finally answered the questions—to be more disapproving than other respondents of the violence described. Those who were said to have had difficulties with this section tended to be just the opposite on both counts. However, excluding either or both of these groups did not alter the basic findings described in this chapter. It should also be noted that 'Don't know' accounted on average for about seven per cent of the cases on these questions; this was more marked, however, for the 'neighbour' responses than for the 'self' ones, as some respondents said they simply did not know what their neighbours would think.

13. Above, Chapter V, pp. 119–120.

14. This assumes that those respondents in the middle category of 'Indifferent' should be grouped with those expressing disapproval, i.e. that approval of violence even in these situations is to some extent contrary to norms; one might equally argue, however, that *disapproval* in such situations is to be considered the unusual response, and that the 'Indifferent' group should be treated as having given tacit approval. In fact, however, the results basically are no different if Table VII.2 is based on percent disapproving rather than percent approving.

15. This case was deliberately described so as to include the 'cooling time' which the courts generally recognize as negativing provocation as a defence; the slandered man's attack was characterized as deliberate rather than as being done in the heat of passion. Given this fact, it is surprising that a substantial minority of the sample still felt that they—or their neighbours—could approve of the violence used; presumably the proportion would have been even higher if the attack had been carried out as soon as the rumours had been heard about.

16. Several respondents told our interviewers that it was not clear, from the case as described, what the stranger had been doing in the house; a few speculated that the stranger might have been after the householder's wife—either with or without her consent—rather than his property.

17. In no case was it possible to obtain a coefficient of reproducibility greater than 0.80, given a minimum marginal reproducibility of about 0.65.

18. Robert K. Baker and Sandra J. Ball, *Mass Media and Violence*, a report to the National Commission on the Causes and Prevention of Violence, Vol. IX (Washington, D.C.:

U.S. Government Printing Office, 1969) 342–354. This survey was actually conducted by Louis Harris and Associates; the sample comprised 1,176 adults and 496 teenagers.
19. Robert K. Baker and Sandra Ball, Mass Media and Violence. 346–47. But there was also a remarkably high degree of approval in this sample for a policeman striking an adult male citizen after 'vulgar and obscene' *verbal* provocation, or when the citizen was demonstrating against the Vietnam war and carrying a Vietcong flag: 27 and 21 per cent among adults, and 19 and 27 per cent among teenagers. These grotesque findings may owe to the fact that the fieldwork for this survey was carried out early in October 1968. But they are a reminder—if one were needed—that the degree of legitimacy accorded to the police and other authorities is by no means only a function of the traditional values of the criminal law.
20. Perhaps somewhat surprisingly, responses to the questions about the household intruder cases did not vary according to type or size of accommodation; council tenants and private tenants were about as likely to approve as owner-occupiers.
21. The first cafe argument case, the first and third household intruder cases, and the first rumour-spreading case.
22. The hypothetical situations were, of course, very briefly described, and it may well be that in assessing them our respondents filled in the unstated details in different ways. (Cf. the minority of the sample who displayed some reluctance to answer these questions without more facts than they were given by the interviewer's description.)
23. 'Revenge,' which was mentioned by about five per cent of the sample in both the cafe and rumour-spreading cases, poses something of a problem here, since it can clearly be conceived of in both normative and purely emotional terms. Since we were unable to tell which (if either) of these things these respondents primarily had in mind, we have excluded these cases in this part of our analysis. We have also excluded a small number of responses—at most three per cent—which fell into a miscellaneous 'Other' category.
24. Cf. the ancient common-law offence of affray, the essence of which is 'two or more people fighting in a public place, to the terror of the Queen's subjects:' *Button*. v.*D.P.P.* [1966] A.C. 591, at 626.
25. This is only partly supported by our self-report data; though the number of persons who admitted having done one or more of the six violent acts we asked about was higher in Brixton, there was virtually no difference between Hackney and Kensington respondents. (See above, pp. 100–103). But, of course, the descriptions of the acts referred to in that part of our questionnaire might themselves have been mediated by differential perceptions, or just plain response bias.
26. Above, p. 80.
27. Cf. Donald J. Black, 'Production of crime rates.' (1970) 35 *American Sociological Review* 733.

3. The 'Seriousness' of Crimes

1. See, for example, Dogan D. Akman and Andre Normandeau, 'The measurement of crime and delinquency in Canada,' (1967) 7 *British Journal of Criminology* 129; Karl O. Christiansen *et al.*, 'Method of using an index of crime,' in *The Index of Crime: Some Further Studies*, in Collected Studies in Criminological Research (Strasbourg: Council of Europe, 1970); P. H. Ennis, *Criminal Victimization in the United States*, Field Surveys II; University of Lancaster, Department of Operational Research, *Survey of Police Operations* [Lancaster: 1967, mimeo.]; A. A. Congalton and J. M. Najman, *Unreported Crime* (Statistical report number 12, Department of the Attorney General, New South Wales Bureau of Crime Statistics and Research, 1974) 15–16.
2. G. N. G. Rose, 'Concerning the measurement of delinquency,' (1966) 6 *British Journal of Criminology* 414; G. N. G. Rose, 'The merits of an index of crime,' in *The Index of Crime: Some Further Studies*, Collected Studies in Criminological Research, vol. VII

(Strasbourg: Council of Europe, 1970) 31–52; Nigel Walker, 'Psychophysics and the recording angel,' (1971) 11 *British Journal of Criminology* 191.

3. In this respect our procedure differed from that of Sellin and Wolfgang, who refused to let their respondents refer back to earlier answers or change a score once it had been given: see Sellin and Wolfgang, *The Measurement of Delinquency* 254–55. Wolfgang has defended this procedure on the ground that it has not been followed in similar psychophysical experiments, and also because it leads to paired comparisons rather than judgements of individual items: 'by turning pages back, the observer attends more to the confused multiplicity of pairs than to the ratios requested.' See M. E. Wolfgang, 'On devising a crime index,' in *The Index of Crime: Some Further Studies*, Collected Studies in Criminological Research, Vol. VII (Strasbourg: Council of Europe, 1970) 68–9. It is open to question, however, just how far the essentially non-rational assessments of psychophysical experiments are in fact analogous to the assessment of the seriousness of crimes: 'seriousness' is not, after all, like a particular itch or tickle, or a feeling of hunger. Wolfgang's second point is in any case difficult to understand, since *all* measurement can be regarded as a process of 'paired comparison' between the object being measured and the unit of measurement; 'gut reactions' to such things as brightness or loudness are not in themselves measurement, even though they may furnish a basis for measurement if (as seems to be the case) most people's reactions to the same stimuli tend to be in agreement.

4. The instructions given by the interviewers stressed that 'of course, in one sense all of these acts are serious because they are all crimes; but they are not all equally serious —for example, most people consider murder to be a more serious crime than shop-lifting.'

5. Through an irritating bit of serendipity, we were able to investigate the consequences of *one* ordering of the slips, since a few of our interviewers plainly did not comply with our instruction to shuffle the slips before giving them to the respondents; thus, about 12 per cent of the sample were given the 33 descriptions in the same order. Comparison of this group's scores with those of the rest of the sample revealed no significant or consistent differences, however; consequently we have not excluded these cases from the analysis.

6. It was in order to overcome this problem that Sellin and Wolfgang used a different method of scoring (the 'magnitude ratio' technique developed by S. S. Stevens in his psychophysical research). Briefly, on this method the respondent is allowed to give any numerical score greater than zero to each offence, using a 'standard offence' (theft of one dollar, scored 10) as a base for measurement. It has been found that scores obtained in this way, and those obtained using category scales, have a linear relationship when the latter are suitably transformed: see Thorsten Sellin and Marvin E. Wolfgang, *The Measurement of Delinquency*, Chapters 15–16.

7. The main statistical test used was the Kruskal–Wallis one-way analysis of variance: see S. Siegel, *Nonparametric Statistics for the Behavioral Sciences* (New York: McGraw-Hill, 1956) 184–93.

8. Excluding the 28 respondents who scored all items 11. The N's on which Table VII.6 are based differ slightly from question to question, owing to the fact that not all respondents were able to score every item; in most cases they are rather more than 500.

9. The exact wording was 'injured and sent to hospital,' and 'injured but not sent to hospital.'

10. Thorsten Sellin and Marvin E. Wolfgang found that dollar values of theft items in their study were related by a power function to the magnitude score scales (see *The Measurement of Delinquency* 284–87). We could not make the same comparison; but a broadly similar relationship exists between the mean *category* scale scores given by our sample, and the values of thefts or damage (£10, £50, £100, £1,000).

11. Cf. D. A. Thomas, *Principles of Sentencing*. 162–65. These judicial views may also, of course, be the result of ignorance as to the nature of marijuana.

12. See Thorsten Sellin and Marvin E. Wolfgang, *The Measurement of Delinquency*. 391–94.

13. Akman and Normandeau, 'The measurement of crime and delinquency in Canada,' 140.

14. Mary Durant, Margaret Thomas and H. D. Willcock, *Crime, Criminals and the Law* (London: Office of Population Censuses and Surveys, Social Survey Division, 1972) 116–19. The authors state that there was general agreement between their findings and those obtained, using a similar method, by Banks in her (unpublished) study of young offenders in penal institutions.

15. Peter H. Rossi, Emily Waite, Christine Bose and Richard E. Berk, 'The seriousness of crimes: normative structure and individual differences.' (1974) 39 *American Sociological Review* 224, at 228–29, 231–33.

16. In part this is due to the fact that the scores for the crimes of violence are bounded by the upper limit of 11; it also holds, however, for offences with mean scores comparable to those of the property crimes rated as relatively serious. For example, the mean score for an attack with fists causing minor injuries is 6·71, whereas that for obtaining £100 by forged cheques is 6·60; the coefficient of variation (i.e., the standard deviation divided by the mean) is 0·355 for the first of these offences, and 0·403 for the second. Standard errors for the mean scores shown in Table VII.6 range from about 0·04 to 0·13; most are about 0·10.

17. See Thorsten Sellin and Marvin E. Wolfgang, *The Measurement of Delinquency*. 249–252. It also appears, however, that at least one of these groups—the students— was chosen on grounds of ease of access; Sellin and Wolfgang say they rejected the idea of a random sample even of middle-class persons because it 'would have been an enormous task consuming resources beyond the limits of the study.' (250).

18. G. N. G. Rose, 'The merits of an index of crime.' 34–36.

19. Thorsten Sellin and Marvin E. Wolfgang, *The Measurement of Delinquency*. 263–68.

20. Marvin E. Wolfgang, 'On devising a crime index'. 73. The omitted words are 'The best judgement of the distance to the moon was never yielded by using a national sample.' But surely it was never yielded by the psychophysical judgments of a sample of policemen, judges and law students either?

21. Mary Durant *et al.*, *Crime, Criminals and the Law*. 119–121.

22. P. H. Rossi *et al.*, 'The seriousness of crimes: normative structure and individual differences'. 230–31.

23. Jack D. Douglas, *American Social Order: Social Rules in A Pluralistic Society* (New York: Free Press, 1971) 90–91.

24. Richard Quinney, 'Crime control in capitalist society: a critical philosophy of legal order,' in Ian Taylor, Paul Walton and Jock Young, *Critical Criminology* (London: Routledge and Kegan Paul, 1975) 181, at 198.

25. Richard Quinney, 'Crime control in capitalist society: a critical philosophy of legal order.' 199.

26. Ian Taylor, Paul Walton and Jock Young, 'Critical criminology in Britain: review and prospects,' in *Critical Criminology* at 42.

27. H. F. Moorhouse and C. W. Chamberlain, 'Lower-class attitudes to property: aspects of the counter-ideology.' (1974) 8 *Sociology* 387.

28. At the 5 per cent level or better, as measured by the Kruskal—Wallis H statistic, comparing the nine age-groups used generally in analyses throughout this book.

29. The Kendall coefficient of concordance—roughly a function of the average rank correlations between all classes—is 0·89.

30. Kendall's τ; $z = 5·88$.

31. In particular, unless we make the considerable assumption that the agreement between the different classes' scores for violent offences reflects a real agreement in the perceived seriousness of those crimes—which is tantamount to the assumption that the respondents' use of the 1-to-11 point scale was based on a 'zero' point common to all groups—

we cannot really infer that our lower-class respondents rated property crimes as more serious in any *absolute* sense. A further possibility is that the different groups responded differently to the stimuli—viz. the offence descriptions and the 1-to-11 point scales— which we presented to them; in that our lower-class respondents simply used less of the scale than the upper-class ones did, in recording what they intended to be comparable distinctions between different offences. Inspection of the variances of the scores does not show any evidence for this view; but it still cannot be ruled out completely.

32. H. F. Moorhouse and C. W. Chamberlain, 'Lower-class attitudes to property'. 394. This survey dealt *only* with the expressed attitudes of working-class persons (council tenants); other methodological problems aside, it is possible that a middle-class control group would have expressed even more 'deviant' attitudes to property than the surveyed sample did.

33. P. H. Rossi and his colleagues found some evidence of an association between having been victimized and a slightly lower collective view of the seriousness of crimes in general: see 'The seriousness of crimes: normative structure and individual differences' at 234–35. In relation to our sample, it must be remembered that most of the victimization mentioned was of a relatively trivial kind; a single experience as victim of serious violence or theft would probably increase one's view of the seriousness of all crime, no matter how unrealistically high that view had previously been. Our respondents' own criminality may also be a factor; since there was a negative association between self-reported offences and mean seriousness scores, it may be that doing crime, rather than suffering it, is what mainly tends to affect one's view of its seriousness.

34. Below, pp. 208–209.
35. Above, pp. 121–123.

4. Methodological Implications

1. Unless he is asked about 'injury' or some similarly neutral category of events: see above, p. 14.
2. Above, pp. 79–80.
3. It might be expected that there would be a direct relationship between the responses relating to our hypothetical situations, and the *proportions* (as distinct from the *numbers*) of actual versus threatened assaults reported by our R sample respondents. In fact, no such relationship appears—in part because *self-reported* violence is confounded with both variables. In any case (apart from general questions about the validity of the responses to our hypothetical situations), it may well be that experiences of victimization influenced the respondents' attitudes, rather than that their attitudes influenced the reporting of their experiences.
4. Above, pp. 59, 61.

CHAPTER VIII

Crime and the Social Environment

1. Crime and its Consequences

And now for something rather different. In the preceding four chapters we have been concerned with estimating the incidence of victimization in our three London areas, with definitions of crime, and with reporting to the police and comparisons with statistics of recorded crime. In those chapters, for the most part, victimization was treated as a dependent variable: it was assumed to be influenced, to some extent, by the attributes, attitudes and behaviour of the victim.

We turn now to the question of the effects which crime—and in particular, experience as a victim of crime—may have on people's lives. Does the experience of victimization alter people's attitudes and beliefs about their own environment, or the world in general? How much crime do people believe is occurring in their immediate social environments, and do these perceptions in any way affect their behaviour? What crimes do people most fear, and what sorts of people are commonly seen as potential 'offenders?' In asking questions of this kind, one is, in effect, treating crime as an independent variable—one which operates either through personal experience (e.g. as a victim), or indirectly, though information communicated by friends and acquaintances or through the mass media.

Necessarily, our findings on these points are somewhat speculative. This is not merely because of the uncertainty which almost always attaches itself to survey responses of an attitudinal kind; it is also because there are definite limits to what can be inferred from cross-sectional data of the kind which we collected. Fortunately, the results of our reverse record check[1] suggest that our measure of victimization is a reasonably accurate one, and give us no reason to suppose that certain attitudes or beliefs relating to crime themselves led to spurious reporting of victimization. But, of course, our data on victimization relate only to the year preceding the interviews (i.e. approximately the calendar year 1972). Thus, when we speak, in this chapter, about 'victims' we are referring to those who mentioned one or more incidents as having occurred to them *in that year;* a 'non-victim' is one who mentioned *no* incidents of victimization during that year, though he may have been a victim at some earlier time.[2]

Moreover, we have no data on our sample's attitudes or beliefs *before* that year began; it is thus perilous (to put it mildly) for us to make casual inferences from our data.

For the most part, we will be concerned in this chapter with responses from the R sample. We will, however, give comparative results relating to the MV and T samples, each member of which had reported a crime to the police. The crimes committed against these respondents were, in general, of a more serious kind than those mentioned by the R sample; in addition, their contact with the police (and possibly the courts) may have had effects on their attitudes which were not experienced by the majority of the victims in the R sample.

The general question of public fear of crime has received considerable attention from researchers in the United States over the past decade.[3] It is often said that in that country the fear of crime has led to the inhibition or restructuring, on a large scale, of normal social activities, especially in American cities: people are said to be afraid to walk the streets at night (and sometimes by daylight), and to avoid the use of public transport, preferring to lurk behind doors displaying a complex of locks and spy-holes worthy of the Bank of England. In fact, that kind of inhibition is by no means as great as it may seem from a distance; and the changes which have taken place in many central cities in the United States in the past few years have clearly had many other causes as well. But this is not to say that fear of crime is unimportant in America: even if unjustified by the objective facts, it can nonetheless be very real and disruptive of social relations.

Public concern about crime is no doubt much less widespread in England. Even so, it is far from non-existent; not long before our fieldwork, for example, there had been widespread comment in the press concerning a supposed outbreak of 'mugging' in London, especially in the area of Brixton.[4] We thought it of interest, therefore, to see how far such concern would be expressed by our respondents, and in particular to see how far their views were in any way related to their experiences as victims. In attempting to explore these problems, we worked from the assumption that concern about crime and fear of crime—like crime itself—are likely to vary according to cultural and environmental factors, which may (among other things) modify the effects of direct experience as a victim. We thus tried to focus our questions primarily on the local neighbourhood areas in which our respondents lived. The reader is reminded once again that our three areas were deliberately selected in order to provide contrasts, rather than a representative sample of neighbourhoods in Inner London. As we shall see, there were important differences between the views of respondents in the different areas; these differences suggest that the psychological and social impact of crime is likely to be different, however similar the objective risks of victimization may be.

2. Attitudes to the Neighbourhood

We suspected that asking questions about crime in the abstract would produce different, and less meaningful, responses than asking about the particular place in which a respondent lived. We began, therefore, by trying to elicit a definition of the respondents' home neighbourhoods, and obtaining their subjective evaluations both of the physical characteristics of the area and of the people living in it.

In order to try to understand the ways in which integration or attachment to a local 'home' area might be associated with perceptions and fear of crime, we used a series of questions devised for a survey conducted for the Royal Commission on the Reorganization of Local Government by Research Services Ltd.[1] We first asked all respondents, 'Is there an area around here—where you are living now—which you feel attached to, and where you feel at home?' Research Services found that nearly four in five of their respondents (in a national sample) claimed to possess some feelings of attachment to a 'home' area, and that this tendency was positively correlated with length of residence in the area. In our R sample as a whole, we found that just over three-fifths of the respondents said they felt attached to an area around and including their present homes; about one-fifth said that there was an area *outside* of their home location to which they felt attached, and the rest said that there was no area anywhere to which they felt such a sense of attachment. There were quite marked variations, however, between Brixton, Hackney and Kensington. More than half of the respondents in Brixton claimed that they felt no sense of attachment to the area in which they lived, as compared with one-quarter in Kensington and 40 per cent in Hackney. Of those respondents who said they felt no sense of attachment to their local areas, 29 per cent in Brixton, 20 per cent in Hackney and 11 per cent in Kensington said that they felt 'at home' or attached to some other area (e.g. outside of London), and the remainder said that they felt no sense of attachment to any area anywhere.

As in the study by Research Services, we found that feelings of attachment were associated with length of residence in the area, and to a lesser extent, with age. Of those claiming to feel a sense of attachment to their home area nearly two-thirds had been resident for more than five years, while only 2 per cent had been resident for less than one year. Of the other factors which we examined in relation to a feeling of local attachment, we found that home-ownership was to some extent associated with the tendency to feel attached. Two-thirds of those owning their homes said that they had a local area of attachment, whilst only just over half of council tenants felt this way.[2] Council tenants were in fact less likely to feel a sense of attachment *anywhere* than home-owners, and were less likely than those who rented private accommodation to feel attached to their local area. In both Brixton and Hackney, persons in social classes I and II were less likely than their counterparts in Kensington to express a feeling of attachment to the area in which they lived. This probably reflects the social composition of the three areas, since only a minority of residents in Brixton and Hackney were in the upper two classes, while the majority of respondents in Kensington were in those social groups. We can infer from this attachment to a home area is to some extent dependent on the ability to identify, in terms of status, with other people living in the area. There was a tendency in both Brixton and Hackney for blacks to feel slightly more attached to their home areas than the whites living with them, and in Brixton a feeling of attachment among whites is the lowest of all three areas. Thus it seems that some whites do not feel particularly 'at home' in an ethnically mixed community. Conversely, it may be that blacks' feeling of security is enhanced and the tendency to feel 'at home' becomes more common, as their numbers increase.[3]

There was considerable variation in the *size* of the 'home' area claimed by our respondents.[4] At one end of the scale, there were some who said 'just this street,' while at the other extreme some said e.g. 'all of Kensington' or even 'the whole of London.' It is probable, therefore, that the interpretation of feeling 'at home' or 'attached' also varied. Overall, however, there was little difference in the average size of area mentioned in Brixton, Hackney and Kensington; the majority of respondents in all three areas described their 'home' neighbourhoods as covering a region of about one square mile or less. Neither length of residence nor age, social class, sex or race were associated with variations in size.[5]

We then asked respondents to describe their neighbourhoods and the people who lived around them, and to say how those neighbourhoods differed from adjacent areas.[6] Overall, both the R and MVT samples were divided almost evenly between those who expressed approval or liking of their area, those who gave disapproving or negative comments, and those who gave neutral or non-evaluative replies. In both Brixton and Hackney, however, a majority of respondents gave a negative or disapproving description of the area, while the vast majority of those interviewed in Kensington gave favourable or approving descriptions. In both Hackney and Kensington, approval of the area was associated with an expressed feeling of attachment to it; but this was not the case in Brixton, where a slight majority claiming some feeling of attachment to the area actually expressed disapproval of it. Take, for example, a woman of 65 who had lived for more than 20 years in Brixton, and claimed to have a feeling of attachment to her home neighbourhood. Her description of the area was '[It's] horrible—really horrible. Hardly anybody goes out. People are frightened.... It was lovely when we moved in—people envied us, until [a well-known black musician] bought up houses around here and let them to immigrants.'

In all three survey areas, negative comments were mostly based on the physical characteristics or limited amenities of the respondent's environment— poor housing or shops, litter, noise and the like. But in Brixton (as the response just quoted illustrates) a minority of those disapproving specifically mentioned 'immigrants' as the cause of their disapproval; this was also the case in Hackney. It is important to note, at this point, that very few of our respondents—about 4 per cent in Brixton, 2 per cent in Hackney and none at all in Kensington— mentioned crime even when giving negative comments: in that respect, the illustrative quotation just given is atypical.

When asked about the people living in their neighbourhoods, the majority of respondents in all three areas gave positive or approving answers; but there were interesting differences in the reasons for their approval. In both Brixton and Hackney, those people who approved of their neighbours did so in the main because they were 'nice' or 'respectable'—two-thirds gave this response in Brixton, as did over half in Hackney. On the other hand, the most frequently given reason for approval in Kensington was that neighbours were 'middle class' or 'like me,' presumably reflecting the level of status consciousness of Kensington residents and the extent to which they identify, or would like to be identified, with their neighbours in this respect. The responses from a 43 year old male artist living in the Holland Park area of Kensington are typical in their message, if not necessarily in their presentation. He described the area as 'very expensive... There are many important people living around here... it's very pleasant.' When asked what kind of people lived around him he mentioned 'Lord L---- and television personalities... young stockbrokers and their wives and Lady F----.... it's great!' He naturally felt very attached to the area and would be 'very sorry to leave.... I love living here.'

Paradoxically, the most common reason given for the infrequent *disapproval* of neighbours in Kensington was similarly that they were 'middle class,' which suggests a division of approval and disapproval directly along class lines. But in both Brixton and Hackney, the most frequent negative description of people in the area was that they were 'immigrants' or (what may well come to the same thing) that they were 'mixed' or 'of all different sorts': about half of those who expressed disapproval of their neighbours gave replies of this kind.

Subsequent questions about other aspects of the neighbourhood were generally intercorrelated,[7] and were associated in fairly predictable ways both with an expressed feeling of attachment to the area and with the objective features of the places in question. Thus, those respondents who claimed to have a feeling of attachment to their local neighbourhood were more likely to view it favourably in comparison with others around it; this was so in all three survey areas, though there was an overall tendency for those in Brixton and Hackney to see no real difference between their home areas and adjacent areas. Respondents in Hackney were much less likely to say that they were 'interested in what goes on' in their neighbourhood; this is to some extent a function of social class, but also appears to be due to the relatively large number of council tenants in Hackney, over a third of whom said they were 'not interested at all' in local goings-on.

In all three areas, those people who perceived some change as having taken place in their neighbourhood overwhelmingly expressed disapproval of that change. In Brixton, nearly two-thirds of the sample observed a change for the worse in the area; of these, one-third spontaneously mentioned either immigrants, or immigrants plus the housing or amenities of the area, in relation to this change. Common responses on this question in Brixton were 'It's on the downgrade—there is a colossal coloured element. It's getting out of proportion now' or 'The houses are deteriorating... there's litter everywhere now since they [immigrants] have come.' In Hackney, 30 per cent of those who perceived change for the worse in the area mentioned the physical characteristics of the area, while another 10 per cent mentioned an increase in crime as the source of change. Kensington residents were less likely to see their area as changing, but among those who did mention changes, observation of a deterioration of the physical characteristics of the area seemed to be the major preoccupation. In all areas, those who expressed a sense of attachment to the area were slightly less likely to see a change for the worse, although this was not a strong association.

Predictably, a lack of interest in one's neighbourhood and a feeling that things are changing for the worse are associated with a desire to leave the neighbourhood: this association is most marked in Hackney, where the greatest number expressed a desire to leave the area. Over the whole R sample, more than 80 per cent of those who would be 'very pleased' to leave the area felt that it had changed for the worse. For example, a woman of 38 in Brixton who has been resident there for only 18 months gives this response:

'[The area has] got worse in the year and a half we've been here .... coloured people are coming in more .... we are very pleased to be moving because we're moving to a completely white area with better schooling. The schooling here is bad.'

In general, then, responses to our questions about attitudes to the local neighbourhood give a reasonably consistent picture. Taking a broad view of the three survey areas, we find that our Kensington residents tend to express a high degree of attachment to their local neighbourhoods, and that this is reinforced by a high degree of approval of both the physical characteristics and amenities of the area and the people seen as living in it. In contrast, we find that respondents in both Brixton and Hackney are less likely to feel 'attached' to their home areas, and that they express a greater amount of dissatisfaction both with the physical environment and with the people around them. These tendencies are, on the whole, more marked in Brixton, where a substantial group of people see a deterioration in their environment and associate this with West Indian settlement; in Hackney, dissatisfaction with housing and the physical characteristics of the area produces the strongest desire to move away.

These generalizations are supported by an examination of responses within particular wards of our three areas, though our numbers of cases are too small to permit much statistical analysis at that level of detail.[8] Thus, for example, in Kensington we find a high degree of consensus, and general approval of the area, among residents of the Holland and Queen's Gate wards in the north of the area;[9] this is the most exclusive and fashionable part of the area, with the highest percentage of owner-occupiers. Such negative attitudes as were expressed by Kensington residents generally came from those living in Redcliffe and Earl's Court wards, which contain the 'bed-sitter belt' of poorer quality housing (mostly furnished rooms for short-stay tenants). In Brixton, negative attitudes are most consistently expressed by those living in three wards[10] containing the greatest proportions of West Indians. Within these wards, moreover, it was mainly the *white* population which expressed disapproval of the area. These findings are consistent with a recent study by Alan Marsh of prejudice in Brixton and other London areas of high immigrant settlement.[11] Marsh found that in Brixton, where identification with the local area was low, the degree of proximity of whites to the black population increased their level of prejudice and expressed hostility, and produced an expressed concern for the 'deterioration' of the neighbourhood: he found that 38 per cent of those who saw things as getting worse in the borough blamed 'the blacks', which, as we have seen, was not an uncommonly expressed view in our samples.

We have pointed out that crime was not mentioned spontaneously in respondents' descriptions of their neighbourhoods, and thus did not seem to be an important determinant of general attitudes to the local environment. This conclusion is strengthened by the fact that victimization (within the preceding year) bore no strong relationship to any of our indicators of general attitudes to the neighbourhood. If all victims are lumped together, there is a slight consistent tendency for them to be less approving, and more disapproving, of the neighbourhood itself and the people living there, and to say that they would be pleased to leave; but this is in no case statistically significant, and there was no consistent increase in disapproval as the number of incidents of victimization (of any type) increased.[12]

3. Perceptions of the Prevalence of Crime

We turn now to our respondents' assessments of the amounts and types of crime occurring in their neighbourhoods, and their expressed beliefs about crime and criminals, both in their immediate environments and in London generally. With reference to the local neighbourhood (as defined by replies to earlier questions[1]) we asked 'Just thinking about this neighbourhood, would you say that there is much crime around here?' and 'Do you think that there is more crime around here than in other parts of town, about the same, or less?' On the face of it, both of these questions ask for respondents' views on objective matters of fact; they are not explicitly aimed at eliciting attitudes, expressions of fear, concern, etc. Nor, strictly speaking, do they even ask for respondents' perceptions of *personal* risk of victimization, since a person may believe (rightly or wrongly) that there is a lot of crime in his area, but that he is relatively immune to it. We have only limited information, of course, with which to assess the accuracy of our respondents' expressed beliefs. But we are less concerned here with the correctness of those beliefs, than with the relations between expressed beliefs and concern or fear, and with possible determinants of both.

Over the sample as a whole, respondents were about evenly divided in their assessments of the amounts of crime in their neighbourhoods; 52 per cent said there was 'quite a lot' or 'a great deal,' and 48 per cent said there was 'not much,' 'very little,' or 'none.' Most people saw their own areas as no more crime-ridden than others, however: 39 per cent said there was less crime than in 'other parts of town,' 48 per cent said there was about the same amount, and only 14 per cent said there was more. Responses to the two questions were highly correlated; that is, those who said there was 'quite a lot' or 'a great deal' of crime in their areas were much more likely also to say that there was more than in other parts of town.[2] There were no significant differences between men and women on these questions, nor were there significant or consistent differences by age or social class. Residents of Brixton—in particular, whites—gave markedly higher estimates of crime on both questions, however.[3]

Tables VIII.1 and VIII.2 show that there is a relationship between victimization (within the preceding year) and the responses to our two perceptual questions; but that the relationship is by no means a strong or consistent one, in either case. Specifically, victims as a group were more likely than non-victims to say that there was a relatively high level of crime in their neighbourhoods, and that there was more than in 'other parts of town;' but the proportions giving these responses were virtually unaffected by the *numbers* of incidents of victimizations which the respondents later mentioned. Nor was there evidence of any trends for particular types of victimization.

After asking *how much* crime there was in the neighbourhood, we asked what kinds of crime took place;[4] overall, victims mentioned more kinds of crime in reply to this question than non-victims, though again multiple victimization made no difference to the answers. We also found that the type(s) of crime of which the respondent had been victimized (if he had been a victim at all) had no influence on the numbers or types of crimes believed to take place in the neighbourhood; in all three areas, burglary was the crime most frequently mentioned, followed at some distance by theft, assault and robbery.

We had expected to find a claimed feeling of 'attachment' to the local area would make a difference to the amount of crime which was thought to be taking place there. In fact, however, replies to our question about 'attachment'

Table VIII.1. 'Would you say that there is much crime around here?' by numbers of incidents of own victimization in the preceding year[a]

	How much crime?									
	Very little, none		Not much		Quite a lot		A great deal		Total	
Number of incidents:	No.	Per-centage	No.	Per-centage	No.	Per-centage	No.	Per-centage	No.	Per-centage
None	63	22·2	93	32·8	110	38·7	18	6·3	284	100·0
One	14	12·2	32	27·8	59	51·3	10	8·7	115	100·0
Two	8	13·6	17	28·8	25	42·4	9	15·3	59	100·0
Three or more	7	12·5	12	21·4	58	50·0	9	16·1	56	100·0
Totals	92	17·9	154	30·0	222	43·2	46	9·0	514	100·0

[a]Excludes 31 respondents giving 'Don't know' answers to the 'How much?' question.
$\chi^2 = 25·9$, df $= 9$, $p < 0·01$; comparing all victims versus non-victims, $\chi^2 = 12·1$, df $= 3$, $p < 0·01$

Table VIII.2. 'Is there *more* crime around here than in other parts of town, *about the same*, or *less*?' by numbers of incidents of own victimization in the preceding year[a]

Number of incidents:	More or less crime?							
	Less		About the same		More		Totals	
	No.	Percentage	No.	Percentage	No.	Percentage	No.	Percentage
None	124	42·6	137	47·1	30	10·3	291	100·0
One	41	36·9	51	46·0	19	17·1	111	100·0
Two	18	31·6	26	45·6	13	22·8	57	100·0
Three or more	20	37·0	27	50·0	7	13·0	54	100·0
Totals	203	39·6	241	47·0	69	13·5	513	100·0

[a]Excludes 32 respondents giving 'Don't know' answer to 'More or less?' question.
$\chi^2 = 9·0$, df = 6, $0·10 \, p < 0·20$; comparing all victims versus non-victims, $\chi^2 = 6·5$, df = 2, $p < 0·05$

Table VIII.3. Attitude to local area, and assessment of crime in the area compared with other parts of town[a]

Attitude to local area	Less than elsewhere		About the same		More than Elsewhere		Total	
	No.	Percentage	No.	Percentage	No.	Percentage	No.	Percentage
Positive	89	55·3	63	39·1	9	5·6	161	100·0
Neutral or non-evaluative	78	41·9	83	44·6	25	13·4	186	100·0
Negative	36	22·0	94	57·3	34	20·7	164	100·0
Totals	203	39·7	240	47·0	68	13·3	511	100·0

$$\chi^2 = 43·1, \text{df} = 4, p < 0·01, \gamma = +0·40$$

[a]Based on responses to questions 'What about this area where you are living now, say within a ten minutes' walk from your home. What kind of area is it?' and 'Still thinking about this neighbourhood, do you think that there is *more* crime around here than in other parts of town, *about the same*, or *less*?'. Excludes 34 respondents giving 'Don't know' answers to either or both questions.

—to the local area, or indeed to some other area—were not related at all to perceptions of the amount of local crime. Nor was expressed interest in 'what goes on in this neighbourhood,' though there was a slight tendency for those claiming not to be interested to say that there was little crime, perhaps because they had not bothered to find out whether or not there was. But there were very strong and consistent associations between our respondents' *evaluations* of their local neighbourhood areas, and their estimates of the prevalence of crime in those areas: on all indices of attitude to the local neighbourhood, those giving negative or disapproving views were much more likely to say that there was a lot of crime in the area, and more than in other parts of town. Table VIII.3 illustrates this point.[5]

The associations between attitudes to the neighbourhood and perceptions of crime are independent of, and stronger than, the associations between victimization and perception; they persist, even if victimization is controlled for.[6] In summary, we saw in the preceding section that victimization had at most only a very slight effect on our respondents' general attitudes to their home neighbourhoods; our conclusion in this section is that those general attitudes, whatever else they may be based on, are much more important determinants of the amounts of crime which the R sample claimed was going on in the neighbourhood, than personal experiences of victimization.

4. Fear of Crime, or Personal Safety

After asking our respondents *how much* crime they thought there was in their neighbourhoods, we asked two questions intended to give some indication of their *fears* of crime, or feelings of personal safety and security: 'Do you think that people in this neighbourhood are safe inside their houses at night?' and 'Do you think that it is generally safe to be out on the streets of this neighbourhood after dark?' Somewhat later in the interview we also asked, 'Are you personally concerned about crime in London as a whole?'—with forced-choice answers ranging from 'very concerned' down to 'not concerned at all.'

It is true that the first two of these questions—like the ones discussed in the preceding section, on the prevalence of crime—ostensibly ask about matters of fact (*viz.* safety of 'most people in the neighbourhood') and not about the respondent's own personal fear or lack of it. It seems not unreasonable to assume, however, that replies to such a question will typically reflect, to some degree, assessments of personal risk of an unpleasant event (intrusion into one's private living space, an attack on the street), and thus give an indication of personal fear. To be frank, the question about 'concern' was included because other researchers have also asked it;[1] in retrospect we must admit that we are not at all clear just what it means, since it is not obvious what 'concern' about crime would boil down to in real life, apart from being a ground for expressing concern to an interviewer.[2] As such, however, it seems a reasonable indicator of general attitudes toward crime; moreover, as we shall see, since it referred explicitly to 'London as a whole,' it provides an illuminating comparison with other questions which were focused on the respondent's immediate 'home' neighbourhood.

In the sample as a whole, just over 40 per cent said that they thought it was *not* safe to be out on the streets of their neighbourhood after dark; 18 per cent said that people were not safe in their homes. On both questions the proportions giving answers indicating insecurity were much higher in Brixton than in the other two areas; two-thirds of the white population of Brixton said they thought their streets were unsafe, compared with only one-third of black respondents. Women were slightly more likely to give 'unsafe' answers than men, to both questions. Responses about safety in the home did not vary by age, though those concerning safety on the streets did, with older persons being more likely to say that the streets were unsafe: in Brixton, over 88 per cent of those aged 61 and over gave this answer. On both questions, a feeling that the neighbourhood is unsafe is much more commonly expressed by working-class respondents: 55 per cent of those in social classes IV and V gave this answer, compared with 22 per cent of those in classes I and II. Since neither age, sex, nor social class was related to estimates of the prevalence of crime in the neighbourhood, these associations may perhaps be interpreted as crude indicators of feelings of vulnerability which are unrelated to subjective assessments of personal risk (and which are not related to objective risk itself).[3]

We found that experience as a victim of crime (in the preceding year) did not in general lead to a greater tendency to say that the homes or streets of the neighbourhood were unsafe: indeed, in some cases it actually appeared to reduce the level of fear or insecurity expressed. In the case of those who had been victims of violent crime (assault, robbery or theft from the person) there was a consistent, though not statistically significant, tendency to be less likely to say that the streets were unsafe as the number of incidents of victimization increased. There was no relationship at all between answers to this question and victimization by theft or burglary; but there was a slight tendency for those who had been victims of theft or burglary to be more likely to say that people were unsafe in their houses.

For all types of incidents combined, the non-effects of victimization on responses concerning safety in the home and on the streets are shown in Table VIII.4. It will be seen from that table that differences in responses between non-victims, one-time victims and multiple victims are in neither case statistically significant; and that while there is a slightly greater tendency to say that people are unsafe in their houses as the number of incidents of victimization increases, replies to the question about safety on the streets follow a curvilinear pattern, first falling and then rising again as the number of incidents increases.

Table VIII.4. Beliefs about safety in one's house and on neighbourhood streets, by number of incidents of own victimization in preceding year

Number of victimization incidents:	Are the streets safe?[a]				Are people safe in their houses?[b]			
	Yes		No		Yes		No	
	No.	Percentage	No.	Percentage	No.	Percentage	No.	Percentage
None	159	58·8	115	42·0	229	84·2	43	15·8
One	69	61·1	44	38·9	93	83·8	18	16·2
Two	35	68·8	16	31·4	38	76·0	12	24·0
Three or more	37	54·4	31	45·6	50	75·8	16	24·2
Totals	300	59·3	206	40·7	410	82·2	89	17·8

[a] $\chi^2 = 2·74$, df = 3, $0·50 > p > 0·30$; excludes 39 respondents giving 'Don't know' answer to the question.
[b] $\chi^2 = 4·1$, df = 3, $0·30 > p > 0·20$; excludes 46 respondents giving 'Don't know' answer to the question.

Plainly, then, having been the victim of one or more crimes in the recent past has little, if any, effect on feelings of insecurity where crime is concerned; indeed, the answers to our question about safety on the streets suggest that a bit of experience as a victim may actually *reduce* fear of crime.[4]

In the preceding section of this chapter, moreover, we found that victims showed a slight tendency to say that there was *more* crime in their neighbourhoods, than did non-victims. Perceptions of the prevalence of crime were associated, in the ways that one might expect, with replies to the two questions about safety: that is, those saying that there was 'quite a lot' or 'a great deal' of crime in their neighbourhoods were significantly more likely to say that their homes or streets were unsafe. And when these estimates of the prevalence of crime are controlled for, any hope of a relationship between victimization and feelings that the neighbourhood is unsafe vanishes completely. A reasonable interpretation, then, is that the experience of victimization has some tendency to make people believe that there is a lot of crime in their neighbourhood; and that it is this belief (which, of course, has many other sources as well) which tends to lead them to believe that the neighbourhood is unsafe.

At this point an important *caveat* is necessary. We are *not* to be interpreted as saying that experience as a victim of crime has *no* effect on people's fears of crime or feelings of personal insecurity. For one thing, as the right-hand side of Table VIII.4 shows, even our R sample data do not go that far; if our sample had been twice as large, the association in that table would have attained statistical significance, which scarcely constitutes convincing defeat of a hypothesis. For another thing, as will be recalled from Chapter IV,[5] the great majority of the incidents mentioned by our R sample were of a relatively unserious kind; in both objective and subjective terms, serious crime was very rare, and we should thus expect that the aggregate effects of victimization on the sample would be correspondingly slight. In our MVT sample—whose experiences of victimization were generally more serious, and led in at least one case per person to the police being called—the general level of expressed insecurity is higher than in the R sample, as is the proportion saying that crime is very prevalent in the neighbourhood.[6] The social and psychological consequences of serious personal victimization are illuminated in a recent study by Lejeune and Alex of a number of victims of 'mugging': experiences of this kind can have dramatic effects on one's perception of the world, and can radically alter attitudes to other people and to oneself.[7]

What can surely be said, on the basis of our data, is that expressed feelings of fear of crime or insecurity[8] appear to have many sources, and to be strongly influenced by beliefs, attitudes and experiences which have nothing whatever to do with crime. Our sample's general attitudes to their neighbourhoods are a case in point. It will be recalled[9] that substantial proportions of our sample— including a majority of those living in Brixton—described their immediate environs in negative terms: they disliked the area itself and the people in it, were not interested in what went on there and would have been pleased to move elsewhere. It will also be recalled that these negative general feelings were

Table VIII.5. Attitudes to the local neighbourhood and safety on area streets, controlling for level of perceived crime in the neighbourhood[a]

	Level of crime in neighbourhood											
	None, very little, not much						Quite a lot, a great deal					
	Are streets safe?						Are streets safe?					
	Yes		No		Total		Yes		No		Total	
Attitude to neighbourhood:	No.	Percentage	No.	Percentage	No.	Percentage	No.	Percentage	No.	Percentage	No.	Percentage
Positive	80	80·8	19	19·2	99	100·0	31	56·4	24	43·6	55	100·0
Neutral	71	82·6	15	17·4	86	100·0	51	52·0	47	48·0	98	100·0
Negative	28	50·0	28	50·0	56	100·0	33	29·5	79	70·5	112	100·0
Totals	179	74·3	62	25·7	241	100·0	115	43·4	150	56·6	265	100·0

$\chi^2 = 22.6$, df $= 2$, $p < 0.01$
$\gamma = +0.40$

$\chi^2 = 15.6$, df $= 2$, $p < 0.01$
$\gamma = +0.38$

[a]Based on responses to questions 'Just thinking about this neighbourhood, would you say that there is much crime around here?'; 'Do you think that it is generally safe to be on the streets of this neighbourhood after dark?' and 'What about this area where you are living now, say within a ten minutes' walk from your home. What kind of area is it?' Table excludes 39 respondents with 'Don't know' answers on one or more of the three questions.

associated with a high level of perceived crime in the neighbourhood.[10] For this reason, we should expect negative attitudes to the neighbourhood to be associated with a feeling that the neighbourhood is unsafe; and Table VIII.5 confirms that this is the case. The table also shows, however, that attitudes to the neighbourhood affect expressed feelings of safety even when perceived level of crime is controlled for. That is, those with negative views of their neighbourhood are significantly more likely to say that the neighbourhood is unsafe, whether they believe the level of crime is low or high. The relationships shown in Table VIII.5 obtain generally, regardless of which indicators of attitudes to the neighbourhood, safety or prevalence of crime are used.[11] In summary, our respondents' attitudes toward their immediate physical and social environments appear to affect their feelings of safety in two ways: first, directly, and second, by leaving them to perceive more crime as going on (which, in turn, affects feelings of safety).

Further evidence on this point comes from our sample's expressed 'concern' about crime. In addition to referring to a somewhat vague attitude (by comparison with fears or beliefs that the streets, etc. are not safe), our question asked specifically about 'London as a whole,' and not just about the respondent's immediate neighbourhood. No less than 72 per cent of the R sample said that they were either 'Quite concerned' or 'Very concerned' in answer to this question; the proportion was slightly higher in Brixton and slightly lower in Hackney, but the differences were not significant. Answers to this question were related to the levels of crime which respondents perceived in their own neighbourhoods; those saying there was 'Quite a lot' or 'A great deal' were significantly more likely to express a high degree of 'concern.' But victimization had no effect whatever on the level of expressed concern; and the pattern of responses in the MV and T sample was virtually identical with that in the R sample. Nor did social class, age, sex, or any other attribute affect the level of expressed concern. Moreover, none of the respondents' attitudes to their local neighbourhoods was related to expressed concern about crime in London as a whole. It thus appears that while feelings about one's local environment may affect attitudes and beliefs about crime *in that environment*, diffuse and general 'concern' about crime has other sources, even more remote from people's day-to-day experiences and surroundings.

5. Some Discussion

Clearly, the relations discussed in this chapter are complex, and we cannot pretend to have sorted them out in any definitive fashion. It appears, however, that the associations which we found between victimization, perceptions of crime, attitudes to the neighbourhood and feelings of unsafety are consistent with the four-variable model described by Figure VIII.1. This model asserts that negative attitudes to one's neighbourhood lead to perceptions that crime is prevalent there, and (independently) to a feeling that the neighbourhood is unsafe; that recent experience as a victim also has some effect on perceptions

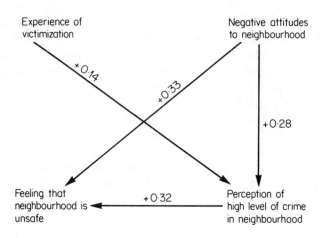

Figure VIII.1.

of the prevalence of crime; and that perceptions of crime lead to feelings of unsafety, which are *not* directly affected by victimization.

Figure VIII.1 also shows the zero-order associations (in terms of the ϕ coefficient, an estimate of Pearson's r) in our data, between four variables.[1] This model predicts that the second-order partial correlation between victimization and feelings of unsafety (that is, the correlation between them, controlling for both perceptions of crime and attitudes to the neighbourhood) should be negligible; in fact, in our data it is slightly negative (-0.07).[2]

The *directions* of causation in such a model (indicated by the arrowheads in Figure VIII.1) cannot, of course, be inferred from the mere existence of correlation; the assumptions which we have made, and the correlations themselves, need some justificatory discussion. First, it is possible that the experience of recent victimization has more of an effect on general attitudes to one's neighbourhood than our data disclosed ($\phi = +0.08$); if this were so, it would be necessary to add a fifth arrow to our model. If there were such an association, it would seem intuitively most plausible that victimization should cause attitude change, and not the other way around. But this is not necessarily true; disliking one's neighbours, for instance, might easily lead to fights with them, or both things might be caused by some third factor, such as social isolation.

Next, note that even in the four-arrow model shown in Figure VIII.1 we have somewhat arbitrarily ruled out the possibility of reciprocal causation, e.g. negative attitudes leading to increased fear of crime which in turn leads to more negative attitudes. Two-way causation can be handled in recursive systems; but to do so would require over-time or panel data, which we do not have.[3] That apart, we think it is more reasonable to assume that attitudes to the neighbourhood influence perceptions of crime there (and feelings that the area is unsafe) than the other way around. We made the point earlier that when respondents were asked for a description of their neighbourhoods, only a small minority spontaneously mentioned the level of crime as a reason for disapproval; this was also true for those who perceived a change for the worse in their area in recent years. When such negative attitudes were expressed, references to a deterioration of the physical features of the area or to unwelcome immigrants were much more common than a feeling that crime was especially prevalent or increasing.

It is possible, of course, that the association between negative attitudes and perceptions of crime is spurious, and is merely the result of response bias. Since we asked the questions about respondents' views of their neighbourhoods before asking any questions at all about crime, it may be that some respondents, having expressed disapproval of their surroundings, felt obliged to appear consistent in their answers and thus said there was more crime in the area than they really thought there was. But in an important sense, it does not really matter whether or not this is true. The fact remains that respondents who disliked their neighbourhoods—for reasons which mostly had nothing whatever to do with crime—were nonetheless prepared to *say* that there was a lot of crime about, and that they would be unsafe in the streets. If so, then expressed views about crime served as a vehicle for respondents' generally negative feelings about their immediate social environments. In our view, this is not at all uncommon; the 'crime problem' gives a concrete form to feelings—often complex and difficult to articulate—about the state of society generally, and about personal concerns which have nothing to do with lawbreaking or the risk of becoming a victim.[4]

We have also assumed, in Figure VIII.1, that perceptions of crime—a belief that there was a lot of crime in the neighbourhood—caused people to feel that the area was unsafe. Again, the relationship may be artifactual, in the sense that those who said to interviewers that there was a lot of crime in the neighbourhood felt constrained also to say that, e.g. the streets were unsafe, though they did not really believe it. That apart, it may be that irrational feelings of unsafety led respondents to say that there was a lot of crime in the neighbourhood even though they did not know or believe this to be true. In such a case, however, we could at least impute some validity to responses about whether the neighbourhood was unsafe; thus, it does not much matter, in our view, whether the arrow in Figure VIII.1 runs from perceptions to unsafety or the reverse. Our data are consistent with either model.[5]

It is clear, in any case, that none of the four variables accounts for very much of the variance of the others. Apart from errors of measurement, this is undoubtedly due to the fact that the model specifies only two of the many things which may influence beliefs about the amount of crime, and fear or insecurity consequent upon those beliefs. Direct personal experience as a victim plainly has very little effect on people's beliefs about crime, in part because such experience is relatively uncommon and unserious.[6] This is true, of course, for most people's beliefs about most things; we are not suggesting that crime is in any way unique in this respect. Given that fact, however, we need to be very cautious about interpreting literally expressions of fear of, or concern about, crime: these may really be expressions of uneasiness about other aspects of experience, or about the state of the world in general.

Notes and References

1. Crime and its Consequences

1. See above, Chapter III, p. 53.
2. Cf. pp. 74–81 above.
3. See, for example, A. D. Biderman in *Field Surveys I*, at 120 ff; A. J. Reiss, Jr., in *Field Surveys III*, at 99–105; Jennie McIntyre, 'Public attitudes toward crime and law enforcement.' (1967) 374 *The Annals* 34, especially 36–41. See also M. C. Courtis, *Attitudes to Crime and the Police in Toronto: A Report of Some Findings*, University of Toronto, Centre of Criminology, November 1970 (mimeo.); P. R. Wilson and J. W. Brown, *Crime and the Community* (Queensland: University of Queensland Press, 1973) Chapter II; Frank Furstenberg, Jr., 'Public reaction to crime in the streets,' (1971) 40 *The American Scholar* 601–610; Wesley C. Skogan, 'Public policy and the fear of crime in large American cities,' a paper presented at the annual meeting of the American Political Science Association, Chicago, May 1976.
4. Things have changed, of course, since our survey was conducted: in subsequent years, political terrorism has become a far more important problem in London. We think it likely, however, that such acts of terrorism have a very different *meaning* for people, from that which attaches to 'ordinary' crimes—for one thing, they tend to be imputed to a more definite group of offenders, such as the I.R.A. Our concern here is with the more diffuse and anonymous concern which may be associated with such 'ordinary' events as assault, burglary, robbery and rape.

2. Attitudes to the Neighbourhood

1. *Royal Commission on Local Government in England, Community Attitudes Survey*, Research Studies, No. 9 (London: H.M.S.O., 1969).
2. A recent national survey on levels of satisfaction also found that home ownership was positively associated with satisfaction over several aspects of life; particularly among working-class people, there is a sharp cleavage between those who own their own homes and council tenants. See M. Abrams, 'Housing: owners and tenants', *New Society*, 7 August 1975.
3. Some evidence for the general validity of our question about 'attachment' comes from a comparison with sample scores on Srole's anomia scale, which purports to measure feelings of alienation: of those scoring highest on this scale (three or four, out of five), over half said they had no area of attachment anywhere.
4. Those respondents who claimed a local area of attachment were asked to describe it; interviewers recorded street names and local landmarks, and the areas were later plotted on a map.
5. In the Community Attitude Survey (note 1 above, at 16) Research Services Ltd. found that the higher the socio-economic status, the larger the 'home' area claimed. But this was a national sample, and thus included rural areas; within London a different pattern seems not unlikely.
6. Those who had claimed attachment to a local area were asked about that area; those who did not were asked to describe 'this area where you are living now—say within a ten minutes' walk from your home.' This was intended to furnish a physical reference for subsequent questions concerning 'your area,' 'this neighbourhood,' etc. Answers to questions about the neighbourhood, people living there, comparison with other

areas, etc. were recorded verbatim by interviewers, and were field-coded according to whether the response was approving, disapproving, or neutral or non-evaluative.

7. Inter-item γ coefficients were generally in the range $+0.35$ to $+0.50$, in both MVT and R samples.

8. It will be remembered that our three survey areas were based on police sub-divisional boundaries; they did not always encompass complete wards, and the parts of the wards falling within our areas were not always representative of the whole population of the ward (as shown in Census data). In addition, the numbers of cases interviewed in some wards was small.

9. For maps of the three areas see above, Chapter II, pp. 21, 23, 24.

10. Ferndale, Tulse Hill and Town Hall; our survey area included only the eastern part of the latter ward, but that is the part in which West Indians have settled.

11. See Alan Marsh, 'Race, community and anxiety,' *New Society*, 22 February 1973 at 406.

12. This was also the case for the MVT sample.

3. Perceptions of the Prevalence of Crime

1. I.e., either the area of attachment elicited a few questions previously, or 'this area where you are living now, say within a ten minutes' walk from your home,' which those who claimed no local area of 'attachment' had been asked to describe.

2. $\gamma = +0.67$. 'Don't know' answers were given by 31 respondents to the 'How much?' question, and by 32 to the 'More or less?' question; but only nine respondents could not venture an answer to either question, and the remaining 'Don't know's introduce no bias.

3. Dichotomizing answers to the 'How much' question, the difference was statistically significant ($\chi^2 = 13.7$, df $= 2$, $p < 0.01$). Of Kensington residents, 56 per cent said that there was *less* crime in their area than in other parts of town.

4. Except, of course, for the few respondents who said 'None' in reply to the 'How much?' question.

5. The associations are about as strong, regardless of the attitude of measure used: that is, whether we look at responses to 'What kind of area is this?', 'What kind of people live around here?', or 'How does this area differ from others around it?'; it also holds for 'How would you feel about moving away?', with those claiming to be pleased to move seeing much more crime.

6. The converse is not true, however: if *perceptions* of the amount of crime are controlled for, the slight association between victimization and attitudes to the local neighbourhood actually becomes slightly (though not significantly) negative. See the discussion on pp. 211–213.

4. Fear of Crime, or Personal Safety

1. E.g. Philip H. Ennis *Field Surveys II*; and several American polls conducted by the Gallup and Harris organizations.

2. Frank Furstenberg, Jr. has pointed out that several researchers have treated 'concern' and 'fear' as virtually synonymous; his own reanalysis of a 1969 Harris survey in Baltimore showed that the two concepts were very different, and were e.g. very differently related to the risk and experience of victimization. 'Concern' in the Harris survey was actually measured by responses to a question about 'the single most serious problem the government should do something about.' See F. Furstenberg, Jr., 'Public reaction to crime in the streets' at 602–5.

3. When asked *why* they thought the streets were unsafe, respondents most commonly mentioned the risk of a violent attack; if such an attack was not specifically mentioned, an unspecific reference to 'trouble' of some kind was the commonest reply. Yet, as

we have seen (above, p. 205), in all three areas the crime most commonly mentioned as taking place in the neighbourhood was burglary.

4. Cf. Chapter VII, pp. 188–189 above, where a similar pattern emerged from seriousness scores given to hypothetical offences.

5. See above, pp. 74–80.

6. For example, over 70 per cent of the MVT sample said that there was 'quite a lot' or 'a great deal' of crime in the neighbourhood, compared with 52 per cent in the R sample. The relationships discussed in this section, between victimization, attitudes to the neighbourhood, perceived crime and views on safety, also generally hold for the MVT sample.

7. Robert Lejeune and Nicholas Alex, 'On being mugged: the event and its aftermath.' (1973) 2 *Urban Life and Culture* 259–87. The effects are not all adverse, of course: one of those interviewed by Lejeune and Alex remarked that 'When someone becomes aware I've been mugged I suddenly take on the aura of a movie star. People do feel sorry for me, but they're intrigued—almost the same way as if they met someone famous.'

8. Expressed to an interviewer, that is. We are not trying to pass off our data on this point as having any validity other than as expressions of attitudes made in a somewhat artificial context.

9. Above, pp. 200–204.

10. Above, pp. 206–207.

11. I.e., whether the analysis is based on attitudes to the neighbourhood, to local people, to the local area compared with others or a desire to move; on safety in the house or on the streets; on how much crime there is or on whether there is more than elsewhere. Occasionally, the associations do not reach statistical significance, but the trend is clear. Note, too, that while the categories in Table VIII.5 have been collapsed into dichotomies for convenience, the relationships are present in tables based on all categories of each variable.

5. Some Discussion

1. The variables used were 'What kind of area is this?', 'Is it generally safe to be out on the streets?', and victimization (of all types combined) based on screening questions; alternative indicators gave pretty much the same results. The ϕ coefficients in Figure VIII.1 were calculated from tables in which all variables had been dichotomized.

2. For a discussion of this type of analysis see H. M. Blalock, Jr., 'Four-variable models and partial correlations.' (1962) 68 *American Journal of Sociology* 182–94; H. M. Blalock, Jr., *Causal Inferences in Nonexperimental Research* (Chapel Hill: University of North Carolina Press, 1964), Chapter III.

3. Cf. H. M. Blalock, Jr., 'Four-variable models and partial correlations' at 185.

4. Thus, for example, in the United States the Louis Harris organization asked 'In the past year, do you feel the crime rate in your neighbourhood has been increasing, decreasing, or has it remained about the same as it was before?' in five polls during the years 1964–73. From a high of 73 per cent in 1964, the proportion saying 'increasing' fell to 46 per cent in 1967, 35 per cent in 1969; it rose again to 62 per cent in 1970 only to fall to 48 per cent in 1973. Yet during that time, the number of 'index' crimes per 100,000 population recorded in the FBI's Uniform Crime Reports rose at an average 7·7 per cent per year. See the discussion in Hazel Erskine, 'The polls: fear of violence and crime.' (1974) 38 *Public Opinion Quarterly* 131.

5. If the bottom arrow in the model were reversed, it would *not* be expected that the second-order partial between attitudes and perceptions would disappear; in our data that partial is $+ 0·24$.

6. Vicarious experience as a victim—e.g., through personal contact with someone who has

been victimized—is presumably less rare; cf. the discussion of the social network of 'intermediaries' in Robert Lejeune and Nicholas Alex, 'On being mugged: the event and its aftermath' at 279–80. This is something which certainly should be studied in future victim surveys, e.g. by asking 'Do you know anyone who has been (assaulted, robbed, burgled, etc.)?' and relating the answer to the numbers and kinds of persons the respondents says he knows.

CHAPTER IX

Concluding Reflections

1. An Overview of the Findings

Before discussing the implications of our research, let us review briefly some of the main methodological and substantive findings of the London survey:

(1) Of the 241 respondents in our MV sample, over 90 per cent recalled and reported to our interviewers the 'target' incidents of victimization during the preceding year, on which we had information from Metropolitan Police files. Over 97 per cent of the incidents of burglary or thefts from dwellings were reported, and about 89 per cent of the assaults and thefts.

(2) There was a slight, though not significant, tendency for non-reporting to interviewers of incidents to be associated with low educational attainment; but we found nothing else which attained any meaningful association with recall and reporting, and failure to mention incidents appeared to be due primarily to simple memory failure operating in a more or less random fashion among respondents.

(3) The proportion of incidents not reported to interviewers was slightly higher in the first half of the reference period (12 per cent) than in the second (4 per cent).

(4) There were limits to the accuracy and precision of respondents' dating of 'target' incidents; most could give only the month in which the incident had occurred, and only half of those who mentioned their 'target' incidents placed them in the month in which they actually occurred. There was a slight tendency for incidents mentioned by the MV sample to be 'telescoped' forward in time; on balance, however, inaccuracies in time placement within the reference period almost cancelled out.

(5) Of the 54 respondents in the T sample, whose 'target' incidents had actually occurred up to three months before the survey reference period, about 18 per cent wrongly reported the incident as within the reference period.

(6) Inaccuracy of time placement (i.e. forward and backward 'telescoping' of incidents) did not seem in our sample to be strongly associated with any particular attributes either of the incidents or of the respondents themselves.

(7) We found some evidence suggesting the existence of inter-class differences in the subjective assessment of 'seriousness' of property offences, and in nor-

mative patterns relating to the use of violence; these may have led to systematic differences in the definition of situations, and thus in the reporting of victimization to interviewers.

(8) In our R sample, just under 45 per cent of the 545 respondents reported that they had personally experienced one or more of the incidents about which we asked. The gross victimization rate was about the same in Brixton and Kensington, and slightly lower in Hackney.

(9) The great majority of these incidents were not very serious, however; in particular, the amount of serious violence reported by the R sample was extremely small. Many of the offences against property were also of a relatively unserious kind, and indeed were seen by the respondents themselves as not serious.

(10) In common with other researchers, we found that the distribution of reported victimization was extremely skewed, and that the number of 'multiple victims' was far greater than would be expected purely by chance. We found no simple theoretical model which would account for this distribution.

(11) Reported victimization was negatively related to age, and fell off sharply among those over 50; it was positively related to social activity (in the sense of going out in the evenings), and appeared to be somewhat higher among recent in-migrants to our survey areas.

(12) There was also a significant association between violent victimization, and self-reported violence.

(13) It appeared that the police had been notified of less than a third of the incidents of victimization mentioned by the R sample to our interviewers. Reporting to the police appeared to be largely a function both of the objective and the subjectively perceived seriousness of the incident, and/or a belief that the police could do something about the situation; it did not appear to be determined by general attitudes to the police. In all three of our survey areas, and among all groups of people in the sample, there was a generally high opinion of the police; there was, however, a minority who wanted more policemen on the beat, and who complained because they did not see a policeman in their neighbourhoods often enough.

(14) After a number of complicated adjustments, population estimates were calculated, for each of our three survey areas, of the numbers of crimes (of the kinds included in our survey) occuring in the areas. These estimates were far greater than the (adjusted) numbers of those types of crimes recorded by the police in our three areas. Over the sample as a whole, the ratio of survey-estimated to police-recorded crime was over 11 to 1. In other words, it appeared that less than one-tenth of those crimes covered by our survey which *could* have been recorded in the police statistics in 1972 were in fact recorded there.

(15) Further analysis, based on respondents' statements about whether their incidents had been reported to the police, showed that about two-thirds of the survey-estimated crime had probably not been reported. Failure to report incidents to the police could not, however, explain all of the discrep between survey estimates and police statistics.

(16) Respondents' assessments of the relative seriousness of various c

their expressed concern about crime in London, and their beliefs about the safety of their neighbourhood streets, were not related in any clear or consistent way to the experience of victimization. Victimization (within the preceding year) did appear to have a slight effect on respondents' perceptions of the amounts of crime in their neighbourhoods; but these perceptions, and other attitudes to crime and/or personal safety, appeared to be much more strongly influenced by the respondents' general feelings of liking or disliking of their neighbourhoods and the people living in them.

2. Further Problems of Method

We must remind the reader once again that the research described in this book was primarily methodological and exploratory, and that the substantive findings relate to three specially chosen London areas only. The main objective of our work was to explore the feasibility of using a particular research technique —the sample survey, based on structured interviews with members of the general public—as a means of measuring crime. Is it possible, by asking people directly about their own experiences as victims, to get a reasonably accurate picture of the amounts and kinds of law-breaking which have occurred in a given area and period of time? On balance, our answer to this question is Yes; but it is an answer with several important qualifications.

The first of these relates to the sampling method which we used, and the relatively low response rates which were a consequence of that method. It will be recalled that we had to use the electoral register as a sampling frame, since we had names and addresses for our MV and T sample respondents, and did not want our interviewers to know that any of their cases had reported offences to the police. The final response rate, of about 50 per cent, was mainly due to non-contacts, especially of people who had moved from their listed addresses; refusals were not a great problem. Especially in areas like those which we studied in London, some form of 'area sampling' should ideally be used.[1] This would not merely increase the gross response rate, but would ensure a more complete representation of certain groups—e.g. immigrants, and highly mobile or transient individuals—who, on the limited evidence from our R sample, may have very different experiences of victimization from that of longer-term residents, and who may also be very different sorts of survey respondents.

It is also important to note that the reverse record check strategy which we used (with our MV and T samples) can provide at best only a partial validation of the victim survey method, since it is based on incidents which have been reported to (and recorded by) the police; these may well be more salient, and thus more readily reported to interviewers, than incidents of which the police were not notified. The implications of this point can be seen by considering Table IX.1. To say that a victim survey has produced valid results is to say that most crime incidents, whether or not recorded by the police, will be mentioned to survey interviewers: that is, that the ratio N_{+1}/N in Table IX.1 will be close

Table IX.1. Relationships between reporting of crime to survey interviewers, and recording by police

| | | Crime reported to interviewer | | |
		Yes	No	Total
Crime recorded by police:	Yes	N_{11}	N_{12}	N_{1+}
	No	N_{21}	N_{22}	N_{2+}
	Total	N_{+1}	N_{+2}	N

to unity. In practice, however, it is impossible to observe directly the N_{22} incidents which are neither recorded by the police nor reported to survey interviewers. Thus—*faute de mieux*—the reverse record check uses a sample of the N_{1+} crimes which have been recorded by the police, in the hope that the proportion of *those* crimes which are mentioned to interviewers—viz., N_{11}/N_{1+} —will be close to unity (in our MV sample it was over 0·9).

Clearly, however, the ratio N_{+1}/N is a weighted average of N_{11}/N_{1+} and N_{21}/N_{2+} ; it thus depends in part on the proportion of all crimes which are recorded by the police (which, on the evidence from our R sample, was only about one in ten). If—as also seems intuitively likely—those crimes which have not been reported to the police (or recorded by them) are less likely to be mentioned to interviewers than those that have, the findings of a reverse record check may be misleadingly optimistic.[2] Other research strategies—such as 'multiple recapture' methods using two or more interviews of the same sample— might be used in future to investigate this problem.[3]

It should in any case be noted that there is no purely statistical criterion by which the success of a reverse record check may be judged. Presumably, if *all* incidents included in such a study are mentioned to interviewers (so that N_{11}/N_{1+} in Table IX.1 equals 1·0) the findings can be fairly described as 'successful'; our capture of 92 per cent of our MV sample's 'target' incidents is pretty close to that. At the other extreme, if a substantial proportion of victims of recorded crime do *not* mention their experiences to interviewers—as victims of assault did not, in the U.S. Census Bureau's pretests[4]—then the victim survey will seem to be of doubtful utility.

In any case, it must be remembered that our results (so far as recall and reporting to interviewers of 'target' incidents are concerned) were achieved through fairly lengthy interviews which included many other questions about crime, as well as a quite-heavily-probed series of screening questions designed to elicit mentions of our respondents' experiences; and that series of screening questions was itself preceded by some minutes' interrogation designed to help respondents to fix the survey reference period in their minds and to recall salient 'landmark' dates within it. It may well be that without these relatively time-consuming (and thus expensive) preliminaries, we would not have achieved the 'success' we did, in terms of 'target' incidents reported. This is not to rule out the possibility of victim surveying through a series of 'screening' interviews of (say) 30 to 40 minutes, coupled with re-interviewing of victims and (a sample of) non-victims in order to obtain other information. But it seems to us unlikely that we would have achieved the same results if we had merely asked the screening questions by themselves; *a fortiori*, it seems unlikely that the same degree of accuracy can be achieved through the inclusion of two or three questions about victimization in a questionnaire mainly devoted to other matters.[5]

There are other methodological issues on which it seems to us that further research would be profitable. One of these concerns the optimum reference period for such surveys. Our results suggest that it is feasible to use a one-year reference period; but perhaps we would not be so optimistic about this if our fieldwork had been in, say, April or October rather than in January and February. Our data show that both recall of incidents and accuracy of time placement declined as the time between incident and interview increased; but, on balance, the decline was not so great as to lead us to regard a six-month reference period as preferable, especially when effects of forward telescoping into the reference period are taken into consideration. Since very much larger samples are needed in order to get the same degree of precision when using a six-month reference period than a twelve-month one, considerations of cost would seem to support the use of twelve months—but no longer—in future victim surveys. The matter is far from settled, however.

Further research is also needed, in order to try to ensure both the reliability and the validity of questions on the perception of crime, assessments of relative seriousness, concern about crime, fears for personal safety, and the definition of potentially criminal situations. Survey respondents may *say* that they believe that crime is increasing, or that they feel unsafe in their homes; but do they *really* believe or feel these things, or act in accordance with them in their everyday lives? Similarly, our data reveal apparent inter-class differences in the evaluation of the seriousness of property crimes. But are these real differences—and if so, what are their consequences in real-life terms? A combination of research methods—observation and experiments, in addition to survey-type interviewing—is indicated here, before very much confidence can be placed on survey findings.[6]

Comparisons of survey estimates of crime with police statistics pose a host of other problems—especially if the areas surveyed are (as ours were) relatively small parts of cities. Ideally, a victim survey should cover an area coterminous with one or more police force areas (more precisely, with one or more areas for which police statistics are kept). For example, in a survey of the whole of the Metropolitan Police District we would have avoided many of the adjustments which we had to make to our data and the police statistics, to take account of victimization outside of the area of residence, etc. At a minimum, any survey of a city should include its 'natural' suburbs (i.e. those in which commuting workers live); even then, however, there are bound to be problems with tourists and other short-term visitors who may be victims of crime in an area even though they live elsewhere.

Finally, it must be emphasized strongly again that victim surveys can at best produce inferential estimates of the difference between crimes which victims (say that they) reported to the police, and crimes which appear in the police statistics. A different kind of research is needed, in order to discover exactly what kinds of incidents do come to the attention of the police, and to study the ways in which those incidents are dealt with and why. Such a project would best be based on a sample of incidents coming to the notice of the police (through complaints by victims, or in other ways); it would follow the process of disposition forward, rather than trying to reconstruct it retrospectively from interviews or records. In this way it would be possible to obtain a more complete picture of both the police and the public's reaction to crime incidents of various kinds, and to gain a better knowledge of the factors which lead some incidents to be settled informally without being recorded in police statistics of crime.

Bearing in mind all of these problems and limitations, our general conclusion is that the survey of victimization is an important research technique for criminology, and that much can be learned by using this technique which cannot be learned in any other way. In our view, future victim surveys should (so far as possible) be systematically planned to accomplish two major objectives. (1) By far the most important need is for over-time data which will make it possible to study at least medium-term changes in victimization rates and attitudes to crime, and to investigate adequately at least some of the possible consequences of crime. For example, do those who have been victims of property crime in one year really tend to take more precautions against such crime afterward—and if so, does this make any difference to their subsequent experience? The ideal study for this purpose would be a panel study, in which members of the sample were interviewed on two or more occasions over a period of time. (2) There is also a need, however, to carry out comparably-designed victim surveys in different types of areas—for example, in central cities, whole conurbations, medium-sized towns, small towns and rural areas—so as to provide more adequate data on the variations which almost certainly exist between such areas in both patterns of crime and attitudes to it. In our view, it is doubtful how much can be learned at this stage from cross-national comparisons. But victim surveys aimed at the systematic mapping of crime trend and patterns within a single country should certainly be worthwhile, and there seems to us to be no methodological reason why they should not be undertaken.

3. Measurement for What?

Victim surveys can have practical utility because they can provide a much more accurate measure of crime than that which can be obtained from police or other official statistics: they can overcome the long-standing problem of the 'dark figure' of unrecorded crime. But why do we need to measure crime—especially unrecorded crime? This question is not as simple as it may seem.

In fact, there are two separate, but related, questions here. The first is, roughly, 'Why do we need an alternative measure of crime, to that provided by official statistics?' The second is: 'Why should we want to know, in any case, how much crime occurs—regardless of the measuring instrument used?'

So far as the first of these questions is concerned, it may be thought that the real puzzle is why anyone should ever have thought that official statistics of crime (whether compiled by the police, the courts or any other agency) could possibly be an accurate measure of the true volume of criminal behaviour. This belief certainly does seem to have been widely held, by some criminologists as well as by politicians, journalists and the general public; but a moment's reflection on the activities involved in the collection of such statistics should surely be enough to discredit them as a measure of all the crime which in fact takes place. As we have repeatedly stressed, the official statistics are the outcome of a complex series of social and organizational processes (perception, definiton, reporting, and recording), such that at each stage of the process some crimes are excluded; and there is absolutely no reason whatever to think that those crimes which are not excluded—and which thus are eventually recorded in the official statistics—are an unbiased sample of all crimes which in fact occur. (What would it be like if the perception and definition of crimes really were in some sense purely 'random' processes—or if the selection of some crimes for reporting and recording really were just a matter of chance?) Instead, of course, the selection is a purposive one at each stage, so that some crimes—in all probability, those thought (by somebody, for some reason) to be 'serious'— have a greater chance of being ultimately recorded.

It might be argued, from this premise, that official statistics of crime do contain all (or most?) *serious* crime; and there is a sense in which this is perhaps true. Unfortunately, in that sense 'Most serious crime gets recorded' turns out to be tautologous, unless some absolute level of 'seriousness' can independently be specified. For otherwise, in this context the last-crunch criterion for saying that someone regards a crime as serious can only be that he reports (or records, etc.) it as a crime; and it is not illuminating to be told that all crime which someone regards as serious enough to report, gets reported. It might conceivably be that most of the general public, and the majority of agents of social control, were in close agreement on their judgments of seriousness, and on the desirability of reporting or recording incidents of a given degree of seriousness (e.g. in terms of property values or degree of physical injury). Our results, however, do not suggest that this is true; even though there was apparent agreement between different social classes on the assessment of some crimes of violence, there was also evidence of variation in definitional norms and views on appropriate behaviour on the part of the police. Moreover, even if there were consensus on these matters at some one point in time, we would have no guarantee that it would still be present at some later time.

It is true that if the 'dark figure' were small, relative to the total volume of crime, its existence would not matter much. Plainly this is the case for some types of crime, such as murder and armed robbery from banks or other organi-

zations. But in most countries, such crimes account for only a minute proportion of all of the crimes recorded even now in the official statistics. It may well
be that the probability of being recorded is also high for other types of crime.
But at the moment, there is no way of identifying those crimes; and it seems
likely that they would also turn out to be a very small proportion of total
crime, in most places. Statistics which included only those crimes would not
be of much use for anything else; in particular, they would give no indication
of the workload of the police or other agencies of social control. (In England
and Wales, for example, residential and non-residential burglaries involving
thefts of property worth £100 or more account for less than 5 per cent of all
recorded crime.)

It might also be argued that official statistics of crime, while containing
only a biased sample of the total volume of crime, nonetheless gave an accurate
indication of *changes* in that total volume; that, for example, a five per cent
increase in recorded crime reflected a five per cent increase in the true level of
crime. *A priori*, however, this seems unlikely. Of course people's perceptions
of crime and their reporting behaviour, and police recording practices, may not
fluctuate wildly; they may not change very much, in the short term (though
we do not know, at present, how much change occurs). But because the total
volume of crime is almost certainly very much larger than the amount finally
recorded, the latter total is likely to be very sensitive even to small changes in
reporting behaviour, etc. Moreover, it seems a reasonable hypothesis that the
probabilities associated with perception, definition, reporting and recording
of criminal behaviour are themselves correlated, and tend to increase or
decrease together; so that if, for example, people become more sensitized to
crime (and so tend to see more things *as* crime) they also tend to report more
incidents to the police; and that the police tend to deal with crime (and to
record it) in response to what they believe to be public opinion about 'the
crime problem'.

Ultimately, of course, the question how far official statistics reflect real
changes in the total volume of crime is an empirical one. It can only be resolved
by comparing other evidence relating to crime trends (including, in time,
evidence from victim surveys) with trends disclosed by the official statistics; and
the results of such comparisons may well differ in different jurisdictions. Some
highly suggestive evidence on this question has recently been published in the
United States, however. It is reported that the National Crime Panel surveys
of victimization, being conducted by the U. S. Census Bureau, found little
change in victimization rates in 1974, compared with the preceding year.[1] Yet
according to the *Uniform Crime Reports* (collected and published by the
Federal Bureau of Investigation) the recorded number of 'index' crimes per
100,000 increased in 1974 by no less than 16·7 per cent over 1973.[2] The National
Crime Panel surveys are by no means free from methodological problems,
and this one-year comparison must be treated with reserve. Whatever their
limitations, however, it would be very surprising if they failed to detect a real
increase of *one-sixth* in the crime rate in the United States.[3]

It must be emphasized that nothing being said here constitutes an argument against the compilation (by the police, or any other agency in the criminal justice system), of statistics of 'crimes known' to that agency: such statistics may have many operational and administrative uses. The point is that to interpret such statistics as measures of the true volume of crime is to mis-interpret them in a fundamental way, and to impute to them a significance which they almost certainly cannot have. What is needed, therefore, is not so much a change in the official statistics themselves, as a change in people's way of thinking about those statistics. Such a change is one thing which victim surveys can help to bring about. To the extent that they can provide an alter-native picture of trends and patterns in crime, victim surveys can help legis-lators, administrators and the general public to understand the statistics which result in part from the operation of the criminal justice system, and to appreciate the ways in which those statistics may change independently of changes in the true volume of crime.

Even this alternative picture, however, has some important inherent limi-tations. For one thing, it is pretty obvious that the victim survey method is of no use where 'victimless' crime is concerned. This category covers not only those crimes where there is literally no victim (such as receiving stolen property, possessing and selling of drugs, certain conspiracies and many motoring offences); it also includes many crimes of a consensual nature, such as some forms of illegal homosexual behaviour, in which neither party would naturally define himself as a victim no matter what the legal position may be. This last category is important, because of the relevance of consent to the legal definition of some crimes (in particular, assaults and certain sexual offences) which may get reported to interviewers in borderline cases where the putative victim regards consent as having been absent.

Moreover, it seems to us that the victim survey method is likely to be of little use in measuring the majority of crimes committed against businesses and public organizations. There have indeed been some attempts to use the tech-nique to elicit information about such crimes;[4] but the results of these studies seem of little value for several reasons. The victim survey is most accurate when the crimes being measured are those of which the respondent has direct personal knowledge; it is for this reason that the use of a single informant to obtain data on other household members' victimization is of limited value. But this condi-tion is seldom, if ever, fulfilled in the case of crimes against businesses or other non-individual victims. The most that can usually be expected is that *some* member of the organization (for example, a store manager, security officer or foreman) will have *indirect* knowledge or belief (through hearsay, or some inferential procedure such as periodic stocktaking) of circumstances which seem to him or somebody else to have involved a crime against the organization. In fact, most shops' and manufacturers' inventory procedures yield no more than an overall figure for 'inventory shrinkage', of which theft forms only a part (and an unknown part at that).[5] This does not mean that such crimes cannot be studied—or even measured—at all; there have been, for example, a number of excellent observational studies of thefts from workplaces, in both America and England.[6] It does mean, however, that they probably cannot be measured at all accurately by victim surveys; and, given that theft from work-places is probably the commonest type of theft in industrial societies, this represents a considerable omission.[7]

It is also important to note that victim surveys cannot be used to measure most crimes *by* businesses or businessmen. They thus exclude most if not all forms of so-called 'white-collar crime' (including price-fixing and other regula-tory offences, consumer frauds, Food and Drug Act offences, bribery and corruption). By their nature, victim surveys (like official crime statistics) tend to focus on the 'traditional' violent and property crimes committed by relatively poor and powerless individuals; it would be difficult if not impossible to use them to measure those forms of crime and kindred venality which the middle classes find most congenial. (The Pandora's Box known as 'Watergate', for example, would at most have amounted to a single second-rate burglary of an office building, in a survey of victimization; the further villainies of unindicated co-conspirators, corporation presidents and like would probably not be captured by the most astute of screening questions.) Victim surveys may present a clearer and more complete picture of *some* forms of criminality than has heretofore been available; but they do not give the *whole* picture, and their virtues should not lead us to overlook their limitations.

This brings us to the second question, to wit: 'Why should anyone want to know how much crime occurs, in any particular time and place?' In recent years considerable research has been done, in a number of countries, on trying to devise 'social indicators' which will describe the quality of social life in objective and quantitative terms—just as, for example, economic indicators such as the unemployment rate, gross national product per capita, new invest-ment and the balance of trade are used to describe the state of the economy. At first sight it may seem reasonable to regard the crime rate as such an indi-cator—as a measure of 'public safety', for instance. But is it really? Certainly there have been, and still are, many times and places in which high crime rates have accompanied, and contributed to, an existence compounded of great misery, poverty and terror: in this sense, as Hobbes saw long ago, a minimum degree of order is a necessary condition of tolerable social life. But where crime is a social problem of those dimensions—as it has been in some urban ghettoes in the United States,[8] and as it often appears to be in contemporary Northern Ireland—it scarcely needs statistics or victim surveys to make this clear.

It does not follow from this, moreover, that for *societies in general*, relatively high crime rates can be unambiguously regarded as being in some sense 'bad'; conversely, a relatively low crime rate is not necessarily an indicator of 'social health'. Crime is causally connected, in ways far from being understood, with many other aspects of social life; and it is at least conceivable that, for example, in developed industrial societies a certain amount of property crime is a neces-sary consequence of an otherwise healthy socio-economic system, so that a relatively crime-free society would also be an economically or culturally stagnant one. Again, the costs of crime must be balanced, in any rational accounting, against the costs of social control; the measurement of crime is a preliminary to that balancing, but no more. Moreover, even if crime rates (or the risk of becoming a victim) are relatively high, it does not follow that people tend to perceive their lives as being 'worse' in any way; our own findings, and those of other investigators, show few clear or consistent relationships between experience as a victim, and expressed concern about personal safety, the 'crime problem' or the quality of life. It is open to question how far people's subjective perceptions on such matters should be treated as decisive—especially since the measurement of such perceptions is as yet in its infancy and is fraught with methodological difficulties.[9] What does seem clear is that people's attitudes do not necessarily correspond in any straightforward way to the objective facts of their situation. Victim surveys can help to illuminate the relations between crime and its social context and consequences, in a way that other statistics of crime cannot. But until these relations are better understood, 'social indicator' uses of the method should be treated with reserve.

These somewhat cautionary remarks should not be interpreted as implying that there are no more immediate practical purposes to which victim surveys can be put. One potentially important use of such surveys is the evaluation of crime prevention programmes. Such programmes—especially if they involve efforts to make the public more conscious of crime and of the precautions which should be taken against becoming a victim—often tend, at least in the short run, to lead to an increase in the reporting of crimes, and thus to a rise in recorded crime rates: this may give a misleading impression that the crime prevention programme has been counterproductive. But victim surveys carried out before and after such a programme could conceivably show not only whether criminal victimization had really increased, but whether there had (following the implementation of the programme) been an increase in the reporting to the police of survey-measured incidents.[10]

Finally, the victim survey method can fulfil an important social function by focusing attention on, and providing information about, the victims of crime. This information may be of great importance for public policy; and it cannot, at present, be collected in any other way. (In most jurisdictions police records now include only a minimum of information about victims; and of course no data at all are available from police records on the great majority of victims who for whatever reason do not report incidents to the police.) One issue which emerged from our London survey is the relatively low proportion of victims of violent offences who made claims for compensation to the Criminal Injuries Compensation Board. The fact that not one of the victims in our R sample had applied for such compensation may be due to the present rule that the injury must be one for which at least £50 would be awarded;[11] it is doubtful, on the facts available to us, that any of the injuries suffered by members of the R sample would have qualified under the rules then in operation, and the victims who reported their assaults to the police may well have been advised of that fact. But we also found that only a minority of the MV and T sample—whose injuries were generally more serious—had applied for compensation. Of the 45 incidents of assault or wounding reported to our interviewers by these respondents, there were only four in which an award had been made by the Board; in five others, the respondent stated that a claim had been made to the Board and an award was pending. One person stated that he had obtained damages from the offender; in the remaining cases, or about 80 per cent, it was stated that no claim for damages or compensation of any kind had been made. Unfortunately we were not able to explore the reasons for this in sufficient detail; but it would be interesting to know whether the failure to apply was due to ignorance of the scheme's existence, or to a belief (on whatever grounds) that a claim would not have succeeded if made. The extent of insurance coverage among victims of property crimes also deserves investigation in future surveys.

4. Victim Surveys and Criminological Explanation

If the arguments of the preceding pages, concerning the inadequacies of official criminal statistics as measures of crime, are correct, then they would appear to apply equally to the use of those statistics as data for criminological research. There are, in fact, at least three distinct ways in which victim surveys may contribute to explanatory research in the field of criminology: (a) by providing a more accurate measure of crime rates, (b) by providing data on victimization, and by (c) throwing light on the nature of societal reaction to crime and the working of part of the criminal justice system. The method has different strengths and limitations in each of these three areas, however.

(a) A Measure of Crime for Research Purposes. Many kinds of criminological theorizing take crime rates as their dependent variable. These rates—usually standardized for the population thought to be at risk of committing crimes[1]—may be analysed either on a cross-sectional basis or longitudinally, in relation to other variables assumed to be causally relevant. It should be clear from what has already been said that we regard the use of official statistics to provide the numerator of such rates as dubious practice, in view of the evidence from victim surveys which have been done so far. Theoretically—except for those few crimes which seem very likely to be recorded—the practice was always unsound in any case: if a theory purports to explain the occurrence, frequency or distribution of crime, then it should not be tested by data which are known to leave out a large and non-random proportion of all the crime which occurs. The practice of using official statistics as a measure of crime has sometimes been excused—even justified—in the past, on the ground that they were the only data available. It may be thought that this was a pretty weak argument: why theorize at all, about data which are known to be biased and incomplete? But it should now be thoroughly unacceptable, given that a method exists which can provide more accurate estimates of what theorists are trying to explain.

It has been argued that statistics of recorded crime, though admittedly imperfect, should be the starting-point for studies of recorded crime: McClintock and Avison, for example, have asserted that 'the importance of the undiscovered offence can only be assessed after a full study has been made of the numbers of different kinds of offences that are discovered by, or reported to and recorded by, the police.'[2] It is difficult to see why this should be thought to be true: indeed, it seems to us to put the cart squarely before the horse. Recorded crime statistics by themselves can contribute nothing whatever to an understanding of the total volume of crime, or of data from a victim survey: one does not need to know how much crime has finally been recorded in order to understand the significance of victim survey estimates. But it *is* necessary to know—or at least to have some hypothesis—about either the total volume of crime, or the processes involved in reporting and recording, in order to understand the significance of the official criminal statistics. The point may be put generally, in terms of sampling. If one already knows the population parameters of a certain phenomenon, it is not necessary to study a sample of that population, unless indeed one is interested in the biases inherent in drawing that sample. But if what one starts with what one knows to be a sample, then it *is* necessary to make some assumptions about either the population or the sampling method, if one is to make any inferences at all about the sample data. No doubt it is often *easier*, in practice, to start with official statistics of crime which are already published or at least collected: perhaps that is why it is so often done. But convenience scarcely constitutes a scientific reason.

Much contemporary research based on official criminal statistics is of course merely descriptive, and does not seriously purport to explain anything. But even at an elementary descriptive level, there seems little point in elaborate analyses of recorded crimes until more is known about the processes which lead some such crimes to be recorded while others are not. As is well-known, statistics of recorded crime in most western countries have shown a steady increase over the past 10 or 15 years. But why should we uncritically accept that that statistical increase is a real one? For example, an analysis of recorded thefts in England and Wales in the period 1955–65 is said to suggest that serious thefts increased faster than petty ones.[3] But it is at least as plausible to suppose that minor thefts have increased at the same rate or even faster, but that the probability of such thefts being recorded has simultaneously declined. The latter hypothesis is consistent both with the evident increase in personal affluence in Britain in the decade 1955–65, and with our findings on the assessments of relative seriousness of property crimes in different social classes;[4] it seems not at all unlikely that as people have come to have more property, they are less inclined to bother about apparent thefts of small amounts of it.

(b) Data for 'Victimology'. On the one hand, the victim survey is a method of measuring crime; on the other, of course, it is a method of identifying victims of crime. Here there are many important theoretical issues awaiting exploration. We discussed a number of these in Chapter IV,[5] and will review them only briefly here; basically, they are concerned with the question 'Why

do some people become victims of crime, while others do not?' Perhaps the most intriguing problems concern the unfortunate minority of 'multiple victims'—in particular, those for whom some form of victimization is more or less of a chronic condition, a way of life. It may well be that the majority of 'one-time' victimization can be regarded as an isolated (and virtually random) phenomenon; there may be as little point in trying to explain why certain persons are victimized once as there is in trying to explain why (as self-report studies suggest) most people commit some form of crime on this or that isolated occasion. But the minority of apparently 'victimization-prone' persons present a different problem. To what extent can repeated victimization be explained by the actions or attributes of the victim himself—and to what extent does it inhere in particular identifiable social situations or places?

Future research on this subject should also deal with a number of issues surrounding the social *meaning* of criminal victimization. In an earlier chapter[6] we considered the possibility that estimates of victimization—including our own—might be distorted by systematic differences in the definition of situations (e.g. those involving assault). Quite apart from this problem of measurement, however, it is plain that an incident recalled as an 'argument', a 'quarrel', or a 'fight' has a different *meaning* for the person involved from one recalled as an 'assault' or a 'threat'—even if the observable physical facts are the same. Here too the chronic or repeated victim is important. In our sample, one West Indian woman living in Hackney reported a large number of incidents involving theft, damage to her apartment, and a variety of assaults. Yet—as further interviews made clear—these incidents (which were almost certainly an underestimate of her actual victimization) were merely small threads in the tumultuous fabric of her life in the slum in which she and her family were housed by the local authority. We presented evidence in the preceding chapter[7] which suggested that personal experience of victimization has little effect on fear of crime or concern about it; part of the explanation of this may be that some of those who suffer the most crime also suffer the most from other things.

(c) Studying Societal Reaction to Crime. Enough has been said, earlier in this book, about the importance of studying the various components of societal reaction to crime and deviance, and the consequences of crime for victims and the community as a whole. Two additional problems may be mentioned, however, on which research is needed to supplement surveys of victimization among the general population. First, once validated attitude data relating to crime and criminal justice are available for the general public, they need also to be obtained for two groups who were probably very largely excluded from our survey: namely offenders, and agents of social control. Our limited self-report data, though not (we think) without interest, themselves require to be validated; in any case, they do not permit us to distinguish between those who had been convicted of crime and those who had not. Moreover, our London sample included no police officer or circuit judge, and so far as we are aware contained only two magistrates. Yet if we are ever to understand the working

of the criminal justice system, we must surely gain some idea of the similarities and differences between the attitudes, values and characteristic perceptions of the people who administer that system, those of the persons with whom they have to deal, and those of the general public (including victims). Is it true—as Sellin and Wolfgang have suggested[8]—that policemen and judges have attitudes characteristic of an 'official' social morality which is basically middle-class? And to what extent does becoming a 'client' of the criminal justice system alter attitudes to that system?

Second, it is important to remember that a survey of victimization can only investigate the earlier stages of the process of societal reaction to crime: that is, the perception and definition of incidents by members of the public, and their decisions to notify the police or some other agency. A victim survey cannot provide adequate information on what happens after that nor can it give a complete picture of the transactions which take place between the police and persons who report incidents to them. We saw in Chapter VI[9] that there appeared to be a substantial gap between our estimates of the numbers of incidents in our three areas of which the police were notified, and the numbers of crimes recorded in the statistics in each area; and we outlined several of the possible explanations for this gap, in terms of the many ways in which reported incidents may properly perceived and dealt with, without being finally recorded as 'crimes known'. But further research is needed, in order to study this part of the process in detail: to learn exactly what type of incidents are reported to the police, how these are handled by the police, and how the treatment of a particular incident is related to the expectations of the person reporting it. (It must be remembered that in many cases in which the police are notified of circumstances amount to an offence, an arrest and prosecution is probably the last thing which the putative 'victim' wants.)

5. A Final Note

When the project discussed in this book was first mooted, about six years ago, it was vehemently opposed by an eminent Polish criminologist who argued that the English criminal justice system had enough of a problem with its recorded crimes; it did not need to know—indeed, could not afford to find out—about crimes which were not recorded. This view seemed to us at the time to be utterly misconceived; and in retrospect it still seems so. The measurement and analysis of the 'dark figure' of unrecorded crime is no mere academic exercise; and the development of a method for carrying out that measurement and analysis is not just in exercise in research technique. On the contrary, an understanding of the great volume of crimes which are not recorded is a necessary first step toward the understanding of those which are.

Of course the practical problems of dealing with recorded crime do not in any way diminish when information on unrecorded crime is provided. The police must still investigate crimes which are made known to them; and— together with the courts, the probation service and the penal institutions—they

233

must still deal with increasing numbers of convicted offenders. Plainly it will not make the jobs of those agencies any easier to be told that those offenders, and the offences which they have committed, account for only a fraction of all crime. That information, however, puts the working of the criminal justice system into its proper perspective: it illuminates the extent to which the system's input depends on the perceptions, beliefs, attitudes and actions of the general public, not only as offenders but as victims. Full realization of that fact may not make the system's workload any lighter; but it may make both the system and its clients more enlightened, and in our view that is an objective worth achieving.

Notes and References

2. Further Problems of Method

1. In this type of sampling, dwellings in the selected area are enumerated and a random sample selected from them; respondents are then selected from dwellings. For a discussion see, e.g. C. A. Moser and G. Kalton, *Survey Methods in Social Investigation* (2nd edn., London: Heinemann, 1971) 118–21.
2. Cf. *Surveying Crime*, the Final Report of the Panel for the Evaluation of Crime Surveys of the Committee on National Statistics (Washington, D.C.: National Academy of Sciences, 1976), Chapter III. We are indebted to Prof. William H. Kruskal for this and other points.
3. For a discussion of 'multiple recapture' methods, used in estimating the size of a closed population (e.g. fish in the sea) where complete enumeration is impossible, see R. M. Cormack, 'The statistics of capture–recapture methods.' (1968) 6 *Oceanogr. Mar. Biol. Ann. Rev.* 455–501; S. E. Feinberg, 'The multiple recapture census for closed populations and incomplete 2^k contingency tables.' (1972) 59 *Biometrika* 591–603; Yvonne M. M. Bishop, S. E. Feinberg and P. W. Holland, *Discrete Multivariate Analysis, Theory and Practice* (Cambridge, Massachusetts: M.I.T. Press, 1975) Chapter 6.
4. See above, Chapter III, pp. 44–51.
5. It may well be that this explains the extremely low rates of reporting of burglary and household theft by respondents in the 1972 General Household Survey conducted by the Government Social Survey. Of 12,603 households included in this survey, only 324, or about 2·6 per cent, reported an incident of burglary or household theft in the preceding 12 months (compared with 11·6 per cent of respondents in our sample). Even allowing for differences between Inner London and the country as a whole, the GHS figures seem implausibly low. The 1972 GHS questionnaire included only two questions on crimes which might have happened to respondents 'within the past year'; these were preceded by a variety of questions having nothing to do with crime. (The 1973 GHS questionnaire had a similar format; questions on victimization were not included in the 1974 survey.)
6. As an example of normative patterns which it would be difficult to discern from survey interviews alone, consider the following. During our pilot work in Peterborough, we occasionally visited a pub patronized largely (though not exclusively) by West Indians. The saloon bar of this pub measured approximately 38 feet by 18 feet; on weekend evenings it could contain 60 or 70 people, many of them clustered at one end where usually two or three games of dominoes would be in progress; and among the West Indian clientele *nobody bumped into anybody else*. The elegant care with which invited bodily contacts were avoided contrasted markedly with the jostling which is accepted

in many 'English' pubs (both working-class and middle-class); it indicated a very different set of norms relating to personal space from those which govern the movements of the indigenous English—perhaps because in many cultures of the West Indies such bumping and jostling is apt to be interpreted as a source of 'trouble'. Such norms are apparently not universal throughout the Caribbean area, however; more research is needed to establish their exact generality among West Indian (or other black) cultures. The point is that this research is unlikely to be based on structured interviews, at least in the first instance.

3. Measurement for What?

1. See *Criminal Victimization in the United States, 1974*, A National Crime Panel Survey Report (Washington, D.C.: U.S. Department of Justice, June 1976).
2. *Crime in the United States, 1974: Uniform Crime Reports* (Washington, D.C.: Federal Bureau of Investigation, 1975).
3. For a brief discussion of the National Crime Panel Surveys see above, pp. 2–3, 44–51; and the Final Report of the Panel for the Evaluation of Crime Surveys, Committee on National Statistics (Washington, D.C.: National Academy of Sciences, 1976). The F.B.I. 'index' crimes (murder, rape, aggravated assault, burglary, theft and car theft) are, with the exception of murder, included in the National Crime Panel surveys.
4. See *Crime Against Small Business*, a report of the U.S. Senate Committee on Small Business (Washington, D.C.: U.S. Gov't Printing Office, 1969); Stephen J. Cutler and Albert J. Reiss, Jr., *Crimes against Public and Quasi-public Organizations*, a report submitted to the President's Commission on Law Enforcement and Administration (Ann Arbor: University of Michigan Department of Sociology, 1967, mimeo.). The National Crime Panel surveys also include commercial robberies and burglaries; but they do not include other sorts of theft (e.g. by employees). One ingenious attempt to study employers' crimes using survey methods is described in Kauko Aromaa, 'The making of a survey on hidden criminality in the field of labour protection laws in Finland, 1972', (1973) 1 *Int. J. Crim. and Pen.* 335–9.
5. Cf. Mary O. Cameron, *The Booster and the Snitch* (Glencoe, Illinois: Free Press, 1964) 9–24; Loren E. Edwards, *Shoplifting and Shrinkage Protection* (Springfield, Illinois: Charles C. Thomas, 1958), especially Chapters 1,24,30.
6. See, for example, Donald M. Horning, *Blue-Collar Theft: a Study of Pilfering by Industrial Workers* (Unpublished Ph.D. dissertation, University of Indiana, 1963); Gerald Mars, 'Dock pilferage', in Paul Rock and Mary McIntosh (eds.) *Deviance and Social Control* (London: Tavistock, 1974); J. P. Martin, *Offenders as Employees* (London: MacMillan, 1962), especially 114–19. In addition, some organizations keep records of crimes committed against them, which are discovered in the course of routine activities: e.g. in Britain the Post Office keeps records of telephone kiosks damaged through vandalism.
7. Thefts *from individuals* at workplaces can of course be measured by victim surveys, as can any other crime which has a personal victim but an organization locus. It seems to us doubtful, however, that even crimes such as commercial burglary can effectively be measured by surveys of individuals.
8. See, for example, Lee Rainwater, *Behind Ghetto Walls* (Chicago: Aldine, 1970).
9. See, for example, Norman M. Bradburn and David Caplovitz, *Reports on Happiness* (Chicago: Aldine, 1965); Norman M. Bradburn, *The Structure of Psychological Well-Being* (Chicago: Aldine, 1969); Angus Campbell and Philip E. Converse (eds.) *The Human Meaning of Social Change* (New York: Russell Sage, 1972); Mark Abrams, 'Social indicators and social equity.' *New Society*, 23 November 1972 at 454; *Social Indicators 1973*, a report compiled by the Office of Management and Budget (Washington, D.C.: U.S. Government Printing Office, 1973). At the time of writing, research on quantitative social indicators is also being undertaken by the O.E.C.D. in several European countries.

10. This was, in fact, precisely the finding of a victim survey carried out in one American city (Portland, Oregon) after the implementation of a 'high impact' crime prevention' programme: see Anne L. Schneider, 'Victim surveys and criminal justice system evaluation', Chapter 8 in Wesley G. Skogan (ed.) *Sample Surveys of the Victims of Crime* (Cambridge, Massachusetts: Ballinger, 1976).

11. See rule 6(a) of the scheme. But compensation is also not payable under a variety of other conditions, e.g. if the victim and offender were living together at the time of the crime: see rules 7, 9, and 17. For the rules governing the compensation program at the time of our survey, see the *Ninth Report of the Criminal Injuries Compensation Board, Cmnd. 5468* (London: H.M.S.O., 1973), Appendix A.

4. *Victim Surveys and Criminological Explanation*

1. Though the question of standardization is itself a complicated one, and crime rates based on the numbers of persons able to commit crimes can in fact be highly misleading. The proper procedure is the standardize in addition for opportunities to commit crime, e.g. property at risk (cars registered in the case of car theft, dwelling-houses in the case of residential burglary). Cf. A. J. Reiss, Jr., in *Field Surveys III (1)*, at 18–20; and the references cited in note 28 on p. 115 above.

2. F. H. McClintock and N. H. Avison, *Crime in England and Wales* (London: Heinemann, 1968) 4. Elsewhere McClintock has written that 'it may seem paradoxical to state that the most important starting point and continual reference point in any study of the "dark figure" phenomenon should be the "known" crime and criminality of the community': see his paper on 'The dark figure' in 5 *Collected Studies in Criminological Research* (Strasbourg: Council of Europe, 1970) 7–8. *Ipse dixit*; he gives no reasons for accepting this 'paradoxical' approach.

3. See F. H. McClintock and N. H. Avison, *Crime in England and Wales* 51–56. McClintock and Avison note that 'increasing affluence' may be a part of the explanation of this apparent increase; elsewhere in their book they adjust the average and aggregate values of property stolen by reference to the Retail Price Index. But this merely reflects (approximately) changes in the replacement cost of certain sorts of property, and not changes in the stock of goods available to be stolen. The end-year values of total consumer durables, at current prices, rose by 93 per cent between 1957 and 1966: see A. R. Roe, *The Financial Interdependence of the Economy* (London: Chapman & Hall, 1971). Personal incomes went up over 93 per cent in the same period, according to the National Income and Expenditure Accounts.

4. See above, pp. 187–189.

5. Above, pp. 97–99.

6. See above, Chap. VII, pp. 190–192.

7. Above, pp. 208–209.

8. Thorsten Sellin and Marvin E. Wolfgang, *The Measurement of Delinquency*. 249–52; and see above, pp. 182–185.

9. Above, pp. 151–155.

APPENDIX

The London Questionnaire

238

UNIVERSITY OF CAMBRIDGE
INSTITUTE OF CRIMINOLOGY

SURVEY OF CRIMINAL VICTIMIZATION, PERCEPTIONS OF CRIME AND
ATTITUDES TO CRIMINAL JUSTICE

FOR OFFICE USE ONLY

INTERVIEW NUMBER

						1

1-10

	INTERVIEWER	SCHEDULE TYPE	CARD TYPE

	DATE	INITIALS
CHECKED & DE-BRIEFED		
EDITED		
PUNCHING CHECKED		

RE-INTERVIEW: YES/NO

FINAL STATUS:

1   COMPLETED
2   TERMINATED
3   NO CONTACT
4   MOVED/DIED ETC.
5   REFUSED
6   OTHER:_____

11

NUMBER OF CALLS: [ ] 12

AREA: [ ] 13

THE CONTENTS OF THIS FORM ARE
ABSOLUTELY CONFIDENTIAL.
INFORMATION IDENTIFYING THE
RESPONDENT WILL NOT BE
DISCLOSED UNDER ANY CIRCUMSTANCES.

NAME: _____

ADDRESS: _____

_____

RECORD OF CALLS (TO BE COMPLETED BY THE INTERVIEWER)

	DATE	TIME ARR.	TIME LEFT	OUTCOME AND REMARKS
1				
2				
3				
4				
5				
6				

(FILL IN FOR ALL RESPONDENTS)

A1   Sex: 1 Male   14
              2 Female

A2   Race: 1 Caucasian
             2 Negroid   15
             3 Asian
             4 Oriental
             5 Other:_____
             X NK

A3   What is your date of birth? (CODE AGE)

    _____/_____/_____   ▢▢
                         16 17

A4   What is your marital status?

    1 Single (never married)
    2 Married (not legally separated) 18
    3 Legally separated
    4 Divorced
    5 Widowed
    X NK

A5   Are you working at the moment?

    1 Yes (full time)
    2 Yes (part time)   19
    3 No
    X NK

(IF RESPONDENT USUALLY WORKS)

A6   What kind of work do you do?
    (WRITE EXACT JOB DESCRIPTION AND
    KIND OF WORK DONE. NOTE IF JOB IS
    FULL OR PART TIME. IF RETIRED, GET
    LAST OCCUPATION) ▢▢▢▢▢▢
                      20 21 22 23 24 25

_____

A6a How long have you been in your present
     job/unemployed/retired?

    1 Less than 3 months
    2 3 months up to 6 months
    3 6 months up to 1 year   26
    4 1 year up to 2 years
    5 3 years up to 5 years
    6 5 years or more
    X NK

(ASK ALL MARRIED WOMEN)

A6b What kind of work does your
     husband do? (GET EXACT JOB
     DESCRIPTION AND KIND OF WORK DONE.
     NOTE IF WORK IS FULL OR PART TIME.
     IF RETIRED, GET LAST OCCUPATION)
                       ▢▢▢▢▢▢
                    27 28 29 30 31 32

_____

(ASK ALL)

A7   What kind of work did your father do?
    (WRITE EXACT JOB DESCRIPTION AND
    KIND OF WORK DONE) ▢▢▢▢▢
                    33 34 35 36 37

_____

(ASK ALL)

A8   Where were you born?

    01 London (this area)   38⁻39
    02 London (elsewhere)
    03 Elsewhere in England or Wales
    04 Scotland
    05 Northern Ireland
    06 Eire
    07 Europe:_____
    08 India
    09 Pakistan East or West
    10 West Indies
    11 Africa East or West
    12 China or Far East
    13 Middle East (inc. North Africa)
    14 Elsewhere:_____
    X   NK

(IF NOT ENGLAND OR WALES)

A8a How old were you when you first came
     to this country? (WRITE AGE) ▢▢
                           40 41

A8b Are you a British subject?   42

    1 Yes
    2 No
    X NK

(ASK ALL)

A9   What kind of secondary school did
    you last attend?
                            43
    1 Grammar
    2 Public, Boarding or Private
    3 Secondary Modern
    4 Elementary
    5 Other:_____
    6 None
    X NK

A10 At what age did you leave that school?
                            44
    1 Never at school
    2 Left before school leaving age
    3 Left at school leaving age
    4 Left after school leaving age
    X NK

A10a Have you had any further education?

    1 Technical College:_____
    2 University (some)
    3 University Graduate   45
    4 College of Education
    5 Other:_____
    X NK

(ASK ALL)

A11 Have you ever served in the forces?

    1 Yes   46
    2 No
    X NK

(IF YES)

A11a Were you ever in action? (SPECIFY)

    1 Yes:_____
    2 No
    X NK   47

(ASK ALL)

A12 Have you ever taken any instruction in any form of self-defence?   48

    1 Yes:_____
    2 No
    X NK

****

B1 How long have you lived at this address?   49

    1 Less than 3 months
    2 3 months up to 6 months
    3 More than 6 months up to 1 year
    4 More than 1 year up to 2 years
    5 More than 2 years up to 5 years
    6 More than 5 years up to 10 years
    7 More than 10 years up to 20 years
    8 More than 20 years
    X NK

(IF LESS THAN 2 YEARS)

B1a Where did you live before?

    1 Same neighbourhood   50
    2 Other part of London
    3 Elsewhere in England or Wales
    4 Other:_____
    X NK

(FILL IN FOR ALL)

B2 Type of accomodation:

    1 House   51
    2 Self-contained flat (shared or not)
    3 Room in parental home
    4 Furnished room(s)
    5 Lodgings
    6 Other:_____
    X NK

(IF ACCOMODATION IS HOUSE OR FLAT)

B2a Do you own this house/flat or rent it?

(IF RENT)

B2b Do you rent it furnished or unfurnished? From the council or private landlord?

    1 Own   52
    2 Rent furnished) from Council
    3 Rent unfurnished)
    4 Rent furnished) private
    5 Rent unfurnished) landlord
    6 Other:_____
    X NK

(ASK ALL)

B2c How many rooms are there in this house/flat, including kitchen and bathroom?

    CODE NUMBER OF ROOMS:
    (USE 9 FOR 9+)   53

(ASK ALL)

B3 Do you have a telephone?

(IF NO)

B3a Is there a telephone nearby which you can use whenever you want? (IF ONLY TELEPHONE IS PUBLIC CALL BOX CODE 3)

    1 Has own telephone   54
    2 Does not own telephone but has use
    3 Does not own telephone and no use
    X NK

(ASK ALL)

B4 Who else lives in this household with you? (CODE AS FOLLOWS:)

OWN FAMILY	NUMBER OF M	F
Spouse/Cohabitee 55		56
Age under 5 years 57		58
Age 6 – 12 years 59		60
Age 13 – 17 years 61		62
Age 18 – 65 years 63		64
Age 66+ years 65		66
OTHER THAN OWN FAMILY		
Age 17 or less 67		68
Age 18 and over 69		70

(ASK ALL)

B5 On average, how many nights a week do you go out?

    1 Every night   71
    2 5 or 6 nights
    3 3 or 4 nights
    4 1 or 2 nights
    5 Less than once a week
    6 Less than once a month
    7 Never
    X NK

(UNLESS NEVER GO OUT)

B5a For what kinds of things? (NOTE ALL ACTIVITIES. PROMPT AS NEEDED)

Freq	Occas		
1	2	Visiting family/friends in their own homes	72
1	2	Cinema/Theatre/Dancing/Bingo or similar public entertainment (including pubs other than 'own local')	73
1	2	Pub ('own local')/Social and Political clubs	74
1	2	Paid employment	75
1	2	Other:_____	76

B5b How do you usually travel when you go out at night?

1 Car (including taxi)
2 Public transport
3 Foot   77
4 Motor bike/scooter
5 Other:_____
X NK

```
┌──┬──┬──┐ ┌──────────┐
│  │  │  │ │        2 │
└──┴──┴──┘ └──────────┘
```

(ASK ALL)   78 79 80   1_5

B6 Is there an area around here - where you are living now - which you feel attached to, and where you feel at home?

1 Yes
2 No   6
X NK

(IF NO)

B6a Is there anywhere else that you feel attached to and where you feel at home?

1 Yes
2 No   7
X NK

B6b What area is that? (PROBE: HOW FAR DOES IT EXTEND?)

(WRITE NAME OF AREA (IF ANY); SIZE BY REFERENCE TO STREETS, BORDERING AREA, LOCAL LANDMARKS, PUBS, ETC.)

_____   8 9
_____
_____

(ASK ALL)

B6c What about this area where you are living now, say within a ten minutes' walk from your home. What kind of area is it? (WRITE IN VERBATIM)

_____   10 11
_____
_____

CODE: APP/DISAPP/NEUT/NON-EVAL

B6d What kind of people would you say live around here? (WRITE IN VERBATIM)

_____   12 13
_____
_____

CODE: APP/DISAPP/NEUT/NON-EVAL

B7 How would you say that this area differs from the others around it? (PROBE: WHAT KIND OF AREA IS IT? ARE THE PEOPLE ANY DIFFERENT?)

(WRITE IN VERBATIM)   14 15

_____
_____
_____

CODE: APP/DISAPP/NEUT/NON-EVAL

B8 How interested are you to know what goes on in this neighbourhood?

1 Very interested
2 Quite interested   16
3 A little interested
4 Not interested at all
X NK

B9 Do you think that this neighbourhood has changed much in recent years?

1 Yes
2 No   17
X NK

(IF YES)

B9a In what ways? (WRITE IN VERBATIM)   18 19

_____
_____

CODE: APP/DISAPP/NEUT/NON-EVAL

(QUESTIONS B10 TO B16c REFER TO NEIGHBOURHOOD AREA JUST ELICITED)

B10 Suppose that you had to move away from this neighbourhood. How would you feel about it?

1 Very sorry
2 Quite sorry   20
3 Neither sorry nor pleased
4 Quite pleased
5 Very pleased
X NK

(UNLESS ANSWERED '3')

B10a Why would you be sorry/pleased? (WRITE IN VERBATIM)   21 22

_____
_____
_____

(ASK ALL)

B11   Just thinking about this neighbourhood, would you say that there is much crime
around here? (SHOW CARD A) Would you say that there is:

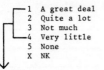

      1 A great deal
      2 Quite a lot   2 3
      3 Not much
      4 Very little
      5 None
      X NK

(IF NOT NONE)

B11a What kinds of crime are committed around here?
(TICK EACH TYPE OF CRIME MENTIONED AND THEN ASK FOR <u>EACH ONE</u>:)

B11b What kinds of people do you think are responsible for (MENTION TYPE OF CRIME)?
(PROBE: WHAT AGES? PEOPLE FROM AROUND HERE OR FROM OTHER PARTS OF TOWN?)

CODE		WRITE IN KINDS OF PEOPLE	CODE		LOCAL	ELSEWHERE	OTHER AND UNSPECIFIED	NK	
THEFT	2 4		2 5		1	2	3	X	2 6
BURGLARY	2 7		2 8		1	2	3	X	2 9
DAMAGE	3 0		3 1		1	2	3	X	3 2
CAR THEFT	3 3		3 4		1	2	3	X	3 5
ASSAULT	3 6		3 7		1	2	3	X	3 8
ROBBERY	3 9		4 0		1	2	3	X	4 1
SEX CRIMES	4 2		4 3		1	2	3	X	4 4
DRUG USE	4 5		4 6		1	2	3	X	4 7
OTHER:	4 8		4 9		1	2	3	X	5 0

(IF ANSWERED "NONE" TO B11)

B11c Supposing that a crime, for example a theft or burglary, was committed in this
neighbourhood, what kinds of people do you think would probably be responsible
for it? (PROBE: WHAT AGES? PEOPLE FROM AROUND HERE OR FROM OTHER PARTS OF TOWN?)

      1 Local
      2 Elsewhere
      3 Other and unspecified   5 1
      X NK

      1 Young people
      2 Adults - 'professional'   5 2
      3 Adults - other
      4 Immigrants
      5 Both adults and young people
      6 Age not specified
      X NK

(ASK ALL)

B12 Still thinking about this neighbourhood do you think that there is <u>more</u> crime around here than in other parts of town, <u>about the same</u>, or <u>less</u>?

    1 More
    2 About the same   53
    3 Less
    X NK

B13 Do you think that people in this neighbourhood are safe inside their houses at night?

    1 Yes
    2 No   54
    X NK

B14 Do you think that it is generally safe to be out on the streets of this neighbourhood after dark?

    1 Yes
    2 No   55
    X NK

(IF NO)

B14a In what ways do you think that it is unsafe?

    1 Risk of violent attack
    2 Risk of other 'trouble' of specific kind, e.g. drunks, drug addicts
    3 Risk of being molested
    4 Unspecific or vague reference to trouble
    5 Prostitution   56
    6 Combination of above
    7 Other:
    X NK

(ASK ALL)

B15 Are there any areas in this part of London where you think you would not be safe on the streets after dark, if you were alone and on foot?

    1 Yes
    2 No   57
    X NK

(IF YES)

B15a Which areas?

    (WRITE IN VERBATIM)

    58 59 60 61

(IF ANSWERED YES TO B15)

B15b Why do you think you would not be safe in (FIRST AREA MENTIONED)?

    1 Risk of violent attack
    2 Risk of other 'trouble' of specific kind, e.g. drunks, drug addicts
    3 Risk of being molested
    4 Unspecific or vague reference to trouble
    5 Prostitution   62
    6 Combination of above
    7 Other:
    X NK

B16 When were you last in that area?

    1 Less than 1 week ago
    2 1 - 3 weeks ago   63
    3 1 month or more, less than 3
    4 3 months or more, less than 6
    5 6 months or more, less than 1 year
    6 A year or more ago
    7 Never been there
    X NK

(UNLESS NEVER BEEN THERE)

B16a Has anything ever happened to you in that area?

    1 Yes
    2 No
    X NK   64

(IF YES)

B16b What happened? (GET DETAILS VERBATIM)

    65 66 67 68

B16c How do you feel about what happened then? (PROBE: DO YOU AVOID THE AREA?) (WRITE IN VERBATIM)

    69 70

(ASK ALL)

Now I would like to ask you some questions about London as a whole, and not just about this neighbourhood.

(SHOW CARD B)

B17 Are you personally concerned about crime in London as a whole? Would you say you are:

    1 Very concerned
    2 Quite concerned   71
    3 A little concerned
    4 Not concerned at all
    X NK

                                  3

    72 73 74 75 76 77 78 79 80   1 − 5

(ASK ALL AND SHOW CARDS C1 - C11 IN RANDOM ORDER)

B18 I would like you to look at these cards and for each one tell me whether you think that in London as a whole, in recent years, these crimes have been getting more frequent, staying about the same, or getting less frequent.

(READ CARDS AND NOTE EACH RESPONSE)

	1	2	3	X	
FRAUD	+	O	–	NK	6
RAPE AND OTHER SEX CRIMES	+	O	–	NK	7
PEOPLE GETTING ATTACKED AND ROBBED IN THE STREET	+	O	–	NK	8
MURDER	+	O	–	NK	9
BURGLARY	+	O	–	NK	10
VANDALISM	+	O	–	NK	11
THEFT OF CARS	+	O	–	NK	12
MOTORING OFFENCES (OTHER THAN PARKING OFFENCES)	+	O	–	NK	13
PEOPLE FIGHTING IN PUBLIC PLACES	+	O	–	NK	14
SHOPLIFTING	+	O	–	NK	15
USE OF ILLEGAL DRUGS	+	O	–	NK	16

(ASK ALL)

Now I would like to ask you some questions about the police.

C1 Do you have a close friend or relative who is a policeman?

1 Yes
2 No
X NK   17

(IF NO)

C1a Do you know a policeman well enough to call him by name if you meet him, (either on or off duty)?

1 Yes
2 No
X NK   18

(ASK ALL)

C2 How often do you see a policeman in this neighbourhood?

1 Every day
2 At least once a week
3 Less than once a week   19
4 Never
X NK

(ASK ALL)

C3 When was the last time you had any contact with the police?

1 Less than 1 month ago   20
2 1 month or more, less than 3
3 3 months or more, less than 6
4 6 months or more, less than 1 year
5 A year or more ago
6 Never had any contact
X NK

C3a What were the circumstances? (WRITE IN VERBATIM. IF CRIME VICTIMIZATION, DO NOT PROBE)

21 22

_____

_____

_____

(FOR CONTACT OTHER THAN CRIME VICTIMIZATION)

C3b Were you satisfied with what the police did on that occasion?

1 Yes - very
2 Yes
3 Indifferent   23
4 No
5 Very dissatisfied
X NK

(ASK ALL)

C4 Are you satisfied with the job that the police are doing in this neighbourhood?

1 Yes
2 No   2 4
X NK

(IF NO)

C4a In what ways are you dissatisfied?

(WRITE IN VERBATIM)

25 26

_____

_____

_____

(ASK ALL)

C5 What sort of job do you think the police do in general? (SHOW CARD D) Do you think it is:-

1 Very good
2 Good   2 7
3 Fair
4 Poor
X NK

(IF NOT GOOD)

C5a In what ways could they do better?

(WRITE IN VERBATIM)

28 29

_____

_____

(ASK ALL)

C6 If you called the police in an emergency, do you think that they would respond immediately?

1 Yes
2 No   3 0
X NK

C7 Do you think that in general the police are fair in dealing with people?

1 Yes
2 No   3 1
X NK

(IF NO)

C7a In what ways are they unfair?

(WRITE IN VERBATIM)

32 33

_____

_____

_____

C8 Are there any things which you think the police should be spending more time on?

1 Yes
2 No   3 4
X NK

(IF YES)

C8a What sorts of things? (WRITE IN VERBATIM)

35 36

_____

_____

C8b Why do you think the police are not spending enough time on these things? (WRITE IN VERBATIM)

37 38

_____

(ASK ALL)

C9 One thing the police do is try and control demonstrations, public meetings, picketing and the like. Have you ever been present at a demonstration where the police were present?

(IF YES)

Did you approve of the way in which the police behaved?

(IF NO)

From what you know, do you approve of the way the police generally behave at demonstrations, etc?

3 9

1 Was present - approved
2 Was present - did not approve
3 Never present - approve
4 Never present - disapprove
X NK

C10 Do you think that the police ever behave differently towards different kinds of demonstrators, for example, students, Trade Unionists, immigrants?

1 Yes
2 No   4 0
X NK

(IF YES)

C10a Which kinds of people and in what ways do the police behave differently? (WRITE IN VERBATIM)

41 42

_____

_____

_____

Now I want to describe some situations which might occur in real life, and then
ask you some questions about them. These will be situations in which a person
does something, and what I'd like you to tell me is whether you think that
most people in this neighbourhood would approve or disapprove of what the person
did, and how strongly you think they would probably feel about it. (SHOW CARD E)
You might think that they would strongly approve, or approve, but not strongly,
or disapprove or strongly disapprove; or of course you might think they would
just be indifferent, and wouldn't feel anything much one way or the other about it.

After that, I'd also like you to tell me how you yourself would feel about the
same incident -- because you might well have different views from other people
about some of the things.

Do you understand? (MAKE SURE THEY HAVE THE IDEA)

Here is the first case:

>   A man, who is driving his car in a crowded street, accidentally
>   knocks another man off his bicycle. The cyclist, who is not
>   injured, gets up and hits the driver with his fists knocking
>   him down.

D1 How do you think that most people in   1 Strongly approve
    this neighbourhood would probably feel   2 Approve
    about what the cyclist did in hitting   3 Indifferent   43
    the driver?   4 Disapprove
                                                  5 Strongly disapprove
                                                  X NK

D2 How would you yourself feel about what   1 Strongly approve
    the cyclist did?   2 Approve   44
                                                  3 Indifferent
                                                  4 Disapprove
                                                  5 Strongly disapprove
                                                  X NK

D3 What do you think the cyclist was feeling when he hit the driver
    of the car? (WRITE IN VERBATIM)

    _____
                                                                          45

>   Now suppose that the man in the car had been driving
>   recklessly when he knocked the cyclist off his bike,
>   and then the cyclist had hit him.

D4 If it had happened that way, how do you   1 Strongly approve
    think that most people in this neighbourhood 2 Approve   46
    would feel about what the cyclist did?   3 Indifferent
                                                  4 Disapprove
                                                  5 Strongly disapprove
                                                  X NK

D5 How would you yourself feel about it?   1 Strongly approve
                                                  2 Approve
                                                  3 Indifferent   47
                                                  4 Disapprove
                                                  5 Strongly disapprove
                                                  X NK

Here is the next case:

> Two men, of about the same age and size, are sitting in a
> cafe or restaurant, and they begin to have an argument.
> The first man loudly and repeatedly insults the second man.
> The second man hits the first man with his fists, and knocks
> him down.

D6 How do you think that most people in   1 Strongly approve
    this neighbourhood would feel about   2 Approve
    what the second man, who was insulted,   3 Indifferent   48
    did in hitting the first man?   4 Disapprove
                                                 5 Strongly disapprove
                                                 X NK

D7 How would you yourself feel about it?   1 Strongly approve
                                                 2 Approve   49
                                                 3 Indifferent
                                                 4 Disapprove
                                                 5 Strongly disapprove
                                                 X NK

D8 What do you think the second man was feeling in that situation?
    (WRITE IN VERBATIM)

_____   50

D9 Suppose a policeman had come in then and witnessed the whole scene.
    What should the policeman do? (SHOW CARD F) Should he:-

            1 Arrest the first man and take him to court
            2 Arrest the second man and take him to court   51
            3 Arrest both men and take them to court
            4 Stop the fight but take neither man to court
            5 Do nothing at all
            6 Other:_____
            X NK

> Now let us suppose that the first man, instead of just
> insulting the second man, also hits him. The second man
> then hits the first man with his fists, as before, knocking
> him down.

D10 If it had happened this way, what do   1 Strongly approve
    you think that most people in this   2 Approve
    neighbourhood would feel about what   3 Indifferent   52
    the second man did?   4 Disapprove
                                                 5 Strongly disapprove
                                                 X NK

D11 How would you yourself feel about   1 Strongly approve
    what the second man did?   2 Approve
                                                 3 Indifferent   53
                                                 4 Disapprove
                                                 5 Strongly disapprove
                                                 X NK

D12 If a policeman had witnessed that scene, what should he do? (SHOW CARD G)
    Should he:-

            1 Arrest the first man and take him to court
            2 Arrest the second man and take him to court   54
            3 Arrest both men and take them to court
            4 Stop the fight but take neither man to court
            5 Do nothing at all
            6 Other:_____
            X NK

248

Here is another situation:

A man who lives in this neighbourhood is returning to his home
late at night when he sees a stranger leaving his house. The
stranger does not appear to be carrying anything. The householder
approaches the stranger who starts to run away. The householder
hits him with his fists and knocks him unconscious.

D13 How do you think most people in this   1 Strongly approve
neighbourhood would feel about what   2 Approve
the householder did in hitting the   3 Indifferent   55
stranger?   4 Disapprove
                                            5 Strongly disapprove
                                            X NK

D14 How would you yourself feel   1 Strongly approve
about what the householder did?   2 Approve   56
                                            3 Indifferent
                                            4 Disapprove
                                            5 Strongly disapprove
                                            X NK

D15 What do you think the householder was feeling when he hit the stranger?
(WRITE IN VERBATIM)

_____

57

Now suppose that the same man is returning to his home late
at night, and sees a stranger leaving his house, carrying
what appears to be some of his property. The householder
approaches the stranger who tries to run away. The householder
picks up a brick or other object and hits the stranger with it,
causing him serious injuries.

D16 What do you think most people in this   1 Strongly approve
neighbourhood would feel about what   2 Approve
the householder did in hitting the   3 Indifferent   58
stranger with the brick?   4 Disapprove
                                            5 Strongly disapprove
                                            X NK

D17 How would you yourself feel about it?   1 Strongly approve
                                            2 Approve
                                            3 Indifferent   59
                                            4 Disapprove
                                            5 Strongly disapprove
                                            X NK

Now suppose that a householder is asleep in bed, and he wakes up
and hears an intruder in another part of the house. On finding
the intruder in the kitchen, the householder picks up a blunt
instrument and strikes the intruder with it, causing him serious
injuries.

D18 How do you think most people in this   1 Strongly approve
neighbourhood would feel about what   2 Approve
the householder did in hitting the   3 Indifferent   60
intruder with a blunt instrument?   4 Disapprove
                                            5 Strongly disapprove
                                            X NK

D19 How would you yourself feel about it?   1 Strongly approve
                                            2 Approve
                                            3 Indifferent
                                            4 Disapprove   61
                                            5 Strongly disapprove
                                            X NK

D20 What do you think the householder was feeling when he hit the intruder?
     (WRITE IN VERBATIM)

_____

6 2

        Now suppose that a man living here in this neighbourhood
        has been spreading malicious rumours about another man
        in the neighbourhood, such as that he has been stealing
        from his employer, or that he has been having an affair
        with another man's wife. Although these things are not
        true, many people might believe that they are. The
        second man finds out what the first man has been saying
        about him; and after several days' thought, goes to the
        house of the first man and hits him with his fists
        knocking him down.

D21 What do you think most people in this   1 Strongly approve
     neighbourhood would feel about what   2 Approve
     the second man, who had the things said   3 Indifferent   6 3
     about him, did in hitting the first man?   4 Disapprove
                                                  5 Strongly disapprove
                                                  X NK

D22 How would you yourself feel about it?   1 Strongly approve
                                                  2 Approve
                                                  3 Indifferent   6 4
                                                  4 Disapprove
                                                  5 Strongly disapprove
                                                  X NK

D23 What do you think the man who had the things said about him was
     feeling when he hit the first man?
     (WRITE IN VERBATIM)

_____

6 5

        Suppose that the second man, still using his fists,
        had caused the first man serious injuries.

D24 What do you think most people in   1 Strongly approve
     this neighbourhood would feel   2 Approve
     about what the second man did if   3 Indifferent   6 6
     it had happened like that?   4 Disapprove
                                                5 Strongly disapprove
                                                X NK

D25 How would you yourself feel about it?   1 Strongly approve
                                                2 Approve
                                                3 Indifferent   6 7
                                                4 Disapprove
                                                5 Strongly disapprove
                                                X NK

250

Now I would like to read you some statements about various things, and I would like
you to tell me whether you agree or disagree with them, and how strongly you agree
or disagree. What I am interested in is your own <u>personal</u> opinions on these things.

As I read each statement, I would like you to tell me how you feel about it --
whether you agree strongly, or agree but don't feel strongly about it, or whether
you disagree, or disagree strongly -- as on this card (SHOW CARD H).

All right? (MAKE SURE THE RESPONDENT UNDERSTANDS)

Here is the first statement:

		Strongly Agree	Agree	Disagree	Strongly Disagree	NK	
E1	There's little use in writing to public officials because often they aren't really interested in the problems of the average man.	4	3	2	1	X	68
E2	A person isn't really mature enough to vote at 18.	4	3	2	1	X	69
E3	Nowadays a person has to live pretty much for today, and let tomorrow take care of itself.	4	3	2	1	X	70
E4	Most children of 12 don't really know right from wrong.	4	3	2	1	X	71
E5	In spite of what some people say the lot of the average man is getting worse, not better.	4	3	2	1	X	72
E6	If a child of 15 breaks the law, he should be dealt with by his parents rather than going to court.	4	3	2	1	X	73
E7	It's hardly fair to bring children into the world with the way things look for the future.	4	3	2	1	X	74
E8	Courts nowadays are much too easy on criminals.	4	3	2	1	X	75
E9	These days a person doesn't really know whom he can count on.	4	3	2	1	X	76
E10	Violence deserves violence.	4	3	2	1	X	77
E11	It's important to be kind to people even if they do things you don't believe in.	4	3	2	1	X	78
E12	"An eye for an eye, a tooth for a tooth" is a good rule for living.	4	3	2	1	X	79
E13	It is often necessary to use violence to prevent violence.	4	3	2	1	X	80

1-5

		Strongly Agree	Agree	Disagree	Strongly Disagree	NK
E14	There are so many loopholes in the law that it's difficult to bring criminals to justice.	4	3	2	1	X 6
E15	When a person harms you, you should turn the other cheek and forgive him.	4	3	2	1	X 7
E16	When someone does wrong, he should be paid back for it.	4	3	2	1	X 8
E17	Many people only learn through violence.	4	3	2	1	X 9
E18	The police are getting so much power that the average citizen has to worry.	4	3	2	1	X 10
E19	Even if you don't like a person, you should still try to help him.	4	3	2	1	X 11
E20	A man has a right to kill another man in a case of self-defence.	4	3	2	1	X 12
E21	A man has the right to kill a person to defend his family.	4	3	2	1	X 13
E22	A man has the right to kill a person to defend his house.	4	3	2	1	X 14

E23 Some people say that stealing or damaging property is as bad as hurting people. Others say that damaging property is not as bad as hurting people. What do you think?

    1 Stealing or damaging property is as bad as hurting people   15
    2 Stealing or damaging property is not as bad as hurting people
    X NK

E24 Do you think it would be worse to become a permanent cripple, or to lose an uninsured home through fire, or are they equally bad?

    1 Becoming a cripple is worse
    2 Losing a home is worse   16
    3 They are equally bad
    X NK

(IF ANSWERED 1 OR 2)

E24a Would you say it would be a lot worse, or just somewhat worse?

    1 A lot worse
    2 Somewhat worse
    X NK   17

252

(ASK ALL)

Now I am going to show you a number of descriptions of acts which are crimes.
For each one I want you to indicate how serious you think it is. Of course,
in one sense all of these acts are serious because they are all crimes; but
they are not all equally serious -- for example, most people consider murder
to be a more serious crime than shoplifting.

What I want to know is how serious you <u>personally</u> think each crime is, and not
what the law says or how the police or courts would act, or what anyone else
would say. You indicate this by giving each crime a score from 1 to 11.
For example, if you think that the crime is <u>not</u> very serious then give it a <u>low</u>
score, like 1 or 2. If you think that it's of about <u>medium</u> seriousness then give
it about 6. If you think that it is <u>very</u> serious then give it a <u>high</u> score,
like 10 or 11, as on the scale on these. (GIVE SLIPS OF PAPER AND PENCIL)
Now if you will look at these you will see the descriptions of the different
crimes. I would like you to fill in the scale for each crime by putting a
circle around the score which indicates how serious you think the crime is.

(MAKE SURE THAT THE RESPONDENT UNDERSTANDS THE PROCEDURE)

Please take your time. You may check back as you go along, and if you want
to change anything, just cross out your previous answer and circle the new
score that you want.

(WHEN THE RESPONDENT HAS FINISHED, ASK:)

Would you like to check back to make sure that you are satisfied with the way
you have scored all the crimes? If you want to change anything, please feel
free to do so.

FOR OFFICE USE ONLY

1 - 5

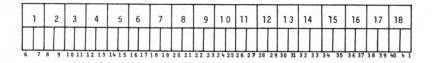

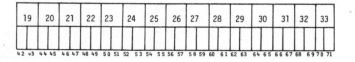

QUESTIONS F1 - F33

1   The offender breaks into a person's house and steals property worth £10.

2   The offender drives recklessly causing £100 worth of damage to another person's property.

3   The offender, a salesman, steals £10 from the till in the shop in which he works.

4   The offender buys property which he knows to be stolen.

5   The offender attacks a victim with a knife or other sharp weapon and the victim dies.

6   The offender, using physical force, robs a victim of £25, but the victim is not injured.

7   The offender steals property worth £10 from another person's car.

8   The offender attacks a victim with a blunt weapon. The victim is injured, but is not sent to hospital.

9   The offender rapes a woman, but causes her no other injury.

10 The offender attacks a victim with his fists. The victim is injured but is not sent to hospital.

11 The offender breaks into a person's house. When he is discovered by the owner of the house, he beats him with his fists, but leaves without taking anything.

12 The offender attacks a victim with a knife, or other sharp weapon. The victim is injured and is sent to hospital.

13 The offender breaks into a person's house. When he is discovered by the owner of the house he leaves without taking anything.

14 The offender, an accountant, steals £100 by altering his company's financial records.

15 The offender sells marijuana to a person aged 15.

16 The offender steals £10 from another person's wallet or bag.

17 The offender, using physical force, robs a victim of £25. The victim is injured, but is not sent to hospital.

18 The offender throws a brick through the window of a private house, causing £50 worth of damage.

19 The offender steals materials and spare parts worth £10 from the factory in which he works.

20 The offender defaces public property causing £50 worth of damage.

21 The offender steals materials and spare parts worth £100 from the factory in which he works.

22 The offender drives recklessly, injuring another person who is sent to hospital.

23 The offender rapes a woman and beats her with his fists, causing her physical injury so that she is sent to hospital.

24 The offender obtains £100 by cashing forged cheques.

25 The offender steals property worth £100 from another person's car.

26 The offender breaks into another person's house and steals £10.

27 The offender, using physical force, robs a victim of £25. The victim is injured and is sent to hospital.

28 The offender steals property worth £10 from a shop.

29 The offender assaults a police officer with his fists. The police officer is injured and is sent to hospital.

30 The offender sells marijuana to an adult.

31 The offender attacks a victim with a blunt instrument and the victim dies.

32 The offender assaults a police officer with his fists. The police officer is injured, but is not sent to hospital.

33 The offender sets up a bogus company and through it fraudulently obtains £1,000 from a big manufacturer.

(ASK ALL)

I would like to ask you about some things which might have happened to you
during the past year. Can you think back to what you were doing a year ago –
that is the (beginning/middle/end) of (month) 1972?

Can you remember some of the things which you did in the past year – for example,
did you go away on holiday? When was your birthday? Did you change your job?
Were you off work at any time? Were there any deaths, births, marriages,or
illnesses in your family? Any other things that you particularly remember?

(TRY AND GET EXACT DATES OF ANY EVENTS, AND WRITE THEM DOWN)

_____

_____

_____

_____

_____

(IF NECESSARY, TRY AND GET RESPONDENT TO REMEMBER, AND PLACE HIS EVENTS
IN RELATION TO THE FOLLOWING EVENTS:)

JANUARY 1 ....NEW YEAR'S DAY

MARCH 31 ....GOOD FRIDAY

APRIL 2 ....EASTER SUNDAY

MAY 29 ....WHITSUN BANK HOLIDAY

AUGUST 28 ....AUGUST BANK HOLIDAY

NOVEMBER 5 ....GUY FAWKES DAY

DECEMBER 25 ....CHRISTMAS DAY

(AFTER NOTING HIS DATES AND PROBING ABOUT MEMORY OF OTHER EVENTS, RUN THROUGH
THEM QUICKLY IN CHRONOLOGICAL ORDER, E.G. "so your birthday was March 5th,
then you went to Grimsby at the beginning of last August for 2 weeks, then
when your children went back to school in September you were off ill with the
'flu for a fortnight ... etc.....")

(THEN CONTINUE)

Now I want to ask you about some things which may have happened to you in that period.
I want you to think carefully about each one, and tell me if anything of that kind
did happen to you in the past year, and if so how many times it happened.
Please take your time and think carefully, and if you remember something which
happened to you which might fit the description I give, let me know. It doesn't
matter who else was involved, or whether you think it was serious or not.

(INTERVIEWER: CODE 0 IF NONE;CODE NUMBER OF INCIDENTS IF YES -- IF NUMBER IS
                GREATER THAN 9, CODE 9 IN BOX AND WRITE ACTUAL NUMBER IN RIGHT
                HAND MARGIN;   CODE X IF "NOT KNOWN". PROBE ON EACH "NO" RESPONSE)

Here are the things I would like to know about:

G1   Did anyone break into your house/flat in the past year?
      (PROBE: Did anyone get into your house/flat without   6
      your permission?)

G1a   Did anyone try to break into your house/flat, or try
      to get in without your permission?   7
      (PROBE: Did you find the lock or catch on a door or
      window tampered with?)

G2   Was anything stolen from inside your house/flat,
      even though the house/flat itself wasn't broken into?   8
      (PROBE: Did anyone just walk in and take something?)

G3   Did anyone physically attack you or assault you, in any
      way, during the past year?   9
      (PROBE: Did anyone hit you, or use any other kind of
      violence against you?)

G3a   Did anyone try to attack you, or assault you, or molest
      you in any way?   10
      (PROBE: Anyone -- even someone you knew? For example, in
      an argument or quarrel?)

G4   In the past year, did anyone threaten you in any way with
      violence of any kind?   11
      (PROBE: Anyone -- even someone you knew? Were you in
      any situation in which violence might have been used
      against you - for example, an argument or a quarrel?)

G5   Was anything taken from outside your house/flat in the
      past year? For example from the garage or doorstep?   12
      (PROBE: A bicycle, milk money, dustbin, clothes off
      the washing line?)

G6   Did you have anything stolen from your pocket or
      briefcase/bag during the past year?   13
      (PROBE: For example, when you were out shopping/
      at work -- even if you got it back later?)

G6a   Did anyone try to take anything belonging to you
      in those circumstances?   14

G7 Did anyone steal anything else from you, at any other time or place during the past year?
(PROBE: Did anyone take anything belonging to you which they had no right to take? Even someone you knew?)

☐ 15

G7a Did anyone <u>try</u> to steal anything else from you, at any time in the past year, or try to take anything else which they had no right to?
(PROBE: When you were out in the evening? IF HAD HOLIDAY: When you were on holiday?)

☐ 16

G8 Do you own a car?

```
┌─1  Yes
│  2  No
↓  X  NK
```

17

(IF YES)

G8a Was your car stolen during the past year?
(PROBE: Did anyone take your car and use it without your permission – even if you got it back later?)

☐ 18

G8b Was anything stolen <u>from</u> your car?
(PROBE: For example, any property which you had left in the car, or parts of the car itself?)

☐ 19

G8c Did you find your car tampered with in any way – for example, did anyone apparently try to get into it or start it, without your permission?

☐ 20

(ASK ALL)

G9 Do you own a motorbike or motor scooter?

```
┌─1  Yes
│  2  No
↓  X  NK
```

21

(IF YES)

G9a Was your motorbike/scooter stolen during the past year?
(PROBE: Did anyone take your motorbike/scooter without your permission – even if you got it back later?)

☐ 22

G9b Was anything stolen <u>from</u> your motorbike/scooter?
(PROBE: Any parts of the motorbike/scooter itself?)

☐ 23

G9c Did you find your motorbike/scooter tampered with in any way – for example, did anyone apparently try to start it without your permission?

☐ 24

(ASK ALL)

G10 Did anyone deliberately damage any property belonging to you during the past year?
(PROBE: For example, a window in your house/flat, or anything you had left outside the house/flat?)

☐ 25

(ASK ALL)

G11 In the past year, did anything else happen to you which you think might have involved a crime of any kind?
(PROBE: Anything which was against the law?)

```
┌─1 Yes
│  2 No                                                    26
│  X NK
↓
```

(IF YES)

G11a Can you tell me briefly what happened?
(RECORD BRIEF DETAILS AND ASK "Anything else?" UNTIL REPLY IS "NO". CODE TOTAL NUMBER OF INCIDENTS MENTIONED)

```
                                                    ┌──┬──┐
                                                    │  │  │
                                                    └──┴──┘
                                                    27 28
```

_____

_____

_____

_____

```
                                                    ┌──┬──┐
                                                    │  │  │
                                                    └──┴──┘
                                                    29 30
```

(FOR EACH INCIDENT, UP TO FIFTH, ASK:)

G11b Did you inform the police about (MENTION INCIDENT)?

INCIDENT NO:	1	2	3	4	5
YES	1	1	1	1	1
NO	2	2	2	2	2
NK	X	X	X	X	X
	31	32	33	34	35

(IF NO)

G11c Why didn't you inform the police?

INCIDENT NO:	1	2	3	4	5
Didn't think crime serious enough	1	1	1	1	1
Didn't think the police would come	2	2	2	2	2
Didn't think police could do any good	3	3	3	3	3
Thought it was a private matter	4	4	4	4	4
Didn't want to get involved	5	5	5	5	5
Fear of retaliation	6	6	6	6	6
Police already on the scene	7	7	7	7	7
Somebody else called the police	8	8	8	8	8
Combination of the above	9	9	9	9	9
Other:	0	0	0	0	0
NK	X	X	X	X	X
	36	37	38	39	40

(ASK ALL)

G12   Did you <u>see</u> any (other) incident in the past year which you think might have
      involved a crime?
      (PROBE: For example, a fight or an assault? Or someone taking something
      that did not belong to him, or deliberately damaging property?)

        ┌─1   Yes
        │ 2   No   41
        │ X   NK
        ↓

(IF YES)

G12a Can you tell me briefly what it was?
      (RECORD BRIEF DETAILS AND ASK "Anything else?" UNTIL REPLY IS"NO". CODE
      TOTAL NUMBER OF INCIDENTS MENTIONED)

                                                                    ┌──┬──┐
                                                                    │ │ │
                                                                    └──┴──┘
                                                                     42 43

      _____

      _____

      _____
                                                                    ┌──┬──┐
      _____   │ │ │
                                                                    └──┴──┘
                                                                     44 45

(FOR EACH INCIDENT, UP TO FIFTH, ASK:)

G12b Did you inform the police about (MENTION INCIDENT)?

INCIDENT NO:	1	2	3	4	5
YES	1	1	1	1	1
NO	2	2	2	2	2
NK	X	X	X	X	X
	46	47	48	49	50

(IF NO)

G12c Why didn't you inform the police?

INCIDENT NO:	1	2	3	4	5
Didn't think crime serious enough	1	1	1	1	1
Didn't think the police would come	2	2	2	2	2
Didn't think police could do any good	3	3	3	3	3
Thought it was a private matter	4	4	4	4	4
Didn't want to get involved.	5	5	5	5	5
Fear of retaliation	6	6	6	6	6
Police already on the scene	7	7	7	7	7
Somebody else called the police	8	8	8	8	8
Combination of the above	9	9	9	9	9
Other:	0	0	0	0	0
NK	X	X	X	X	X
	51	52	53	54	55

(UNLESS LIVES ALONE, ASK:)

G13 Did any of the things I have mentioned happen to anyone else in your household in the past year? (MENTION THEM INDIVIDUALLY, E.G. Your wife, your son, your lodger?)

(PROBE: Did anyone have anything stolen from them? Was anyone attacked or assaulted? Was anybody threatened with violence?)

```
┌─ 1  Yes
│   2  No
│   X  NK                                            5 6
↓
```

(IF YES)

G13a Just briefly what happened?
(RECORD BRIEF DETAILS AND ASK "Anything else?" UNTIL REPLY IS "NO". CODE TOTAL NUMBER OF INCIDENTS MENTIONED)

57 58

_____

_____

_____

_____
59 60 61 62

(FOR EACH INCIDENT, UP TO FIFTH, ASK:)

G13b Did you inform the police about (MENTION INCIDENT)?

INCIDENT NO:	1	2	3	4	5
YES	1	1	1	1	1
NO	2	2	2	2	2
NK	X	X	X	X	X

63 64 65 66 67

(IF NO)

G13c Why didn't you inform the police?

INCIDENT NO:	1	2	3	4	5
Didn't think crime serious enough	1	1	1	1	1
Didn't think the police would come	2	2	2	2	2
Didn't think police could do any good	3	3	3	3	3
Thought it was a private matter	4	4	4	4	4
Didn't want to get involved'	5	5	5	5	5
Fear of retaliation	6	6	6	6	6
Police already on the scene	7	7	7	7	7
Somebody else called the police	8	8	8	8	8
Combination of the above	9	9	9	9	9
Other:	0	0	0	0	0
NK	X	X	X	X	X

68 69 70 71 72

(ASK ALL)

G14   Have any of the things I mentioned <u>ever</u> happened to you, or to any member of
       your family, not just in the past year, but at any time?

```
 ┌──1  Yes
 │   2  No                                                    7 3
 │   X  NK
 ▼
```

(IF YES)

G14a   Just briefly tell me what happened?
       (RECORD BRIEF DETAILS AND THEN ASK "Anything else?" UNTIL REPLY IS "NO". CODE
       TOTAL NUMBER OF INCIDENTS MENTIONED)

       _____   ┌──┬──┐
                                                                               │ │ │
       _____   └──┴──┘
                                                                               7 4 7 5
       _____

       _____   ┌──┬──┬──┬──┬──┐ 76-
                                                                             │ │ │ │ │ │ 80
       _____   └──┴──┴──┴──┴──┘

(FOR EACH INCIDENT, UP TO FIFTH, ASK:)   ┌──┬──┬──┬──┬──┐
                                                                             │ │ │ │ │ 7│
G14b   Did you inform the police about (MENTION INCIDENT)?   └──┴──┴──┴──┴──┘
                                                                                  1 - 5

INCIDENT NO:	1	2	3	4	5
YES	1	1	1	1	1
NO	2	2	2	2	2
NK	X	X	X	X	X
	6	7	8	9	10

(IF NO)

G14c   Why didn't you inform the police?

INCIDENT NO:	1	2	3	4	5
Didn't think crime serious enough	1	1	1	1	1
Didn't think the police would come	2	2	2	2	2
Didn't think police could do any good	3	3	3	3	3
Thought it was a private matter	4	4	4	4	4
Didn't want to get involved	5	5	5	5	5
Fear of retaliation	6	6	6	6	6
Police already on the scene	7	7	7	7	7
Somebody else called the police	8	8	8	8	8
Combination of the above	9	9	9	9	9
Other:	0	0	0	0	0
NK	X	X	X	X	X
	11	12	13	14	15

(ENTER TOTAL NUMBER OF INCIDENTS MENTIONED IN G1 - G10 HERE: ┌────┐)
                                                              └────┘

(IF RESPONDENT MENTIONED ANY VICTIMIZATION IN G1-G10, GO BACK AND FILL IN AN INCIDENT
FORM FOR <u>EACH ITEM MENTIONED</u>)

(ASK ALL)

We've been talking about people who break the law, and situations where you might have been the victim of a crime. But most people have done something which was against the law at some time in their lives. I'm going to show you some cards which have a number of things which are crimes listed on them. I'd like you to look at each list and tell me <u>how many</u> of these things you have ever done, at any time in your life. I'd also like you to say whether you have done them once, or more than once. You don't have to tell me <u>which</u> of the things you have done, or to tell me anything about any particular incident. Just tell me <u>how many</u> of the things you have ever done <u>once</u>, and <u>how many</u> you have done more than once. All right?

SHOW CARDS TO RESPONDENT IN FOLLOWING ORDER, DEPENDING ON SCHEDULE TYPE (MARKED AT TOP OF COVER SHEET). IF NECESSARY READ ITEMS TO RESPONDENT BEFORE HANDING THE CARD TO HIM.

> SCHEDULE TYPE 1: I J K
> SCHEDULE TYPE 2: K I J
> SCHEDULE TYPE 3: J K I

I1 CARD I Things done once ☐ 16   Things done more than once ☐ 17

  CARD J Things done once ☐ 18   Things done more than once ☐ 19

  CARD K Things done once ☐ 20   Things done more than once ☐ 21

(IF RESPONDENT ANSWERS "NONE" IN ALL CASES, ASK:)

I2 Have you ever done anything which was a crime?
  (PROBE: Anything - even if the police weren't involved, or nobody found out about it?)

┌─1 Yes
│ 2 No   22
│ X NK
↓

(IF YES)

I2a Can you tell me something about it?

  (WRITE IN VERBATIM)   ☐☐
                                              23 24

_____

_____

_____

_____

I3 Have you ever been arrested or charged with a crime of any kind, even if you didn't do it?

┌─1 Yes
│ 2 No   25
│ X NK
↓

(IF YES)

I3a Can you tell me something about it?
  (WRITE IN VERBATIM)   ☐☐☐
                                            26 27 28

_____

_____

_____

_____

INTERVIEWER'S ASSESSMENT OF RESPONDENT:

Was respondent: 1 Very co-operative   29
                 2 Somewhat co-operative
                 3 Not co-operative

RESPONDENT'S UNDERSTANDING OF QUESTIONS:

                 1 Very good
                 2 Good   30
                 3 Fair
                 4 Poor

COMMENTS AND NOTES/OR DE-BRIEFING:

(NOTE ESPECIALLY ANY SECTIONS OR QUESTIONS WITH WHICH RESPONDENT HAD DIFFICULTY
OR SEEMED RETICENT, AND ANY FURTHER VIEWS OR FEELINGS ABOUT ANY SUBJECTS WHICH
HE MAY HAVE EXPRESSED; AND WRITE A SHORT DESCRIPTION OF RESPONDENT HIMSELF/HERSELF)

UNIVERSITY OF CAMBRIDGE

INSTITUTE OF CRIMINOLOGY

SURVEY OF CRIMINAL VICTIMIZATION, PERCEPTIONS OF CRIME AND

ATTITUDES TO CRIMINAL JUSTICE

CRIME INCIDENT FORM

THE CONTENTS OF THIS FORM ARE ABSOLUTELY CONFIDENTIAL.
INFORMATION IDENTIFYING THE RESPONDENT WILL NOT BE
DISCLOSED UNDER ANY CIRCUMSTANCES.

CASE NO.

) BE COMPLETED FOR EVERY INCIDENT MENTIONED IN QUESTIONS G1 - G9)

ᵤestion_____ Incident No._____ of total:_____   1—6

ᴇFER BACK TO EACH QUESTION WHERE VICTIMIZATION WAS MENTIONED. IF RESPONDENT MENTIONED MORE
ᴴAN ONE INCIDENT OF EACH TYPE, TAKE THEM IN ORDER BEGINNING WITH THE FIRST, E.G. "You said
ᵒu had some things stolen. Can you tell me a little more about the (first, next, etc.)
ᵢme this happened?"

ᴴEN ASK ALL:

ᴸ Can you tell me as accurately as possible when this happened?

_____day/date_____month_____year   7 8 9 10 11

(IF NECESSARY PROBE FOR SEASON AND RELATE TO EVENTS THE RESPONDENT USED TO DEFINE THE
PAST YEAR AT THE START OF SECTION G)

ᴸa INTERVIEWER: HOW RELIABLE DO YOU THINK THIS ESTIMATE IS?

        1 Completely reliable
        2 Probably reliable
        3 Doubtful   1 2
        4 Very doubtful
        X NK

² Can you tell me exactly where this happened? (PROMPT TO GET STREET NAMES; LANDMARKS;
BUS OR TUBE LINE/STATION/STOP; NAME OF PUB, ETC., TO LOCATE EVENT PRECISELY)

                                                                13 14 15

²a INTERVIEWER: HOW RELIABLE DO YOU THINK THIS DESCRIPTION IS?

        1 Completely reliable
        2 Probably reliable
        3 Doubtful   1 6
        4 Very doubtful
        X NK

264

H3   Will you please describe the incident as fully as you can?

(WRITE IN VERBATIM)

_____

_____

_____

_____

_____

_____

_____

_____

(ASK AND/OR FILL IN QUESTIONS H4–H13b AS APPROPRIATE)

CRIMES AGAINST THE PERSON (INCLUDING ROBBERY)

H4   Were you the only person who was (assaulted/attacked, etc.)?

    1 Yes
    2 No   21
    X NK

(IF NO)

H4a Who else was attacked, etc.)?
     (WRITE IN VERBATIM)

                22

_____

_____

H5   Were you physically injured in any way?

                23
    1 Yes
    2 No
    X NK

(IF YES)

H5a What were your injuries?

          24 25

_____

_____

H5b Did you need any medical attention?

(IF YES) What kind?

    1 No medical attention   26
    2 G.P. or police doctor
    3 Hospital less than 1 day
    4 Hospital more than 1 day
    5 Other:_____
    X NK

(IF DETAINED IN HOSPITAL)

H5c Total time spent in hospital:
     (WRITE IN VERBATIM)
                    27

_____

H6   Do you have any permanent disability of any kind resulting from this incident? (WRITE IN VERBATIM)

                    28

_____

H7   Did you lose any time from work as a result of the incident? (WRITE IN VERBATIM)

                    29

_____

_____

H8   Have you had any money as compensation for your injuries?

(IF NO)

Have you tried to get compensation? 3

    1 Yes – Criminal Injuries Comp. Board
    2 Yes – damages from offender
    3 Yes – Other:_____
    4 Claim made but no payment
    5 Claim pending
    6 No claim made
    X NK

CRIMES AGAINST PROPERTY (INCLUDING ROBBERY)

H9 How was the crime first discovered?

  1 Offender caught in the act
  2 Offence discovered later   31
  3 Other:_____
  X NK

(IF CRIME WAS BURGLARY)

H10 How did the offender get into
    the house? (WRITE IN VERBATIM)

  _____   [ ]
  _____   32
  _____

(ASK ALL)

H11 What was the total value of the
    property taken/damaged in £ ?   [|]
  £_____   33 34

H11a Description of property:

  _____
  _____   [|]
  _____   35 36

(IF PROPERTY STOLEN)

H12 Was any of the property recovered?

  1 All recovered
  2 Some recovered   37
  3 None recovered
  X NK

(IF SOME PROPERTY WAS NOT RECOVERED OR
WAS DAMAGED)

H13 Was the property (lost/damaged)
    insured?

  ┌─1 Yes   38
  │ 2 No
  │ X NK
  ▼
(IF YES)

H13a Did you make an insurance claim?

(IF NO)

H13b Do you intend to make a claim?

  1 Yes
  2 No - but intend to claim   39
  3 No - do not intend to claim
  X NK

H13c Did you collect on the insurance,
     get restitution or damages from
     the offender, or get money from
     any other source?
                                        40
  1 Insurance payment received
  2 Insurance claim pending
  3 Court damages/compensation/
    restitution
  4 Money from other source:_____
  5 More than one of the above
  X NK

(ASK AND/OR FILL IN QUESTIONS H14-18 IN ALL CASES)

H14 Do you know who was responsible for the crime?

  ┌─1 Yes   41
  │ 2 No──────────→ (IF NO) H14a Who do you think was responsible for it?
  ▼ X NK   (DO NOT PROMPT)

(IF YES)

H14a Who was it? (PROMPT AS NEEDED: HOW OLD? MALE OR FEMALE? WHAT SORT OF PERSON?
     ENGLISH, WEST INDIAN, IRISH, ETC? (USE RESPONDENT'S OWN CATEGORY))

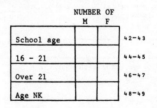

| | NUMBER OF | | |
	M	F	
School age			42-43
16 - 21			44-45
Over 21			46-47
Age NK			48-49

Race/
Nationality:_____

  [|]
  50 51   52 53

266

(ASK ALL)

H15 Who first discovered that the offence had been committed?

    1 Police
    2 Respondent   54
    3 Other member of household
    4 Neighbour
    5 Passer-by
    6 Other:_____
    X NK

(UNLESS POLICE DISCOVERED OFFENCE)

H15a Was the offence reported to the police?

    1 Yes
    2 No   55
    X NK

(IF NO)

H15b Why didn't you inform the police?
      (WRITE IN VERBATIM)

_____ 56

_____

H15c Did you take any other action?
      (WRITE IN VERBATIM)

_____ 57

(IF YES TO H15a)

H15d Who reported the offence to the police?

    1 Respondent
    2 Other member of household   58
    3 Neighbour
    4 Passer-by
    5 Other:_____
    X NK

H15e Where was the offence reported?
      (GET EXACT DETAILS)

_____ 59

_____

(IF RESPONDENT INFORMED POLICE)

H15f Why did you report it to the police?
      (WRITE IN VERBATIM)

_____ 60

H15g Were you satisfied with what the police did?

    1 Yes   61
    2 No
    X NK

(IF NO)

H15h Why were you dissatisfied?
      (WRITE IN VERBATIM)

_____ 62 63

_____

(ASK ALL)

H16 Were (any of) the offenders arrested by the police? (ARRESTED INCLUDES SUMMONSED)

    1 All   64
    2 Some
    3 None
    X NK

(IF ALL OR SOME ARRESTED)

H16a Do you know what happened to them?

    1 Prosecuted   65
    2 Cautioned
    3 Other:_____
    X NK

(IF PROSECUTED)

H16b Were those taken to court found guilty?

    1 All found guilty
    2 Some found guilty   66
    3 None found guilty
    X NK

(IF SOME OR ALL FOUND GUILTY)

H16c Do you know what sentences were imposed?

(IF YES)

H16d What were they? (WRITE IN VERBATIM)

_____ 67 68

(IF RESPONDENT KNOWS SENTENCES)

H16e Do you think those sentences were the right ones? (PROBE: TOO HEAVY? TOO LIGHT?)

      (WRITE IN VERBATIM)   69 70

_____

(ASK ALL)

H17 Has this experience caused you to change your outlook or your behaviour in any way?
      (WRITE IN VERBATIM)   71 72

_____

H18 You will remember that in a previous section you were asked to give a score to some crimes on a scale of seriousness from 1 to 11. (SHOW CARD P) I would like you now to give a score from 1 to 11 for the incident you have just described, to show how serious you think it was.

      CODE SCORE GIVEN:

                      73   74

      75 76 77 78 79 80

Bibliography

This Bibliography gives the full publication details of works which have been referred to in an abbreviated form in the Notes and References.

Abrams, Mark. 'Social indicators and social equity.' *New Society*, 23 November 1972.
Abrams, Mark. 'Housing: owners and tenants.' *New Society*, 7 August 1975.
Akman, Dogan D., and Normandeau, André. 'The measurement of crime and delinquency in Canada.' (1967) 7 *British Journal of Criminology* 129. .
Amir, Menachim. *Patterns of Forcible Rape*. Chicago: University of Chicago Press, 1971.
Anttila, Inkere. 'The criminological significance of unregistered criminality.' (1964) 4 *Excerpta Criminologica* 411.
Arbous, A. G., and Kerrick, J. E. 'Accident statistics and the concept of accident proneness.' (1951) 7 *Biometrics* 340.
Aromaa, Kauko. *Arkipäivan Väkivaltaa Suomessa [Everyday Violence in Finland]*. Helsinki: Kriminologinen Tutkimuslaitos, 1971.
Aromaa, Kauka. 'The making of a survey on hidden criminality in the field of labour protection laws in Finland, 1972.' (1973) 1 *International Journal of Criminology and Penology* 335.
Aromaa, Kauko. 'Victimization to violence: some results of a Finnish survey.' (1973) 1 *International Journal of Criminology and Penology* 245.
Aromaa, Kauko. *The Replication of a Survey on Victimization to Violence*. Helsinki: Institute of Criminology, 1974.
Aromaa, Kauko, and Leppä, Seppo. *Omaisuusrikosten Yksitöuhrien Tarkastelua [A Survey on Individual Victims of Property Crimes]*. Helsinki: Kriminologinen Tutkimoslaitos, 1973.
Austin, J. L. 'A plea for excuses.' In J. L. Austin, *Philosophical Papers* (edited by J. O. Urmson and G. E. Warnock). Oxford: Oxford University Press, 1961.
Baker, Robert K., and Ball, Sandra. *Mass Media and Violence*. A staff report to the National Commission on the Causes and Prevention of Violence. Volume 9. Washington, D.C.: U.S. Government Printing Office, 1969.
Banton, Michael. *The Policeman in the Community*. London: Tavistock, 1964.
Bauer, Raymond A. (ed.). *Social Indicators*. Cambridge, Massachusetts: M.I.T. Press, 1966.
Biderman, Albert D. 'Surveys of population samples for estimating crime incidence.' (1967) 374 *Annals of the American Academy of Political and Social Science* 16.
Biderman, Albert D. 'A proposed measure of interpersonal violence.' Washington, D.C.: Bureau of Social Science Research, Inc., 1971. Mimeographed.
Biderman, Albert D. 'When does interpersonal violence become crime?' Washington, D.C.: Bureau of Social Science Research, Inc., 1973. Mimeographed.
Biderman, Albert D., and Reiss, Albert J., Jr. 'On exploring the dark figure of crime.' (1967) 374 *Annals of the American Academy of Political and Social Science* 1.

268

Biderman, Albert D., *et al. Report on a Pilot Study in the District of Columbia on Victimization and Attitudes Toward Law Enforcement.* President's Commission on Law Enforcement and Administration of Justice, *Field Surveys I.* Washington, D.C.: U.S. Government Printing Office, 1967.

Bishop, Yvonne M., Fienberg, S. E., and Holland, P. W. *Discrete Multivariate Analysis: Theory and Practice.* Cambridge, Massachusetts: M.I.T. Press, 1975.

Black, Donald J. 'Production of crime rates.' (1970) 35 *American Sociological Review* 733.

Blalock, Hubert M., Jr. 'Four-variable models and partial correlations.' (1962) 68 *American Journal of Sociology* 182.

Blumenthal, M., *et al. Justifying Violence: Attitudes of American Men.* Ann Arbor: University of Michigan Institute for Social Research, 1972.

Bradburn, Norman M. *The Structure of Psychological Well-Being.* National Opinion Research Center Monographs in Social Research. Number 15. Chicago:Aldine, 1969.

Bradburn, Norman M., and Caplovitz, David. *Reports on Happiness.* Chicago: Aldine, 1965.

Cain, Maureen. *Society and the Policeman's Role.* London: Routledge and Kegan Paul, 1974.

Cameron, Mary. *The Booster and the Snitch.* Glencoe, Illinois: Free Press, 1964.

Campbell, Angus, and Converse, Phillip E. (eds.). *The Human Meaning of Social Change.* New York: Russell Sage, 1972.

Carr-Hill, R. A. *The Violent offender: Illusion or Reality?* Oxford University Penal Research Unit, Occasional Paper Number 1. Oxford: Basil Blackwell, 1971.

Christiansen, K. O. 'Method of using an index of crime.' In *The Index of Crime: Some Further Studies.* Collected Studies in Criminological Research, Volume 7. Strasbourg: Council of Europe, 1970.

Coleman, James S. *Introduction to Mathematical Sociology.* New York: Free Press, 1964.

Congalton, A. A., and Najman, J. M. *Unreported Crime.* Statistical Report number 12, Department of the Attorney General, New South Wales, Bureau of Crime Statistics and Research, 1974.

Cormack, R. M. 'The statistics of capture–recapture methods.' (1968) 6 *Oceanogr. Mar. Biol. Ann. Rev.* 455.

Cumming, E., Cumming, I., and Edell, L. 'The policeman as philosopher, guide and friend.' (1964) 12 *Social Problems* 276.

Curtis, Lynn A. 'Victim-precipitation and violent crime.' (1974) 21 *Social Problems* 594.

Cutler, Stephen, J., and Reiss, Albert J., Jr. *Crimes against public and quasi-public organizations.* A report submitted to the President's Commission on Law Enforcement and Administration of Justice. Ann Arbor: Department of Sociology, University of Michigan, 1967. Mimeographed.

David, Martin. 'The validity of income reported by a sample of families who received welfare assistance during 1959.' (1961) 57 *Journal of the American Statistical Association* 680.

Davis, James A. 'Hierarchical models for significance tests in multivariate contingency tables: an exegesis of Goodman's recent papers.' In H. L. Costner (ed.), *Sociological Methodology 1975.* San Francisco: Jossey Bass, 1975.

Departmental Committee on the Criminal Statistics. *Report, Cmnd. 3448.* London: H.M.S.O., 1967.

Douglas, Jack D. *American Social Order: Social Rules in a Pluralistic Society.* New York: Free Press, 1971.

Durant, Mary, Thomas, Margaret, and Willcock, H. D. *Crime, Criminals and the Law.* London: H.M.S.O., 1972.

Ennis, Philip H. *Criminal Victimization in the United States: A Report of a National Survey.*

President's Commission on Law Enforcement and Administration of Justice, *Field Surveys II*. Washington, D.C.: U.S. Government Printing Office, 1967.

Erskine, Hazel. 'The polls: fear of violence and crime.' (1974) 38 *Public Opinion Quarterly* 131.

Fienberg, S. E. 'The multiple recapture census for closed populations and incomplete 2^k contingency tables.' (1972) 59 *Biometrika* 591.

Feller, William. 'On a general class of "contagious" distributions.' (1943) 14 *Annals of Mathematical Statistics* 384.

Ferber, Robert. 'On the reliability of responses secured in sample surveys.' (1961) 50 *Journal of the American Statistical Association* 788.

Furstenberg, Frank, Jr. 'Public reaction to crime in the streets.' (1971) 40 *The American Scholar* 601.

Gastil, R. D. 'Homicide and a regional culture of violence.' (1971) 36 *American Sociological Review* 412.

Gibson, H. B., Morrison, S., and West, D. J. 'The confession of known offences in response to a self-reported delinquency schedule.' (1970) 10 *British Journal of Criminology* 277.

Goffman, Erving. *Relations in Public*. London: Allen Lane, 1971.

Gould, Leroy C. 'The changing structure of property crime in an affluent society.' (1969) 48 *Social Forces* 50.

Gray, Percy G. 'The memory factor in social surveys.' (1955) 50 *Journal of the American Statistical Association* 344.

Greenwood, M., and Yule, G. Udny. 'An inquiry into the nature of frequency distributions representative of multiple happenings with particular reference to the occurrence of multiple attacks of disease or repeated accidents.' (1920) 83 *Journal of the Royal Statistical Society* 255.

Hood, Roger, and Sparks, Richard. *Key Issues in Criminology*. London: Weidenfeld and Nicolson (World University Library).

Horning, Donald M. *Blue-Collar Theft*. Ph.D. dissertation, Indiana University, 1964.

Hotson, Bernard E. *Thefts from Gas and Electricity Pre-payment meters*. Cambridge: Institute of Criminology, 1968. Mimeographed.

Institute for Local Self-Government. *Criminal Victimization in Maricopa County*. Berkeley, California, 1969.

Jaeger, Carol M., and Pennock, Jean L. 'Consistency of response in household surveys.' (1961) 50 *Journal of the American Statistical Association* 320.

Kitsuse, John, and Cicourel, Aaron. 'A note on the use of official statistics.' (1963) 11 *Social Problems* 131.

Lange, David L., Baker, Robert K., and Ball, Sandra J. *Mass Media and Violence*. A staff report to the National Commission on the Causes and Prevention of Violence. Volume 11. Washington, D.C.: U.S. Government Printing Office, 1969.

Latané, B., and Darley, J. M. *The Unresponsive Bystander: Why Doesn't He Help?* New York: Appleton–Century–Crofts, 1970.

Lejeune, Robert, and Alex, Nicholas. 'On being mugged: the event and its aftermath.' (1973) 2 *Urban Life and Culture* 259.

McClintock, F. H. *Crimes of Violence*. London: Macmillan, 1961.

McClintock, F. H. 'The dark figure.' In *Collected Studies in Criminological Research*, Volume 5. Strasbourg: Council of Europe, 1971.

McClintock, F. H. and Avison, N. H. *Crime in England and Wales*. London: Heinemann, 1968.

MacIntyre, Jennie. 'Surveys of public attitudes to crime.' (1967) 374 *Annals of the American Academy of Political and Social Science* 43.

Mars, Gerald. 'Dock pilferage.' In Paul Rock and Mary McIntosh (eds.), *Deviance and Social Control*. London: Tavistock, 1974.

Marsh, Alan. 'Race, community and anxiety.' *New Society*, 23 February 1973.

Martin, J. P. *Offenders as Employees*. London: Macmillan, 1962.

Martin, J. P., and Wilson, Gail. *The Police: A Study in Manpower*. London: Heinemann, 1969.

Mellinger, G. D., *et al.* 'A mathematical model with applications to the study of accident repeatedness among children.' (1965) 60 *Journal of the American Statistical Association* 1046.

Moorhouse, H. F., and Chamberlain, C. W. 'Lower-class attitudes to property: aspects of the counter-ideology.' (1974) 8 *Sociology* 387.

Mulvihill, Donald J., and Tumin, Melvin M. *Crimes of Violence*. A staff report to the National Commission on the Causes and Prevention of Violence. Volume 11. Washington, D.C.: U.S. Government Printing Office, 1969.

National Research Council. *Surveying Crime*. Final report of the Panel for the Evaluation of Crime Surveys, of the Committee on National Statistics. Washington, D.C.: National Academy of Sciences, 1976.

Neter, John, and Waksberg, Joseph. *Response Errors in Collection of Expenditures Data by Household Interviews: an Experimental Study*. U.S. Department of Commerce, Bureau of the Census, Technical Paper number 11. Washington, D.C.: U.S. Government Printing Office, 1965.

Neter, John, and Waksberg, Joseph. 'A study of response errors in expenditures data from household interviews.' (1964) 59 *Journal of the American Statistical Association* 17.

Politz, A. and Simmons, W. 'An attempt to get at the "not at homes" in a sample without callbacks. I., (1949) 44 *Journal of the American Statistical Association* 9.

Price, J. E. 'A test of the accuracy of crime statistics.' (1966) 14 *Social Problems* 214.

Quinney, Richard. 'Crime control in a capitalist society.' In Ian Taylor, Paul Walton and Jock Young (eds.), *Critical Criminology*. London: Routledge and Kegan Paul, 1975.

Reiss, Albert J., Jr. 'Systematic observation of natural social phenomena.' In H. L. Costner (ed.), *Sociological Methodology 1971*. San Francisco: Jossey-Bass, 1971.

Reiss, Albert J., Jr. *The Police and the Public*. New Haven: Yale University Press, 1971.

Reiss, Albert J., Jr. Appendix A to *Crime Against Small Business*, a report of the Small Business Administration. Senate document number 91–14, 91st Congress, 1st session. Washington, D.C.: U.S. Government Printing Office, 1969.

Reiss, Albert J., Jr. *Studies in Crime and Law Enforcement in Major Metropolitan Areas*. President's Commission on Law Enforcement and Administration of Justice, *Field Surveys III*, Volume 1. Washington, D.C.: U.S. Government Printing Office, 1967.

Reynolds, Paul Davidson, *et al. Victimization in a Metropolitan Region: Comparison of a Central City Area and a Suburban Community*. Minneapolis: Minnesota Center for Sociological Research, 1973. Mimeographed.

Rose, G. N. G. 'Concerning the measurement of delinquency.' (1966) 6 *British Journal of Criminology* 414.

Rose, G. N. G. 'The merits of an index of crime.' In *The Index of Crime: Some Further Studies*. Collected Studies in Criminological Research, Volume 7. Strasbourg: Council of Europe, 1970.

Rossi, Peter H., Waite, Emily, Bose, Christine, and Berk, Richard E. 'The seriousness of crimes: normative structure and individual differences.' (1974) 39 *American Sociological Review* 224.

Royal Commission on Local Government in England. *Community Attitudes Survey*. Research Studies, Number 9 (by Research Services Ltd.). London: H.M.S.O., 1969.

Royal Commission on the Police. *Final Report. Cmnd. 1728 of 1964*. London: H.M.S.O., 1964.

Rubinstein, Jonathan. *City Police*. New York: Farar, Strauss and Giroux, 1973.

Schafer, Stephen. *Restitution to Victims of Crime*. New York: Quadrangle Books, 1960.

Schneider, Anne. 'Victim surveys and criminal justice system evaluation.' In Wesley G. Skogan (ed.), *Sample Surveys of the Victims of Crime*. Cambridge, Mass.: Ballinger, 1976.

Scott, Marvin B., and Lyman, Stanford M. 'Accounts, deviance and social order.' In Jack D. Douglas (ed.), *Deviance and Respectability*. New York: Basic Books, 1970.

Segal, Marshall H., Campbell, Donald T., and Herskovits, Melville J. *The Influence of Culture on Visual Perception*. Indianapolis: Bobbs-Merrill, 1966.

Seidman, David, and Couzens, M. 'Getting the crime rate down: political pressures and crime reporting.' (1974) 8 *Law and Society Review* 457.

Sellin, Thorsten, and Wolfgang, Marvin E. *The Measurement of Delinquency*. New York: John Wiley, 1964.

Skogan, Wesley G. 'Citizen reporting of crime: some national panel data.' (1976) 13 *Criminology* 535.

Skogan, Wesley G. *Public Policy and the Fear of Crime in Large American Cities*. A paper presented to the annual meeting of the American Political Science Association, Chicago, May 1976.

Smigel, E.O. 'Public attitudes toward stealing as related to the size of the victim organization.' (1956) 21 *American Sociological Review* 59.

Stephan, Egon. *Dunkelfeld und Kriminalstatistik [Dark Figure and Criminal Statistics]*. Freiburt: Max-Planck Institute, n.d. Mimeographed.

Sudman, Seymour, and Bradburn, Norman M. *Response Effects in Surveys: A Review and Synthesis*. National Opinion Research Center Monographs in Social Research, number 16. Chicago: Aldine, 1974.

Sudman, Seymour, and Ferber, Robert. *Experiments in Obtaining Consumer Expenditures in Durable Goods by Recall Procedures*. Urbana, Illionois: Survey Research Laboratory, 1970.

Svalastoga, K. 'Homicide and social contact in Denmark.' (1956) 62 *American Journal of Sociology* 37.

Taylor, Ian, Walton, Paul, and Young, Jock. 'Critical criminology in Britain: review and prospects.' In Ian Taylor, Paul Walton and Jock Young (eds.), *Critical Criminology*. London: Routledge and Kegan Paul, 1975.

Thorndike, F. 'Applications of Poisson's probability summation.' (1926) 5 *Bell System Technical Journal* 604.

Turner, Anthony G. 'Methodological issues in the development of the national crime survey panel: partial findings.' Washington, D.C.: Law Enforcement Assistance Administration, National Criminal Justice Information and Statistics Service, Statistics Division, December 1972. Mimeographed.

Turner, Robert. 'Inter-week variations in expenditure recording during a two-week survey of family expenditure.' (1961) 10 *Applied Statistics* 136.

U.K. Government Social Survey. *The Survey of Sickness*. London: H.M.S.O., 1952.

U.S. Department of Commerce, Bureau of the Census. *Victim Recall Pretest (Washington, D.C.): Household Survey of Victims of Crimes*. Unpublished report, June 10, 1970. Mimeographed.

U.S. Department of Justice, Law Enforcement Assistance Administration: National Criminal Justice Information and Statistics Service.

    Crime in Eight American Cities: Advance Report. Washington, D.C.: U.S. Government Printing Office, 1974.

    Crime in the Nation's Five Largest Cities. Washington, D.C.: U.S. Government Printing Office, 1975.

    Criminal Victimization Surveys in Thirteen American Cities. Washington, D.C.: U.S. Government Printing Office, 1975.

    Criminal Victimization in the United States: January–June 1973. Volume I. Washington, D.C.: U.S. Government Printing Office, 1974.

    Criminal Victimization in the United States, 1973 Advance Report. Volume I. Washington, D.C.: U.S. Government Printing Office, 1975.

    Criminal Victimization in the United States: A comparison of 1973 and 1974 Findings. Report SD-NCP-N-3. Washington, D.C.: U.S. Government Printing Office, 1976.

Crimes and Victims. A Report on the Dayton-San Jose Pilot Survey of Victimization. Washington, D.C.: U.S. Government Printing Office, 1974.

National Institute of Law Enforcement and Criminal Justice, Statistics Division. *San Jose Methods Test of Known Crime Victims.* Statistics Technical Report No. 1. Washington, D.C.: U.S. Government Printing Office, 1972.

Statistics Division. *The Cleveland-Akron Commercial Victimization Feasibility Test.* Statistics Division Technical Series, Report number 2. Prepared by Karen Joerg. Mimeographed, n.d. (probably 1971).

Viano, E. 'Victimology: the study of the victim.' (1976) I *Victimology* 3.

Von Hentig, H. *The Criminal and his Victim.* New Haven: Yale University Press, 1948.

Walker, Nigel D. 'Psychophysics and the recording angel.' (1971) 11 *British Journal of Criminology* 191.

Weiss, Carol H. 'Validity of welfare mothers' interview responses.' (1969) 32 *Public Opinion Quarterly* 622.

Wheeler, Stanton. 'Criminal statistics: a reformulation of the problem.' (1967) 58 *Journal of Criminal Law, Criminology and Police Science* 317.

Wilks, Judith A. 'Ecological correlates of crime and delinquency.' Appendix A in the President's Commission on Law Enforcement and Administration of Justice, Task Force report on *Crime and its Impact–an Assessment.* Washington, D.C.: U.S. Government Printing Office, 1967.

Wolf, Preben. *Vold i Danmark i Finland, 1970/71. En Sammenligning af Voldsofre.* Projekt Noxa, Forskningsrapport No. 1. Copenhagen: Nordisk Samarbe jdsrad for Kriminologi, 1972. Mimeographed.

Wolf, Preben and Hauge, Ragnar. 'Criminal violence in three Scandinavian countries.' In *Scandinavian Studies in Criminology*, Volume 5. London: Tavistock, 1975.

Wolfgang, Marvin E. 'On devising a crime index.' In *The Index of Crime: Some Further Studies.* Collected Studies in Criminological Research, Volume 7. Strasbourg: Council of Europe, 1970.

Wolfgang, Marvin E. *Patterns in Criminal Homicide.* Philadelphia: University of Pennsylvania Press, 1958.

Wolfgang, Marvin E. and Ferracuti, Franco. *The Subculture of Violence.* London: Tavistock, 1967.

Woltman, Henry and Bushery, John. *A Panel Bias Study in the National Crime Survey.* Paper prepared for presentation at the annual meeting of the American Statistical Association, Atlanta, Georgia, August 1975. Washington, D.C.: U.S. Department of Commerce, Social and Economic Statistics Division. Mimeographed.

Yost, Linda R. and Dodge, Richard W. *Household surveys of the Victims of Crime, Second Pretest (Baltimore, Maryland).* Unpublished report dated November 30, 1970. Mimeographed.

Index

accuracy of recall, 4, 35, 38–42, 218; in Baltimore pretest, 47–48; in Main Victim sample, 56, 59–61; in San Jose pretest, 49–50; in Washington pretest, 45–46

age and victimization, 84–85, 104, 109, 148

Akman, Dogan D., 185, 186

alcohol use and victimization, 114–115

Alex, Nicholas, 209, 216, 217

anomia scale, 9, 138, 214

Anttila, Inkeri, 12

Aromaa, Kauko, 34, 90, 110, 111, 112, 234

assault, in Baltimore pretest, 47–48; definition of, 106–107; in Main Victim sample, 55; in San Jose pretest, 49, 69; in Washington pretest, 45–46. *See also* violence, victim–offender relationships

attitudes, to crime, 8–9, 167–168; to neighbourhood, 200–204, 209–211, 212–213; to police, 117–118

Avison, N. H., 230, 235

Baker, Robert K., 175

Ball, Sandra J., 175

Baltimore, Maryland, *see* U.S. Census Bureau pretests, U.S. President's Commission victim surveys

Bentham, Jeremy, 1

Biderman, Albert D., 14, 87, 112–113

bounding of interviews, 39, 50–51

Bradburn, Norman, 40–41, 71, 72

Brixton, 11, 20–22, 26, 147; assaults in, 79–80, 85; attitudes to police in, 125–132, 135–136; fear of crime in, 207–208, 209–211; prevalence of crime in, 205; reporting of crimes to police in, 118, 156–158, 164; residents' attitudes

to, 200–204; self-reported crime in, 101; seriousness of crime in, 107, 188

burglary, in Main Victim sample, 53–54; in Register sample, 77–78; reporting to interviewers of, 45, 47, 49, 55–56, 59, 70–71, 87

Chamberlain, C. W., 187, 197

classification of crime incidents, 5, 13, 14, 55, 75, 144–146

Coleman, James S., 89, 92–93, 111, 112

commercial victimization, *see* victimization, commercial

concern about crime, 10–11, 207, 211, 215, 219–220, 228

consensus on crime seriousness, 8–9, 185–188

'contagious' Poisson distribution, *see* Poisson distribution

crime, effects of, on community 10–12, 67, 198, 204–211; on victims, 54, 209, 216–217

crime incident forms, 19, 70, 74–75, 106, 263–266

crime rates, and criminological research, 1, 229–230

Criminal Injuries Compensation Board, 14–15, 77, 228–229

criminal statistics, *see* statistics of crime

'dark figure' of unrecorded crime, 1–2, 6, 142, 167, 232; estimation of, 150–160, 223–225; and reporting to police, 137–138, 150, 230. *See also* recording of crimes by police, reporting of crime to police

David, Martin, 42

definition of situations as crime, 5, 14, 43, 168, 190–191

273